Williamson County, Tennessee

Wills and Inventories, Book I & II

1800-1818

Abstracted by

Louise Gillespie Lynch

Book Publishers

Southern Historical Press, Inc.
Greenville, South Carolina

Please direct all correspondence and orders to:

www.southernhistoricalpress.com
or
SOUTHERN HISTORICAL PRESS, Inc.
PO BOX 1267
375 West Broad Street
Greenville, SC 29601
southernhistoricalpress@gmail.com

ISBN #0-89308-471-9

Printed in the United States of America

PREFACE

Before a County WILL BOOK may come into being, there must be a Court of Record with authority to govern the residents in an orderly and just manner. Thus five men met at a local house in the Town of Franklin early in the year 1800, bearing their official Commissions to organize the law-making body for a new county in the State of Tennessee.

The following first entries in the First Minute Book of the Court of Pleas and Quarter Sessions tell the story of who the men were and what they did on the Morning of the First Day, nearly a hundred and seventy years ago:

"State of Tennessee
Williamson County Monday February 3rd 1800
Pursuant to an Act of the General Assembly of this State passed at Knoxville on the twenty Sixth day of October Seventeen hundred and ninety nine for dividing the County of Davidson and Laying off a County on the Southward thereof by the name of Williamson and establishing a Court of Pleas and Quarter Sessions therein to be held on the first Monday in February Eighteen Hundred, appointing and Commissioning the following Gentlemen for that purpose (to Wit) John Johnston Senior James Buford James Scurlock, Chapman White and Daniel Perkins
"Be it therefore remembered that pursuant to the before recited act James Buford James Scurlock, Chapman White and Daniel Perkins the gentlemen named in the aforesaid Commission of the Peace met this third day of February Eighteen hundred at the house of Thomas McKay in the Town of Franklin and proceeded to qualify themselves for the purpose aforesaid by taking the Several Oaths requisite to be taken by Justices of the peace in the following manner (to wit) James Scurlock being qualified by one of the Justices of Davidson County and he then administered the Several necessary Oaths to Daniel Perkins Chapman White and James Buford the other members present
"The Court thus Constituted proceeded to elect a clerk and made Choice of Nicholas Perkins Hardeman who gave bond of Five thousand dollars with Security as the law directs and took necessary Oaths as by law required for his qualification as Such. . ."

Be it noted that the choosing of a CLERK was the first official act of the newly-sworn Court, and it was his hand that entered in his new ledger the Minutine incident to a decedent's death, heirs, legatees, real and personal property, sales purchases, etc. The compiler of this book, Will Book Number One, has thoughtfully included in her carefully transcribed Abstracts many of the above details (often omitted by Abstractors) and has strived in every way to provide researchers with all available genealogical information. In presenting this volume to the public, Mrs. Lynch has most capably filled a long-standing void in the published records of her native county.

Katherine W. Ewing (Mrs. Albert, Jr.)
Nashville, Tennessee

COMPILER'S NOTE:

Question marks have been used in this book to indicate words and names that are partially or wholy illegible in the original volume. In instances of uncertain interpretation of names, I have had to copy them as I saw them; where names were spelled in several different ways in the original, all spellings are here indexed.

Since recognition of the visual and phonetic variants of name-spellings is of inestimable value to researchers, it is suggested that for every possible way in which the desired name could have been written at the time-period, 1800-1812, both as to the way it might LOOK or SOUND.

Full texts of records herein
abstracted may be ordered
from the office of the
Williamson County Court Clerk
by providing him with the name
of the deceased, the type
and date of the instruments
in point, and the original-
volume page numbers which
will be soon on the left
margins in this transcription.

Louise Gillespie Lynch,
Compiler

State of Tennessee

Williamson County Monday February 5th 1820

Pursuant to an act of the General Assembly of this State passed at the session with the twenty sixth day of November eighteen hundred and ninety nine providing the County of Williamson and laying off a County in the southwest thereof by the name of Williamson and establishing a Court of Pleas and Quarter Sessions therein to be held on the first monday in February, eighteen hundred, the Justices are Commissioned the following Gentlemen for their respective (to wit) John Johnston, Senior, James Bigford, James Bearlock, Chapman White and Marie Perris

Be it therefore remembered that pursuant to the before recited act James Bigford, James Bearlock, Chapman White and Marie Perris the gentlemen named in the aforesaid Commission of the peace met this third day of February eighteen hundred at the house of Thomas McCray in the town of Franklin and proceeded to qualify themselves for the purpose of holding the several Courts requisite to be taken by Justices of the Peace in the following manner (to wit) James Bearlock being qualified by each of the Justices of Williamson County and the then administered the several preceding Oaths to Marie Perris, Chapman White and James Bigford the other members present

The Court this Constituted proceeded to attack and made Choice of the State Hardeman who gave bond of this Honorable dollars with security with the hundred and took security oath as by law required for his qualification as such

HICKMAN CO. DICKSON CO.

WILLIAMSON

FRANKLIN

MAURY CO.

DAVIDSON CO.

BEDFORD CO.

RUTHERFORD COUNTY

Adapted from
Mathew Rhea's Map of Tennessee
(1832, Columbia)

WILL BOOK VOL. 1

WILLIAMSON COUNTY, TENNESSEE

P. 1. JAMES HOPKINS, Will, July 18, 1800; Wife Elizabeth;
Children, John, Elizabeth, Jonathan, Hannah, Jason, (the
plantation I now live on), Winifred, Keziah, Bitha, and James
Pickering. Daughter Lucy; Son John, Whereas I own 540 acres of
land on Waters of Stones River, Land divided between sons John,
Jonathan and James Pickering, as they become of age. I have
rec'd $50 of John Pickerin in part pay for 100 acres of land on
Stones River. Note on John Blackamore. Exr.: wife, Elizabeth
and brother, Joseph Hopkins. Proven Feb. 9, 1800. May sessions
1800.

P. 3. JAMES HOPKINS, Inventory and Valuation. Returned to court
Aug. session 1800. By Elizabeth Hopkins, Exr. Signed:
Samuel McCutchen and Samuel Edmiston.

P. 4. JOHN STEWARD, Dec'd. Inventory Nov. 1800. By Thomas
Steward, Admr. Appraised Sept. 6, 1800 by John Johnson,
Daniel Perkins, and Samuel McCutchen. Many Items, Large Bible,
books and chest. Note on Christopher Moses, Dec. 4, 1798, Va.
Currency; Note on Frederic Fishers, Dec. 4, 1798, Va. Currency;
Note on John Carpenter, Feb. 3, 1798, Va. Currency; Note on Noel
Watkins, March 2; Note on John Weakley; Acct. on Alexander Gower;
Acct. on William McDowels, Pa. money dated Oct. 24, 1767; Acct.
on Frederic Hebel, Pa. money; Acct. on Elisha Gowers; Bond on
Thomas Malloy for 274 acres of land; Notes on: Thomas Weakley,
Hannah Denton, Moses Moody, Hannah Holmes, Thomas Holemans,
Thomas Stewart, Adam Binkleys, John Nash. Nov. 4, 1800; Thomas
Stewart, Admr. Nov. sessions 1800.

P. 7. JOHN HIGHTOWER, Dec'd. Inventory May session 1801. By
Polly Hightower, Admrx. Many items and several books.
Sales Account of John Hightower; sold March 25, 1802. Those
buying: Richard Hightower, William Sanders, Polly Hightower,
William Orton, John McCuiston, Alexander Smith. May sessions
1802.

P. 8. WILLIAM BELL, JR., Dec'd. Will Oct. 5, 1803. Father,
William Bell, Sr.; Sisters, Elizabeth Bell and Sally Bell;
Brothers, James Bell, Thomas Bell, Stenson Bell, John Bell, and
Sterling Bell; Brothers-in-law Matthew Cunningham and Joseph
Payton. Test.: Henry Childress and James Love. Dated Oct. 6,
1802. Proven Feb. sessions 1803.

P. 8. GILES PARMELY, Dec'd. Will Oct. 5, 1803. Feb. 26, 1803.
Samuel Burton and Henry Skidmore. Notes to be used for
oldest son, Ephraim Parmely. Exr. Ephraim Parmely. Wit.:
Edward Elam and Samuel Parmely. Proven Aug. session 1803.

P. 9. BENJAMIN LEE, Dec'd. Will Oct. 11, 1803. Nephew Braxton
Lee tract of land on Marrow Bone Creek and slaves Anthony,
Lucy, and Ben. Nephew John Lee and wife Jenny Lee, 50 acres
of land. Relation Benjamin Lee (son of Braxton); Friend Chapman
White, slaves: Tom, James, and Lucy, after the death of wife.
Wife Mary Lee. Exr. Chapman White, Aug. 18, 1802. Test.: John
P. Neal and Caleb Mandley. Proven Nov. session 1802.

Inventory of the estate of BENJAMIN LEE, Dec'd.; 6 slaves:
Tom, James Anthony, Ben, Henry, and Lucy. Feb. 7, 1803.

P. 10.   YOUNG MCLEMORE, Dec'd. Will, Dec. 31, 1803. Daughter
         Sukey Gray, Negroes: James, Nan, Essin, Joyce, Lydia,
and Stephen; Grandson Young A. Gray, Slave, Benjamin and land I
now live on; Grandson James McK. Gray, Negroes: Furry and Abram;
Grandson Henry K. Gray, negros: Hardy, Jinney, and Hester;
Granddaughter Sukey McL. Gray, negros: Jack, Beck, Effey, and
Davy; Grandaughter Sally L. Gray, negros: Harper, Dudley, and
Lucy; Granddaughter Polly M. Dickson; James Gray, his wife and
children, a suit of mourning from the estate; James Gray Land I
bought from Gen'l Robertson; James M.K. Gray (son of James Gray)
and Henry K. Gray. Exr.: Friends, James Gray and William Dickson and Young A. Gray. Wit.: Thomas Masterson, Abraham Maury,
Jr., A. Maury. Degraffenreid and Nathan Farmer. Proved April
session 1804.

P. 12.   Inventory of YOUNG MCLEMORE, April 9, 1804. Bond on
         Abraham Maury, Elijah Williams, Henry Walker, Henry G.
Kearney, Robert Johnston, and John Farmer. Signed: J. Gray.

P. 13.   ELIJAH EWINGS, Dec'd. Will, March 2, 1804. 380 acres
         land on Harpeth; Wife Nancy Ewings, land including the
mill; daughter Amelia, land goes to her at the death of the wife.
Exr.: Wife, Nancy Ewings. Wit.: Thomas Stuart, Ann Hay, and
Thomas Bond. Proven April session 1804.

P. 14.   Inventory of ELIJAH EWINGS, Dec'd. June 28, 1804. 1
         chest and other items. Nancy Ewings, Exr.

P. 14.   JESSE EVANS, Dec'd. Will, Nov. 21, 1804. Wife Mary
         Evans, the plantation, tools, stock and furniture;
daughters Rebecca Evans and Rachel Evans; son John Evans, Plan-
tation goes to him at the death of wife; Sons Daniel Evans and
Robin Evans; daughters Patsy Nash and Sarah Jackson. Test.:
Burwell Temple and Samuel Jackson. Exr.: Daniel Evans and Robert
Evans. Proven Jan. session 1805.

P. 16.   Inventory of JESSE EVANS, Dec'd. Jan. 14, 1805.
         Several items and chest. Exr.: Daniel Evans and Robert
Evans.

P. 16.   WILLIAM WILKINS, Dec'd. Will Aug. 23, 1805. Wife is
         now with child (name of wife not given); sons John and
James; Negros Judy, Milly and Conkard, to be divided between
sons and daughters (not named). Proved Jan. session 1806.

P. 18.   Inventory of Goods, Chattels rights of Credit of
         WILLIAM WILKINS, Dec'd. Jan. 31, 1806. Those buying:
William Neelly, Rebecca Wilkins, Augusta Willis, William Kindrake,
James Wilkins, Robert Wilkins (stud horse). The above property
sold to pay debts. More inventory listed. Judgment against
Thomas Due and Rus Porter. April 14, 1806. James Wilkins, Admr.

P. 19.   WILLIAM GARDNER, Dec'd. Will Feb. 13, 1805. Wife
         Jane Gardner, land and stock, Negro Simon; sons Richey
and William land where I now live, when they are grown. son
William to be given negro Philip at the death of wife; sons
Thomas and John; daughters Jane, Hannah and Ann (has married
daughters, names not given); Negro Dolly shall live where she
wishes, at the death of wife. Exr.: Wife Jane Gardner. Wit.:
Nicholas Scales, Joseph Sumners, William McKnight. Proven
April sessions 1806.

P. 21.   HANNAH MONTGOMERY, Dec'd. Will, Feb. 21, 1806. Daugh-

2

ter Mary Montgomery, Bible, other items; granddaughter Jane
Montgomery; son David Montgomery; son-in-law Thomas Aydelott and
Mary Montgomery, Exr. Wit.: John Pope, and James Neelly, Feb.
21, 1806. Proven July session 1806.

P. 22.   Inventory of the Estate of HANNAH MONTGOMERY, Dec'd.
          April 13, 1807. Note on David Montgomery; Accounts of
William Bailey and Greenham (Grunham?) Taylor. Exr.: Thomas
Aydelott.

P. 22.   WELCOM HODGES, Dec'd. Will, Junt 6, 1807. Sons
          Philip Hodges, James Hodges, each one-fourth of land;
daughters Elizabeth and Lydda, each one-fourth land; Betsey
Cottingim, rest of estate. Exr.: Burton Jordan and Samuel
Shields. Wit.: David Floyd, John Keeth, and Elizabeth Beaver.
Proven July sessions 1807.

P. 24.   RICHARD WINDROW, Dec'd. Will, Nov. 21, 1805. Daughters
          Elizabeth Windrow, Sally Windrow, Millinder Windrow,
Jane Sea, and Nancy Brown; son John Windrow, 160 acres land and
land he sold to Rosewell; son Henry Windrow, 160 acres land in-
cluding plantation where I now live; wife Millinder Windrow.
Exr.: son John Windrow and John Sea. Wit.: Green Hill, A. Maury
Degraffinreid, William Hill. Proven July sessions 1806.

P. 26.   Inventory of the estate of RICHARD WINDROW, Dec'd.
          Signed, John Windrow.

P. 27.   AMMON DAVIS, Dec'd. Will, Dec. 23, 1806. Brother
          John Davis; daughter Sally Davis, the land on Mill
Creek if she should live till maturity. Exr.: Brother, James
Davis. Wit: Arthur Pearce, Peter Pinkston, and George Shannon.
Proven April session 1807.

          Inventory of AMMON DAVIS, Dec'd. (no date). Several
items, 1 case of Holster Pistols, Bible, and silver watch.

P. 28.   NANCY BENTON, Dec'd. Will, Jan. 19, 1807. As the
          daughter and one of the heirs of Jesse Benton Dec'd. of
the state of North Carolina, being heir to property in the state
of Tennessee, of land lying on Harpeth and Duck Rivers, Cumberland River and Tennessee River, and other rivers emptying into
the Mississippi River. Negros in Tennessee granted by my
father's will; Two sisters Polly Benton & Susannah Benton; deceased sister Peggy Benton, also being one of her heirs, (she
being one of the heirs and devisees of Jesse Benton). Exr.:
Thomas H. Benton. Wit.: Thomas H. Benton, Samuel Benton, John
Record. Proven April sessions 1807.

P. 29.   SUSAN LOVE. Nuncupative Will June 10, 1807. Whereas
          on the 14th day of Dec. 1806, Susan Love departed this
life at Franklin, Williamson County, A few hours before her death
expressed her will, Eldest daughter of her brother William, that
is, Peggy Love, whole of her estate. Wit.: Harrison Boyd, Rhoda
Boyd, Thomas H. Benton, Charles Boyles, Jenny Bright, and Mary
Williamson. June 11, 1807. Proven July sessions 1807.

P. 30.   JOHN DICKEY, Dec'd. Will, Dec. 5, 1807. Wife Mary
          Dickey, 60 acres of land purchased of Ray Sand as agent
of the heirs of Nathaniel Green; wife Mary Dickey the following
slaves: Friday, Nanny, Old Lona, Ned, and Labina; friends Moses
G. Frierson and David Frierson; daughter Sarah Blakely; grandson Isaac Edwin Frierson; son Benona Dickey. Exr.: Moses G.

3

Frierson, David Frierson, and son Benona Dickey. Wit.: H.
Patterson, Abram Maury and Samuel Frierson. Proven Jan. sessions 1808.

P. 33.   JANE GARDNER, Dec'd. Will, Sept. 5, 1807. Son John
         Gardner the Negro Harry; son Richey Gardner the negro
Simon; son William Gardner; son Joseph Richey. If negro Simon
should outlive Richey and William, he should be set free. Son-
in-law William Berry; daughters Martha, Molly Sumners, Nancy
Sumners, Rebecca Sumners, Anne Patterson, Polly Downing, Jane
Gardner, and Hannah Gardner. Due from John McKey, 40 pounds.
Exr.: John Gardner and Nicholas Seales. Wit.: John Sumners,
Joseph Sumners, and James Patterson. Proven Jan. session 1808.

P. 36.   Inventory of JANE GARDNER, Dec'd. April 12, 1808. 1
         Bible, books, testaments, chest, cupboard, other items.
Exr.: John Gardner. Comissioners: John Baldridge and William G.
Boyd. April session 1808.

P. 37.   WILLIAM APPLEBY, Dec'd. Will, Nov. 3, 1807. Wife
         Agnes; son John Appleby, 100 acres of land out of a
500 acre land survey in Livingston Co., Ky.; son James Appleby,
$50 in cash; son William Appleby, 100 acres of land in aforesaid
survey; son David Appleby, bay mare; daughters Elizabeth McCurdy,
Grissy McCurdy, and Jean Little (each $3.00 in cash.); sons
David and Samuel Appleby the remainder of land. Exr.: Trusty
friend, David McCurdy and John Appleby. Wit.: John Record and
John Calvert. Proven July session 1808.

P. 39.   Inventory of WILLIAM APPLEBY, Dec'd. Oct. 12, 1808.
         In state of Georgia for wagon to Nathaniel Hill $70;
Notes on sundries left in hands of James Appleby in the state of
Georgia. Price of a horse in Ga. from Stephen Gra?? $75.00;
book by James Lamaster $1.60; 3 years lease of land in Ga.
Exrs.: David McCurdy and John Appleby. Returned Oct. sessions
1808.

P. 40.   WILLIAM GREEN, Dec'd. Will, Feb. 23, 1809. Son Thomas
         Green; wife Mary Green, negro man Daniel. Exr.: Wife
Mary Green and son Thomas Green. Wit.: James White and John
Andrews. Proven April sessions 1809.

P. 41.   JOHN LOWRANCE, Dec'd. Will, June 7, 1808. Wife Eliza-
         beth; son Abraham Lawrence, $250 on note by James Mc-
Alroy in the state of Georgia for a shot gun; $250 coming from
son Samuel Lawrence in Ga. for payment for negro man; daughter
Polly Lawrence; son John Lawrence; daughter Margaret Harris $20;
daughter Sarah Harris $20; daughter Nancy Thomas $2; money in
Georgia for support of wife and children. Exr.: wife, Elizabeth
Lawrence and trusty Friends, Jacob Lawrance and Allen Leeper.
Wit.: David McCurdy and James Coffey. Proven Oct. session 1808.

P. 43.   WILLIAM BULLOCKS, Dec'd. Will, Jan. 13, 1807. Wife
         Frances; daughter Elizabeth; sons Nathan and Amos.
Exr.: Friend, John Williamson and wife, Frances Bullock. Wit.:
John Williamson, Henry Bailey & Jones Glover. Proven Oct.
session 1808.

P. 44.   Inventory of the Estate of WILLIAM BULLOCK, Dec'd. Note
         on Nathaniel Wych; Negro, Jane; 1 Bible, Testament,
books, Gun, chest, and many other items. Exr.: John Williamson
and Frances Bullock.

P. 45.   EPHRAIM ANDREWS, Dec'd. Will, July 18, 1807. Wife
         Ann; six children: George, Knacy H. (tract of land
adjacent Benjamin Bugg line), Stacy, Elizabeth Young (other
half of land I now live on joining Biggers and Barrens line, and
the negros Pat, Vine, Nelson with their increase), Nancy, Ephraim (one half of land I now live on); daughter Rebekah Kyle
$1.00; grandson Howard Young. Exr.: Wife Ann, son Knacy Andrews
& Benjamin Bugg. Test.: Miles Malone & William Boring. Proven
Jan. session 1809.

P. 46.   Inventory of the Estate of EPHRAIM ANDREWS, Dec'd.
         April 6, 1809. 2 walnut chests, Bible and testament,
and books; many other items; Negros: Will, Jeffery, Dick, Abram,
Warrick, Jacob, Starling, Jack, Bob, Bill, Jenny, Darcas, Doll,
Suck, Aim, Sizo, Lucy, Young Doll, Rachel, Dilse, Tom (in the
state of Va. in possession of George Andrews and William Drum-
right, hired from April 10, 1798); bond on Kimbro Ogilvie, Miles
Malone, Julis Neal, William Neelly, N. B. Hardeman; Account on
W. Williams in Va. Exr.: Benjamin Bugg, Knacy Andrews, and Ann
Andrews.

P. 48.   JAMES GRAY, Dec'd. Will, Jan. 20, 1807. Wife Suckey
         Gray, the land I now live on which is to be conveyed
to me by a representative of James Robertson whose bond I hold;
daughter Lucy Kearny, negros Joe, Joan, Jack, Nelly, Charles,
Judith, Hardy, Anderson, & Minty; daughter Suckey Booker, negros
Jenny, Ephraim, Kissy, Deliah, & James; daughter Sally S. R.
Gray; two youngest boys James M. and Henry K., the land and
negroes of wife when she dies; Suckey Booker and Sally S. R.
Gray, rights to undivided land on Diers or Spring Creek of 3840
acres granted to Joseph and James Gray, North side of Cumberland
River in Stewart County; son Young A. Gray, one half of lands in
state of Georgia; other half of lands in Ga. to three youngest
children; Friend, William Dickson, guardian of James until he is
of age; son Young A. Gray, guardian of son Henry K. Gray until he
is of age, also slaves Starling, Bill, Sarah, Franky, & Patsy.
Exr.: wife, Suckey Gray, friend William Dickson and son Young
A. Gray, Friend, Peter R. Booker. Test.: John Hicks and Harrison Hicks. Proven July session 1809.

P. 51.   JOHN HIGGINS, Dec'd. Will, June 8, 1809. Wife Martha,
         land; sons John and Albert; balance of estate sold and
equally divided between children (not named). Exr.: Wife, Martha
and John Holbert. Wit.: Jeremiah Burns, John Pigg, and Meriman
Landrum. Proven July session 1809.

P. 52.   LUKE SMITH, Dec'd. Will, May 28, 1809. Wife Sione;
         sons Senneah Smith and William Smith; daughter Molinde
Smith; Accounts on Elijah Hunter, Billington Taylor, Green
Williamson; balance due of Sion Records, Sept. 7, 1809, supposed
good; Samuel Brooks, signs note; John Carter, note, supposed
good for nothing; Martin Hall and Washington Thompson, note,
Dec. 1, 1805, supposed to be a bad debt; James Jordan, note in-
dorsed to Hardy Murfree by Daniel Ross, payable May 1, 1808,
doubtful debt; James Mulherrins, note, payable Jan. 1, 1809,
good; Edward Givin and John Hudson, note, due Jan. 1, 1810, good;
Howell Adams, note, payable May 1, 1808; John Hollam, Jr., note
Jan. 1, 1809, good; Charles Stephens, William Gray, note, Sept.
2, 1806, doubtful; Slaves: George (yellow), Peter, Frank, Tom,
Daniel, Will, Dacey, Fortune, Ned, Bob, Sally, Bett, Hetty,
Charlotte, Kitty, Selvy, (Hardy, Maggy, Harriot, are children of
Selvy), Jancy and her children; Dred & Nancy, Abley and her
children; Moses, Edy, Jacob, and Ben, Harvy, Tom Frank, Brister,

5

Phillis, Cloey, Frances, Hanner; 500 pounds of ginned cotton
now in Casse Lytle's Gin; Note on Henry Morres; Thomas Ryan
Butler, note, doubtful and another note also, doubtful due
Oct. 31, 1787; Samuel Bartons note payable April 7, 1794; Credit
of North Carolina currancy, bad debt; Draft on John Wright,
Dec'd. merchant of Franklin, good; many slaves on plantation
where H. Murfree lived and on West Harper on tract of land called Martin Tract; 1 large Bible; many other items. Returned Oct.
session 1809 by David Dickinson, Admr.

P. 91.   Inventory of Goods and Chattel rights and credits of
          BENJAMIN CODINGTON, Dec'd. Presley Hardin, Garner Mc-
Connico, and James Neelly appraised goods. An accepted order
given by John Green to the estate on David Hudspeth, Kentucky
money. August session 180(1 ?). Catherine Codington, Admrx.

P. 92.   Additional Inventory of the Estate of BENJAMIN CODING-
          TON, Dec'd. Returned July session 1806.

P. 92.   Additional Inventory of the Estate of BENJAMIN CODING-
          TON, Dec'd. Bonds on: John Greenlee and R. Hay, Garner
McConnico, Richard Puckett. Sales of BENJAMIN CODINGTON, Dec'd.
held Sept. 3, 1803 and June 7, 1803. Names of those buying:
Presley Hardin, Richard Puckett, Joseph Braden, William McMullin,
William Fluallen, Isaac Bateman, Samuel Merritt, Eli Stacy,
Gustis Holland, John Spencer, Burrell McLamore, David Huston,
Benjamin Davis, Dann Hill, Williamson McMullin, Samuel Currey,
Henry Walker, Richard Orton, John Harness, Henry Kerney, William
Glover, William Davis, William McGah, James Williams, Michael
Kinnard, Jr., James Neely, Moses Chambers, John McKnight, George
Davidson; (does not mention the Bible). Isaac Lay, Admr. in
right of his wife.

P. 95.   Settlement of the Estate of BENJAMIN CODINGTON, Dec'd.
          Expenses: Richard Puckett and Garner McConnico as
guardians, John Parks, receipt. Returned Jan. session 1807.

P. 96.   Settlement of the Property of JOHN HIGHTOWER, Dec'd.
          Sold March 25, 1802. Expenses: Lambert Clayton, John
Hurlery, for bringing family here, Richard Orton, Roger B. Sappington, Jesse Wharton, Alexander Davidson, Stephen Childress
for a judgment obtained by John Rodgers and William Smith in
Hamilton Dist; paid to John Dickinson; Richard Hightower for
board and clothing the children; hire of Negro, Luke; hire of
Negros for years 1802, 1803, 1804, 1805, 1806 and 1807; hire of
Negro, Reuben; hire of Negro to William Sanders. Polly Hightower, alias Polly Sanders, Admrx.

P. 97.   Inventory of Goods and chattels rights and credits of
          ELISHA CASH, Dec'd. Feb. session 1802. Account of
Presley Hardin, Eli Stacys, Howard Cash as Exr. of Joseph Cash,
36 pounds in North Carolina money, this is disputed and an uncertain debt; 1 negro Harry. William Williams, Admr.

P. 98.   Sales of Property of ELISHA CASH, Dec'd. Sold March 3,
          1802. Those buying: Joseph Rolston, John William,
William Williams, Henry Cook, Samuel Curry, Presley Hardin,
Elijah Williams, John Hardin, John Goff, Robert Road, William
McMullin, Peter Edwards, John Rankin, Chapman White. Returned
May session 1802. William Williams, Admr.

P. 99.   Inventory of Daniel Cox, Dec'd. Feb. 4, 1802. Ret.
          Feb. session 1802. Newton Cannon, Admr.

P. 99.   Sales of Daniel Cox, Dec'd.   Sold at public March 8,
          1802 (No names are given). May session 1802. Newton
Cannon, Admr.

          Settlement of Daniel Cox, Dec'd. Estate. Sold Feb. 3,
          1803. Oct. 28, 1803. Newton Cannon, Admr. Returned
to Nov. session 1803.

P. 101.   Inventory of the Estate of ANDREW MCMULLIN, Dec'd. Aug.
          Session 1802. Signed, Mary McMullin.

          Sale of the Estate of ANDREW MCMULLIN Oct. 5, 1802.
          Those buying: Mary McMullin (1 chest and furniture),
James McMullin, John Spencer, John Grimes, Richard Orton, John
Goff, Eli Stacy. Nov. session 1802.

P. 102.   Inventory of JARED MCCONNICO, Dec'd. Bible, 1 old
          Bible, books and other items. May session 1803. Jared
McConnico.

P. 103.   Sales of the Estate of JARED MCCONNICO, Dec'd. May 26,
          1803. Those buying: Thomas Walker, John Williams,
Samuel Curry, Eli Stacy, Joseph C. Cornwell, Ann McConnico,
David McNin, William Glover, Keziah McConnico (bought most of
the property sold including books). Returned to _____ session
180_.

P. 105.   Inventory of the Property of JONES GLOVER, SENR., Dec'd.
          Jan. 10, 1803. Many items including 1 Bible; bond of
Thomas Mason; the following Negros: Abigail, Tempathy, Arthur,
Hannah, Molley, Jemima, Mingo, Tillman, Burrell, Thomas. Re-
turned Feb. session 1803. John Williamson and Jones Glover,
Admr.

P. 106.   Sales of Property of JONES GLOVER, Dec'd. Feb. 28, 1803.
          Those buying: John McKinney, John Williamson, James
Neelly, Esq., Lancaster Glover, Burrell McLemore, William Glover
(Bible), James B. Thompson, Edmond Withers, Thomas Price, Baalam
Newson, William Glover, Jesse Weathers, Lazarus Dotson, Presley
Hardin, Richard Williams, John Spencer, George Stramlor, Jones
Glover, Reuben Dotson, Richard Puckett, William Bullock, Amos
Bullock, John Huston, David Huston, Benjamin Adams, George Neelly,
Henry Petty. Negroes sold: James Glover bought Milley (woman)
$112.00 & Mingo (boy) $210.00; William Glover bought Arthur
(man) $620.00; Burrell McLemore bought Aby (woman) $206.00;
Richard Williamson bought Tom (boy) $220.00; Lancaster Glover
bought Tempy & Tillman (woman & child) $580.00; Burrell McLemore
bought Minney (girl) $490.00; Benjamin Adams bought Hannah (girl)
$311.25; Burrell McLemore bought Burrell (boy) $340.00; John
Williamson and Jones Glover, Admrs.

P. 108.   Inventory of the Estate of NOBLE STOCKETT, Dec'd. Many
          items, One Bible, and books; 1 Negro name Jim about 20
years old. May session 1803. Robert Hulme & Susanna Hulme,
Admrs.

P. 109.   Sales of the Estate of NOBLE STOCKETT, Dec'd. Those
          buying: Robert Hulme (negro, Jim, $400.00), James
McCutchen (sliver watch), James Borland, Robert Clayton, John
Porter, Henry Martin, Samuel McCutchen, John Porter (Bible),
Thomas Garrott, John McCutchen, David Campbell, G. Hulme, Thomas
Connally, Jonathan Hopkins, George Martin, James Gault, Thomas
Speaks, William Thomason, Ephraim Brown, William Stockett. Aug.

Aug. session 1803. Robert Hulme & Susanna Hulme, Admrs.

P. 111. Inventory of the Estate of WILLIAM MURREY, Dec'd.
         Taken Aug. 1, 1803. Thomas O. Due, Admr. Aug. session
1803.

         Inventory of the Estate of METCALF DEGRAFFENREID, Dec'd.
         Nov. 7, 1803. Many items. The following negroes:
Jerry age 49, Ned age 40, James age 30, Solomon age 28, Matt age
24, Ben age 14, Ross, age 12, Jack age 12, Godfrey age 9, Dover
age 9, Maho (?) it age 6, Thomas age 3, Silon (woman) age 42,
Jenny age 35, Abba age 31, Charity age 16, Nancy age 14, Mariah
age 5, Minncy age 14, Sawyer age 5. Returned Nov. session 1803.

P. 113. Sales of METCALF DEGRAFENREID, Dec'd. Jan. 9, 1804.
         Those buying: Mary Ann Degrafenreid (bought most of the
household goods, furniture, and some livestock), Chapman White,
Henry Cook, Philip Maury, Nathan Farmer, Jordan Solomon, Edmund
Cook, Abram M. Degraffenreid, Francis Gunter, Henry Walker, Ro-
bert Guthrie, William White, William Bright, William McKey,
Henry Holliday, Adam Whiteside, Abram Maury, Sen., Robert Davis,
Joseph C. Cornwell, John White, Thomas Masterson. Returned Jan.
session 1804. Henry Cook, one of the Admrs.

P. 115. Sales of part of the Slaves of the Estate of METCALF
         DEGRAFENREID, Dec'd. Jan. 1, 1805. Negro Man, Solomon
sold to C. White $460.00; Negro boy Ben sold to Wm. Williams
$301.00; Negro boy Jack sold to R. Puckett $290.00. Jan. session 1805. Henry Cook, Admr.

P. 116. Inventory of the Estate of JESSE BLACKSHARE, Dec'd.
         July 26, 1803 by Hannah Blackshare and Stephen German,
Admrs. Bond by Joseph Mairs, dated June 25, 1803 for 126 acres
of land on waters of big Harpeth; bricklayers tools, shoemakers
tools, 3 Bibles, 2 Testaments, other books; 1 Tame Door, many
other items. Nov. session 1803.

P. 117. Account of the sales of JESSE BLACKSHARE, Dec'd. Those
         buying: Hannah Blackshare (Bible, books, cradle, blowing
trumpet and many other items), John Porter, John Campbell, Tho-
mas Blackshare, Jacob Garrett, Francis Hodge, Jacob Garrott (1
new Bible), John Settle (1 new Bible), Aaron Averell, Darling
Perry, Micajah West, James McCutchen, John McCutchen, John Hulme,
William Hulme, Robert Hulme, Reuben Huggins, Phillip Walf (Warf?),
George Martin, John McAfee, George Y. Peyton, James Wilson,
Martin Stanley, Abraham Little, Stephen German, Samuel McCutchen,
Miles McAfee. Returned Jan. session 1804.

P. 119. Settlement of the Estate of JESSE BLACKSHARE, Dec'd.
         Debts due from: James McNeelly, interest on money due
from Sept. 2, 1803. Debts to be paid to: Dr. Hayes, James Mc-
Cormac for making coffin $3.00; John Dickson (suits vs. Robert
and George Hulme); Dederick and Tatum; Stephen German; Paid to
Joseph Mairs and Silvanus Castleman. Returned July session 180?.

P. 120. Inventory of the Estate of JOHN JORDAN, Dec'd. Sally
         Jordan, Admrx. April 4, 1804. Returned to April
session 1804.

         Sales of the Estate of JOHN JORDAN, Dec'd. May 4, 1805.
         Those buying: Sally Jordan, Burton Jordan, John Browder,
James Downing. Sale of the Negroes: Sally Jordan bought girl,
Tiller $350.00, girl Jane $107.00, boy Ace $310.00, boy Ben

8

$100.00 July session 1805. Sarah Jordan, Admrx.

P. 121. Inventory of the Estate of JAMES MOORE, Dec'd. James
        Riggs and Peter Fitch, note, desperate debt; Samuel
Southerland & Alexander Chisnhall, note, desp. debt; William
Baldridge & James McCullock, note, desp. debt; Ashby Dunnagan
and John Ray, note, desp. debt. David Robinson and John Moore,
Admrs. Return April session 1805.

P. 122. Sales of the Estate of JAMES MOORE, Dec'd. Those
        buying: Catherine Moore, James Neely, Josiah Peck, John
Neelly, Joel Hobbs, Jesse White, John Alsap, David Cummins,
Betsy Moore, Abraham Walker, John Moore, James Waldriss, David
Robinson, David Dobbins, Thomas Dixon, Seth Barnes, James Hobbs,
Frederick Pinkley, James Faris. Slaves sold: (no names of
slaves given) Catherine Moore, woman and child, 2 girls; Betsy
Moore girl. Sold on June 6, 1805. David Robinson & John Moore,
Admrs. July session 1805.

P. 126. Inventory of the Estate of DAVID DAVIS, Dec'd. Oct.
        16, 1805. Several items, 15 head of wild hogs, the
gitting uncertain. Sarah Davis, Admrx. Oct. session 1805.

        Additional Inventory of the Estate of DAVID DAVIS,
dec'd. Negro woman named Doll. Other items.

P. 127. Sales of the Estate of DAVID DAVIS, dec'd. Nov. 23,
        1805. Those buying: Sarah Davis (wild hogs and other
items), Samuel Wilson, Abraham Rodgers, Thomas Wilson, Arthur
Pierce, Edward Stepleton, Thomas Holton, James Davis. Jan.
session 1806. Sarah Davis, Admrx.

P. 128. Inventory of the Estate of EDMUND COOK, dec'd. Bond in
        the hand of H. Cook of part of stud horse due, Jan. 1,
1806; one bond on H. Cook, due Jan. 1, 1806. The following
slaves: Charles age 21, Sam age 18, Bob age 4, Levina age 5,
Nancy age 24, Juner age 22 (woman), Joham age 2, Milley age. 2.

P. 129. Sales of the Estate of EDMUND COOK, dec'd. Those buy-
        ing: Mary Cook, Henry Cook. Mary Boyd, Admrx. Jan.
sessions 1806. Return April session 1809.

P. 130. Settlement of the Estate of EDMUND COOK, dec'd. Bond
        on Henry Cook; goods bought at sale by Mary Cook and
A. Boyd. April 8, 1809. April session 1809. G. Hulme & John
Witherspoon.

P. 131. Inventory of the Estate of THOMAS STRICKLAND, dec'd.
        Taken Oct. 9, 1804 by Zilpha Strickland, Admrx. Oct.
session 1804.

        Sales of the Estate of THOMAS STRICKLAND, dec'd. Those
buying: Jan. 4, 1805 were Zilpha Strickland, Joseph Slocumb,
Riley Slocumb, Barnabus Beel, Nathan Garner, John Garner, Bri-
tain Garner, John Johnston, Richard Orton, Thomas West, Abraham
Whitesides, Isaac Crow, John Blackman, Enock Bateman, John
Patton. Zilpha Strickland, Admrx. Jan. session 1805.

P. 132. Inventory of the Estate of JOHN HENDERSON, dec'd. Note
        on Robert Magnoss; many items. Oct. session 1804.
John McCalpan, Admr.

P. 133. Sales of the Estate of JOHN HENDERSON, dec'd. Nov. 1,

1804. Those buying: John McCalpan, Senr., George Mayfield, Benjamin White, William McCalpan, George Steward, John Gamble, Henry Rutherford, John McCalpan, Jr. Jan. session 1805. John McCalpan, Admr.

Inventory of the Estate of MOSES MCHUGHES, dec'd. 1 chest, 2 Bibles, 2 Testaments, books, other items. Note on William Miller of Kentucky for 80 pounds of Virginia Currency, due first day of Sept. next, thirty of which is to be paid in property, fourty four shillings like currency on William Hall of the state aforesaid. April session 1804. Jane McHugh.

P. 134. Sales of the estate of MOSES MCHUGH, dec'd. Those buying: Jane McHugh (books and many items), John Garrett, John Hinds, Nathaniel Armstrong, Samuel White, John White, Ephraim Brown, Jacob Garrett (Garrot), William Young, John Hartley, James McNeilly, Robert Hulme, Lemuel Edmiston, James M. Neelly, James McCormac, Samuel McCutchan, Nancy McHugh, James M. McHugh, Polly McHugh, Guilliam Clarke, Lancolot Armstrong, James Gault, Charles Brown (no mention of the Bible). Jane McHugh, Admrx. July session 1804.

P. 137. Settlement of the Estate of MOSES MCHUGH, dec'd. Expenses: travel expenses to Kentucky to collect note on William Miller. Paid to the administratrix of which she is entitled to her dower as the widow of Moses McHugh, dec'd. Board and clothing for Jane McHugh, infant daughter of Moses McHugh, dec'd., age 7 years, until the second Monday in Oct. 1806, which is 3 years at $4.00 per year. Board and clothing for Sarah McHugh, infant daughter of Moses McHugh, dec'd., aged 3 years and 6 months, until the second Monday in Oct. 1806 which is 3 years at $4.00 per year. Returned to Oct. sessions 1807.

P. 138. Inventory of Goods and Chattels of WILLIAM ORTON, dec'd. Oct. 8, 1803. Notes on James Owen, Isaac Nolen, John Hill, Robert Chapman due Dec. 25, 1803; note on William Wallis due Dec. 10, 1803; note on R. Chapman due June 25, 1804; note on Samuel Jentry and John Champ endorsed by John Hill, due Dec. 25, 1803. Account against Robert Williams (verbal) and William Wallis (livestock); stock at Pinkston's, hogs running wild about John Hills, sow running at Reading Wormbells (Wombwell?); account of John Garner (minor) $12.00. Reading Wombuell, Admr. Nov. session 1803.

P. 139. Inventory of the Estate of JOHN GARRETT, dec'd. Large Bible, chest, many items. Ret. _____ session 1806. Thos. Garrett & Jacob Garrett.

P. 140. Sales of the Estate of JOHN GARRETT, dec'd. Those buying: Thomas Speaks, Jenney Garrett, George Stramlar, Jacob Garratt (chest & Bible), John D. Garrott (trunk), Jonathan Botts, William Ivey, Robert Johnston, John Boyer, Henry Martin, William Cowen, Samuel Meddleton, William Honell, John Alsup, Daniel A. Dunham, John Compton, John Jones, Hardy Murphrey, John McCollum, Joseph Dawson, John Porter, Benjamin Dunn, James Jackson, Bartholomew Stovall, James Hartgrave, Dempsey Nash, Isaac Wright, George Hulme, Seven Edney, John Crowder, John Blair, Thomas Garrott, Izrael Mayfield, John Harding, Patrick Deviling, David Wren, Daniel Cowen, Lemuel White, John Pruet, James David John Hulme, Robert Hulme, John Campbell. Returned July session 1806.

P. 144.   Sales of the balance of property of JOHN GARRETT, dec'd.
          Those buying: William Mattocks, John Jones, Henry Hun-
ter, Isaac Wright, John D. Garrett, Jacob Garrett, Thomas Alsup,
Daniel Dunham, James Hartgrave, Jonathan Betts, Thomas Garrett.
Jan. session 1807. Jacob Garrett & Thomas Garrett.

P. 145.   Inventory of the Estate of JAMES GAY, dec'd. Clothing
          and personal items. July 15, 1806. July session 1806.
J. Going, Admr.

          Supplementary Inventory of the Estate of JAMES GAY,
dec'd. Black horse of little value. Oct. session 1806. John
Goyne, Admr.

P. 146.   Sales of the Estate of JAMES GAY, dec'd. Aug. 9, 1806.
          Those buying: John Baldridge (horse), John Goyne
(clothing), Jesse Tarkington (clothing). Oct. session 1806.
John Goyne, Admr.

          A supplemental Account of the sales of the Estate of
JAMES GAY, dec'd. Made Oct. 8, 1806. Black horse sold to Elijah
Richardson. Jan. session 1807. John Goyne, Admr.

P. 147.   Settlement with John Goine, Admr. of JAMES GAY, dec'd.
          Expenses: Jesse Wharton (services), Peter R. Booker,
Dr. Sappington; expenses when he was sick. April 14, 1808.
Signed, G. Hulme and Sion Hunt. July session 1808.

P. 148.   WILLIAM MCKNIGHT. Nuncupative Will. On Nov. 3, 1805
          by accident of horse running away with wagon, William
McKnight received a bodily bruise which caused his death. His
wishes are no sales of his property but family keep it together
and when family grows up, it be divided equally between them.
(no names given). Given April 15, 1806. Proven by the oaths of:
David Shannon, John McKnight, and Samuel McKnight. April session
1806.

P. 149.   Inventory of WILLIAM MCKNIGHT, dec'd. Note on Matthew
          McGaugh due Oct. 1, 1806; note on Isaac Williams due
March 1, 1806; note on John Perryman; judgment against Heatwell
Miles; bond on Julius Sanders and William Logans for 228 acres
of land, doubtful debt. July session 1806. David Shannon and
John McKnight, Admr.

P. 150.   Inventory of the Property of JAMES PATTON, dec'd.
          James Patton and Margaret Patton, Admrs. Returned
Jan. session 1807.

          Account of Sales of the Estate of JAMES PATTON, dec'd.
Those buying: Margaret Patton (most of the slaves (no names
given), and the household items); Charity Upshaw, John Davidson,
Robert Patton, James Patton. Sold March 16, 1807. April session
1807.

P. 152.   Inventory of the Goods and Chattels of JOHN INGRAM,
          dec'd. Note on Wiltshire G. Pool, desperate debt.
Return Jan. session 1807. Thomas Ingram, Admr.

P. 153.   Account of the Sales of the Estate of JOHN INGRAM,
          dec'd. Those buying: Susanna Ingram, Senr., Frances
Ingram, Thomas Ingram (watch), Samuel Ingram, John McCuistian,
Alexander Raulston, James Neal, Susanna Ingram, Junr., Benjamin
Arthur, Elijah Downing, Nicholas Scales, Wilson Davis, Minos

11

Cannon, Johnson Wood. The following slaves were sold: Susanna Ingram, Negro man Tibe $351.00; Frances Ingram, Negro man Andrew $450.00; Susanna Ingram, Negro woman & child $350.00; Thomas Ingram, negro boy $405.00; John McCuistian, negro girl $340.00; Samuel Ingram, negro boy $270.00; Thomas Ingram, negro Betsy ? (boy) $150.00; Susanna Ingram, Jr., negro girl $161.00.

P. 155.   Inventory of Chattell Estate of WILLIAM BRIDGES, dec'd.
            taken Oct. 15, 1806. October session 1806. Terry
Bridges, Admr.

            Sales of the Estate of WILLIAM BRIDGES, dec'd. Those
buying: Nancy Bridges, Charles Campbell, Patrick Campbell. George
Hulme, John Campbell, Thomas Pruet, John McCollum, John Prewett
(lease of land), Thomas Hulme, Ephriam Brown, James Brown, James
Miller, C. Trunkhouser, Robert Prewett, Robert Pruet, Samuel
Edmiston, Terry Bridges, William Young, James McHugh, Patrick
Devilling. Jan. session 1807. Terry Bridges, Admr.

P. 156.   Inventory of the Property of CATHERINE MOORE, dec'd.
            Sold Nov. 27, 1806. Those buying: John Moore, Jesse
Sparkman, Jediah Peck, Thomas Latta, Jesse White, Charles Robin-
son, William Sparkman, John Armstrong, Frederick Mabary, Caleb
Manley, Gray Sims, Elisha Hunter, Senr., Samuel Andrews, Sion
Record, Jacob Patterson, Thomas Taylor, Thrasher McCollum, Swan-
son Johnson, Ezekiel Harrelson, Robert Page, William Lea, David
Dobbins, Moses Sprinkles, James Huey, Betsy Moore, Henry Moore,
David Robinson, John Neelly, William Neelly, Robert Wilkins,
Cloud McCollum, Jacob McCollum, William Simpson, Alexander Moore,
John Robinson, John Farrar, Elijah Hunter, Carter Bethell, George
Glascock, Luke Patterson, Gilbert Patterson, William Harrelson.
The Negro, Diana, was sold to Sion Record but the names of the
other slaves sold were not given. Jan. session 1807. David
Robinson & John Moore, Admr.

P. 161.   Inventory of the Estate of WILLIAM RUTLEDGE, dec'd.
            taken Jan. 5, 1807 by Alexander Rutledge, Admr. Debts
as follows: Jesse Foster, John Folks, Alex Rutledge, William
Alexander, Humphrey Baker, Robert Ore, Edward Elam, John Hail,
Presley Hampton, Old Mr. Fielder. Money rec'd. of Edmiston &
William Irvine. Jan. session 1807. Alexander Rutledge, Admr.

            Sale of the Estate of WILLIAM RUTLEDGE, dec'd. Sold
on Jan. 26, 1807. Those buying: Alexander Rutledge, Margaret
Rutledge, William Rutledge, Elijah Rutledge, Alexander Roulston,
Thomas Sutherland, Wilson Davis, Thompson Wood, Robert Winsett,
Robert Paisley, James Patterson, James Gault, Johnson Wood, John
Barnhart, James Wilburn. April session 1807. Alexander Rutledge,
Admr.

P. 162.   Inventory of the property of JOHN P. PERKINS, dec'd.
            Many items, Negroes hired to William McKey until
12-25-1807; Negro woman hired to Philip Maury until 12-25-1807;
Negro woman hired to Jonathan Phillips until 12-25-1807; Riding
carriage, old stage wagon; obligation on Nathaniel Harris of
Petersburg, Va. payable on Jan. 1, 1807, doubtful debt; note on
Philip Maury, doubtful debt; note on William Mackey due 12-25-
1807; note on Peter Perkins paid Nov. 1, 1802 (& Leah Perkins);
an obligation on William & Michael Robertson for 440 acres of
land lying in Davidson Co. on the east side of Harpeth one mile
above the narrows. Negroes sold: Abraham & Pammey in possession
of William McKey, hired until Dec. 25, 1807; Negro woman, Annekey
hired to Philip Maury until Dec. 25, 1807; Negro woman, Milkey,

12

hired to Jonathan Phillips; one negro boy named William, about
8 years and 1 child 5 or 6 months, in possession of said Phillips;
1 negro boy, about 16, named Peter. Taken on May 11, 1807. July
session 1807. Daniel Perkins.

P. 164.   Inventory of the Estate of WELCOME HODGE, dec'd. 160
           acres of land, many items, Desk, 2 trunks, shot gun
and pouch. July session 1807. Edmond Hodge, Admr.

P. 165.   Account of the Sales of the Estate of WELCOME HODGE,
           dec'd. Sold on August 13, 1807. Those buying: Edmond
Hodges (table), Reuben George, Alexander Rolston, James Billin-
sly, William Beavers (trunk), Nathaniel Kimbro, John Depriest
(desk), Moses Triel, James Downing, Robert Orr, William Towler,
Robert McClellen (shot gun), Barnet Elliott, Sterling Brown,
Benjamin Arthurs. April session 1808. Edmund Hodges, Admr.

P. 166.   Inventory of the Estate of Samuel Clark, dec'd. Note
           on Jonah Ellot (Elliot?) & Col. Christmas; Acct. on
Alexander Ray, John Marine, James House, Senr., John Hall,
William House, James House, Jr., George Busso, Jacob Ragger,
James Downing, Arthur Fuller; Note on Israel McCarrel, Isaac
Rogers, Riley Murry, Thomas Miles, Ephraim Givens; 2 years lease
of cleared land; large walnut chest, large trunk, Bible, walnut
table. The following negroes: negro man named Watt about 35 years
old, negro man Dick 25 years old, negro man Judah about 18 years
old; 2 children, Allen and Lewis; 2 girls over 12, Orrey and
Molley; 1 girl under 12, Mary; 1 boy under 12 years, Frank. July
session 1807. William Martin & Virginia Clark, Admr.

P. 167.   Additional Inventory of the Estate of SAMUEL CLARK,
           dec'd. Clothing and receipt for hire of negroes (not
named). Oct. session 1807. William Martin & Virginia Clark,
Admr.

P. 168.   Account of the Sales of the perishable Estate of
           SAMUEL CLARK, dec'd. Sold August 15, 1807. Those
buying: Virginia Clark (crop growing, table, trunk, clothing of
the deceased, chest, books & many items), William Martin, William
Nolen, Bartholomew Stovall, William House, Joseph Howell, Isaac
Mason, Abram Walker, Jacob Waggoner, John Matthews, Benjamin
Gambrel, Richard Orton, James Downing, Izrall McCarrell, George
Busseo, Abraham Mason, John Depriest, Lawson Hobson, (no mention
of the Bible). Oct. session 1807. William Martin & Virginia
Clark, Admr.

P. 170.   Inventory of the Estate of JOHN NOLAND, dec'd. Taken
           July 10, 1807. Account on William Hooker. July
session. Thomas Hooker and Easter Nolon, Admr.

           Account of the Sales of the Estate of JOHN NOLEN,
dec'd. Sold Aug. 10, 1807. Those buying: John Nolen, Ester
Nolen. Jan. session 1808. Esther Nolen, Admrx.

P. 171.   Inventory of the Estate of JASON WADSWORTH, dec'd.
           50 acres of land, household items. Oct. session 1807.
Obediance Wadsworth, Admrx.

           Account of Sales of the Estate of JASON WADSWORTH,
dec'd. Sold at public auction April 2, 1808 (does not give
names of persons buying). July session 1808. Obedience Wadsworth, Admrx.

P. 172.   Inventory of the Estate of EDITH HAY, dec'd. April
           session 1807.

           Additional Inventory of the Chattel Estate of EDITH
HAY, dec'd. Note on Nathaniel Wych, due 4-11-1808. April
session 1808. Richard Hay.

           Account of the Sales of Personal Estate of EDITH HAY,
dec'd. May 9, 1807. Those buying: Richard Hay, Amos Bullock,
Balaam Hay, William Glover, John P. Gibson (negro, Cheary),
Edith Hay, John Black, note on Nathaniel Wych, William Williams,
James Gibson, Francis McCall, Richard Bently, John Geary, Joel
Stephens. July session 1807.

P. 173.   Settlement made July 9, 1808 between David Squire and
           James Hicks, commissioners appointed to settle on be-
half of the heirs of EDITH HAY, dec'd. with Richard Hay, Admr.
of said estate. Note on John B. Gibson, Joel Stevens, John
Geary, Edith Hay, William Glover, William Williams, Nathaniel
Wych, Balaam Hay, Richard Hay, John Black, James Gibson, Richard
Bentley, Amos Bullock. Expenses: paid to Patrick Gibson for
selling estate; cash paid to John Atkins on one of the legatees;
cash paid to John Lindsey for said dec'd.; four legatees, each
$105.2½. July session.

P. 174.   Inventory of the Estate of MICHAEL WARREN, dec'd.
           Many items, 2 chests, 2 trunks. Oct. session 1807.
David Craig & Alexander Miller.

P. 175.   An Account of the Sales of the Estate of MICHAEL
           WARREN, dec'd. Those buying: Ezekiel Lampkins, John
Elliott, Alexander Miller, John B. McMahon, Thomas Adams, John
Miller, John Gillespie, Thomas Reardon, Robert Sellers, Alex
Montgomery, Isaac Sellers, Thomas Caldwell, Matt Johnston,
William Gurley, David D. Thomas, James Fitzgerald, John Lindsey,
Alexander Gillespie, George White, Samuel Cox, David Craig, James
Craig, John Collie, Olsimus Kindricks, William McLin (& McLain),
William Blakely, David Orton, Robert McLain, William Adams,
William M. McClean, Mark Edwards, David Hines, John F. Cousart,
Isaac Brooks, John Hood, John Jamison, James Copeland, Henry
Davis, John Ray, Alexander Miller. Sold Nov. 5 & 6, 1807. Oct.
session 1808. David Craig & Alex Miller, Admr.

P. 177.   Inventory of the Chattel Estate of DEMPSEY KENNEDY,
           dec'd. Oct. 13, 1807. John Kennedy, Admr. Oct.
session 1807.

           Inventory of the Estate of THOMAS ROGERS, dec'd. (lease
of 7 or 8 acres of land). Oct. session 1807. William Beard,
Admr.

           Account of the Sales of the Estate of THOMAS ROGERS,
dec'd. Sold Nov. 5, 1807. Those buying: Robert Calvert, John
Mitchell, (Sawn?) Johnston, Joel Hobbs, John McCracken, John
McDaniel, William Beard, Moses Parks, Stephen Brooks, William
Wittet, Greenberry Rogers, James Swanson, George Glascock,
Sophia Rogers. Jan. session 1808. William Beard, Admr.

P. 178.   Charles Campbell, Admr. of the Estate of JOHN CAMPBELL,
           dec'd. made the following Inventory: James Campbell
due the estate $1.50; John Brady due the estate $9.00; John
Campbell due the estate $12.00; John Pruett due the estate $4.00;
Patrick Campbell book; Charles Campbell for schooling $6.00.

April session 1808. Charles Campbell, (signed).

           Inventory of the Estate of JOHN SHUMATE, dec'd. Bible,
many items.

P. 179.   Inventory of the Estate of WILLIAM DAVIS, dec'd. Note
           on Richard Venable; note on William Tolley and William
Churchwell (payable in beef). Jan. session 1808. Elizabeth
Davis, Admrx.

           Account of the Sales of the Estate of WILLIAM DAVIS,
dec'd. Sold Feb. 5, 1805. Those buying: John McKnight, James
McKnight, Robert McKnight, Jr., Samuel B. McKnight, Robert Mc-
Knight, Senr., Matthew McGaugh, John Boyd, James Shannon, Thomas
Shannon, Andrew Keigler, Matthew Benthall, Jacob Buckley, Elizabeth Davis, James Elliott, Polly Shannon, David Shannon. July
session 1808. Elizabeth Davis, Admrx.

P. 180.   Inventory of the Estate of JOHN GAMBLING, dec'd. Negro
           girl named Del, about 13 years of age. Jan. session
1808. John White, Admr.

P. 181.   Account of the Sales of the Estate of JOHN GAMBLING,
           dec'd. Those buying: Polley Gamblin, William Hutche-
son, William Wilson, John White (chest), Gorsham Hunt, David
Tate, William Snell, Samuel White, James White, Thomas Cox, Ivy
Burnum, Joshua Burnham, William Robbins, Isaac Acuff, David T.
Alexander. April session 1808. John White, Admr.

P. 182.   Inventory of the Chattell Estate of JONATHAN DAVID,
           dec'd. Many items; various livestock running on the
range on Duck River. Account for Isaac Bells $2.00, Simon Hinds,
Abner Vaughn for $ .50, William Clayton for $7.50, John Davis
for $9.50, Wright Williams for $1.00, Zachariah Martin for $1.00.
Jan. session 1808. Amos Davis, Admr.

P. 183.   Additional Inventory of the Estate of JONATHAN DAVIS.
           dec'd. 87½ cents in the hands of Jonathan Martin.
Oct. session 1808. Amos Davis, Admr.

           Account of the Sales of the Estate of JONATHAN DAVIS,
dec'd. Feb. & March 1808. Those buying: Nancy Davis, John
Fowlkes, John Davis, Mathias Rosenbum, Stephen Clayton, Hartwell
Hyde, William Clayton, David Smith, Richard W. Hyde, Samuel
Venable, John Eaton, Matthew Benthall, John Depriest, Wiltshire
Jordan, William Edmondson, Oliver Williams, John Pillow, Morgan
Fitzpatrick, Wright Williams, Samuel Fitzpatrick, Amos Davis,
Hannah Fleming, Jesse Davis, Daniel Davis, John Clark, Joseph
Jackson, Edmund Rivers, John McClellan, John Perryman, James
McKnight. Sold on Feb. 5 & March 30, 1808. Amos Davis, Admr.
Debt due Estate from Simeon Haynes (Pd. Dec. 1808). Jan.
session 1809.

P. 185.   Inventory of the Estate of JOHN PAGE, dec'd. July 8,
           1808. 1 trunk, 2 chests, many items. July session
1808. Lovey Page, Admrx.

P. 186.   Account of the Sales of the Property of JOHN PAGE,
           dec'd. Those buying: Henry Ingram, Lovey Page (trunk
& chest), Josiah Wooldridge, Peter Pinkston, Thomas Parsons,
William Lock, Amos Rounsavall, Hugh McBride, John Nichols, Joel
Vaughn, Jeremiah Wade, Charles Stevens, William Bennett, Henry
Stevens, Levy Ferrell, James Hungerford, William Stevens, Jr.,

James McBride, Edward Stevens, William Stevens, Jr., Nathan
Scruggs, David Shannon, Senr., John Watson, Joseph Howell, Arthur
Fulghum, Lewis Stevens, John McKnight, Andrew Craig, Lazarus
Crawford, Andrew Pickins, William Alexander, Richard Wood, Joel
Stevens, Turner Pinkston, Coleman Wheaton, William Gurley,
William Mansker, George Mansker, Nathan Scruggs, David Shannon,
David Page, Senr., John McLelland, Robert McLennon, John Patter-
son, John West, William Baker, John Depriest, James Downing,
Henry Jordan, Beverly Ridley, John Crawford, William Lock, Joel
Stevens, William Stevens, Senr. The estate is indebted to Peter
Pinkston for crying the sale, $4.00; Joel Vaughn as clerk, $1.75,
David Shannon as clerk, $1.00. Jan. session 1809.

P. 189.   Inventory of the Estate of THOMAS SHARP, dec'd. taken
            Feb. 9, 1808. Account against Charles Patterson and
B. Watkins. Saddlers tools, sorrel horse, 1 old saddle and bridle, needles, 1 cloth coat and 1 cotton coat, a pr. stockings, 1
blanket great coat, 1 pr. overalls of velvet, 1 pr. overalls of
nankeen, 1 pr. overalls of tow and a worn pr. of cloth, 6 hander-
chiefs, 2 shirts, 1 pr. boots, 1 hat, 1 pr. of flannel slips and
shirts of flannel, 1 waistcoat of swansdown, 1 old waistcoat of
swansdown, 2 other waistcoats, 1 doz. sadlers awls, and 100
tacks, 3 remnants of silk tast ?, 1 pocket knife, 1 lancet, 1
thinble, 4 horse shoes, 1 ink stand, 1 wallet and saddle blanket,
1 pr. of scissors, 1 vial of snuff as medicine, 1 pinch back
ring, 1 breast pin. April session 1808. Jacob Hardner.

P. 190.   Account of the sales of the Estate of THOMAS SHARP,
            dec'd. Sold May 10, 1808. Those buying: B. Wadkins,
Jacob Hardner (velvet pantaloons, breast pin & pinch back ring),
Peter Pinkston, Ludwell Estes, Clayton Talbott, James Dial,
Charles Patton, Martin Stanley, John Sappington. July session
1808. Jacob Hardner, Admr.

P. 191.   Inventory of the estate of BURWELL THORNTON. dec'd.
            Taken April 16, 1806. April session 1806. Ed Swanson.

        Account of the Sales of the Estate of BURWELL THORNTON,
dec'd. Sold June 21, 1806. Those buying: Edward Swanson, John
Gatling (crier), David Lemaster. Edward Swanson, Admr.
July session 1806.

P. 192.   Inventory of the Property of WILLIAM S. MULLIN. dec'd.
            3 chests, 1 candle stand, 2 cupboards, Note on William
Mullin, Joshua Mullin, Jesse Mullin, Henry Key, Charles Campbell,
Daniel Cowan, Sarah Robertson, John Gordon, Elijah Renshaw.
April session 1806. Mary Mullin & J. T. Ellison, Admr.

P. 193.   An Additional Inventory of the Estate of WILLIAM S.
            MULLIN, dec'd. Several items, 1 sun dial, account
against William Young. Mary Mullin & J. T. Elliston, Admr.

        An Additional Inventory of the Estate of WILLIAM S.
MULLIN, dec'd. Account on William Mullin, Jr., Hanks for corn,
W.S. Marr for hire of negroes, Capt. Domombro, Josiah Mullin,
Sneed, Lintz. April session 1807. Mary Mullin & J.T. Elliston,
Admr.

P. 194.   An Additional Inventory on the Estate of WILLIAM S.
            MULLIN. dec'd. Account on Joseph T. Elliston. Oct.
session 1807. Mary Mullin & J. T. Elliston, Admr.

        Account of the Sale of the Estate of WILLIAM S. MULLIN,

dec'd. Slaves sold but no names given. No names of buyers
given. July session 1806. Mary Mullin & J.T. Elliston, Admrs.

P. 196. Inventory of the Estate of SAMUEL HOUSTON, dec'd.
Carpenters tools, many items. April 12, 1809. Test:
Thomas Bell & David Houston. April session 1809. Sidney Hous-
ton, Admr.

Inventory of the Estate of JOHN TAPLEY, dec'd. Negro
men Sam, Napper, Lawson; negro women Aggy & Fanny; judgement
against Stephen Chipley for $18 per month for 6 months for the
hire of 2 negros, a desp. debt.; note on Robert McLemore, Thomas
Newman, Charles Smith, John Dabney, Thomas H. Perkins; cash in
hands of Thomas Edmiston, 1 set of surveying instruments, cash
in hands of Thomas Perkins which he rec'd. of Edward Warren, an
obligation on Robert Grinder in favor of John Tapley & Thomas H.
Perkins to make a deed to a tract of land lying on the waters of
west Harpeth granted to Robert Hays by virtue of John Grinders
warrent for his services in the Continental War; an order drawn
by Nelson on John Anderson for $70 in favor of Peter Perkins and
by him assigned to John Tapley, cash $260.36½ - supposed to be
part of the price of a negro, John Tapley sold to Robert McLemore,
which money we have paid to said McLemore a quantity of corn,
Sundry papers in Peter R. Bookers hands. April session 1809.
Thomas Perkins & Thomas Edmiston.

P. 197. Memorandum of Property sold and Negroes hired belong-
ing to the Estate of JOHN TAPLEY, dec'd. Those buying:
David Squire, Thomas H. Perkins, Robert McLemore, Daniel McMahon,
Edmond Chitwood, John McCandless, Joseph Harris, Amos Bullock,
Thomas Edmiston, Samuel E. Goodridge, Richard Huse, Edward War-
ron, Caleb Manley, George Stramlar, Peter Perkins, John Wither-
spoon, Nicholas T. Perkins, George Davidson, Gregory Wilson,
Zachariah Drake, Hondley Stone; negro woman Aggy sold to David
Squire; negro woman Fanny sold to Caleb Mandley; negro man Napper
sold to George Strumlar; negro man Sam sold to Peter Perkins;
Negro man Lawson sold to Robert McLemore.

P. 199. Inventory of the Estate of ROBERT CARLILE, dec'd.
Many items, chest, shoemakers tools. April session
1809. Stephen Childress, Admr.

Inventory of the Estate of JAMES JOHNSON, dec'd.
Lease of 10 acres of land. Jan. session 1809. James Gault &
Grace Johnson, Admr.

Inventory of the Estate of JAMES MAYFIELD, dec'd. Oct.
session 1808. John Mayfield.

P. 200. A Supplemental Inventory of the Estate of JAMES MAY-
FIELD, dec'd. Debt on John McColpan. Jan. session
1809. John Mayfield, Admr.

Account of the Sales of the Estate of JAMES MAYFIELD,
dec'd. Those buying: John Wooton, James Walker, James Mayfield,
John Mayfield, John Champ, Francis Donalson, I. L. Fielder. Jan.
session 1809. John Mayfield, Admr.

P. 201. Inventory of the Estate of MICHAEL ROBINSON, dec'd.
Taken July 9, 1808. Receipt from James Robinson.
July session 1808. David Robinson, Atty. in fact for William
Cocke, Exr.

Inventory of the Estate of FRANCIS MCCALL, dec'd.
Debt on Jacob Whitehead. Oct. session 1808. Cathren McCall &
Thomas McCrary.

P. 202.   Account of the Sales of the Estate of FRANCIS MCCALL,
           dec'd. Sold Dec. 10, 1808. (no names given) Return
Jan. session 1809.

P. 203.   Inventory of the Perishable Estate of JOHN PATTON,
           dec'd. Negro man named Jim; negro woman and child.
Jan. 9, 1809. Jan. session 1809. Lawrence Bass, Admr.

        Additional Inventory of the Estate of JOHN PATTON,
decd. Debts: Mrs. Robertson, desperate; William Caldwell, desperate; Moses Akins, desperate; David Cummins, sperate; Archibald McReynolds, desperate; Patrick Lyons, desperate; Joel Lewis,
desperate; James Walker, desperate; John Childress, Jr., desperate; Samuel Mitchell, desperate; Spear Roach, desperate; John
Dillihunty, desperate; John Gillespie, desperate; John Boyd,
desperate; John Boyd, desperate; Daniel Joslin, desperate; David
McGavock. sperate; John C. Phillips, desperate; John May, desperate; John Brownlee, desperate; Gen'l. James Robertson, desperate;
Sam'l. Donelson, desperate. In the above list of accounts some
of the persons therein named have left the country and probably
will not return, others are insolvent, and others have accounts
against the estate. Added to the above list: Thomas Tallots,
William T. Lewis, Huch Blacke, Account. April session 1809.
Lawrence Bass, Admr.

P. 204.   Additional Inventory of the Estate of JOHN PATTON.
           dec'd. Andrew Fitzpatrick & James Wilson, debt
sperate; Philip Fishburn, North Carolina Currency, desperate;
George Patton, debt sperate; William Love and transferred by
William T. Lewis, debt desperate; debt desperate are Robert
Franklin, John Crump, George S. Allen, Michael Salter and John
Shackleford; William Parkers, due bill desperate; Robert Hayes,
obligation for 400 acres of land, desperate; William Caldwell,
note for corn, desperate; judgment against John Maclin, desperate. April session 1809. Lawrence Bass, Admr.

P. 205.   Schedule of the Sale of the Personal or Chattel
           property of JOHN PATTON, dec'd. Sold Feb. 20, 1809
(no names given). April session 1809. Lawrence Bass, Admr.

P. 207.   Account of the Sales of the Estate of ROBERT CARLILE,
           dec'd. Sarah Carlile, the widow, (several items and
chest), Stephen Childress, Eli Spurlin, John Porter, Thomas H.
Perkins, George Marlin, James Black, Hardin Perkins. Jan.
session 1810. Stephen Childress, Admr.

        Additional Inventory of the Estate of JOHN HIGGINS,
dec'd. Whiskey in Kentucky. Jan. session 1810.

P. 208.   Inventory of the Estate of ARTHUR FREEMAN, dec'd.
           Negro man, Ben; many items; a claim for money in
Virginia (amount unknown); gold breast pin. Jan. session 1810.
Polly Freeman, Exr.

P. 209.   Account of the sales of the Estate of WILLIAM LOVE,
           dec'd. Those buying: David B. Love, John Marr, John
House, John G. Love (200 acres of land), Thomas Mayfield, William
Hess, Henry Hughah. Jan. session 1810. Joseph Love, Exr.

Inventory of the Estate of JAMES CRAFTON, dec'd.
Negroes: Ellick, Lindey, Eny, Moses, Mary, Sam, Moriah, and
Charles. Several items. Jan. 10, 1810. Jan. session 1810.
John Crafton & Daniel Wilkes.

P. 210.   We, David Shannon and Oliver Williams, two of the
          Justices of the Peace for the County of Williamson,
being appointed as commissioners by the county court at Jan.
session 1810, to settle with Sarah Davis, widow and admrx. of
David Davis, dec'd. _____   Having sold the estate -----.
Expenses to: Peter R. Booker, R.P. Currin, Arthur Pearce, Margaret Davis, Daniel Perkins, John Page. Jan. sessions 1810. O.
Williams and D. Shannon.

          Account of the Sales of the Estate of JOHN HIGGINS,
dec'd. Those buying: Martha Higgins, James Higgins, Albert
Higgins, Abraham Beller, William Higgins; 65 gal. whiskey sold
$22.00. Jan. session 1810. John Halbert, Exr.

          Expenses incurred in the Estate of WILLIAM C. HILL,
dec'd. Jan. 1, 1810. William Parham in Acct. with orphan of
William C. Hill, dec'd.; negro woman, Cloe (keep); board of
Martha, James C., and H. W. Hill for 1809: cash paid Nichols &
McAlister rect. Jan. session 1810. William Parham, Guardian.

P. 211.   Account of the Sales of the Estate of SAMUEL HOUSTON,
          dec'd. Sold May 27, 1809. Those buying: Lydia Hous-
ton (most of the items), David Hoiuston, John Marr, Charles
Boyles, Josiah Wooldridge, James Heiuston, Grove Sharp, Henry
Ingram, Samuel Williams. Jan. session 1810. Lidey Hewston.

P. 212.   Settlement with Sampson Sawyers, Admr. in right of his
          wife, on the Estate of SAMUEL CLARK, decd. Account
to John & Thomas Childress, Deadrick & Sommerville, William Polk;
note, Benjamin Gabriel; account: John Sappington, Samuel Clark,
William Nolen, Richard Henderson, William S. Henderson, Abraham
Whitesides, George Bussuy; Jason Thompson, note; Thomas Light-
foot, account; William Martin's account for cash paid; Thomas
Steward for advice. For boarding and schooling 4 infant child-
ren of the deceased, 2 years and 6 months, or up to this date,
Jan. 12, 1810, $300.00. For keeping 3 negro children up to this
present date, $56.00. William Martin expenses to North Carolina
to settle the benefit of said deceased. Jan. session 1810.
Sampson Sawyer, Admr. in right of his wife and William Martin,
Admr. of the Estate of SAMUEL CLARK. dec'd. Jan. 12, 1810.
Comm: S. Green & O. Williams.

P. 214.   JOSEPH COLES. Will, July 20, 1809. Brother, Thomas
          Cole and sister Elizabeth Cole (the land lying on
little Harpeth, containing 320 acres); Elizabeth Cole, 1 negro
boy named Jack; brothers Samuel Cole & John Cole; sister Nancy
Cole $100.00; sister Mary Cockey 25¢; brother Philip Cole 25¢;
half-brother William Cole $1.00; Exr.: brother Thomas Cole.
Wit.: Daniel Perkins, Sam'l McCutchan, & Sam'l Edmiston. Proven
Jan. session 1810.

P. 215.   EVAN MITCHELL. Will, Aug. 16, 1809. Wife Charity
          (negro woman Jenny); daughter Elizabeth Benton; son
Hamblen Hares; son David Alen (Jenny goes to him at wife's death)
Exr.: Wife Charity. Test.: James Allison and William Ogilvic.
Proven April session 1810.

P. 216.   JOHN T. PRIEST. Will, Nov. 1, 1809. Wife Mary; sell lots in town of Franklin; nine youngest children: Jenney, James, John, Moses, Fanney, David, Elizabeth, Abram, and Rhodey Love. Two other children already provided for, Thomas and Mary Rivers. Exr.: Mary Priest. Wit.: Abram Maury and Robert Davis. Proven April session 1810.

P. 217.   JOSEPH COALES, dec'd. Inventory. Legatees: Thomas Coale, Elizabeth Coale (negro boy Jack), Samuel Coale, John Coales; note on John D. Garrett, Samuel Edmonston, Car. Allen, Thomas Sappington, John Duffield, Ephraim Brown, William Sneede. April session 1810. Thomas Coale, Exr.

Property sold by Thomas Coale, Exr. of JOSEPH COALE, dec'd. Sold April 7, 1810. Those buying: Thomas Cole (50 gal. whiskey $20), John McCutchan, Joseph Stockett, T. W. Stockett. April session 1810. Thomas Coale, Exr.

P. 219.   Settlement of the Estate of JOSEPH COALE, dec'd. Cash paid - Charles A. Burton - funeral expenses; Bradford (printer); by cash - note on John D. Garrett, Samuel Edmondson, Carr Allen; bal. of Thomas Sappington; acct. of John Duffield, Ephraim Brown, William Sneed. April session 1810. S. Green & John Crawford.

P. 220.   The remaining part of the contract between JONATHAN DAVIS, dec'd. and Simon Hinds. April session 1810. Amos Davis.

The following negroes given are in the Inventory of SAMUEL CLARK, dec'd. Watt age 35, Dick age 25, Orra age 18, Mary age 13, Lewis age 4, Frank age 12, Jude age 20. Milley age 17, Allen age 6, Caroline age 1. Feb. 13, 1810. Given by William Martin, one of the Admrs. April session 1810.

P. 221.   The hire of the negroes of the Estate of SAMUEL CLARK, dec'd. Feb. 24, 1810. April session 1810. William Martin & Sampson Sawyers.

Account of the Sales of the Estate of JAMES CRAFTON, dec'd. Feb. 9, 1810. John Crafton was the only person buying. April session 1810. Daniel Wilkes, Admr.

P. 222.   Inventory of the Estate of WILLIAM BERRY, dec'd. Feb. 23, 1810. April session 1810. James Miller & James Berry, Admr.

Inventory of the Estate of MICHAEL KINNARD, dec'd. Note on George Kinnard, Michael Kinnard, John Kinnard, Lewis Stevens, Nathaniel Kinnard, Anthony D. Kinnard, James Thompson, James Jones, William Matthews, George Staton; 2 slaves (no names given). April session 1810

P. 223.   JOHN CHAMPS. Will. The estate left to me by my father; wife not named; children not named. Exr.: Brothers, Thomas Champs & Robert Champs. Test.: John Mayfield & John L. Fielder & Robert Olive. Proven July session 1810.

Thomas Champs qualifies as the Exr. of the Estate of JOHN CHAMPS, dec'd. Oct. session 1810.

P. 225.   Division of the Estate of SAMUEL CLARK, dec'd. July 9, 1810. Widow Virginia (now the wife of Sampson Sawyer); negroes Dick & Lewis valued at $660.00. July session

1810. John H. Crockett, S. Green, Wm. Christmas, John Smith.

P. 226.   Inventory of the Property of JOSEPH ROBERTS, dec'd.
           July 7, 1810. 1 set of cabinet makers tools, a quan-
tity of plank (not known how much). about 3 acres of ground of a
lease for one year after this. July session 1810. William
Brown, Admr.

           Memorandum of the Estate of THOMAS G. CALDWELL, dec'd.
1 negro boy, about 17 years old named Peter; 1 receipt on Charles
Polk for 2 horses valued at 80 pounds to be paid in land on Elk
River; 1 note on Lydal B. Estep; 1 note on William German (said
German is insolvent). July session 1810. Mary Caldwell.

P. 227.   List of the Vendue of WILLIAM BERRY'S Estate. March
           30, 1810. Those buying: James McCutchen, David Mc-
Cord, George Allen, Martha Berry, William Alexander, Charles
Adams, John Depriest, Jesse Linisy, Valentine Allen, David Spain,
William Hickman, James Andrews, Henry Scales, Edward McNeal,
Alexander Johnson, Adam Summers, James Miller, Thomas Berry,
William Beaty, John Eaton, James Berry, Amos Davis, John Clark,
William Walls, John Brim, William Banks, John Bostick, Adam
Miller. April 30, 1810. July session 1810. James Miller &
James Berry, Admr.

           Allowance for the widow and children of WILLIAM BERRY,
dec'd. for 1 year. April 30, 1810 by William Wilson, Robert
Donnalson, & Abram Summers. July session 1810. James Miller &
James Berry, Admr.

P. 229.   An Inventory of the Estate of EVAN MITCHELL, dec'd.
           1 negro girl Jenny $400.00; other items. July 7. 1810.
James Allison, J.P. July session 1810. Richard Ogilvie, Kimbrough Ogilvie, and Henry Bailey.

P. 230.   Inventory of the Estate of JOHN PRIEST, dec'd. 1 deed
           from Abram Maury to John Priest dated Nov. 5, 1809,
for 2 lots in Franklin no. 66 & 76 not recorded; 1 note from
Robert Bevile to John Priest due Oct. 7. 1809, desperate. Of
the above property there was sold on the 4th of May 1810 by
Thomas Hulme, to satisfy three executions against John Priest,
dec'd. One of the instance of John Sample, one of the instance
of Ro. P. Currin, one of the instance of Thomas Masterson. July
session 1810. Mary Priest, Ext.

P. 230.   By order of the court of Williamson County, April
           session 1810, we have measured the lines of the land
deeded to JOHN PATTON, dec'd. out of grant No. 43 that was formerly granted to William Collingsworth for 640 acres and that
there was deeded to John Patton 367 acres. The said John Patton
has deed to James Wilson 48 acres and 150 poles of that land and
the balance of the land being divided among the heirs of said
John Patton in the following manner to wit: Sally Patton - 106
acres her dower, (between Franklin Road and Beesley's fence, near
Crocketts field); No. 1 - Hannah Patton 21 acres; No. 2- John
Patton 22 acres; No. 3 - John Cunningham and Polly his wife 19
acres; No. 4 - Drucilla Stainback, formerly Drucilla Patton (on
west link of little Harpeth) 24 acres; No. 5 - Betsy Patton
(side of Franklin Road) 20 acres; No. 6 - Thomas Patton (on
Crockett's line) 20 acres; No. 7 - Nancy Bass, formerly Nancy
Patton (on west side of Little Harpeth); No. 8 - James Patton
19 acres; No. 9 - George Patton 19 acres; No. 10 - William Patton
20 acres. Given July 10, 1810. J. Bruff ?, John Holt, James

Bradley, Samuel Wilson, and James Davis, Surveyor. July session
1810.

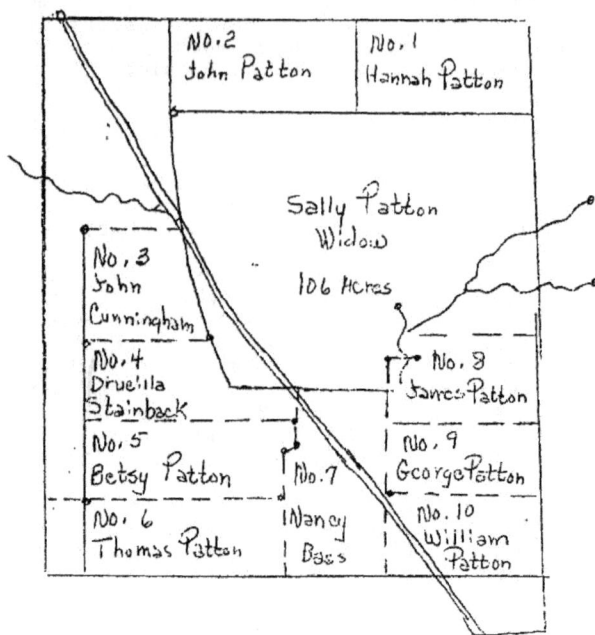

No.2 John Patton

No.1 Hannah Patton

Sally Patton Widow 106 Acres

No.3 John Cunningham

No.4 Drue'ila Stainback

No.8 James Patton

No.5 Betsy Patton

No.7 Nancy Bass

No.9 George Patton

No.6 Thomas Patton

No.10 William Patton

P. 235.   Inventory of the goods and Chattels rights and credits
         of JOHN CHAMP, dec'd.   4 negroes: Ailse, Nance, George
and London; 3 notes on John Mayfield; 1 note on Tolliver Brady
and John L. Fielder. Oct. session 1810. Thomas Champ.

         Account of the sales of the Estate of WILLIAM HUNNELL,
dec'd. Sold on Nov. 20, 1809. Those buying: Robert Caniday,
Benjamin Brown, Peter Honoll (Hunnell?), Andrew McMahon, Richard
Hart (1 set of coopers tools), Joseph Dewery, John Jones, Henry
Inman, Hugh Allison, Elisha Williams, Samuel Williams, James
Prickett, Ambrose Cobb, Isiah Davey, Andrew Mahan.

         Account of the sales of the Estate of WILLIAM HUNNEL,
dec'd. Sold on Dec. 30, 1809. Those buying: Robert Cannady,
Robert Shannon, Andrew McMahon, Jered Puckett, Peter Honoll,
Thomas Rieves, William Conney, James Conney, David Witherspoon,
Hugh Allison, Peter Honoll. Given Oct. 8, 1810. Returned Oct.
session 1810. Hugh Allison.

P. 237.   Inventory of the Estate of JAMES MCCUTCHEN, dec'd.
         Many items, 1 walnut chest, 1 small Bible, books; note
on Jonathan Hopkins, Robert Hulme, Robert Clayton. Oct. session
1810. Hannah McCutchen, Admrx.

         A Supplemental Inventory of the Estate of EPHRAIM
ANDREWS, dec'd. 1 negro Jerry, 1 negro Milley; bond on Benjamin
Bugg, Knacy Andrews, Richard Locke. Jan. session 1811.

22

P. 238.   List of the Sale of the Estate of JAMES MCCUTCHAN,
           dec'd. Nov. 3. 1810. Those buying: Hannah McCutchan,
William Sargent (walnut chest), John Porter, David Pinkerton,
John McCutchan, Elisha Reynolds, John McAffee, William McCutchan,
Thomas S. Robertson, Neal Hopkins, Jason Hopkins, Winifred Hop-
kins, Robert Hulme, John S. Fielder. Jan. session 1811.

P. 239.   Inventory of the good and Chattels rights and credits
           of THOMAS HOPE, dec'd. Notes on William Perry, William
Hemphill, David P. Anderson, Edley Ewing, John Clark, Basil
Berry, William Berry, Daniel Perkins, William Sargent, John Pre-
wett, John Harvey; $10 sent to Widow Hope; $4 lent to Mary Ann
Taylor. Jan. session 1811. Thomas Berry, Admr.

P. 240.   Settlement of the Estate of JOHN PRYOR, dec'd. with
           Hendley Stone, Admr. in right of his wife Elizabeth,
the Admrx. of the said estate and a guardian for Peter Pryor and
Green Pryor, orphans of the said John Pryor. Dec. 29, 1810.
Jan. 15, 1799 - bal. due as recorded from Pittsylvania Court,
Virginia - settled Jan. 15, 1799. Jan. 29, 1799 - To cash paid
John Brown pro. act. May 12, 1807 - To cash paid Col. Peter
Perkins as pr. award of admr. debt, damages, & etc. Bal. due
Mr. (Wm.?) Stone. Peter Pryor & Green Pryor, orphans of John
Pryor, dec'd. Hendley Stone, guardian to said orphans. Jan.
1804 - Boarding, clothing, schooling and expenses from the year
1804. Balance from Virginia as recorded by hire of Sundry
negros and rent of lands in Pittsylvania, Virginia from Dec. 1803
up to present date. Jan. session 1811. Daniel Perkins, N.
Perkins, Sr., Edward Warren, S. Childress.

P. 241.   List of the Property sold by Thomas Champ, Exr. of the
           Estate of John champ, dec'd. Oct. 30, 1810. Those
buying: Andrew Baldrige, John Mayfield, Dr. John White, Frederick
Owen (chest), Mary Champ (Bible). G. Hunt, Nelson Fields, John
Campbell, John Hill, Frederick Owen, Senr., John S. Fielder,
Christian Hughes, Robert Baldridge, James Moore, James Walker,
Robert Henderson, Joel Riggs, Peter Reaves, Richard Hightower,
John McCalpan, Nimrod Williams, Nathaniel Herbert. Jan. session
1811. Thomas Champ, Exr.

P. 242.   Settlement of the Estate of JOHN PAGE, dec'd. An
           order given in Oct. session 1810. Jan. 14, 1811.
S. Green & Nicholas Scales.

P. 243.   Balance due the estate of JOHN PAGE, dec'd. A will
           appeared by the within settlement an allowance made to
the Admrx. of John Page, dec'd. for her services. An allowance
made for the maintainance of four small children for two years.
Jan. 19, 1811. Jan. session 1811. S. Green & James Black.

           Dr. William Parham, guardian, in account with the
orphans of WILLIAM C. HILL, dec'd. Jan. 1, 1811 - To John
Warren for the hire of a negro man, Broomfield. To Talbott &
Reed for the hire of a negro man, Isham (note 1810). To Potts
for the hire of negro man Toby (note 1810). To Jacob Hardner -
note for the hire of negro man, Lewis (note 1810). To Sion
Record & John Wilkins for hire of negro boy, Jerry (note for
1810). To the hire of Easter and her child (self - 1810). To
the hire of Phil, a negro boy (self). By cash paid Edward Harrison for boarding and schooling of James C. and Henry W. Hill.
By cash paid D. Caldwell for Martha James and H.W. Hill, Nichol
and McAlister for J.C. & H.W. Hill #4, Henry W. Hill #5, James
C. Hill #5, Martha Hill #6, 7, & 8; Cash paid Boarding Martha

Hill for year 1810. To cash paid John Branch for a chest for
Martha Hill #9; cash paid Nielson King and Mitchell #10. Jan.
session 1811.

P. 244.   THOMAS SIMMONS. Will, Oct. 5, 1794. Of Caswell
          County, North Carolina. Wife Priscilla, plantation of
157 acres and the slaves: Phillis, Fanney, Tom, Rachel and Isbell. Children: Hannah Graves, Martha, Priscilla, Keziah, Sarah,
and Thomas, to divide the following slaves between the children
just mentioned (old Lucy, Milley, Dilcoy, Young Lucy, and Reuben);
son Alexander, 170 acres land and negro Aaron; son Thomas, 157
acres land and negro Sam. Exr.: Thomas Graves and Thomas Simmons (son). Test.: Charles Taylor and Butler Murphey. Proven
Oct. session 1794. April session 1811. Thos. Simmons, Admr.

          Inventory of the Estate of THOMAS SIMMONS, dec'd.
which was by his will loaned to his son, Alexander during his
life, then by his will to be divided between all the children of
said Thomas, dec'd. Taken by me the Exr. of said Thomas this
April 11, 1811. The following negroes: man named Aaron, boy
Charles, boy Lee, woman Philis, boy Reuben, boy Stephen. Proven
April session 1811. Thomas Simmons, Exr. Returned April session 1811.

P. 246.   An Account of the Sales of the Estate of EPHRAIM
          ANDREWS, dec'd. Sold 21st, 22nd, 23rd, 24th, and 25th
Jan. 1811. Returned by Knacy Andrews and Benjamin Bugg, Exr.
April session 1811. Those buying: James Allison, Joel Stevens,
John Ogilvie, John Robenson, Peter Pinkston, George H. Allen,
William A. Price, Will Stevens, Hugh Pinkston, William Alexander,
John R. Tankersley, Ephriam Bugg, Robert McConnel, John Watts,
Elijah Mayfield, William Tucker, Senr., Josiah Wilson, Work
Smith, John Baker, Edward Scruggs, Greenberry Dean, Isiah White,
John Dalton, Tapley Andrews, Julian Neal, Benjamin Little, John
Oslin, Curtis Hooks, William Borin, William Logate, Loamine
Steavens, William Young, David Pinkston, Thomas Wilson, Thomas
Allison, Alexander Bennett, Clement Walls, James Joyce, Gideon
Hansley, Alexander Johnston, John Pillow, Richard Ranolds, George
Kinnard, Nelson Chapman, George Melbane, Charles Dowd, Richard
Ogilvie, George Manco, Joseph Glover, ? Allen, Kimbro Ogilvie,
Lewis Mance, Hugh McBride, Abram Cole, Lancaster Glover, Richard
S. Locke, Robert Rogers, Patrick Gibson, Obediah Driskell,
Nicholas Neal, Michael Kinnard (account on Joel Stevens), Charles
Stevens (account on William Stevens). The following slaves:
Knacy Andrews old negro Will, woman & 2 children Dolly, Dolly &
Jerry, mulato boy John, negro girl Lucy; John Erwin negro girl,
Size; Thomas Bradley negro woman Amy, negro boy child Bob;
Cornelius Matthews negro Dick; Ephraim Andrews negro Abraham,
negro woman & her children Susan, Will & Milley, ($10) 2 old
negroes, Jeffrey & Jenney; Benjamin Bugg woman and 2 children
Darcus, Rachel & Dilcey, negro Jacob, negro Worick & negro boy
Starling.

P. 251.   Settlement of the Estate of WILLIAM MULLIN, dec'd.
          Interest against William Mullin, Jr.; account against
Joshua Mullin, John Gordon, William Young, Jesse Mullin, Ben
Shaw, ? Hanks, J.T. Ellison, Charles Campbell, Henry Key, Mrs.
Robertson. A judgment on Chapman and others. Account against
Daniel Cowen. Comm.: Oliver Williams & Sion Hunt. April 11,
1811. Joseph T. Ellison, Admr. April session 1811.

P. 253.   Feb. 10, 1807 thru Jan. 9, 1809. Polly Pate, dr. to
          Lancaster Glover, her guardian, expenses for clothing,

expenses from Virginia, and for 12 months schooling. Feb. 10,
1807 thru Jan. 15, 1809 - Elizabeth Pate, Dr. to Lancaster
Glover, her guardian, expenses from Virginia, for clothing and
12 months of schooling. Feb. 10, 1807 thru Jan. 1808 - Nancy
Pate, dr. to Lancaster Glover, her guardian, expenses for clothing, 9 months of schooling, expenses from Virginia. April 4,
1807 thru 1810 - Porson G. Pate, dr. to Lancaster Glover, his
guardian, expenses from Virginia, 9 months schooling, 83 days
schooling, school supplies and hat. Lancaster Glover, guardian,
dr. to Polly, Elizabeth Pate, Nancy Pate, & Porson G. Pate,
heirs of Hardy Pate, dec'd., interest on $400 from Dec. 25, 1804
to April 8, 1811. Interest on $159.93 7 mills from Feb. 28.
1803 to April 8, 1811. Returned April session 1811.

P. 254.   Settlement of the Estate of JOHN JORDAN, dec'd. March
           9, 1811. By amount paid John Anderson as part and
receipt. By amount paid Sheriff. Benjamin McCuistion, Admr.
in right of his wife.

P. 255.   JAMES BUFORD. Will, April 10, 1811. Daughter Sicila,
           son Hennery, daughter Frankey, sons Spencer & Charles,
daughter Charlotte, negro boy Harry; son Edward, negroes Dick &
Stephen, the plantation where I now live after giving James
Luster the one fifth part, provided he make Hennery Buford a
title to the tract of land whereon Hennery Buford lives in
Virginia. If not, Hennery Buford is to have the part left to
James Luster; daughters Katharine and Pricila; grandson Duncan
C_mmeron. The following negroes to be divided between my three
daughters, Charlotte, Pricilla & Catherine (negroes: Andrew,
Suckey, Darby, Pate, Jude, Gloster, Fanny, and Sam and their
increase); son James, negro Peter. Exr.: Sons James, Spencer,
Charles and Edward Buford. Wit.: Elisha Dodson, Gabriel Buford
and Alexander Mebane. Proven July session.

P. 257.   Inventory of the Estate of CHARLES TAYLOR, dec'd.
           Note on George Stramlar. July 13, 1811. July session
1811. Henry Atkinson, Admr.

P. 257.   April 27, 1811. The amount of the Sail of the property
           of THOMAS SIMMONS, dec'd. which was loaned to his son
Alexander, during his life, then to be sold and equel devided
amungst all his sisters and brothers. Those buying: Thomas
Simmons (six negroes, Aaron, Phillis, Charles, Rulien, Lee &
Stephen and a trumpet), Daniel Adams, Jordan Solomon. July
session 1811.

P. 258.   Inventory of the Sale together with all the debts due
           and accounts coming to the estate of MICHAEL KENARD,
dec'd. under the Admr. of Lewis Stevens and Michale Kinnard.
Notes on Demand Nov. 4, 1810 on the following: George Kennard,
Lewis Stevens, James Thompson, Nathaniel Kennard, William
Matthews, Anthony Kennard, John Kennard, Michael Kennard, John
Stevens & George Seaton. Notes on demand Feb. 12, 1811 on the
following: Nathaniel Kennard, Richard Rodes, Cary Morgan, George
Seaton, John Kinnard, Anthony Kennard, John Curry, Robert More,
George Bennett, William Caldwell. Notes on demand Feb. 17, 1811
on the following: Nelson Chapman, James Thompson, Nathaniel
Kennard, Michael Kennard, Betty Hooks, Mark Michel, Curtis Hooks,
Anthony Kennard & Lewis Stevens; note on George Kennard on demand
Feb. 23, 1811; note on Benton Harris, rec'd. May 12, 1810; note
on John Kennard on demand Jan. 17, 1811; $1 account against
Loamie Stevens. July session 1811. Michael Kennard & Lewis
Stevens.

P. 259.   Account of the sales of the Estate of WILLIAM BULLOCK,
            dec'd. Dec. 10, 1810. Those buying: Amos Bullock,
Nathan Bullock, Elizabeth Bullock, William May, Sylvanus Sturdu-
vant, George Sleeker, Jacob Rowland, Charles Boyles, John Hay,
Thomas Jones, James House, George Neelly, George Davidson, James
Terryl (negro girl Jane), Amos Bullock (note due from Nathaniel
Wyche). July session 1811. John Williamson, Exr.

P. 260.   JOHN NOWLIN. Will, Sept. 23, 1808. Bartholomew
            Stovall and his wife Aggy Stovall $1.00; son Golsby
Nolen $1.00; Son-in-law John Duffy and his wife Salley Duffey
$1.00; wife Anney Nolen; 2 sons Littleberry Nolen & Davis Nolen
(most of his estate). Exr.: William Nolin and his son Gen'l
Lee Nolin. Wit.: William Christmas and Jordon Solomon, John
Job, and Gen'l. L. Nolin. Proven Oct. session 1811.

P. 261.   Inventory of the estate of JOHN NOLIN, dec'd. Oct.
            session 1811. Many items, 2 chests, 2 tame deer, 1
Bible and Books. Negro men Abel and Ned. Accounts on the
following persons: Isaac Mason, Israel McCarrell, Augusty Holland,
Edmund Chitwood, William Little, William Osteen, William Price,
William M. Grider, James Downing, William Rutledge, Peter Gillum
& Jesse Hurd, George Manker, Senr., A. Fergerson, H. Bell (bad
debt), William Venable, William Fielder, John Chitwood, Old
William Venable, John Harkings, Jesse Osteen, Alex McDonald,
Nathaniel Aldridge, William Wilkockson, Armer McCrary, John
Taylor, Alex Simpson, William Brooks, Daniel Willis. Oct.
session 1811. Gen'l. L. Nolen, Exr.

P. 262.   Account of the sales of the Estate of JOHN NOLEN. dec'd.
            Those buying: William Nolen, Senr., Walter Kennard
(tomahock); negro men Ned and Abel (buyers names not given).
Jan. session 1812.

P. 264.   WILLIAM CHRISTMAS. Will. Tract of land I now live
            on, on Mill Creek; tract of land which I purchased of
Bennett Philips; adjoining land which I purchased of Henry Butler and one of John Buchanan; grandson William Christmas Marrs,
plantation where I live and the following negroes: boy Abram,
girl Mary, now in the possession of his father Josiah Marrs;
wife Abegal; daughter Sally Jane Dyer, my clock and case; daughter Polley Graves Connelly, 1000 acres of land on the clear fork
on Cumberland River; daughters Sally Jane Dyer and Patsey Green,
all the negroes except Bobb. Oct. 31, 1811. Exr.: Sherwood
Green & Joel Dyer, sons-in-law. Wit.: B. Searcy, James Vaulx.
Proven Jan. session 1812.

P. 267.   Inventory of the Estate of WILLIAM CHRISTMAS, dec'd.
            Many items, the silver cup and fork worn by Col.
Christmas on his arm. Negroes: Jubels, Bobb, Adam, and Dinah.
Notes on the following people: John Davis, John Allen, Sherwood
Green, Edward Gregory, Gideon Pillow, Richard Howard, William
McGimsey, Arthur Harris, William Wakefield, John K. Campbell,
John Crawford, John Murrey, Samuel Weakley, William Dickson,
B.G. Stewart, R. & D. Shores, William McClure, A. Stubblefield,
Joseph Coleman, Moses Fisk. John C. McLemore (800 acres of land
warrent), Sampson Sawyers, Henry Lyons, Patrick Lyons, William
P. Anderson, Hugh T. Bell, William Christmas, John Coleman, Enoch
P. Connell, Ephraim B. Davidson, John Griffin, John Givin, Thomas
Harney, Thomas Johnson, Lewis Evans, Elm Holmes, Thomas Shute,
Edward Wilson, William Luton, Dawsey Hudson, John Jones, William
B. Ross, John Haywood, Benjamin Mancue, Stephen Debow. P. M.
Eackem(?), William P. Anderson, Calvin Wheaton, William G. Magison,

Elisha Pruett, John Currey, W. Brackin, James Coock, John Moore,
Simpson Harris, Moses Fisk, John Andrews, John Bowen, Joseph
Collins, Thomas Clonlan, Henry Conway, Robert H. Dyer, Augustin
Davis, Garrott Gooloes heirs, William Green, John Haywood,
Turner Lane, William Montgomery, G.S. Nolin, William Mitchell,
Edward Mitchell, William Outlaw, Henry Pughe, Rouben Searcy,
Robert Searcy, Robert Weakley, James Ralston, William Good,
Benjamin Blackman, McLemore & Givins, Philips & Campbell, Mc-
Lemore, Watkins & Mitchell, Co. William Moore, William Nelson,
Stephen Montgomery, John Overton, Robert Prince, Abner Pillow,
Francis Taylor, James Taylor, Joseph Woolfork, William Verill,
Edward Jinnins, Edward Givins, William Dickson, John Primm.
Account by Dr. William Dickson for 1 note on James Tygard. April
session 1812. Returned April session 1812. L. Green & Joel
Dyer, Exr.

P. 271.   Account of the sales of the Estate of WILLIAM CHRIST-
           MAS, dec'd. Those buying: Sherwood Green, Benjamin
Gamble, Joel Dyer, James Scott, Josiah Hall, Nelson Foilds,
Thomas Griggs, Isaac Battle, Caleb Willis, Izrael McCarrel, James
Haley, Ansolum Nolen, William L. Watson, Isaac Nicholson, James
Bradley, Isaac Mason, Willie L. Davis, Henry McClure, Allen
Nolen, William Nolen. April session 1812. L. Green & Joel Dyer,
Exr.

P. 272.   JOE PARRISH. Nuncupative Will, Nov. 27, 1811. Debt
           due me by Hinchey Petway for balance of land conveyed
by me to the said Hinchey (adjoining town of Franklin), tract of
land I now live on which lies east of the Mill Creek running
through it; wife Susannah; daughter Caroline who is married to
the said Hinchey; minor children not named. Wit.: Abram Maury,
Senr. and Chapman White. Proven Jan. session 1812.

P. 274.   Inventory of the goods and chattels rights and credits
           of JOEL PARRISH, dec'd. 14 negroes: Amos, Molley,
Bobb, Clary, William, Nancy, Tom, Michael, Mariah, Frank, Milly,
Isral, Dilcy, and Julia; note on John Sappington; many items, ox
cart, and chest. April 13, 1812. April session 1812. Chapman
White & Abram Maury, Admr.

           WILLIAM HIGGINS, dec'd. Nuncupative Will. Sworn to
me by William Halbert and Martha Barnett; wife Phoebe, support
until she could go to her friends; 60 acres of land lying on the
head of Harpeth, and other property to be sold to pay the doctor
and his other debts. Jan. session 1812. Proven Jan. session
1812.

P. 275.   Inventory of the Property of WILLIAM HIGGINS, dec'd.
           60 acres of land head of Harpeth. Jan. session 1812.
John Higgins, Admr.

           Account of the sales of the Estate of WILLIAM HIGGINS,
dec'd. Those buying: William Ray, John Windrow, Thomas Hendrix,
William Halbert, James Higgin (slaymakers tools), James Hefflin,
John Lamb, Halbert Higgins, Beverly Harris, John Webb (60 acres
land), John Pigg, John Patterson, Morimon Landrum, William Powell,
Jarvis Jones, James Ray, William Taylor, Thomas Carson. April
session 1812. John Higgins, Admr.

           JOHN SEAY. Will, March 24, 1811. Wife Jenny Seay,
150 acres of land where I now live; four children, Eli A. Seay,
Martha A. Seay, Elizabeth W. Seay, and Polley Any Seay; to my
children, my part of my father's estate which is coming to me,

when the children come of age and to be equally divided between
them. Exr.: Beloved friends John & Henry Windrow. Wit.: Benjamin Carr and Samuel Brown. Proven Jan. session 1812.

P. 277.   Inventory of the personal Estate of JOSEPH POTTS,
          dec'd. Return Oct. term. Negro man Peter and negro
woman Sarah and three children; set of carpenters tools, other
items. Samuel Crockett, Admr.

          ANN STEWARD. Will, Nov. 3, 1803. Jinea Kee 1 chest;
          Nancy Kee spinning wheel and reel; loving daughter
Jinea Key my cloke not made up; Margaret Stewart satin bonnet;
Joseph Elexander bay horse; Sarah Stewart satten gown; daughter
Jenny Kee rest of wearing apparel; Nancy Kee money when she comes
of age; Joseph Elexander money to be put in Donnald Purkins
hands. Exr.: Charles Brown. Wit.: Ephraim Brown, John Johnson
& Charles Brown. Proven Jan. session 1812.

P. 279.   Inventory of the goods and chattels rights and credits
          of ANN STEWARD, dec'd. Jan. 18. 1812. Many items,
books; bond on Robert Smith, Robert Bitticks & Thomas Berry,
Jonathan Cooper & Thomas Berry, Henry Stuart and Sam'l McCutchen,
William Sneed & Sam'l McCutchan, William Carpenter & Henry
Stuart, Nathan Reeves & Wm. Sneed. Jan. session. Thomas Stuart,
Admr.

P. 280.   Account of the sales of the Estate of ANN STEWART,
          dec'd. April 2. 1811. Those buying:
Joseph Alexander, Ezekiel Davsin, Hugh Barr, Joseph Alexander,
Thomas Berry, Larence Young, Thomas Malone, Andrew Jemmerson,
John Mayfield (2 Bibles), Joshua Burham, Nancy Kee, John Porter,
Vincent Greer, Barnet Markim, John S. Campbell, John Hull, Jacob
Garrett, John Dilling, Charles Brown, Curnelis Mackfadin. April
session 1812. Stephen Childress, Auctioneer.

P. 282.   List of sales of the Property of CHARLES TAYLOR, dec'd.
          Sold Oct. 17. 1811; (no names given). Oct. session
1811. Henry H. Jackson, Admr.

          Inventory of the Property of MARTHA EVANS, dec'd.
Lease of land for 1 year; negro man and other items. Jan. session 1812. Thomas Clark & John Evans, Admr.

          Account of Sales of the Estate of MARTHA EVANS. dec'd.
Sold Feb. 12, 1812; (no names given of persons buying). April
session 1812.

P. 283.   Inventory of the Estate of JOHN DOWD, dec'd. Jan.
          session 1812. John Dowd, Charles Dowd, and James
Wilkins.

          Account of the Sales of the Estate of JOHN DOWD. dec'd.
Jan. 24, 1812. Those buying: James Wilkins (pistol). Isaiah
White, Jean Dowd, Anderson Powell, Andrew McCorkle, William
Carson, Polly Powel, Thomas McElwen, Thomas Gillespie, Clem
Wall. Charles Dowd, Nelson Chapman, David Gillespie, Greanberry
Deen.

          1 year allowance of Jean Dowd and family allowed to
them by David Gillespie and David Crisman. $2 paid to Nelson
Chapman for crying the sale. April session 1812.

P. 285.   Inventory of the Estate of GEORGE HUDLOW, dec'd. Jan.

11, 1812. Note on Charles Boyles; walnut chest, other
items; note on Jack Camden. Jan. session 1812. Barbara Hudlow.

Inventory of the Estate of WILLIAM STONE. dec'd. Jan.
9, 1812. 7 negroes: Cloe, Ben, Milley, Harry, Lewis, Season, and
Manuel; 122 acres of land. Jan. session 1812. Jane Stone &
William Stone, Admr.

P. 286. Account of the Property sold at the sale of WILLIAM
STONE, SENR., dec'd. Feb. 14, 1812. Those buying:
G.S. Nolen, John McCutchan, E. Riggs, Robert Carethers, Caleb
Willis, Ambrose Owen, John S. Fielder, John Hill, Thomas Bellue,
Thomas Simmons, Izrael McCarrel. Gurson Hunt, William McEnlers,
John Mayfield, Rowley Stone, David Lovet, John Boyd, James Ful-
ton, John Holt, Edward Stone, Jane Stone, James Jobe, John
Carothers, A.B. Morton, William Nolen, Jabez Owen, Agnes Stone,
James Love. April session 1812.

P. 287. Inventory of the Estate of DUDLEY PORTER, dec'd.
William Duncas due $5.00; David McCord due $9.00;
Kizey Shinol due $10.00; William Wilson 50 gal. whiskey. April
session 1812. Sarah Porter, Admrx.

P. 288. Inventory of the goods and chattels of PETER RIEVES.
dec'd. April 12, 1812. Several items; small negro
boy. April session 1812. James Owen, Admr.

Inventory of the Estate of LITTLEBERRY EPPERSON. dec'd.
March 30, 1812. April session 1812.

Inventory of the Estate of JAMES BUFORD, dec'd. Large
Bible, notes on the following people: Nicholas Lavender, Richard
Roods, Joseph Teat, Samuel Braddon, Bud Lavender, Neil Johnson,
Samuel Bond, William Sallen, Joshua Barnes, Peter Edwards, John
House, Benagy Goodman, George Glascock. George Crow, Thomas
Kelly, James Fitzgerald, Robert Alexander. Accounts due the
estate from the following persons: 1809 - Samuel Dotson, David
Lone, William Tleppon(?), James Alexander; 1808 - Andrew Cuff,
William Wells, Peter Ragsdale; 1809 - Hugh Smiley, William Fisher,
1811 - Richard Barnes, John Whealy, Charles Duisey; accounts in
James Hewey's hand of collection of James McCraven, Henry Davis,
Armistead Mays; Thomas McElevee note. Oct. session 1811. Spen-
cer Buford, Charles Buford, James Buford & Edw. Bufford.

P. 290. Account of the sales of the Estate of JAMES BUFORD.
dec'd. Those buying: William Gurley, Edward Buford
(Bible), Spencer Buford, Charles Buford, James Giddens, Alexander Clark, Daniel Derryberry, Cornelious Mathis, Malachi Nicholson, Alexander Mebane, Jeremiah Brady, Archibald Beasley, Cornelius Wilson, George Glascock. Allen Hill, Daniel Carter, Caleb
Manley, George Mebane, Elisha Hassell, Ezekiel McKearley, William
Ginley, Somerset Moore, Edward Ragsdale, Elisha Dodson, James
Davis, Bluff Lavender, Thomas Stags(?), William Blakely, Charles
Hulsey, Beverly Reese, Charles Boyles, Samuel Harrass. Jan.
session 1812. Amos Duncan, Thomas Old.

P. 295. Settlement of the Estate of MICHAEL WARREN. dec'd.
Nov. 3, 1811. Jan. session 1812. David Craig &
Alexander Miller.

Settlement of the Estate of ROBERT CARLILE, dec'd.
Allowance for widow and children, paid to William Childress for
debts and costs. Oct. 14, 1811. Oct. session. Stephen Child-

29

ress, Admr.

P. 296.   William Parham, guardian, in Account with the Orphans
           of WILLIAM C. HILL. dec'd.   Jan. 1, 1812.   Hire of the
following negroes: negro man Broomfield, negro men Isham, Toby,
Lewis; negro boys Jerry & Phil; negro woman and her child, Ester
& child.   Jan. 1, 1812 - deduction for the boarding of Martha
Hill for the year 1811, to Lewis S. (?); boarding of James Hill
for the year 1811.   Returned to Jan. session 1812.

P. 297.   Settlement of the Estate of JONATHAN DAVIS, dec'd.
           Dec. 19, 1811.   Jan. session 1812.   Admrs. Amos Davis,
Nicholas Scales & Archer Jordan.

P. 298.   Settlement of the Estate of J. PATTON, dec'd.   Money
           rec'd. of John & Thomas Williamson, James Wilson, David
Cummins, David McGavock, John Nicholos; appointed to adjust
accts.: John Witherspoon & Hinchey Petway.   Jan. 16, 1812.   Jan.
session 1812.   Lawrence Bass, Admr.

           Inventory of the Estate of SAMUEL CLARK. dec'd.   Jan.
1, 1812.   Negroes: Wat, Frank, Jude, Anne, Molley, Mary, Allen,
Caroline and their children born since, namely, Jacob and Ruth;
Sherwood Green, guardian; one-fifth part deducted for widows
part; hire of the negroes for the years 1810-1811.   Expenses:
one-fifth part of the hire of the negroes was paid to the widow
as her equal share of the estate; maintenance of the said heirs
of the year 1810; whiskey at the hiring of the negroes, 1811;
books and school supplies for Salley & Martin; merchandize for
Sally Clark.   Nov. 27 - Cash paid William Martin for Samuel
Clark note, payable to Richard Hopkins; cash paid N. Wyche for
the schooling of Salley and Martin; cash paid I. Sawyers for
extra charges.   April session 1812.

P. 300.   William Parham, guardian, in Account with the Orphans
           of WILLIAM C. HILL, dec'd.   Balance due the orphans
for the years 1808, 1809, 1810, and 1811: paid Henry W. Hill a/c
against William Parham, guardian; paid to Doct. Crockett, acct.
March 1812.   April session 1812.   T. Saunders, D. Dunn, G. Hill,
D. Dickinson, & I. Reese.

P. 301.   Division of the Negroes of the Estate of WILLIAM C.
           HILL, dec'd.   Martha Hill gets the following negroes:
Lewis, Phill, Bromfield; James Hill gets the following negroes:
Toby, Jerry, and Mouring; Henry W. Hill get the following
negroes: Isham, Esther and child, Chloe.   March 30, 1812.   G.
Hill, T. Saunders, D. Dickinson, D. Dunn, & I. Reese.   April
session 1812.

P. 302.   Settlement with the guardian of Peter Pryor and Green
           Pryor, orphans of JOHN PRYOR, dec'd. to Hendley Stone.
Expenses: Jan. 1811 - surveying land in Wilson County and search-
ing to get duplicate warrent; To Sion Hunt for board and school-
ing of orphans for 2 months; taxes on land in Wilson County, 1812
and in Virginia, 1811.   Paid to William Hamilton for boarding,
to Blackburn for schooling, to Hambleton for boarding.   Credits:
Hire of Suckey and 3 children to Hobs; Frank to Col. Perkins;
Jude and 3 children to Col. Perkins; Hannah and 3 children to
Corder; Sam to David Dunn; Cloe to David Witherspoon; Joe to
Daniel Perkins; Jesse to Daniel Perkins; George to James Hews.
By the rent of the land in Virginia, say the River Plantation.
March 30, 1812.   April session 1812.   N. Perkins, Daniel Perkins,
Edward Warren, & Robert McLemore.

P. 305.   SAMUEL WILSON. dec'd. Will, July 30, 1804. Wife
          Martha; oldest daughter Margaret; 2 sons Robert &
Josiah my plantation when Robert comes of age; Polley, Betsy,
Respah(??) and Sally be schooled. Exr.: Martha Wilson, Robert
Wilson & Zacheus Wilson. Wit.: Aron Wilson, Zacheus Wilson &
Moses Wilson. Proven July session 1812.

P. 306.   JOHN SHEPARD. Will, Aug. 26, 1811. Wife Jane. Test.:
          J. B. Thompson & William Hunter. Proven July session
1812.

P. 307.   PATRICK MCCUTCHEN. Will, April 29, 1812. Brothers
          James McCutchen, Samuel McCutchen, the legal heirs of
my brother John McCutchen, dec'd., the legal heirs of my brother
William McCutchen, dec'd., to the legal heirs of my sister, Sarah
McMutt, dec'd., to the legal heirs of my sister, Margaret
Buchanan, dec'd.; wife Hannah, tract of land I now live on and
slaves; Patrick McCutchen, fourth son of my brother, Samuel, all
my rights in the undivided tract of land for which Matthew Talbot
gave his obligation to James and Samuel McCutchen; Elizabeth
Larkins, daughter of John Larkins by his first wife Margaret, the
land where I now live after the death of my wife; negro slave
Jack age 24, negro slave Ben age 19, negro slave Rose age 26 and
her children, Elisa age 11, Scintha age 7, Thomas age 4, Harriett
age 2, and Maria age 2 months; the slaves mentioned are to be
given to wife Hannah, during her lifetime and then to be liber-
ated and set free; James Marshall, my wife's brother. Exr.:
wife Hannah; brother Samuel McCutchen and friend James Marshall.
Wit.: Thomas Hardeman and William Marshall. Addition to the
Will: Patrick McCutchen be joint legatee with Elizabeth Larkin
in the land. Proven July session 1812.

P. 310.   PETER PERKINS. Will, Jan. 26, 1813. Granddaughter
          Agnes Stone, silver and wife's wearing apparel; grand-
daughters Polly Stone and Ruth Stone; my four favorite slaves,
Bob, Esther, Charles, and Hannah to be set free and my Exrs. to
look after them. (They also got some livestock); son Nicholas;
Brother Harden; Peter Hairston of Stokes Co., North Carolina,
has a power of authorizing him to sell the Snow Creek Iron Works
and lands there; Nicholas Scales one-third part of lands, if
sold; children of Hendley Stone, had by my daughter, Betsey.
Exr.: son Nicholas Perkins; nephew Nicholas Scales. Wit.: Anne
P. Scales, Thomas H.P. Scales, and John Bostic. Proven April
session 1813.

P. 311.   Inventory of the Estate of Col. PETER PERKINS, dec'd.
          Taken Feb. 9, 1813. April session 1813. Gold watch,
books, old acct. books, many items.

P. 313.   WILLIAM OGILVIE. Will, March 2, 1811. Son Richard
          Ogilvie, the land I now live on, 315 acres; daughter
Nancy Allison, negro man Pompey and the woman Juniper; cattle in
the care of Henry Arthur in Rutherford Co.; children Harris
Ogilvie, Smith Ogilvie, Kimbrough Ogilvie, William Ogilvie, John
Ogilvie, Sally Allison, Patty Manire, and Nancy Allison; the
whiskey made at the distillery on the farm. Exr.: Son Richard
Ogilvie; and son-in-law, James Allison. Wit.: John Manier, John
White, & Jacob Boring. Proven April session 1813.

P. 314.   Inventory of the Estate of WILLIAM OGILVIE, dec'd.
          Note on Richard Ogilvie. April session 1813.

P. 315.   JORDON REESE. Will, Jan. 18, 1813. Wife Sally Reese,

31

500 acres of land I now live on, and the negroes: Aaron (which
came to my said wife), Daniel my gardiner, Old Dilcy Maria,
Betty, Little Daniel, Hanibal, Rusey, and Terey; daughter Elizabeth Old, the slaves and furniture I have lent her and land lying
in Williamson County that I have given her and her husband Thomas
Old; three grand children Sally Hobbs (negro Judea), Ann Hobbs
(negro Hannah) and Hartwell Hobbs (negro Sam); son Herbert Reese
the land which I gave to him in Dinwiddie Co., Virginia, and
which he has sold to Doct. Hardeway, also the negroes heretofore
given him and the stock left in his possession by me at the time
of my removal to the Western Country; son Beverly Reese, land
lying between White Oak Creek and Case Road, (reserving one acre
to the meeting house) containing 1400 acres, also 8 negroes: Big
Bob, Charles, Ceasar, Little Bob, Charlotte, Winney, Rheuben, and
David; daughter Matilda Reese, 500 acres of land lying on west
Harpeth beginning where Pattons road crosses west Harpeth thence
south from the bank of west Harpeth where said road crosses with
said road to the cross road east with said cross road to Allen
Hill's line thence north to west Harpeth thence down west Harpeth
with its meanders to the beginning, also 8 negroes: Little Dilcey,
Moses, Jerry, Mercka, George, Selina, Brister, and Chelsey;
daughter Jane Watson, 500 acres land which I have deeded to her
and her husband, John Watson, also the slaves lent them; son
Patrick Reese, 1200 acres land where I now live reserving the
500 acres for wife, Sally Reese, also 12 slaves: Sam, Peter,
Edmund, Little Aaron, Ben, Lew, Jim, Fanney, Gillum, Sook, Lewis,
and Tom; daughter Nancy Hobbs $1.00.   Exr.: Thomas Old and John
Watson, my sons-in-law & friend, Abraham North. Wit.: James
Hicks, Leonard Dunn & Fendall Crump. Proven April session 1813.

P. 316.   Inventory of the Estate of JORDAN REESE, dec'd. Slaves
           mentioned in the will; 1 ridding Carrage, pictures,
silver, 500 acres land, many items; property not specifically
divided.   Slaves: Gardiner, Frank, Frank Will, Stephen, John,
Miles, Jinny and her child Ursey, Biddy, Jim, Venture, Judy,
Jack, Billy, Oliver, and Isaac; notes due the estate of the
following people: Young A. Gray, Turner Sanders, James McKinney,
John Watson, Nelson Jones, David C. Jones, Thomas Worsham, Robert
Worsham, Robert Ritcher, Herbert Reese & Stephen Shaw, Robert and
Leonard Dunvant, Polly Bonner & Herbert Reese, Lewicing Jones &
William Wills, William French & Brook Dunvant, Benjamin Bevell &
William Wills, Gabriel Baughn & Clement Olds, William Good &
Herbert Reese, William Featherton & Daniel Beasly, Isham R.
Trotter, William C. Wills, Abraham North, John Tally, George R.
Claiborne, Elijah Olds, George Smith, Joseph Moore, Patrick
Poytress & Sim Woodard, John Allen & Labone Epps, Linn Woodard &
Patrick Pottress; receipt given by Beverly Reese to Herbert
Reese; receipt for Jordan Reese; note on Thomas Woodard; slaves
devised to Patrick Reese, a minor; Sam, Peter, Edmund, Little
Aaron, Ben, Lew, Jim, Fanny, Gillum, Sook, Lewis, and Tom.
April 13, 1813.

P. 318.   BENJAMIN BUGGS, dec'd. Inventory. April 13, 1813.
           2 Bibles, books, many items; note on Jesse Bugg and
John Williamson; the following negroes: Charles, Allen, Peter,
Jacob, Terry, Warrick, Dorcas, Lucy, Rachel, Jenney, Viney, and
Dilcey, and Elenor. April session 1813.

P. 320.   Inventory of the Estate of PATRICK MCCUTCHEN. June 6,
           1813. Many items, 3 chests. July session 1812.

           Account of the Sales of LITTLE BERRY EPPERSON, dec'd.
and a Supplementary Inventory, June 6, 1813. Bible. May 12,

1812. Account of the Sale. Those buying: Ann Epperson (Bible), James Joyce, William Dickinson, James Armstrong, Francis Smith, Sally Allen. July session 1812. James Joyce, Admr.

P. 321.   JAMES SULLARD. dec'd. Will, March 20, 1812. Brother
          Samuel Sullard; note on Joseph Johnson. Exr.: L.W.
Mansker and Henry Flowers. Wit.: R.W. Shannon, David Thaigler,
James Davis. Proven Oct. session 1812.

P. 322.   JANE WHEATON, dec'd. Will, April 22. 1812. 2 sons
          Sterling Wheaton & John Lord Wheaton, they be educated
in Raleigh. North Carolina, and they be raised by their Uncle
Doct. Sterling Wheaton; slaves and stock in a bank. Exr.:
Friend, John Lord of Wilmington and Doct. Sterling Wheaton of
Raleigh, North Carolina. Wit.: James Shannon, William Black, J.
Bruff, and Eliza Bruff. Proven July session 1812.

P. 323.   JOHN MANIRE, dec'd. Will, April 30, 1808, of the
          county of Garrard and state of Kentucky. Exr.: wife
Betty Manire and son-in-law Daniel Hubbard. Wit.: Achilles
Finnell, James Finnell, & John Hubbard. I hereby certify that I
have removed and settled myself in Williamson County and do not
see cause to alter my will. Dec. 9, 1809. Wit.: Thomas Wilson,
James Ridley, John Wather(?). Oct. session 1812. Proven Oct.
session 1812.

P. 324.   ROBERT WINSETT, dec'd. Will, May 13, 1812. Wife
          Milley Winset, negroes, Rachel & Jack; son Jason, land
I gave gift deed to; reserving Rachels first child to go to my
daughter, Silvey Brown and the second child to my daughter, Ann
Winsett; negro man James to be sold; son William Winset, land
left him by gift deed; son John Winset, note of $110.00; son
Amos Winset, $1 and land he lives on; son Silvo Winset, $1 and
land he lives on of gift deed; son Jesse Winset $30. Exr.: wife
Milley Winset; son William Winset and son Amos Winset. Test.:
Daniel Brown, Silas Winset & James Gillespie. Proven Oct. session 1812.

P. 326.   ANDREW HARRIS. dec'd. Will, April 28, 1812. Wife
          Ede, negroes: Nancy & Hillard and the plantation;
children Cassandra, Samuel, Josephus, Edward, Patsy, Meekezeno
Caro, and Sidney; 1250 acres of land left to me by my father and
for which I have his deed of conveyance to be equally divided
amongst children as soon after it is purchased from the Indians
as my Exr. shall deem it practical. Exr.: wife Ede; son
Josephus, Ephraim Sampson and George Burnet. Test.: Robert
Guthrie, James House, Jr., Andrew Cowsort, and Glen Owen. Proven
Oct. session 1812.

P. 327.   DAVID CRAIG, JUNR., dec'd. Inventory of the Estate.
          Oct. session 1812.

P. 328.   JOHN SHEPPARD, dec'd. Inventory of the Estate. July
          session 1812.

          DUDLEY PORTER, dec'd. Sales Account by Sarah Porter,
Exr. Those buying: Sara Porter, James Berry, Mordica Pillow,
William Walls, John Brim, William King, William Webster, James
Busby, David McCord, Robert McClenen, James Miller, John Porter.
July session 1812.

P. 329.   JOHN SEAY, dec'd. Inventory of the Estate May 10,
          1810. July session 1812. John Windrow.

33

P. 330.   Settlement with Lancaster Glover, guardian, for Nancy
            Sammons, otherwise Nancy Pate of her part of the es-
tate of her father, HARDY PATE. dec'd. Expenses from Virginia,
paid to Currin & Mason, paid to Petway & Maury. July 15, 1812.
John Witherspoon & C. Boyles.

            WRIGHT RIGGS, dec'd. Inventory of the Estate; 1
silver watch, 1 chest, book account, amount unknown. Oct.
session 1812. David Riggs, Admr.

P. 331.   Settlement of the Estate of WILLIAM WILKINS, dec'd.
            by James Wilkins, Exr. April 3, 1812. To John
Sappington Physician Account: Wm. Williams, Edward Jones, Edward
Swanson, John Hardeman, John Record, Samuel Dobbins, Joseph
Braden, James Thompson, R. P. Curren, Mr. Wright. Jan. session
1812.

P. 332.   Settlement with Lancaster Glover, guardian for Persons
            Pate. April 13, 1813.

P. 333.   Sale of the Estate of WILLIAM STONE, dec'd. Those
            buying: James Fulton, Alexander McDaniel, Jane Stone,
John Ray (Bible). Cubb Willis, William Nolin, Gurshum Hunt,
William Stone, John L. Fielder, John Waters. April session, 1813.

            Account of the Sale of GREEN HOUSE, dec'd. No names
given. James House, Admr.

P. 334.   Inventory of the Estate of JOSEPHUS HARRIS, dec'd.
            April session 1813. Edith Harris, Admrx. Those buy-
ing: the saddle and bridle bid off by Edith Harris for Zens
Harris, infant, Murrey Gramner, Morses Gazetter, Duncan Logick,
Edward Harris. The patent right of a certain washing machine
for the company of Giles, claimed under Eli F. Hill of New
York; a note on land on Cheatham of Columbia, Maury Co. April
session 1813.

            Settlement of the Estate of MICHAEL KINNARD. dec'd.
Paid to Robert Mitchel & Col, John Sample & Co., William P.
Harrison, Robert McCoy, George Kinnard; William Tait, note given
to Felix Grundy, George Bennett rec. and filed here with Peter
Pinkston for a judgment obtained by Bennett Smith against the
dec'd.; voucher on Thomas Releiugh, John Curry, William Culwell.
Oct. 15, 1812. April session 1813. Lewis Stephens & Michael
Kinnard, Admrs.

P. 335.   Oliver Williams, guardian of Nancy Jordan, dtr.
            April 19, 1812. To her proportion of the Estate of
JOHN JORDAN, dec'd.; to cash rec'd. of Stephen Wood by sale of
negroes in the hands of William Jordan; interest from 9-7-1808
to 4-19-1812. April 13, 1813.

P. 336.   Nicholas Scales, guardian of Susanna G. Jordan, her
            share of the Estate of JOHN JORDAN, dec'd; to cash
rec'd. of Stephen Wood by sale of Negroes in the hands of William
Jordan; interest from 9-7-1808 to 4-19-1812. April 13, 1813.

            SALLY L.R. GRAYS, Supplemental Inventory of the
Estate. Tract of land in Stewart, acres unknown; account
against Robert Stockett. April session 1813. Young A. Gray,
Admr.

            RICHARD WILLETT. dec'd. Account of the Sales. Those

34

buying: Charlotte Willet, John Floyd, James Pugh, Edward Russel,
Samuel Andrews, James Cranshaw, Reuben Huggins, William Willet.
April session 1813. Charlotte Willet, Admrx.

P. 337.   Agreeable to an order of the county court of William-
           son. To us directed Jan. session 1813, we met at the
house of Frederick Davis and examined the accounts of Samuel
Wilson, guardian of David Page and Jacob Page and John Page,
minor offins of JOHN PAGE, dec'd. and find said Samuel Wilson in
an account current with said orphans as follows to wit. as
guardian for David Page; note on William Stephens, Henry Stephens, Robert McCleland, Charles Stephens, David Craig. Jan. 1,
1813. William Denson, Richard Puckett & O. Williams.

P. 338.   Settlement with Frederick Page, Patsy Page, minor
           orphans of JOHN PAGE. dec'd. with Owen T. Watkins,
their guardian; note on Henry Stephens, Andrew Johnston, David
Squire, Eli Morgan; to cash paid P. Pinkston for crying negroes
at hire, for pare shoes for Milly, Young A. Gray for medicine
and attendance on the negro Milly. (met at Frederick Davis
house). Jan. 25, 1813. William Denson, O. Williams, and Richard
Puckett.

P. 339.   Settlement with Samuel Crockett, guardian of Stokley
           Page and Harvey Page, minor orphans of JOHN PAGE, dec'd.
Judgment against John L. Fielder for hire of negroes; note on
Henry Rutherford for hire of negroes; expenses for schooling.
April 13, 1813. O. Williams, William Denson, and Richard Puckett.

P. 340.   Inventory of the Estate of THOMAS BALLOW, dec'd. 1
           negro woman, 1 chest, and several items. April session
1813. Ann Ballow and Alex Smith.

P. 341.   Account of the Sale of the Estate of JOHN CRAWFORD,
           dec'd. Those buying: James Whooton, Henry Rutherford,
Elizabeth Crawford (bureau), James Rutherford, Matthew Johnston
(desk). John Gray, John West, Samuel Crawford (negro Lewis).
Michael Long, John White, Alexander Crawford, Nicholas Perkins,
Abraham Socress, James Walker, Duncan Robertson (negro girl
hired). Ryley Slocolmb (negro girl hired). G.C. Rutherford
(negro boy hired); the bailing cloaths and rope belonging to the
firm of Rutherford and Crawford; Elizabeth Crawford and Henry
Rutherford, Admrs. Additional Sales: Surveying instruments and
books - Henry Rutherford, James Campbell. Andrew Ewing. April
session 1813.

P. 342.   The valuation of the Estate of JAMES CRAFTON, dec'd.
           The division between the widow and his four children,
George Crafton, Dennis Crafton, Richard Crafton, and Daniel
Crafton; the slaves are divided as follows: Dennis Crafton -
Mary and Charles, Widow Crafton -'Elick, George Crafton - Mariah
and Sam, Daniel Crafton - Moses, Richard Crafton - Scinda and
Enee. April session Jacob Halfacre, Freeman Walker, James
Harder, Eloc Alexander, and Robert Davis.

           July session 1812. Settlement of the Estate of JAMES
CRAFTON, dec'd. To Doct. Samuel Crockett, Nicholas Wilbourn for
medicine & attendance of the family, Jacob Halfacre for a cow
killed by a negro of the dec'd., Wm. P. Harrison, D.C. of Wmson.
Co. Court, Wm. Hulme, sheriff of Wmson. Co. for taxes. Robert
Davis for schooling of children. Oct. 1, 1812. Oct. session.

WILL BOOK # 2

P. 1.   ANTHONY SHARP, dec'd. Inventory. Returned Oct.
session 1812. Taken Oct. 10, 1812. 3 Bibles, books,
furniture, livestock and many items. Negroes: man Moses aged
38 years, Adam aged 31 years, woman Rachel aged 40 years, Chiana
aged 18 years, boy Harwell aged 15 years, Peter aged 13 years,
girl Lydia aged 14 years, Rose aged 12 years, Lina aged 11 years,
boy Sandy aged 9 years, girl Esther aged 8 years, boy Stephen
aged 6 years and Redden aged 2 years; 1 moiety of a land warrent
to Anthony Sharp & Thomas Dugan-Duplicate #332 for 123½ acres;
1 moiety of a land warrent to Anthony Sharp & Thomas Dugan-
Duplicate #333 for 623 acres; 1 moeity of a land warrent to
Anthony Sharp & Thomas Dugan-Duplicate #326 for 355 acres; bond
on Nicholas Perkins due Feb. 1, 1812 & Feb. 1, 1813; Jacob
Harder due Aug. 14 & 17, 1811; James Stanley due Dec. 25, 1812;
one cotton Receipt on Jacob Harder for 248 3/4 lb.; one bond on
Thomas Blackemore due Dec. 8, 1792; David Allen due Dec. 25,
1809; Francis McKinney due March 1, 1813; Joseph Davis due June
9, 1805; Edmund Harrison due June 7, 1812; Elisha Haerdon due May
1, 1791; James Elliot (balance); David Allen due Sept. 16, 1809;
James Marlin due Sept. 24, 1804 & March 1, 1805. Henry Cook,
Admr. and Peggy Sharp, Admrx.

P. 2.   ANTHONY SHARP, dec'd. Account of Sales. Sold on Nov.
2, 1812 and Returned Jan. session 1812. Those buying:
Peggy Sharp (large Bible and many items), Henry Cook, John J.
Henry, Caleb Manley, James Gray Jones, Benjamin Gholston, John
Stacy, George Neely, Daniel Carter, Benjamin White, Richard
Orlon, John Gholston, William Banks, (Credit by Mrs. Sharp for
sundries charge her), A. Andrews, Isaac Henry, Alexander Lester,
Frederick Lester, George Martin, Stephen Smith; Jane Sharp, 1
bed & furniture, side saddle; Sally Sharp 1 bed & furniture, bay
filly; Nancy McFail, late Nancy Sharp 1 bed & furniture. Returned to court Jan. session 1813.

P. 4.   ANTHONY SHARP. Personal estate divided among his
several legatees, (to wit), We, Abram Maury, Senr.,
Stephen Childress, Nicholas Perkins, Sion Hunt & Thomas Old, commissioners appointed by county court in Jan. session 1813. 1
share-John J. Henry, who drew Violet at $325 and Sina at $530;

37

1 share-Elizabeth Jones, who drew Lydia at $280 & Sandy at $275;
1 share each: Ann McPhail, who drew Hartwell at $350; Sally N.
Sharp, who drew Peter at $350; Searcy D. Sharp, who drew Chane
at $375; Sumner M. Sharp, who drew Rachel at $300 & Stephen at
$200; Peggy N. Sharp who drew Rose at $230 & Esther at $225.
January 12, 1813. Returned to April session 1813.

P. 5.   Inventory of the estate of ROBERT WINSETT, dec'd.
           Returned Jan. session 1813. Negro men Jim age 28
years, Jack age 19 years, negro woman Rachel 18 years, negro
family child Hannah born June 25, 1812; many items, money scales,
and books. Dec. 29, 1812. Mille Winsett, Amos Winsett & William
Winsett, Exr.

P. 6.   DAVID CRAIG, JR., dec'd. Account of sales of the
           estate. Those buying: Margaret Craig, James Craig,
Samuel Buchanan, David Craig, John Stephens, John McKinsey,
Ebenezer Alexander, John Pillow, Andrew Cole, John P. Shelburn,
Mary Craig Jr., John Crafton. Returned to Jan. session 1813.

P. 7.   JOHN CRAWFORDS, dec'd. Inventory made and Returned
           Jan. 1813. 9 negroes: Lewis, Judy, Suke, Nancy, Jane,
George, Nathan, Amerky, and Anderson; livestock, furniture, sur-
veying instruments, other items. Elizabeth Crawford & Henry
Rutherford, Admrs. Returned Jan. session 1813.

           RICHARD WILLETT, dec'd. Inventory Returned Jan.
session 1813. Livestock, furniture, many items. Account against
John Wilkey for making 1 mans and 1 womans saddle; account
against Andrew Dorton. (writing on bottom of page torn off).

P. 8.   ANDREW HARRIS, dec'd. Inventory Returned Jan. session
           1813. 332½ acres land in Williamson County where he
was living when he died; 1250 acres on Tennessee River, the
Indian title not extinguished; two negroes, Hilliard and Nancy;
household items, including 1 washing machine, furniture, bureau,
chest with drawers, cupboard, many items; property sold on the
12th Nov. last for which there is notes taken on: George Burnet
to be discharged in Carpenters work; account against Joseph
Harris for boarding himself and horse; the patent right to a certain washing machine for the county of Willson by purchase under
Ely F. Hill of New York. Signed Ede Harris, E. Sampson & G.
Burnet.

           JOHN ATKINS, dec'd. Inventory; returned Jan. session
1813. Livestock, furniture, tools, note on James Terbivill.
Balaam Hay, admr.

           GREEN HOUSE, dec'd. Inventory; returned Jan. session
1813. Horse, saddle, sword, clothing and cash. (the name of
Admr. not given.)

P. 9.   JOHN CRENSHAW, dec'd. Inventory returned Jan. session
           1813. Horse, livestock, furniture, 1 silver watch,
clothing, crops and cash. Joseph Crenshaw, Admr.

           SALLY L. R. GRAY, dec'd. Inventory returned Jan.
session 1813. 1 negro man Harper; 1 negro man Dudley; 1 negro
girl Lycy; 1 negro girl Clementina; 1 horse & 2 mares. (A
supplemental inventory received in Book #1, page 336). Young
A. Gray, Admr.

           STEPHEN ELAM, dec'd. Inventory and appraisment.

Returned Jan. session 1813; given Jan. 3. 1813. 1 still valued
at $64.00, 7 mash tubs $7.00, casks $3.00; 1 key, ½ bushel & 1
giggin at $1.00; livestock. furniture, other items; 1 note on
Amos Devers and Walter Owen; 1 note on Wilie Smith, William H.
Balew, Wm. H. Balew and Canper Bennett; a bond for the conveyance of 100 acres of land assigned by George Parker to Stephen
Elam, dec'd.; a article between the widow and James Patterson
for the rent of the farm where the widow now lives; a article
between the widow and Charles Burnes for 64 gallons of Whiskey
for the rent of the still till the first day of June next. No
admr. named.

P. 10.   JACOB ROLLAND. dec'd. Account of sales which was sold
           on Nov. 21, 1812. Returned Jan. session 1813. Those
buying: Mrs. Polly Rolland (most of the items that were sold,
also 1 negro man Jack. $50.00; 1 negro woman $52.00; 1 negro
woman Doll $360.00). Andrew Cowsart & Jacob Dooly.

P. 11.   SAMUEL WILSON, dec'd. Account of sales. Returned
           Jan. session 1813. Sold on Oct. 22, 1812. Those
buying: the widow, 1 note on John Potts to Samuel Wilson.

P. 12.   The articles mentioned with their prices were valued
           by John Walker, John Ogilvie and James Reid. Furni-
ture and other items. Zacheus & Martha Wilson, Exr.

           JAMES MCCUTCHEN, dec'd. Estate settlement. Returned
Jan. session 1813. Hannah McCutchen, Admrx. Received from:
George Hulm, No. 1; William Mars No. 2; Petway & Maury No. 3;
Winfred Hopkins No. 4; John McCutchen No. 5; James Campbell
No. 6 & 7; Jonathan Cooper No. 8; John McCutchan No. 9; receipts
produced by Jason Hopkins for Hannah McCutchen, Admrx. of JAS.
MCCUTCHEN, dec'd. Jan. 11, 1813. S. Hunt & G. Hulm.

P. 13.   WILLIAM M. LOVE. Estate settlement with Joseph Love,
           Admr. The estate of the dec'd. has been sold and
divided to the legatees as directed in the will. To: William
Ewing for Voucher #1; Maxamillion Redding #2; David B. Love #3;
Samuel Love #4; John G. Love #5; James Love #6; Edley Ewing #7;
Martha Wilson #8; Dr. Newman #9; Dr. Hickman #10; Clerk of
Williamson County for voucher #11; Jeremiah Gurley for #12.
Returned Jan. session 1813. Signed: Richard Puckett & Samuel
Shelburn.

P. 14.   JAMES C. HILL. Account with William Parham, guardian.
           January 1812. Boarding for year 1812 paid to Banks &
Cannon; paid Dr. Crockett; paid Nicholas Hardeman expenses for
making this return; credit: hire of negro Toby to Mr. Blackman;
hire of negro Jerry to Thomas Hiter.

           HENRY W. HILL in account with William Parham, guardian.
To Nicholas P. Hardeman for making this return; credit: hire of
negro Isam to William Lyntz and hire of negro woman & child kept
for their victials & clothes for the year 1812. Returned April
session 1813.

           PETER REEVES, dec'd. Account of sales. Returned April
session 1813. Those buying: Sarah Reeves (Rieves), Frederick
Owen, James Owen, Ambrose Owen, Robert Rieves, John Watson,
Terry Bradley, William Alfred, Robert C. Rieves, Thomas Ballow,
William Hickman, John Hill, Gasham Hunt, William Alfred, Charles
Beasley, Everit Owen, William Wevster, Nelson Fields, William
Bibb hire of 1 negro boy. James Owen, Admr.

P. 15.   JOHN ADKINS, dec'd. Account of sales. Returned
          April session 1813. Those buying: Molly Adkins (most
of the items sold), John McKinney, Patsey Adkins, Balaam Hay,
Polly Johnston Adkins, Amos Bullock; a balance remaining not
sold of the estate of JOHN ADKINS, dec'd.: 1 cart wheel & the
irons of one; 1 foot and one clevis; one open ring; 1 old mans
saddle; come to my knowledge since the day of sale. Balaam Hay,
Admr.

          Hendley Stone, guardian. Account for Peter & Green
Pryor, orphans of JOHN PRYOR, dec'd. A settlement for 1812 &
Returned April session 1813. Expenses for books, clothing
tuition for schooling to Maj. Maury for Peter & Green's board;
taxes for land in Wilson Co. 1812; taxes on their part of lands
in Virginia 1812; Credits for 1812: by hire of Negro Sukey &
children to Hobbs, girl Cloe to Hobbs; negro Hannah & 3 children
to D. Witherspoon, Jude & 3 children to Col. Perkins, Frank to
Col. Perkins, Jesse, Joe & Sam to Daniel Perkins, George to
James Hews; rent of land in Virginia 1812. April 7, 1813.
Signed: N. Perkins, Daniel Perkins, Robert McLemore & Edward
Warren.

P. 18.   JAMES WILSON, dec'd. Division of partition of his
          land among the several legatees entitled to a share.
Returned Jan. 7, 1813. State of Tennessee, Williamson County.
Agreeable to an order of Court issued to us from said County we
the undersigned subscribers have laid off & divided a certain
tract of land containing 700 acres lying & being in Williamson
County on the ridge above Harpeth Licks between the heirs &
legatees of JAMES WILSON, dec'd. (to wit): To John Gouly lot #1,
Josiah Hodges #2, Jacob Howdeshell #3, Vilate Wilson #4, Hannah
Hodge #5, Samuel Wilson #6, Joseph Wilson #7, James Wilson, Jr.
#8. October 17, 1812. General L. Nolen, surveyor. Thomas
Wilson, Josiah Wilson, Richard Reynolds, David Edmonston, Comm.

P. 18.   JAMES SHELBURNE, dec'd. Inventory. Returned July
          1813. 100 acres of land; 5 negroes: Louisa, Mary,
Ritta, Linda & Acy; livestock, books, carpenters tools, other
items. Sarah B. Shelburne & Samuel Shelburne, Admr.

P. 19.   EPHRAIM ANDREWS, dec'd. Settlement with Knacy Andrews,
          surviving executor of said EPHRAIM ANDREWS, dec'd.
To bond on: Benjamin Bugg, Richard S. Lock, William Neelly,
Knacy Andrews, Kimbro Ogilvie; cash received from James Ridley
& Lanier for leather; value of negro Tom left with Drumright &
Andrews in Virginia; cash paid Robinson for spirits for sale;
particular bequest to Howard Youn(?); cash allowed to Knacy
Andrews for services to Benjamin Bugg; cash paid John Hardeman
for services; by amount paid to W. Drumright & George Andrews,
two of the legatees in the following items: Their order in favor
of Jesse Bugg; cash paid Agent W. Drumright & Gee; Negro fellow
left with them in Virginia; by amount received by Benjamin Bugg
of the executors & legatee in the following its: cash received
by said Bugg of J.R. Tankersley; Paid to K. Ogilvie, Dalton &
C. Matthews; by amount of EPHRAIM ANDREWS portion of the whole
being one sixth part--in compliance with the order of the county
of Williamson County made at April Term 1813. We, James Allison,
Thomas Wilson, & Jacob Garret make the following report: That we
met on the 29th June 1813 at the house of Knacy Andrews & after
examing all the documents which to our knowledge had any refer-
ence to the estate of EPHRAIM ANDREWS, dec'd. as transacted by
Knacy Andrews, surviving exr. of said EPHRAIM ANDREWS, find the
account as stated: Benjamin Bugg has received over and above his

portion; Knacy Andrews as surviving exr. is entitled to a credit;
Knacy Andrews accountable for the sum, directed by the will of
EPHRAIM ANDREWS, dec'd. to be kept for the use of Howard Young.
Several items hereto subjoined & were copied from the inventory
returned before the death of the old Lady relict of credits of
the forgoing account though they have been investigated (viz) a
bond on Julian Nail which was received by the old Lady, one on
Miles Malone rec'd by the Old Lady, one on N.P. Hardeman paid by
the old Lady, cash lent to Ehpraim Andrews, Junr., a bond supposed to be collected by said EPHRAIM ANDREWS of W. Williams of
Virginia, 2 bonds left for collection in Virginia. June 29,
1813. Jacob Garrett, James Allison, & Thomas Wilson.

P. 21.   BENJAMIN BUGG, dec'd. Estate sold May 20, 1813. Those
          buying: Mrs. Nancy Bugg (Bible, furniture & other
items; hire of Negroes, Allen & Moll & negro woman & 4 children
till expenses of maintaining negro woman & 4 children Christmas
next), George Kennard, David Lancaster, Jesse Bugg, Richd.
Tankersley, John R. Tankersley, James Burgess, Robert Rogers,
James Price (hire Jacob), James Joyce, Richard S. Locke, Knacy
Andrews, W. Kennard, Thomas Ridley, Gabriel Walker, William
Withrow, John Robinson, William Young (hire of girl), David
Pinkston (hire of Peter), John Carothers (hire of Charles), John
Dalton, Jesse Kanaday, John Boyd, Nicholas Lenier, James G.
Jones, Alexander Johnston, William Alexander (hire of Sterling),
Richard Ogilvie, William Jackson, James Williams. Returned
July session 1813. Nancy Bugg, David Pinkston, & Ephraim M.
Bugg, Admrs.

P. 23.   STEPHEN ELAM, dec'd. Estate sold Feb. 10, 1813.
          Those buying: Jacob Adams, Peter Johnston, Moses Rid-
ley, William Holbert, David Merchant, James Allison, David Lawry,
James Neal, Peter Pinkston, Meriannam Landrum, -----(?) -elam,
Daniel Maxwell, George Oliver (1 still), John Ogilvie, William
Wilson, Robert Wilson, Dianna Elam, John Robertson, James Roy,
Joseph Boyd, Spencer Rennels, Josiah Dixon, Drury Bennett, Rachel
Phillips, William Phillips, Joseph Bell, Willice Carson, William
Hodge, Kimbro Ogilvie, Wilson Calhoon, Kenchen Pate, Francis
Nunn, James Ferguson, Wm. R. Nunn, Benj. Russell, Rich. Smith.
Rich. Ogilvie, John Hail, David Flemin, Robert Rogers, Levie
Measels, Matthew Elam, Reuben Reynolds. Moses Ridley & Dianna
Elam, Admr.

P. 25.   THOMAS BALLOW, dec'd. Estate sold May 14, 1813. Those
          buying: Ann Ballow, Nathaniel Herbert, John Hill,
David Lunn, John Hill (Petersburg), Arthur Fulgum, Abner Marcum,
Wm. Shumake, Robt. Henderson, Ephraim Stanfield, Alexr. Smith,
Henry Rutherford, Willie Roy, John Winders, Wm. M. Calpin; due
Thos. Ballow, dec'd. for his attendance in a cause of law between
the heirs of Jesse Thomas, Senr., & Jesse Thomas, Junr. Ann
Ballow & Alexander Smith, Admr.

          SALLY L. R. GRAY, dec'd. Account of sales Returned
July 1813. Negroes: Dudley, Lucy sold to Young A. Gray $856;
Clementime sold to Peter R. Booker $475; Harper sold to Geo.
Neely at $280; 3 horses bought by James M. Gray. Young A.
Gray, Admr.

          WM. OGILVIE, dec'd. Account of sales Returned July
1813 sold May 10, 1813. Those buying: Jas. Allison (Bible),
John Ogilvie, James Shumate, Wm. Hooker, Wm. Webb, John Adkinson,
John Meneer, Richard Ogilvie, Wm. Tucker, Geo. Julin, Anthony
Walk, Geo. H. Allen, Henry Bailey, Chas. Calhoon. Jas. Allison

& Richard Ogilvie, Exr.

P. 26.   JORDAN REESE, dec'd. Division of Chattel Estate.
         Those buying: Patrick Reese many items & following
negores: Boy Stephen $400; man Oliver $385; girl Juda $75. John
Watson many items & following negroes: man Little Frank $450;
woman Bidd $262.50; Blacksmith Isaac & tools $250. Beverley
Reese many items & negroes: man Will $375; man Jim $375; boy
Billey $275. Thomas Old several items & following negroes:
1 yellow man Gardner $450; man Jack Miller $381.25; boy Miles
$75. Matilda Reese items & following negroes: man Big Frank
$391.66 2/3; boy John $208.33 1/3; Jinney & child Ursula $362.50.
April 23, 1813. Hinchey Petway, Edw. Swanson, Wm. Parham, &
David Dickinson.

P. 27.   Sherwood Green, settlement with the heirs of S. CLARK,
         dec'd. To hire of negroes for year 1812 debt; credit
by cash paid for whiskey at the hiring of negroes; cash paid
Nelson Fields for crying negroes; Leather for Martin Clark &
making shoes; 1 pr. of leather shoes for Salley Clark and 1 pr.
of morocco shoes for Salley Clark; boot for Martin Clark; to
Samuel Bradford for Martin schooling; to James Davis for Martin
board; note payable to Samuel Staples by SAMUEL CLARK, dec'd;
cash paid following: Nelson Fields to cry the negroes; spelling
books for Wm. & Samuel Clark; paper & books for Salley & Martin
Clark; to Robt. Edmonston for Sallys' board; Nathaniel Wyche for
Sallys' schooling; Sampson Sawyers. July 13, 1813. C. H.
McAlister & H. Petway, commrs.

P. 28.   Settlement with Michael Kinnard & Lewis Stephens,
         admrs. MICHAEL KINNARD, dec'd. At April session of
court. Relative to vouchers not included in the return to last
court; credit by John Dickinson; Account & vouch #1 filed here
with John Haywoods; Voucher #2 for services rendered to est. as
admr. July 17, 1813. Richard Puckett & Samuel Shelburne.

P. 28.   Settlement with William Brown, Admr. & JOSEPH ROBERTS,
         dec'd. June 17, 1813. We, Gersham Hunt & James Davis
have settled with William Brown, Sr. Adm. of JOSEPH ROBERTS,
dec'd. Wm. Brown charges $10 for his trouble.

P. 29.   Settlement with Joshua Cutchan, guardian of orphans
         of MOSES MOORE, dec'd. Amos Moore 1813-clothing &
expenses; 1812-in account with Joshua Cutchen guardian for Amos
Moore orphan. March 1st cert. from Clerk of Edgecomb Co., No.C.
dated Feb. 1812. Chas. M. Callister & Hinchey Pettway, Comm.
Settlement with Joshua Cutchen, guardian to Esther Moore, dau. of
MOSES MOORE. March 1813-1 yrs. board & tuition cert. from the
clerk of Edgecomb Co., N.C. dated Feb. 1812. Hinchy Petway &
Charles McAlister, comm.

P. 30.   WM. NORTON, dec'd. Inventory. Returned Oct. 1813.
         Household furnishings, very few items. Sam'l Andrews
& Eliza Norton, Admr.

         RICHARD PUCKETT, dec'd. Inventory. Returned Oct.
session 1813. Taken by Garner McConico & Wm. Denson. *Plantation, furniture, stock. cash, note due July 22, 1801; note on
Sam'l Witherspoon & Richard Orton; notes on following: 1806-
Robert Crafton & Sam'l Shelbourn; 1801-Samuel Curry & Eli Stacy;
1801-John Harnes & David McEwen; 1807-Eli Stacy; 1810-Jared
Puckett; 1813-Geo. Davidson & Moses Chambers; 1810-Jared Puckett;
1813-Harvey Puckett; 1812-Jese Johnston & Jasiah Wooldredge;

42

1813-Richard Orton & Henry G. Kearney; 1807-Samuel Shelbourn;
1806-Samuel Shelbourn & Robt. Crafton; 1809-Richard Orton &
Moses Chambers; 1810-John M. Neal; 1808-Jared Puckett; *silver
watch. family books, 160 gal. spirits, 2 negro men, 1 negro
woman & 3 children. Receipt given by John Norton to James Tomlinson for a bond on James & John Mays & Jeremiah Down of Wilkinson Co., Miss. territory for the sum of $420 for collection.
Garner McConnico.

P. 31.   Jacob Coddington. Receipt to Garner McConnico Oct.
          1813. Received of Garner McConnico, adm. of RICHARD
PUCKETT my deceased guardian the sum of $413.71 & 3 mills for my
part of money in my said, dec'd. guardians hands with the interest also for rent of land to this date. Test: Wm. Denson & B.
Randolph.

          Garner McConnico settlement as guardian for John
Coddington a minor orphan of BENJ. CODDINGTON, Oct. 11, 1813.

P. 32.   ISAAC CROW, dec'd. Inventory. Returned Oct. session
          1813. 8 negroes: Leah, Crecy, Levan, Flora, Isaac,
Hetta, Geo. & Sutha; furniture, livestock. 2 Bibles, 1 Testament,
books, 1 small pocket book. 2 pr. knitting needles, many other
items. Oct. 13, 1813. John Atkinson & Andrew Herron, Admr.

P. 33.   JAMES SHUMATE. dec'd. Inventory. Oct. session 1813.
          1 negro girl, 140 acres of land, livestock, books,
farm & household equipment & other items.

          Sarah Porter settlement return Oct. session 1813,
admrx. of DUDLEY PORTER, dec'd. Paid to David McCord, Kizza
Shinault, Bazil Berry & James Berry. Signed: Jacob Garrett, W.
Wilson & S. Shelbourn.

P. 34.   JAMES SHELBOURN. dec'd. Supplimentary Inventory.
          Returned Oct. session 1813. A suppliment to an inven-
tory of JAMES SHELBOURN Estate, dec'd. returned by Sarah B.
Shelbourn & Samuel Shelbourn, Admrs. at July session 1813. Not
many items. Allotment to go to the widow & children for their
maintainance by Oliver Williams, Thos. Ridley, Freeman Walker &
James Harden. July 31, 1813.

P. 35.   JAMES SHELBURNE. dec'd. Account of sales. Returned
          to Oct. session 1813. Sold on Aug. 16, 1813. Those
buying: Horatio Pettience, Robert Crafton, Sarah B. Shelburne
(Bible), Freeman Walker, Finch Scruggs, Wm. Radford, John Craf-
ton, John Radford, Dicey Whitlock. Peter Pinkston, Thos. Mayfield,
Joel Stephens, Mordica Pillow, William Radford, Daniel Wilson,
Andrew Cole, Daniel Wilkes, Richard Hay, Joseph Clark, David
Lancaster, Aaron Ascue, Henry Walker, Sally Sammons, Betsy
Carroll, Joseph Fitz, John P. Shelbourne, Henry Stephens, Andrew
Craig.

P. 36.   GURDON SQUIER, dec'd. Inventory. Returned Oct.
          session 1813. household furniture, books, 2 horses,
other items, watch. Notes on Martin Stanley & Jas. G. Jones,
Thos. J. West & John West, Zacheriah Jackson & P. Beasley, Joel
T. Rieves & Jason Hopkins, John & James Neelly, Garner McConnico
& T.P. Hardeman, Thos. Hiter, David Squier, Geo. Hulme & H.
Lyon, Henry Lyon, John J. Henry & Geo. Hulme, Henry Walker &
N.P. Hardeman, Wm. Bright, James G. Jones.

P. 38.   GEORGE REYNOLDS. Will. Returned Oct. 1813. Wife

43

Susannah Reynolds-my mantion house & plantation adj.
the same & then to be for my youngest son, Richard Reynolds, the
liens of said tract of parcel of land to begin at the N. end of
the lane between Mr. Stone & myself, run east to old corn crib
& thence s. to back line, thence E. to Pryor Reynolds line; also
to wife: 1 negro man Lewis, Lucy & Bob & after her death to be
devided between all my children; son Pryor Reynolds, 100 ac. of
land part of tract I now live on to begin at the N.E. corner of
said tract at a Walnut running W. & S. to the south line for
compliment; son Geo. Reynolds the balance of land and when he
comes of age $100 in property; son Thomas Reynolds a negro woman
named Fanny & child Anney & their increas; dau. Elizabeth Hew a
negro girl Silvey; dau. Susannah Hews negro girl Elley; dau.
Jincey Bennett $190 in lieu of a boy Isaac, sold by Walter
Binnett & the money he rec'd (said boy sold to Rich. Hews); dau.
Nancy Reynolds a negro girl Easter; dau. Polly Reynolds a negro
boy Willis; dau. Sarah Reynolds a negro boy Miles; dau. Beatheny
Reynolds shall have a negro purchased for her in value to Miles;
I have a claim of lands in Virginia known by the name of Charles
Oakes old place, if ever it is secured, I wish it sold & divided
equally between my children. Sife, Susannah Reynolds executrix,
son Pryor Reynolds & son-in-law Richard Hews exr. May 21, 1813.
Wit.: H.D.L.G. Stone, Edw. Warren, John T. Bennett, & John
Witherspoon. Probated Oct. session 1813.

P. 39.   GURDON SQUIER, dec'd. Account of sails sold Nov. 2,
          1813 and returned to Jan. session 1814. Those buying:
James Jordan, Stephen Thomason, David Squier (books), William
Banks, Samuel Cox (watch), Joseph A. Martin, John J. Henry,
David Shannon, Benjamin Marritt, Olvier Crainshaw, Wm. Compton,
Wm. Saunders, Mary Squier, Geo. Morgan, Joseph Leadbetter, James
G. Jones (books), Gersham Hunt, Samuel Winstead, Mary Squier
(books), William Gourley, Hinchey Petway, Wm. Nolen, Nelson
Fields, Richard Orton; hire of Jenny (negro) from Oct. 3 till
Xmas.

P. 41.   Inventory of the estate of GEO. REYNOLDS, dec'd.
          Returned at Jan. session by Susanna Reynolds & Pryor
Reynolds. 1 negro man Lewis age 40, 1 negro woman Lucy age 36,
1 negro man Bob age 17. 1 negro girl Ester age 15, 1 negro boy
Willis age 13, 1 negro boy Miles age 5; livestock, furniture,
3 guns, books; bond on H. Cook, Nicholos Perkins; 1 negro girl
named Silvey 12 yr. lent to Elizabeth Hughes by Geo. Reynolds in
his life time; 1 negro named Elly lent by said Geo. Reynolds in
his life time to Susanna Hughes aged 10 yr.; 1 negro woman named
Fanny & her child Anny lent to Thos. Reynolds by Geo. Reynolds
dec'd. in his life time.

P. 42.   Inventory of the estate of HENRY CHILDRESS, dec'd.
          Jan. 7, 1814. 1 negro man named Geo. age 38 or 40,
1 negro woman Milley age 30, 1 negro boy Jessie age 12, 1 negro
boy Perry age 9; lewyed on by an execution before administration
granted 1 girl Esther age 7, 1 girl Lotte age 5, 1 boy Allen age
3, 1 boy Nelson age 1; livestock, furniture, books, farm equipment & crop of corn, other items. John Childress & Wm. Smith,
Admr. N.B. negro boy Perry was lewyed on by an execution at the
site of Daniel A. Dunham & now in the hands of Samuel Core(?)
Constable.

P. 43.   PETER PERKINS, dec'd. Account of Sales. Jan. session
          1814. Those buying: Wm O. Perkins (gold watch),
Nicholas Perkins, Thos. H. Perkins, Hendley Stone, Wm. Bright,
John Gholson, Benj. Gholson, John Corhan, Black Chares, John

Evans, Capt. Andrews, John S. Campbell, James Hungerford, James
McGavock, Joseph Clarke, John Bostic, Peter Hollyday, Richard
Hughes, Henry Holiday, Richard Vaughan, Matthew Lee, David Pin-
kerton, James G. Jones, Jason Hopkins, David H. Bareshear, Robt.
Gray, Wm. H. Armistead, Armistead Atkinson, Geo. Reynolds (1
stage wagon), John Crouch, Comelius Crenshaw, Jas. Corham, Henry
Lester, Frances Carter, James Wilkey, Jacob Tillman, David P.
Anderson, Martin Trentham.

P. 46.   Account of the sales of the property of RICHARD
           PUCKETT, dec'd. sold Nov. 11 & 12, 1813 by Garner
McConnico, Admr. & returned to Jan. session 1814. Those buying:
John Adam Layground, Henry Puckett (cupboard). Robt. C. Puckett
(walnut chest), Sally G. Puckett (truck), Nowel Watkins, Michael
Kinnard, Reuben Dobson, Alexander White, Elizabeth Puckett,
Stephen Barfield, Freeman Walker, Moses Francis, Wm. Walker,
Henry Stephens, Jas. Harder (books), Jas. Cavendar, Josiah Wool-
dridge, Thos. Hanes, Alexander Lester, Senr., Thos. Walker, John
Braddenn, James Short, Thos. West, James G. Jones, Ruffin Brown,
Wm. Marshall. Peter Pinkston, Stephen Thomason, Andrew Johnston,
Felston Andrew, Anderson Berryman, Oliver Williams, Joel T.
Rivers, Jonathan Wood, Henry Ingram, Jesse Johnston, Martin
Standley, Henry Allen, Geo. Bennet, Freeman Walker, Berry Nolen,
John Stacy, Geo. Bennett, James McConico, Lewis Stephens, Berry
Noles (lot of Law Books), Drury Pullam, Zachariah Jackson, Sam-
uel Merrit, John Duglass, Baalam Hay, John Broadenax, John Henry
(silver watch), Michael Long, Reuben Dobson, Noel Watkins; John
H. Nichols 1 negro man Jack $530; Stephen Barfield for Garner
McConnico 3 negroes: Guameny his wife & also her child Winney
$569.26; Henry Puckett 1 negro boy Fill $389; Dan Hill 1 yellow
girl Rhody $288.50 & also sold on Dec. 23, 1813 & returned to
Jan. session 1814.

P. 50.   ISSAC CROW, dec'd. Account of sales sold 25th & 26th
           of Nov. 1813 & returned to Jan. session 1814. Those
buying: John Atkinson, Wm. Glenn, Beverly Reese, Thos. Ragsdale,
Joanah Crow (dishes & furn.), Matthew Weightman, Felix Stagg,
Elisha North, Henry Reams, Archibald Beasley, Benj. Jones, Jacob
Lankston, Alexander Bennett, Wm. Gurly, Aaron D. Coharn, Clem
Wall, Wm. Adams, Jeremiah Trainum, John Golson, Joseph Blythe,
James Crow (pistols, shot gun, 2 Bibles & testament & many other
items), Joshua Reams, Samuel Bird, David McAlister, Edw. Ragsdale,
Loamy Stephens, Wm. Yarbrough, Benajiah Goodman, Cabb Manly,
Isaac Bezle, Gabriel Bleuford, Pleasant Watkins, John Burns,
Andrew Herrin, Wm. Cannon, Stephen Hargroves, Geo. Ganter, J.G.
Jones, Hardy Bizle; hire of the negroes for 12 mo. from Dec. 10,
1814, man Levan to John Atkinson, woman Leah to Thos. Wallis, boy
Isaac to Andrew Herrin, girl Het to Andrew Herrin, woman &
child Flora to James G. Jones, woman Crecy to Joanah Crow, boy
Geo. to Wm. Hill; note on Jason Hopkins due Sept. 29, 1813 given
Sept. 19, 1811; note on Wm. Parks given March 8, 1810; note on
Benj. Chitty given Dec. 25. 1813; note on Little Berry Chun &
Wm. Chun due Jan. 12, 1813, desperate; note on Robt. Steel due
Dec. 25, 1811 credit paid Feb. 17, 1812. insolvent; note on Wm.
Patton due June 1813; note on Jason Hopkins due Sept. 29, 1814;
note on Lewis Smoade due Nov. 11, 1810, runaway; note on Wm.
Patton to be paid in Stone Mason work: note on Wm. Johnston due
June 23, 1809, moved to state of Ga.; note on Thos. due Dec. 25,
1811 and one due June 12, 1810; 3 notes signed J. Crow; 1 note
which appears to have been given by John Epps to Petway & Maury
& Isaac Crow & Archie Beasley discharged by Isaac Crow to S. Cox,
desperate; Receipt signed by L.B. Aams given to Isaac Crow on
Charles Kavannas which Adams was to pay to Isaac Crow when

45

collected, desperate. Book Accounts-1st book. June 21, 1810,
Thos. Pouge & Wm. Cheatham; April 15, 1808-Wm. Hobes, Matthew
Wallis, Thos. Herrin, Francis Cannaday, Robert Calvert, Thos.
Polke, John Dizart, Wm. McCollister. 2nd book: Feb. 15, 1811,
Denney Dun, Henry Lester, Charles Kavanaugh, Grove Sharp, Wm.
Hourley, Thomas Wallis; March 10, 1811-March 29, 1811, Thomas
Wallis, Jeremiah Deans, John Barns; March 28-1812-Stephen Smith;
Aug. 31, 1812-John Whaley, Joseph Blye, Wm. Cheatham; Jan. 20,
1812-Thos. Nealy; Dec. 24, 1811-Peter Edwards, Hardy Bezzell,
Stephen Smith, Wm. Medalne, & Geo. Allen. John Atkinson and
Andrew Herron, admr.

P. 55.   RICHARD SMITH, dec'd. Inventory. Returned Jan.
          session 1814 by Oliver Williams, admr. Horse, saddle,
& bridle & axe. "He was one of the soldiers that was wounded in
the battle of Tallushatchee & has died with the wound he received
in the battle. There will be some money owing to him for his
services as a soldier by the United States, amount of pay unknown." O. Williams, Admr.

          WM. NORTON, dec'd. Supplemental Inventory. Jan. 4,
1814.   Samuel Andrews & Eliza Norton, admr.

P. 56.   JOHN HODGE, dec'd. Inventory returned Jan. 1814 by
          Wm. Hodge. Horse, saddle, 1 piece of Morrocco, & etc.

          RICHARD PUCKETT, dec'd. Additional inventory Jan.
session 1814 by Garner McConnico, Admr.

          Widow Crow, allotment Oct. session 1813, estate of
ISAAC CROW, dec'd. allotment for widow & children. Met at her
house Oct. 27, 1813. Edward Ragsdale, John Miller, John Adnrews,
& Ephraim Andrews, Commr.

          BENJAMIN BUGG, dec'd. Jan. session 1814. Hire of
negroes for 12 months: Charles to Robert Carrothers, Allen &
Jacob & Nelly to Nancy Bugg, Darcass & child to Nancy Bugg,
Contra Loose & 4 children to lowest bidder, Peter to James Price,
Sterling to David Pinkston, Rachel to Wm. Young. David Pinkston,
Nancy Bugg & E. M. Bugg, Admr.

P. 57.   JOHN ATKINSON, dec'd. Supplemental return of sales
          Jan. session 1814. Those buying: Drury Clouton, Mary
Atkinson, given by Balasm Hay, Admr. Supplement income also
given; note on James Terbaville; Acct. on Wm. Harris. Balasm
Hay, Admr.

          JAMES SHUMATE, dec'd. Account of sales. Jan. session
1814. Those buying: Claiborn Williams, Thos. Shumate, Samuel
Gentry, Benjamin Russel, Moses Admonston, Thos. Anderson, Widow,
Shadrock Harris, Aney Shumate, David Rigs, Frank Hogh, Watson
Owen, Claiborn Williams, Samuel Flemnir, Joseph H. Bell, Daniel
Maxfield (Mafield), Jas. Toyl, Richard Ogilsvie, John Ogilsvie,
Kimber Ogilsvie, Marshall Hail, Jacob Adams (Bible & prayer book),
Richard Reynolds, Amos Devers, Drury Wals. Joseph H. Bell, Admr.

P. 58.   LYDIA HEWSTEN, Admrx. settlement made by Charles Mc-
          Alister & Hinchey Petway Esq. Returned to Jan. session
1814. For schooling to Hardin Moor; pd. to Roy for schooling;
pd. to Mason Craft, to Robt Davis, to Bedick, for Alse in taxes
& midwifes fee; Ruth & Margaret paid to: Merchant Write, Merchant Curren, Petway for shoes, Samole for material for dresses,
Smith for shoes, Smith Gambrick for dress; Rachell paid to :

Smiths for dress, for the support of the youngest child born
after the death of his father for 4 yrs. & 4 mo., for the next
youngest child aged 2 yr. & 7 mo., for the next youngest child
aged 6 yr., for the next youngest child aged 8 yr. to Sam for
expense & travel for collecting notes in Ga. Jan. 4, 1814.

P. 59.   Account of the divident of the Legatees of the heirs
             of HARY MURFREE, dec'd. of the land property. Return-
ed to Jan. session 1814. Lot #1 William H. Murfree 606 acres;
Military Grant #39, tract 342 acres granted to Bryant Smith
March 7, 1786; #223, 640 acres granted to John Mederus Dec. 6,
1797; #3248 & conveyed to Hardy Murfree by deed Nov. 21, 1808;
384 acres, pt. of Thos. Callenders tract; grant #49 dated March
4, 1786 & conveyed to H. Murfree Dec. 5, 1786; 768 acres pt. of
Clement Halls tract grant #47 dated March 14, 1786 & conveyed to
H. Murfree Nov. 21, 1803; 2740 acres Lot #2 Isaac Hilliard &
Mary his wife 1430 acres; apart of Hardy Murfrees survey granted
to H. Murfree 1786. 1430 acres. 320 acres granted to Thomas
Powell #201 dated March 7, 1786 lying in Rutherford Co. on south
side of Murfree's Borough & adj. said town. 640 acres granted to
H. Murfree assinee of Jane Manley, heir of Allen Manley in
County of Willson near Lebanon-conveyed to Murfree by John Davis
& reconveyed to David Dickinson & Wm. H. Murfree, Admr. of H.
Murfree, Dec'd.   490 acres pt. of tract granted to H. Murfree in
the county of Dixon on Turnbull Cr. grant #2380-400 acres part
of Absalom Burges tract in county of Stuart on south side of
Cumberland River. grant #91 dated March 7, 1786. 640 acres
granted to David Bizzle in Wilson Co. grant #146 dated March 14,
1786 & conveyed to H. Murfree Feb. 25, 1803. 62½ acres purchased
of Jacob Thomas in Wilson Co. 773 acres grant #95 granted to
Archibald Henderson March 14, 1786. in Smith co. on Beaver Cr.
287 acres. part of tract granted to Nancy Sheppard in Sumner Co.
on waters of Goose Cr. grant #2294-640 acres granted to Nancy
Sheppard in Jackson Co. at head of Jennings Cr. grant #2311-321
acres part of 6003½ acres of William Slades tract in Wilson Co.
on Cedar Lick Cr. grant #22 dated May 18, 1789 & conveyed to H.
Murfree March 28, 1794.   Lot #3 James Maney & Sally H. his wife
1588 acres part of large survey joins Lot #1 & #2. 252 acres
granted to Ezekiel White in Rutherford Co. on Stones River.
grant #200 dated March 7, 1786-386 acres granted to Dempsey
Jenkins in Rutherford Co. granted March 7, 1780. grant #218-
1508 acres granted to John Pointed in Smith Co. grant #2178
dated May 20, 1793 conveyed to H. Murfree Sept. 8, 1804. 228
acres granted to Isaac Butler March 7, 1786 in Montgomery Co.
on north side of Cumberland River. Grant #245-274 acres granted
to James Colson March 7. 1786 in Montgomery Co. 2 mile below
McAdoo's Cr. grant #238-640 acres granted to Nancy Sheppard Dec.
8, 1787 in Stewart Co. north side of Tenn. River adj. Ky. line.
grant #668 2650 acres. Lot #4-Levenea B. Murfree-1242 acres W.
Harpeth part of grant. 400 acres granted to Henry Winborne March
7, 1786 in Rugherford Co.   grant #194 passing three spring in
tract of land granted to Joseph Mitchell. 216 acres granted to
John Butler March 7, 1786. grant #162 in Rutherford Co. 640 acres
granted to Baker Archer March 7, 1786 #211 in Montgomery Co.
south side of Cumberland River & Haws Cr. 256 acres part of
grant of John Pearce in Davidson Co. south side of Cumberland
River above mouth of Blue Creek & crossing Brush Creek. 228
acres granted to Mosson Williams in Wilson Co. on Stoned Creek.
2982 acres. Lot #5-Martha Ann C. Murfree-1452 acres north east
corner of Lot #4-714 acres granted to John Wells March 7, 1786.
#195 in Rutherford Co. on Stones River, 640 acres granted to
Luticia Archer March 7, 1786. #240 in Montgomery Co. on south
side of Cumberland River above mouth of Red River. 274 acres

granted to John Hargrove Dec. 20, 1791. #1454 Montgomery Co.
north side of Red River 2 miles above Clarksville. 477 acres
part of grant to Nancy Sheppard dated May 20, 1793. #2321 in
Overton Co.-640 acres granted to Nancy Sheppard Dec. 8, 1783.
#666 in Stewart Co. on Indian Creek & at present called Leather-
wood Creek. 640 acres granted to Nancy Sheppard July 11, 1788.
#697 in Davidson Co. Waters of Sulpher Fork of Red River 3385
acres. Lot #6-David Dickinson & Fanny N. his wife-1016 acres
part of Murfees large military survey. 708 acres granted to
Anthony Gains March 7, 1786 in Rutherford Co. on Stones River
grant #112-94 acres part of tract granted to Robertson on waters
of Stones Creek in Wilson Co.-300 acres granted to Wm. Ponder
March 7, 1786.#203 in Rutherford Co. beginning at north east
corner of Anthony Gains survey. 466 2/3 acres part of tract
granted to H. Murfree in Bedford Co. on Rock Creek of Duck River
& joining John Mederus. 200 acres part of tract granted to H.
Murfree in Lincoln Co. on Mulberry Creek. 2784 2/3 acres. Lot
#7-Matthias B. Murfree 1089 acres granted to James Martin in
Wmson Co. known by name of Hurricane tract 265 acres granted to
Joseph Mitchell March 7, 1786. #197. Rutherford Co. on Stones
River adj. tract granted to Henry Winborn & John Mitchells
grant. 203 acres granted to John White March 7, 1786 #165 in
Williamson Co. west fork of Big Harpeth. 390 acres granted to
Benj. Johnson May 20, 1793 #2354 in Davidson Co. opposite the
mouth of Turnbull Creek. 301 acres part of a tract granted to
Nancy Sheppard dated Oct. 29, 1792 in Sumner Co. west fork of
Bledsoes Creek remained of tract taken by John Sawyers 640 acres
granted to Nancy Sheppard Dec. 8, 1787 #667 in Stewart Co. on
Hays Creek & at present called Standing Stone Creek. 640 acres
granted to Nancy Sheppard July 11, 1788 #693 in Robinson Co.
Waters of Sulpher fork of Red River. 3529 acres. Dec. 31, 1813.
O. Williams, John Watson, G. McConnico, D. Dunn, Thos. Old, T.
Saunders, & Abram Maury, commissioners.

P. 65.   William Parham, guardian in account with the orphans
           of WM. C. HILL, dec'd. 1814. Jan. 1st. Hire of negro
man Isham for 1813, of Tobey & Jerry. Expense of boarding to
James C. Hill 1813. Geo. Cohoon partitioner made of Harrisses
tract of 1000 acres whereas commossion alloted said Cohoon 350
acres. Oct. session. Commissioners: James Allison, Thos.
Wilson, Wm. Wilson, Kembro Ogilvie, John Ogilvie & Geo. Tilman
to view & lay off 350 acres of land apart of 1000 acres granted
to Harris of which Samuel Harris is an heir. Land on waters
of Big Harpeth the said land being reduced by the interference
of better titles to 728 acres & for that reason the said Cohoon
directed the commissioners to lay off to him the 3rd part of
what remains. Dec. 14, 1813. Geo. Tillman, surveyor.

P. 66.   JOHN COUCH, dec'd. Inventory of the estate taken
           April 5, 1814 and returned Aprile session 1814. Live-
stock, furniture & tools. Susanna Crouch.

           WILLIAM NORTON, dec'd. A list of property, furniture,
& tools & etc. Samuel Andrews & Eliza Norton, Admr.

           JAMES SHELBURN, dec'd. A supplement to a inventory
returned by Sarah B. Shelburn & Samuel Shelburn, Admr. Allotment
for the widow & children.

P. 67.   HENRY CHILDRESS, dec'd. Account of sales. Feb. 2,
           1814 & returned to April session 1814. Those buying:
Elizabeth Childress (several items), Richard Orton, Edw. Ragsdale,
Chapman White, James Brown, Susanna Gray, Pryor Reynolds,

48

Nicholas Perkins, Wm. Smith, Martin Smith, Geo. Hulme, Benj.
Brown (chest, books, gun), Robt. Warren, Gray Jones, Henry Cook,
Athelston Andrews, Benj. Gholston, Richard Hughes, Samuel Cox,
James Toone, Wm. Shute, Joel Hobbs, Wm. Harrison, Jesse Benton,
Harrison Boyd, Angus McPhail, John Dunham; account of negroes
for hire 1814: boy Jessee to Wm. Shute, boy Geo. to James Brown;
crop allowed Elizabeth Childress, widow of HENRY CHILDRESS,
dec'd. from his death, Sept. 20, 1813.

P. 68.   GURDEN SQUIRE. dec'd. Inventory of Estate. Returned
          to April session. Horse, furniture, household items,
books; Note on: Martin Stanley & Jas. G. Jones, Thos. S. West &
John West, Julues Burton & John West, Zachariah Jackson & P.
Beasley, Joel T. Rivers & Jason Hopkins, John & James Neely,
Garner McConico & T.J. Hardeman, Thos. Hiter, David Squire,
Geo. Hulme & H. Lyan, Henry Lyon & John J. Henry, Henry Walker
& N.P. Hardeman, Wm. Bright, James G. Jones. D. Squier, Admr.

P. 70.   RICHARD SMITH, dec'd. Account of Sales sold Feb. 6,
          1814. Returned to April session 1814. Those buying:
James McGuire, William M. Simpkins. O. Williams, Admr.

          Supplemental Inventory of RICHARD SMITH, dec'd.; note
on Roger B. Sappinton and Edwin Smith assumption for $10 doubt-
ful. April 7, 1814. O. Williams, Admr.

          RICHARD PUCKETT, dec'd. Inventory. Note on: Samuel
Witherspoon & Richard Orton, Robt. Crafton & Samuel Shelburn,
Samuel Curray & Eli Stacy, John Harnes & David McEwen, Jared
Puckett, Geo. Davidson & Moses Chambers, Harvey Puckett, Jessee
Johnson & Josiah Wouldridge, Richard Orton & Henry G. Kearney,
John McNeal; furniture, silver watch, books, livestock, farm
implements, slaves & cash. Receipt given by John Norton to
Jas. Tomlinson for a bond on James & John Mays & Jeremiah Dower
of Wilkinson Co., Miss. territory. Garner McConnico.

P. 72.   JOHN HODGE, dec'd. Amount of property sold. Wm. Hodge,
          Admr. Those buying: Kimbro Ogilvie, Walter B. Owen,
Mashach Haile, John Robertson, Francis Hodge, Thomas Shumate,
Thomas Maxwell. Wm. H. Hodge, John West. Wm. Hodge, Admr.

          JOSEPH POTTS, dec'd. Account of Sales sold Dec. 6,
1811. Returned to April session 1814. Those buying: Abner Holt,
Thomas West, Alexander Smith, David Johnston, Peter Pinkston,
Stephen Barfield, Wm. Sneed, Turner Pinkston, Ana Reed, Thomas
Malone, Robt. E. Beasley, Hugh Pinkston, John Blackman, Simon
Bateman, Terry Bradley, Agnes Potts, Wm. McEwen, James Armstrong,
Abner Holt, James McEwen, Samuel Crockett, John Corethers, James
McGavock, Henry Talley; Agnes Potts hire of Peter & woman &
children. Isaac Little & Samuel Crockett, Admr.

P. 74.   Allotment to Elizabeth Childress, widow of HENRY
          CHILDRESS, dec'd. Returned to April session 1814.
April 8, 1814. R. P. Curren, James Gordon, & William Banks,
commissioners. John J. Henry (J.P.)

P. 75.   DAVID JOHNSON'S Bill of Sale; Stills, horses, mare,
          cows, hogs, sheep, & furniture sold to Robert Johnston,
March 4, 1814. Wit: Jas. Armstrong, David Johnston, John Reed.
April session 1814.

          David Johston bill of sale to Robert Johnston. Negro
man named Lige 32 yrs., man named Ben 32 yrs, man Jared 24 yrs.,

man named Congo 19 yrs., woman Poll 31 yrs., woman Zilf 26 yrs., woman Fill 19 yrs., woman Seal 19 yrs., boy Frank 10 yrs., boy Dick 9 yrs., boy Virgil 6 yrs., boy Isaac 3 yrs., boy Ben 1 yr., boy Jim 4 yrs., boy Moses 1 yr., boy Daniel 3 months, girl Silva 5 yrs. Test: James Armstrong, John Reed, & David Johnston. April session 1814.

P. 76.   We, Philip Beasley, John W. Beasley, Ephraim W. Beasley & James Hicks, heirs & representative (& Ann Beasley widow & relict of) ROBERT BEASLEY, dec'd. have agreed to make a partition of the personal estate & possessions. The names of negroes are as follows: Sam, Isaac, Peter, Ned, Aggy, & Delilah. The said Ann Beasley, the widow, agreed to take a childs part of the estate, as her dower consisting of the following negroes: Sam, Peter & Aggy; certain livestock & furniture. Philip Beasley get negro Isaac. James Hicks get negro Delilah & Ephraim. W. Beasley to get equal in money. Jan. 7, 1814. Wit: Isham Cole, Jr., Elenor Cole, John Gray, Senr.

P. 77.   MARTIN ADAMS. Bill of Sale to William Hope. Martin Adams of Davidson Co. have sold to Wm. Hope of Wmson. Co. the following slaves: Rose about 22 yrs., Tom 5 yr., Sealy 3 yr., Billy 2 mo., Nancy 13 yr. Dec. 8, 1813. Wit: Thos. Berry & S. Hunt.

Jan. 7, 1814. Settlement with Lydia Hewstin, Admxr. of SAMUEL HEWSTIN, dec'd. Money, negro woman Aylee & her child, Nelson; Hinchey Petway, guardian to the orphan of SAMUEL HEWSTIN, dec'd. Test: Jacob Tillman & C. White.

Richard Willett. Account of Sale of the property of R. M. WILLETT, dec'd. sold on Sept. 30, 1813. Returned to April session 1814. Charlotte Willett, Admrx.

P. 78.   Finch Scruggs. Bill of Sale. Finch Scruggs, exr. of JESSE THOMAS, dec'd. sold to James Cockrill, 1 negro man, Dick. Sept. 24, 1813. Wit: N. Dillard.

Wm. Hope bill of sale to Daniel Jermain; sold negro woman about 22 yrs. old & 3 children, named Tom, Sally, & Billy of ages 5, 3 yrs. & 2 months. Dec. 8, 1813. Test: Thomas Berry & S. Hunt.

DAVID EVINS for the love & affection I have for my daughter Martha Galaspie Evins convey to her, my yellow girl named Suck about 11 yrs. old & increase of the girl goes to any children that my wife Jenny & I may here after have. Jan. 5, 1814.

P. 79.   WALTER BENNETT, SENR. Deed of Gift. Love & affection for my grandchildren: John Bennett, Jenny Bennett & Elizabeth Bennett, children of Geo. Bennett, the following negro slaves: Ned now hired to Joel Hobbs, negro boy Jack purchased of Wm. Brown of Randolph Co., N.C. Whenever the youngest of children arrives at age of 18 yrs. the said slaves will be sold & equally divided between them at which time the mother of said children, Anna Bennett, shall be entitled to a childs part during her natural life. Oct. 29, 1812. Wit: Wm. P. Harrison & Robt. McLemore.

P. 80.   Hendley Stone, guardian account for Peter & Green Pryor, heirs of JOHN PRYOR, dec'd. credit for 1813 Jan. 1st & returned to April session 1814. Jan. 1st hire of Jude &

3 children to Col. Perkins, boy Frank to Walter Jenkins, girl
Cloe to David Squire, Sukey & 3 children to Joel Hobbs, boy Geo.
to Henry Perkins, boy Sam to Daniel Perkins, boy Joe to Walter
Jenkins, boy Jesse to Thos. H. Perkins, Hannen & 3 children to
Wesley Witherspoon; rent of land in Virginia; met at house of
Hendley Stone 26th day of March 1814. Expenses: for clothing,
school supplies, medicine, etc. Signed: N. Perkins, Sr., Daniel
Perkins, Robert McLemore, & Edward Warren.

P. 82.   JOHN ATKINSON, dec'd. Settlement. Balaam Hay, Admr.
          Note on: John McKenney due 10th Feb. 1813, James
Terbaville due 25th Dec. 1812, Balam Hay due 6th Feb. 1813,
Molly Atkinson due 6th Feb. 1814, Amos Bullock due 6th Feb.
1814, Wm. Turnage due 6th Feb. 1814, Polley J. Atkinson due 6th
Feb. 1814, Patsey Atkinson due 1st Feb. 1814, Charles Boyles due
6th Feb. 1814; collected from: James Terbaville 15th Oct. 1813,
Wm. Harris 15th Oct. 1813; note on: Drury Clanton due 6th Feb.
1814, Molley Atkinson due 6th Feb. 1814; collected from: Jas.
Terbaville 17th Sept. 1813, Jas. Sneed 17th Sept. 1813, admrs.
of Benj. Adams; receipt from Wm. Ramsey for cost 19th Mar.; note
to J. Tuberville with interest from 6th Decr. 1811. Account
Berry Nolin & G. Hulme.

P. 83.   Henry Cook, guardian of Henry Cook, a minor orphan of
          EDMUND COOK, dec'd. 1809-paid Boyd for boarding,
clothing, schooling, & taxes on negroes; 1810-paid schooling with
Jno. T. Tolbert, clothing, board, etc.; 1812-paid G. Hulme for
schooling, clothing; 1813-paid A. Boyd for boarding & etc.;
1814-expenses for clothing. Credit: 1809-hire of negro woman
Nuney; 1810-hire said negro Suk for nothing; 1811-by hire of said
negro, by hire of Isham; 1812-by hire of Nuney & Isham; 1813-
by hire of Nancy & Isham. 1st April 1814. G. Hulme & John
Witherspoon.

P. 83.   Henry Cook, guardian for John Cook, minor orphan of
          EDMUND COOK, dec'd. 1809-paid A. Boyd for boarding
& clothing & schooling; 1810-paid John T. Talbot for boarding,
clothing & schooling; A. Boyd for boarding, clothing & schooling;
1811-paid Jackson for schooling, A. Boyd for boarding & clothing & schooling; 1812-paid A. Boyd for boarding, clothing &
schooling; 1813-paid A. Boyd for boarding, clothing & schooling,
G. Hulm for boarding, clothing, & schooling; 1814-paid for pr.
shoes; 1810-hire of Bob; 1811-hire of Bob & Lovy; 1812-hire of
Bob & Lovy; 1813-hire of Bob. 1st April 1814.

P. 84.   Henry Cook, guardian of Geo. E. Cook, minor heir of
          EDMUND COOK, dec'd. 1809-paid A. Boyd for clothing,
boarding, & schooling; 1810-paid John T. Tolbert for schooling;
1811-paid Wm. J. Boyd for boarding & schooling; 1812-paid A.
Boyd for boarding & schooling; 1813-paid schooling with S. Bradford, paid A. Boyd boarding & clothing; 1809-hire of Sam; 1810,
1811,1812, 1813-hire of Sam; 1811, 1812, 1813-hire of Melley.
April 1st 1814.

P. 87.   We the comm. appointed by court for the purpose of
          dividing among the heirs of ANTHONY SHARP, dec'd. the
tract of land which was assigned to his widow, containing 877
acres & which has been sold by Geo. Hulme & Peggy his wife,
formerly the widow Sharp, to the heirs of said ANTHONY SHARP,
dec'd. Lot #1-Sumner M. Sharp 80 acres; Lot #2-John J. Henry
68 acres; Lot #3 Sola N. Sharp 73 acres; Lot #4 John P. Broadnax 72 acres; Lot #5 Angus McFale 130 acres; Lot #6 James G.
Jones 100 acres; Lot #7 Peggy N. Sharp 162 acres; Lot #8 Searcy

D. Sharp 192 acres.

P. 91.   JESSE BENTON, dec'd. Division of the land. We, the
comm. in obedience to an order of the County court,
which order is annexed by & the consent of all the Legatees &
agreeable to the provisions of the last will of JESSE BENTON,
dec'd. late of North Carolina, have proceeded to divide the
following tract of land. (Natchez Road runs through property).
Lot #1-Samuel Benton 257 acres; Lot #2 Nat'l Benton 369 acres;
Lot #3 Thos. H. Benton 216 acres; Lot #4 Jesse Benton 283 acres;
Lot #5 Mary Benton 200 acres. D. Dunn, S. Saunders, & O.
Williams. Test: N. Perkins, W. Smith, Archibald Lytle, Nich.
Scales.

P. 93.   Division of the negroes of JESSE BENTON, dec'd.
Returned July session 1812. JESSE BENTON, late of
N.C. 6 negroes not prop. belonging to afore said estate but as
property given by the late Col. Thos. Hart of N.C. to the heirs
of the above said JESSE BENTON, dec'd. negroes valued at $800,
making a div. of $160 each legatee. Lot #1 drawn by Thos. H.
Benton, old Tom & wife Dorcas, cash rec'd. $159 & $160.00; Lot
#2 Jesse Benton, Chloe valued at $100.00, received from #4 & #
4 $60.00=$160.00; Lot #3 Nat'l. Benton, Judith $350.00, paid
to #1 $159.99, paid to #2 $30.01=$160.00; Lot #4 Mary Benton,
Mitchell boy $200.00, paid to #2 $30.00, paid to #5 $10.00=
$160.00; Lot #5 Samuel Benton, Sam small boy $150.00, from #4
$10.00=$160.00. Thursday 16, July 1812. Probated court July
session 1812.

JAMES SHELBURN, dec'd. Allotment. July session 1813.
Sarah B. Shelburn, widow & relict of JAMES SHELBURN, dec'd.
Oliver Williams, Thos. Ridley, Freeman Walker & James Harder,
Comm. 31st July 1813.

P. 94.   Jacob Coddington to G. McConnico receipt. 12th Oct.
1813. Garner McConnico Admr. of RICHARD PUCKETT,
my dec'd. guardian $413.71 & 3 mills part of money & rent of
land. Jacob Coddington. Test: Wm. Denson & B. Randolph.

DUDLEY PORTER, dec'd. Settlement. Sarah Porter,
Admrx. Paid to: David McCord, Kizza Shinault, Bazel Berry,
James Berry for maintainance of family 1 yr. Sign: Jacob
Garrett, W. Wilson, S. Shelburn.

P. 95.   Susanna Crouch. Allotment April session 1814. Widow
& relict of JOHN CROUCH, dec'd. 11th Apr. 1814. Henry
Cook, Edward Warren, Wm. Bond.

ELIZABETH HOLSTEAD. Will. Proven July session 1814.
Dau. Julia Jones, house & lot where I now live; Holland White,
bed & furniture; Elizabeth White, looking glass. Julia Jones,
Edrx. May 13, 1814. Wit: Robt. Daves & Wm. Manning.

P. 96.   JOSEPH BROWN. Will. Proven July session 1814.
JOSEPH BROWN of Dixon Co., Tenn. wife Ann Brown, personal estate during her life & then divided between children.
Dau. Polly Worly, negro child Matilda, first child of my negro
woman Peggy; dau. Sarah Mitchell, negro woman Peggy & if Peggy
should have another it goes to dau. Elizabeth Handlin & should
Peggy have 3rd child, to dau. Philopina Dickerson & should
Peggy have 4th child it goes to dau. Ann Potter & all the rest
that she has to dau. Sarah Mitchell; Dau. Ruth Mendenall, horse
or either personal property after death of wife, exr. to procure

freedom for negro man David for meritorious services. Exrs:
wife Ann Brown & trusty friend John Hall of Leatherwood.   19
June 1812. Test: Alex Martin, John Shelton, Mathew Morgain.
Codicile - gr. son Joseph Worley, rifle gun.   June 1812. Probated July session 1814.

P. 97.   DAVID LEWIS, dec'd.   Will.   Proven July session 1814.
         12 Feb. 1814. Wife Hannah Lewis, all personal & real
estate; children: Sarah Lewis, David Lewis, Wm. Lewis, Elizabeth Lewis, Benj. Lewis, & Nancy Lewis; worthy friend Francis
Jackson, exr. Test: John Hill & Francis Jackson.

P. 98.   JOHN CROUCH, dec'd.   Account of Sales.   30th Apr. 1814.
         Susanna Crouch, Admrx. several lots of carpenters
tools & etc. No buyers names given.

         Settlement of JOHN CROUCH. No. 1, balance of a note
due Wm. Shute; No. 2, John S. Campbell proven account; No. 3,
Pryor Reynolds account; No. 4, Sterling Gunter proven account;
No. 5, Isaac Potter for making coffin; No. 6, exr. of Col. Peter
Perkins proven account; No. 7, Nicholas Perkins proven account;
No. 8, allowance for 1 yr. 3rd Oct. 1814. Nicholas Scales,
John Witherspoon, James Black.

P. 99.   NATHANIEL BROWN. Noncupative Will. 16 day May 1814.
         In a low state of consumption. Bro.-in-law Benj.
Rutherford use of stock until 15 Sept. next & then exr. to sell
same & cash arising be divided between my bro. & sister, Richard
Brown & Sister Brown. Bro. George Brown, childs part of land
which my father Ephraim Brown gave me lying at head of McCutchens
Creek. Bro. John Brown, saddle, rifle & shot pouch; sister Ruth
Brown, dog irons & account which Hugh Bell, on Big Harpeth below
this, owes me; Bro. Thomas Brown $5.00 for & in consideration
of the love I have for him. Test: Robert Neelly. Produced by
Sam'l Edmiston. July session 1814 by oaths of Charles Brown &
Samuel Edmiston. Chas. Brown, Admr.

         NATHANIEL BROWN, dec'd. Inventory & Sail buyers:
Matthew Lee, Thomas Brown, Charles Brown, Joseph Pinkerton,
Joshua Green, Geo. H. Pewitt, Wm. Robins, Wm. Cooper, Hugh Barr.
Sold on 6th Aug. 1814. Sale at the house of Benj. Rutherford.
Charles Brown, Admr.

P. 100. JANE WHEATON. Inventory. Betwixt the 2nd Monday in
         Oct. 1812 & 2nd Monday in Jan. 1813 skedule of per-
sonal property came to knowledge & control of Thos. T. Maury,
Admr.; part of Lot #15 in Nashville between Watter & Market St.
with single story dwelling house; part of Lot #175 in Nashville
fronting Watter St. with a small 2 story hewed log house; Lot #
22 in Franklin fronting on Church St. including a small 2 story
frame house, small brick house & log kitchen & framed small
house. In Davidson Co. the following slaves: 10 in number,
Mary (old & of little value); Hagar & 3 children; Polly & 1
child; Harriet, Lucy & Orid; furniture in Wmson. Co.; bureau,
sugar chest, large trunk. other furniture & household items.
List of notes on following: J. Bruff due 26 June 1809. Thos. J.
Read due 27 Aug. 1812; several notes on E. Marshall due 1808 &
1809. Thos. T. Maury, Admr. Jan. 1813.

P. 101. JOSEPH POTTS, dec'd. Settlement. Paid to Abner Holt,
         Henry Tally, John H. Crockett, Doct. S. Crockett, &
Peter Pinkston. 6th July 1814. Samuel Crockett, Admr.

WM. NORTON, dec'd. Supplemental inventory. Notes on Jesse Yocom to Thos. Ballow & was assigned to Wm. Norton. Samuel Andrews & Eliza Norton, Admr. July session 1814.

P. 102.   JOHN CRAWFORD, dec'd. Division of slaves. April term 1814. Elizabeth Crawford widow, Washington P., James J. & Henry R. Crawford, heirs & allotment to the said widow, a certain negro woman named Sukey 21 yrs. of age, & her 2 youngest children, Anderson & Bedford. The balance of negroes Judea, Nancy, Jean, George, Nathan, & Anerkey. 20 May 1814. Commissioners: David McEwen, Robert Carothers, Robt. Hodge, Jason Hopkins, Ewen Camerson, Daniel McMahan, John White, Martin Stanly, Alexander Smith, James Crockett, Wm. Shute, & James McEwen, Sr. Probated in court, July session 1814.

ANTHONY SHARP, dec'd. Settlement. 7th July 1814. H. Cook, Admr. paid to the following: H. Cook, J. J. King, Thomas H. Benton, Stephen Smith, Thos. L. Robertson, P. Russel, Petway & Maury, Caleb Manly, John White, John Haywood, A. Balchas, Banks & Cannon. Received from: A. McKnowen, N. Perkins, John J. Henry, James G. Jones, J. Stanley, Lewis Fauts, Mrs. Sharp.

P. 103.   ANTHONY SHARP, dec'd. Settlement with Margaret Hulm late Margaret Sharp, Admrx. of ANTHONY SHARP, dec'd. Cash Paid: H. Petway, John Gee, James Geordan for 6 months service in making & gathering crop, Garner McConico, Edw. Ragsdale, for lime delivered at David McEwens; cash received from Perry Taylor. April term 1814. Geo. Hulm, Admr. in right of his wife.

P. 104.   THOMAS CALDWELL, dec'd. Account of sales sold 21st of Sept. 1810. Those buying: Mary Caldwell (most of furniture & some livestock & negro boy Peter), James Stephens, Charles Boyles, Richard Orton, Andrew Caldwell, John Haly, G. Manly, James Cambell.

P. 105.   CLEMENT SMITHSON, dec'd. Inventory taken Oct. 1, 1814. 125 acres of land, livestock, farm tools, household furniture, 2 negro women, 1 boy & child, 1 Bible & 1 Testament. Nancy Smithson & Horatio Pettus. Probated in court Oct. session 1814.

JAMES BERRY, dec'd. Estate Inventory. Oct. term 1814. 4 negroes, livestock, furniture, pistols, stud horse in hands of Wm. Wilson; rent of ground from James Buzby. Notes on: John Watt, Azariah Anderson, Sal. Campbell, Joseph morris, Jonathan Mobly, David Berry & John Allen. Rebecca Berry, Admrx. Alex. Johnson & Bassel Berry, Admr. Oct. session 1814.

P. 106.   JOSEPH BROWN, dec'd. Inventory. Returned Oct. session 1814. Livestock, furniture, farm tools, rifle gun, shot bag, & etc., negro man, woman & 2 children. Ann Brown, Exrs.

DAVID LEWIS, dec'd. Estate Inventory. Oct. session 1814. Household items, livestock & farm implements; widow traded off bay horse & saddle, 1 gun & heifer; killed sow & pigs. Francis Jackson.

P. 107.   JOHN BENSON, dec'd. Inventory. Returned Oct. session 1814. 2 horses, saddle, bridle & clothing. Samuel Williams.

JESSE GULLEY, dec'd. Inventory. Returned Oct. session

1814. Horse, saddle, bridle & saddle bags, 1 draw on the United States for 3 months & 10 days <u>towe</u> in Capt. Kavender's Cavalry Co. Labon Benson.

BENJAMIN BUGG, dec'd. Inventory. Returned Oct. session 1814. 1 negro boy Starling. David Pinkston, Nancy Bugg, & Ephraim M. Bugg, Admr.

ISHAM EVANS, dec'd. Inventory. Returned Oct. session 1814. Admr. has collected his pay for his services in the army from the paymaster in the amt. of $19.8772. Jason Hopkins, Admr.

WM. C. DEVORIX, dec'd. Inventory. Returned Oct. session 1814. Clothing. William Wilson.

Sherwood Green, guardian for S. CLARK, dec'd. heirs settlement. Oct. session 1814. From last settlement at July session 1813. July 15-Sally Clark's school entrance & expenses; Martin Clark-shoes & expenses; schooling for Martin, Willie & Samuel Clark paid to Sampson Sawyers for boarding the children. Returned to Oct. session 1814.

P. 109. Isaac Mairs, guardian for JESSE BLACKSHARE, dec'd.,
heirs settlement. Oct. session 1814. Heirs: Ezekiel Blackshaire, Elisha Blackshare, Jacob Blackshare, Luke Black-share, David Blackshare, Jesse Blackshare, Elijah Blackshare. Hannah Blackshare, admr. of the estate now Hannah Mairs, wife of Isaac Mairs. Balance of money has been divided between Penny Blackshare & James Blackshare & above named heirs. G. Hulme & Sion Hunt.

WM. C. DEVARIX, dec'd. Supplementary Inventory. Clothing. William Wilson. Jan. session 1815.

HARDY MURFREE, dec'd. Division of slaves. Oct. session 1814. Account current with David Dickinson, Admr. Lot #1 Wm. H. Murfree-1. Ned 50 yrs. $200; 2. Toney 25 yrs. $500; 3. Harry 40 yrs. $500; 4. Sampson (a blacksmith & tools) 35 yrs. $1000; 5. Charles 60 yrs. no amount; 6. Lewis & Betty 60 yr. $200; 7. Peggy & 3 children, Silvey, Nancy & Judy $775; 8. Judy & her child 35 yr. $350; 9. Willis 19 yr. $300; 10. America 60 yr. $75; 11. Judith 60 yr. no amount; 12. Pleasant 60 yr. no amount; 13. Doctor Scott no amount; 14. Lucy 21 yr. $300; 15. Amey 21 yr. $300; 16. Abram 10 yr. $250; 17. Jimmy no amount; 18. Jack no amount; Lot #1 pays D. Dickinson, Levenia B. Burton, Jas. Maney, Martha Murfree & Isaac Hilliard. Lot #2 Isaac Hilliard; 1. Chysick 30 yr. $400; 2. Peggy 25 yr. $325; 3. Jinny 3 yr. $125; 4. Nancy child $75; 5. Phillis 20 yr. $350; 6. Eddy 11 yr. $225; 7. Venus 10 yr. $225; 8. Dick 13 yr. $300; 9. Per-kins 3 yr. $150; 10. John 10 yr. $350; 11. Fortune & Cloe $100; 12. Charles 16 yr. $400; Lot #3 David Dickinson; 1. Rebecca 10 yr. $225; 2. Kitty 16 yr. $375; 3. Lucy 15 yr. $350; 4. Cabe 15 yr. $300; 5. Tony (since dead) 45 yr. $300; 6. Jack 12 yr. $350; 7. Benjamin 38 yr. $375; 8. Frances no amount; 9. Bristow & Phillis his wife $250; Lot #4. Martha Murfree, 1. Brazior (Ned) $550; 2. Sally, Ned's wife $325; 3. Betty her child $100; 4. Hetty her child $200; 5. Charlotte & Kitty (twins) $325; 6. Joseph $140; 7. James $75; 8. Winney $100; 9. Geo. Carr & Cloe $325; 10. Bob $400; 11. Anna $200; 12. Dred $250; 13. Hannah $350; 14. Jack & Trace his wife $150; Lot #5 James Maury; 1. man Will $400; 2. Selvy, his wife & child $300; 3. Magga, her dau. $200; 4. Hardy $200; 5. Harriotte $175; 6. Henry $150; 7. Willis $100; 8. Tim $325; 9. Tinney & child $275; 10. Nat,

her son $250; 11. Warrick, her son $212.50; 12. Dinah her dau.
$150; 13. Eliza $125; 14. Geo. Porter & Lucky his wife $150;
15. Sam $400; Lot #6. Matthias B. Murfree, 1. Peter $75; 2.
Tona his wife $200; 3. Isam her son $250; 4. Venus her dau.
$200; 5. Sarah her dau. $175; 6. Annas her dau. $150; 7. David
her son $100; 8. Daniel $500; 9. Frank $200; 10. Cherry, his
wife $175; 11. David her son $150; 12. Nancy her dau. $150;
13. Lewis her son $130; 14. Henry her son $100; 15. Tom $350;
16. Frank $450; 17. Jesse $400; blacksmith tools; Lot #7.
Francis N. Burton, 1. Abby $275: 2. Eddy her dau. $50; 3. Moses
her son $300; 4. Jacob her son $275; 5. Benj. her son $225; 6.
Levena her dau. $125; 7. Davie $500; 8. Molly & child $325;
9. Hardy her son $150; 10. Henry her son $125; 11. Jack, Molleys
husband $500; 12. Harry $400; 13. Willis $400.

P. 112.   Expenses-1809 paid expense in giving land for taxes
            paid Laurance. Paid: Hary M.; Banks of Receipt;
Postage & letters; Campbell & Bond for Jacob Lawrence; Sheriff
of Maury Co. for double tax; Expense in attending to pay taxes;
Stephen Childress; John Coffee for taxes in Bedford Co. a 5000
acre tract; John Coffee tax on land in Rutherford Co. for 1808;
expenses to Jefferson on business of estate; Jno. Dickinson,
note given by H. Murfree to Frances Prince; James Hicks postage
of a steer; M.B. Murfree expenses to Mulherrins & Nashville;
Eastern Printer in Nashville; James Helbon, expenses to Stones
River & Nashville; Sheff. of Stuart Co. by W. Outlaw, tax for
1809; M.B. Murfree's expenses to Dover & Co.; Michael Moulton
Sheff. in Dixon Co. 1809; negro boy Frank; M. Knights expense to
Nashville; Thos. Talbots bill; Turner Saunders; W. Woodford,
money he advanced to pay taxes 1808-09; Sheff. of Smith Co. for
land tax 1809; Sheff. of Davidson Co. for land tax 1809; M.B.
Murfree's expense on estate business; Sheff. of Dixon Co. by H.
Adams tax 1808; note to Wm. Cool; M.B. Murfree's expense on
estate business; Mrs. Childress for turkeys; W. Waite bond;
Sheff. of Montgomery Co. land tax 1808; M.B. Murfree's expense
to Dover & Charlotte; George Poyzer; M.B. Murfree's expense to
Jas. Mulherrins & Co.; Wm. Patton; Thos. Black; John Barnett
for Isaac Patton in part of his account; Wm. Howell by J. Burgess for stray hogs; Joseph Park for note to Peter Bennett;
expense to Nashville on estate business; Sheff. of Wmson. Co.
tax 1809; James Hicks D.R. Wmson. C.; Sheff. of Jackson Co. tax
1809; Clerk of Overton Co. tax on land 1809; James Pughes expense going to Jackson & Overton; James Nickerson for making H.
Murfree's coffin; H. Murfree's assumption to Joel Hobbs for
Lorance; taxes on John Young's land % B. Bradford receipt; Brad-
fords to redeem Youngs land for 1808; taxes of land receipt in
1809; Joseph Glover for H.M. subscribing for building meeting
house; expenses to Nashville on business; T.G. Bradford, printer;
Sheff. of Maury Co. tax for 1809; Henry Cornway surveyor; Sheff.
of Robertson Co. tax of land 1809; expense in going to Dover,
Stewart & Montgomery Co.; John White; Andrew Jones, exorgh?
Lazarus Carter dec'd.; Murfree's note paid by me with interest;
Sampson Futrell in part for a small negro Murfree bought of him
in 1807; small Buckram back; John & Ab Thompson; expenses at
Nashville attending Feb. court; J. Dickinson fee of suit H.
Murfree vs. Humphrey's & wife; Wm. Waite; Sheff. of Wmson. Co.
tax 1810; Dr. J. Nunan; Robt. Prince; Sheff. of Montgomery Co.
tax 1809; Tristram Patton; Jordan Adkerson; Doctor S. Crockett;
R.P. Currin note to W. Stevens; J. Sample & Co., note; Thos.
Stuarts receipt; Henry Conway, surveyor of Rutherford Co. for
running line between estate & Joel Childress; H. Tatum for land
entry made; H. Murfree's note to Thos. Callen; E.S. Hall & Co.;
Thos. Porter; Robt. Sercy clerk to Comm. for West Tenn.;

Eldridge Newsome; M.B. Murfree's expense to No. C. on estate business; Theo. Black for sheep; Sheff. Jackson Co. tax for 1810; land redeemed year 1809; expenses to Jackson Co; Mathew Figuers in part of bond given to B. Roberts; Robt. Finney atty. for Hardy Ireland on bond; expense to Lebanon on business Jacob Laurance; Sheff. of Stewart Co. tax 1810; expenses to Dover; Sion Record for Bond on Wm. Neelly; Isaac Patton; Isaac Tignor; Isaac Tignor for boarding 1 negro with Son-leg; Sheff. Davidson Co. tax 1810; expense to Nashville & Stones River; Caleb Mandley, Neelson King & Mitchells account; Thos. Stallings; Nias Andrews; Sheff. Smith Co. tax 1810; Sheff. Sumner Co. tax 1810; Sheff. Overton Co. tax 1810; expense to Overton, Smith & Sumner Co.; Sheff. Giles Co. tax 1810; exp. to Columbia; Sheff. Robinson Co. tax of land 1810; Sheff. Montgomery Co. tax of land 1810; expense to Stones River, Springfield, Clarksville & Dover & Smith Co.; Petway & Maury; R.P. Currin & Co.; negro Frank; Oliver Williams surveyor; Sheff. Montgomery Co. tax 1811; Sheff. Stewart Co. tax 1811; for regestering 2 grants; expenses to Montgomery & Stewart Co.; John McCracken for repairing mills; David Squire; Abner Pillow; W. Dobbins; Wm. Woodfork; expenses to Fort Blount; John Dickinson, atty.; Isaac Tignor; James Mulherrin, 274 acres land warrent.

P. 117.   Paid: Sheff. Jackson Co. tax 1812: collector Smith Co. tax 1812; R. Finney expenses to Jackson & Smith Co.; W. Woodfork for small leather book; Wm. Houston Account; Sheff. Dixon Co. tax 1811; R. Finney expenses Dixon & Bedford Co.; taxes Dixon & Bedford Co. 1812; Sheff. Montgomery Co. tax 1812: expense to Hopkins, Kentucky on business; Wm. Neusom; Elizabeth Wright, Admrx.; Sheff. Dixon Co. 1810 taxes; Howell Adams; Isaac Tignor; David Dunn; James Morgan & Mat. B. Murfree's expense to Anesville, Ohio & Clarksbury, Va. to make sale of Ohio lands; chain carrier expense Harpeth lick lands; sheff. Davidson Co. tax 1811; Sheff. Robertson Co. tax 1811; Sheff Giles Co. tax 1811; Sheff. Lincoln Co. tax 1811; expenses to Giles & Lincoln Co.1 bond to Samuel Wilson; Sheff. Rutherford Co. tax 1811; Sheff. Wmson. Co. tax 1811; expenses to Wilson Co.; John Pugh for going & paying taxes in Overton Co. 1810; Sheff. Smith Co. tax 1811; Sheff. Sumner Co. tax 1811; Sheff. Jackson Co. tax 1811; expenses to Jackson, Smith & Sumner Co.; Isaac Tignor; G.T. Bradford; to Turner Saunders season on mares; to Deadrick & Clemm; to W. Thompson chain carrier; to John Newgent chain carrier; M.B. Murfree's expense to Carthage & Fort Blount; Thos. H. Benton; Sheff. Sumner Co. tax 1812; G.G. Washington agt. for Thos. Masterson, dec'd.; Sheff. Lincoln Co. tax 1812; James Geordon & Co. balance Collins note; Joel Childress; Jas. Jackson note sent to Murfree (?) Morgan; Sheff. Rutherford Co. tax (no year); Sheff. Giles Co. tax 1812; Sheff. Stewart Co. tax 1812; to Mathew Figuers balance on bond; Jenkins Whiteside; Sheff. Wmson. Co. tax 1812; T.H. Benton; Sheff. Davidson Co. tax 1812; John Sample & Co.; E.B. Davidson for surveying land in Stewart Co.; G. Bradford Printer(?); Dan' Perkins C. Ranger.

P. 118.   1813. July 16-Yancy Thornton comm. exp; expense in viewing lands in Stewart, Montgomery & Dixon & Davidson Co.; Aug. 16-paid for copies of letters of admr. sent to N.C.; Oct. 9-comm. for valuing land in Wilson & Smith Co.; paid: J.G. Blount 27 Nov. 1809, Dr. Crockett, Jas. Sims exp. to Hosser Town, N.C. going after negroes (Sam & Willie); Nov. 28-paid: Sheriff Montgomery Co. taxes 1813, M.B. Murfree's expense comm., expenses carrying mule to Stone River. 1814. Paid: Mr. Brown; Jan. 12-Sheff. McClannahan, Rutherford Co. tax 1813, John Sample, W. Hulmes Sheff. Wmson. Co. 1813, D. Dickinson expenses to

Nashville, business; Robt. Finneys expenses to Mulherrins; M.C.
Dunn Sheff. Davidson Co. tax 1813; James Pugh. Mar. 12- Sheff.
Lincoln Co.; Sheff. Smith Co.; Sheff. Sumner Co.; P.M. Eachen;
Jas. Turney taxes Overton Co. 474 acres; Samuel Weakley; M.B.
Murfree's to Smith & Sumner Co.; Comm. to Smith, Sumner & Over-
ton co.; copy of grant; taxes in Overton Co.; Henry Lyon busi-
ness of estate. Mar. 28-Buckingham Sheff.; Sheff. Dixon Co.;
M.B. Murfrees expense. May 5-Kavanaughs expenses; John Dickin-
son; Garner McConnico; Oliver Williams; W.W. Cunningham; W.
Smith & Cunningham expenses; Sheff. Overton Co. tax 1811; Sheff.
Overton Co. tax 1813; expenses surveying land & chain carriers.

P. 119.   Paid: M.B. Murfree's expenses (Talbot); M.B. Murfree's
           expenses (Childress); John Davis Surveyor; Wm. Wait
account; M.B. Murfree's to Davidson Co.. July 26-W. Lytle, baing
cotton. Received of W.H. Murfree, part James Mulherrins note
crying sale in Rugherford Co. Paid: D. Dunn, boarding Jone's
child; D. Dickinson, board & clothing for Sally & 5 children bid
off to him. 1-10-1814; comm. exp. Bedford, & Lincoln Co.; James
Sims balance account; Sam'l Dotson balance account; Abner Pillow
account; W. Houston account; balance due on 2 judgment vs. John
& Ire Fly in circuit court of Maury Co.; paid Orsbourne Nicholson
account; expenses at Columbia for estate; Henry Cook account;
Currin & Mason account. 1809 Contra; cash received Oct. 1809-
Inventory. Received: Howell Adams note, Daniel Ross, W. Neelly's
note, Sion Record note, Henry Moore note, E. Hope account, John
& Ire Fly note, Elijah Hunter account, Billington Taylor's
account, Green Williamson, Sam'l Brooks, Jas. Jordom note endorsed
to H. Murfree, part of Jas. Mulherrins note, Jas. Mulherrins &
Jinkin Whiteside note, Edw. Gwinns & John Hudson account cattle,
Edw Gwinns note of Inventory, 2 bank notes of W.H. Murfree.
Aug. 2 Received: Jacob Montgomery note paid Jas. Hilton settle-
ment with Hunter, of Jas. Sims, of E. Cratcher for rent. 1811-
received from Plantation in Wilson Co. Jan. 3 received of Issac
Tignor; Sept. 9 of John Neelly; Dec. 22 Jas. Sims, John Alcorn
for rent, Isaac Rhodes for land warrent. 1813. Received: of
Wm. Houston account, of Thos. Smith, of Thos. Walker. July 14-
of Thos. Walker. Nov. 8- Chas. Mason & D. Balck note.   1814-
Received: of Elijah Hunters note, of Houston, rent of land, of
Trotter, of Jas. Sims, of Sales on plantation in Rutherford Co.

P. 121.   Received of Thos. Cotton for his bond for land; of
           Abner Pillow account; balance due on W. Houstons ac-
count; Dan'l. Cartess note; Malachi Nicholson note; Jas. Sims
account. 1814, July 28-James Twinners account assumed by Jas.
Sims. Received: Orsborne Nicholson's note; Geo. Nichols; W.
Neelly; Jas. Pugh; D. Dickinson; John Willey; Abram Walker note;
W. Simpson; John Griffith; E. Alexander note; Thos. Dollerson;
P. Cheatham; Jas. Cowen; R. Page; W. Sparkman; W. Holts account;
M. Mallory account; N. Shaw account; Thos. Old account; Green
Williamson account.

P. 122.   Received: Howell Tatum, John Sample. Aug. 22-Received:
           H. Cook, rent plantation; Jas. Sims, settlement with
him; Joel Dyers note; Nugent, Bulks, & Garner for corn; Thos.
Durham, rent land Smith Co.; J. Toon, rent land; Wall & Echols,
rent land; J. Trotter, rent land; Francis Carter & Jas. Hicks,
note; W. Lytte; John Carter, note; Hall & Washington Thompson;
T.R. Butters; Moulton Carter; Samuel Barton. Paid: Caleb
Mandley account; Sheff. Jackson, Robertson; D. Dickinson expenses to Smith & Wilson; Turner Sanders.

P. 123.   Paid: John Burgess; Luke Dean, bad notes & Inventory-

58

John Carters, Martin Hall & Co., T.R. Butters, Moulton
Carters, Samuel Barlons, Edw. Gwinn, now in suit in Sumner Co.;
M.B. Murfree's expense to Nashville; balance due on 2 bonds of
D. Dunn; D. Dunn balance his account; McConnico balance due as
comm.; A. Maury, as comm.; Capt. Wilson, as comm. 16 days; T.
Old, as comm. 8 days; Col. Weatherspoon; Sheff. of Rutherford
Co.; R. Searcy; J. Coleman; W. Welch; J.B. Cheatham; D. Moore;
Thos. Stewart; G.W. Mederin in land warrants. 1814: Credits:
Thos. Smith note; rent plantation in Wilson Co.; Aug. 24-Paid:
Martha Ann C. Murfree her proportion in M.B. Murfree's account
current as her guardian; T.N. Burtons proportion; D. Dickinson
as one of legatees; Jas. Maney in bonds his proportion; Isaac
Hilliard his proportion.

P. 124.   HARDY MURFREE, dec'd. Account of the hire of slaves.
           8th Jany. 1813. Negro men: Daniel to John K. Campbell;
Timothy to John Porter; Bristow & Philes his wife to Rich.
Hughes; Peter, his wife & 3 children to David Dunn; Bob to David
Dunn; George Porter to Joel Ferguson; Will to James Pugh; Frank,
his wife & 4 children to Abram Walker; David to Wm. M. Houston;
Ned (blacksmith) to James Ferrel; girl Hannah to Robt. P. Currin;
negro woman Abby & 4 children to Garner McConnico; negro boys to
David Puckett.

P. 125.   HARDY MURFREE, dec'd. Account of Sales. 8 Jany 1813
           Returned Oct. session 1814. Those buying: James
Thurman, David Dunn, Joseph Pollard, Joel Hobbs, John Johnson,
David Black, Fielding Helms, Edw. Tignor, Matt B. Murfree, Rich-
ard Graham, Edw. Russell, James Pugh, David Dickinson, Barnaba
Donelson, Thomas Terry, John Cox, Eli Hope, Robt. Finney, Alex-
ander Shaw; hire of slaves: James Johnston hired Charles; James
Roane hired Old Jack & Truce; M.B. Murfree hired Frank, Jesse,
Jack. Molly & 2 children; David Abet hired Harry & Dred; M.B.
Murfree hired Cloey & Frank; deduct for keeping Cherry & her 4
children hired to the lowest bidder; David Dickson hired George;
James Pugh hired Will; Sally & 3 children to lowest bidder; John
Atkinson hired Bristo & Fillis; Wesley Weatherspoon hired Old
Peter, Janey & 3 children; Zachariah Drake hired Daniel; Joseph
Wright hired Bob; Joseph Cowen hired Tim; Isaac Tignor hired
Geo.; David Dunn hired Fortune & Cloey; Wm. Neelly hired David;
Caleb Henly hired Abby & 3 children; Garner McConnico hired
Moses boy; Balaam Hay hired Isam; Wm. Terrell hired Ned; deduct
for Sally & 5 children hired to lowest bidder. D. Dickinson.

           HARDY MURFREE, dec'd. Account of Sales. 3rd Jan.
1814. Returned to Oct. 1814. Those buying: M.B. Murfree, Alborn
Lowry, James Crithers, Daniel Malory, John Wade, Wm. Wadey,
James Waddel, Adkins Massey, Samuel Waller, Burwell Gunnaway,
John M. Tilford, Robt. Overhall, David Dickinson, Alexander Car-
micale, James Dickson, Bryan (Hare)?, Isaac Johnson, Benjamin
Gilbert, John Fleming, Ezell Gable, James Roane, Henry Trott,
James Sims.

P. 127.   MATTHIAS B. MURFREE, Guardian. Jan. session 1815.
           Expenses for Martha Ann C. Murfree; taxes in Robinson
Co.; expenses to Clarksville; taxes in Rutherford Co., Wmson.
Co., Overton Co., Stewart Co., & Montgomery Co.; due Martha Ann
C. Murfree; account against Wm. H. Murfree & John Berkeley for
hire of negro girl Hana.

P. 128.   GEORGE H. JAMES, dec'd. Will. Jan. session 1815.
           Of Town of Franklin to affectionate wife, all of my
worldly goods. Nicholas Perkins & Turner Saunders, Exr.

59

2nd Dec. 1814. Test: Wesley Malani, Robert Bradley & Robt.
Davis.

SHAROD MILLS, dec'd. Will. Probated Jan. session
1815. Bro. James Mills' daughter Patsy Mills $100; Samuel
Benton, bay colt & the money due me from Kempt Holland & if he
isn't able to obtain that, the money due me from Joseph Crenshaw;
Thomas Smith's son John Crensahw Smith, my watch; to his daughter Elizabeth Burk Smith my trunk; Thomas Smith, my mare, bridle
& saddle, bed & furniture & rifle gun, some cattle, debt that
John P. Elliot owes me, also the things I have at this house &
the balance of my property. I appoint Samuel Benton & Thomas
Smith, exr. 16th May 1814. Test: Andrew Hunter & Nathaniel
Benton.

P. 129. SHAROD MILLS, dec'd. Inventory. Jan. session 1815.
1 bay mare, saddle, rifle, carpenters tools, silver
watch, personal items, pocketbook containing notes on the following: Samuel Benton, John K. Campbell, Joseph Crenshaw, James
Crenshaw, John Kryster, Crenshaw Futwell, Wm. Russel, Nashville
Bank note of $5.00. Thomas Smith, Exr.

P. 130. GEORGE H. JAMES, dec'd. Inventory. Jan. session 1815.
1 negro woman & child, Agnes & Jim; 1 negro boy Hirum;
2 negro girls Ivice & Seally; 1 mare & colt, furniture, silver
watch, etc., notes to amount of $3000. Thos. Bradley, Admr.
Probated Jan. session 1815.

WM. C. DEVORIX, dec'd. Account of Sale. Jan. session
1815. Sold 19th Nov. 1814. Those buying: William Wilson (the
clothing), William Hodge, Frank McLaran. Wm. Wilson, Admr.

JOHN BENSON, dec'd. Account of Sales. Jan. session
1815. Sold Oct. 25, 1814. Those buying: Samuel Williams,
William Williams, Wm. House, John Massey, John Bridges, Catharine Boyet. Samuel Williams, Admr.

P. 131. Rebecca Berry, widdow of JAMES BERRY, dec'd. Allotment. Jan. session 1815. 22nd Oct. 1814. Wm. Wilson,
Nicholas Scales & Watson Gentry, Commissioners.

Nancy Smithson, widdow of CLEMENT SMITHSON, dec'd.
Allotment Jan. session 1815. 20th Oct. 1814. Thos. B. Walthall,
James Williams, & Geo. Kinnard, comms.

Garner McConnico, admr. Recpt. Jan. session 1815.
21 day Nov. 1814. Garner McConnico, Admr. of RICHARD PUCKETT,
dec'd. $413.75 in full of my part of the estate of Benj. Cod-
dington, dec'd. principal & interest in land & rent.

P. 132. JAMES BERRY, dec'd. Account of Sales sold on 19 of
Nov. 1814. Jan. session 1815. Those buying: Rebecca
Berry, Admr. (most of the household furniture & items, livestock,
& etc. Hired the 2 negro women & negro man), John McClaron bought
a coat of JAMES BERRY, dec'd. from Rebecca Berry, Basil Berry,
Jesse Bugg, Reuben Hamilton, Spencer Reynolds, Francis Hodge,
Samuel McKnight, John Robinson, Nathan Adams, John P. Shelburn,
Milton Gambill, Wm. Wilson, Thomas Berry (gun), Moses Worley,
Sarah Porter, David Edmonson, John Fielder, Wm. Stevens, Sr.,
Nicholas Scales, Wm. Stevens, Jr., James Craig, Benjamin Russell,
Isreal McCarrel, Mordecai Pillow, Wm. Burrass, John B. Crafton,
Wm. Wall, Thos. B. Lock, David Shannon, Matthias Rosenbum.
Rebecca Berry, Bassil Berry & Alex. Johnson, Admr.

P. 134. CLEMENT SMITHSON, dec'd. Account of Sale. Jan.
session 1815. Those buying: Nancy Smithson (furniture,
etc.), James Willams, Jacob Garrett, James Shelbourn, John
Roberts, Wm. Harder, Shemey Merrit, Samuel Parks, Susanna Smith-
son, Presley Harden, Edmond Withers, Thos. Sappington, Johathan
West, Willie G. Davis, Henry Walker, Isaac West, Richard Hay,
Wm. Williams, Phenis Thomas, Drucilla Smithson, Horatio Pettice,
Jonathan Welch, John P. Shelbourn, Adam Laground, Wm. Walker.
Nancy Smithson & Horatio Pettice, Admr.

P. 135. LUCY DAVIS KEARNEY, dec'd. Will. Jan. session 1815.
All my property to my six children when they reach the
age of 21 years. (no names given). Sister, Sally Gray's estate
due me; trusty friend Peter B. Booker of Maury Co., Exr. 9th
May 1814. Probated Jan. session 1815. Wit: J. Hicks, Lucy
Gray, James M. Gray.

P. 136. JORDAN REESE, dec'd. Division of lands. 1/5 of land
is specially willed to Patrick Reese. Making a total
to him of 1212 acres & 36 poles. June 6, 1814. James Giddens,
A. Clark & Edw. Swanson.

LUCY D. KEARNEY, dec'd. Inventory. April session
1815. 1st March 1815. Negro named Joe about 50 yrs. old; negro
girl Jinny about 20 yrs. old; negro man Billy about 50 yrs. old.
R. P. Booker, Exr.

KITCHEN DOIL, dec'd. Inventory. April session 1815.
3 head cattle, gun, (very few items). Joshua Doil, Admr.

HENRY WHITE, dec'd. Inventory. April session 1815.
Few household items. Wm. Neelly, Admr.

P. 137. JAMES MOORE, JR., dec'd. Inventory. April session
1815. $720, 3 head horses, other livestock. John
Moore.

DAVID TERRY, dec'd. Inventory. April session 1815.
DAVID TERRY who died in Orleans in Jan. last while in the service of the United States; horse, saddle, bridle, saddle bags
& gun. Thos. Terry, Admr.

JAMES NORRIS, dec'd. Inventory. April 1815. Livestock and household items; by Daniel White & Elizabeth Norris
on 3rd April 1814. Elizabeth Norris, Admr.

DAVID LEWIS, dec'd. Account of Sales. April session
1815. Those buying: Wm. Holbert, Lemuel B. Hall, Wm. Rutledge,
Martin Benson, David Lamb, Jr., Thos. Boatright, Thos. Cole,
Oswald Potts, Wm. S. Webb, Levi Meazeles, Obediah Wade, James
Rey (Key?), Francis Gillespie, Stephen Johnson, Larkin Crutcher,
Wm. Browder, John Johnson, Mary Landrum, Gideon Hensley, John
West, John Webb, Asa West, Wm. Philips, David Lamb, Saunders
Freeman, Jonathan Heslin, Richard Jackson, Thomas Carlton, Wm.
Hogans, Aquilla Lamb, Moses T. Spann, John Hill; to rent of land
until 24th Dec. 1815. Frances Jackson, Exr.

P. 138. GEO. H. JAMES, dec'd. Account of Sales. Those
buying: Andrew Herrin, Terry Bradley, Wm. Sample, Wm.
Banks, Hugh F. Bell, Stephen Barfield, Archibald Potter, Peter
Pinkston, Amsey Jones, Mrs. Lyan, Zachariah Drake, David Squire,
Ephraim Beasley, Thos. Bradley, Thos. Wm. Smith, Robt. P. Currin,
Thos. Haines, Thos. Bradley, Robt. McCrackin, Moses Wooten, John

61

White, John P. Brodenax, Frederick Brodenax, Stephen Childress,
Andrew Campbell, Jason Hopkins, Edw. Ragsdale, Benj. Gholdson.
Thos. Bradley, Admr.

P. 140.   Henry Cook, guardian for Searcy D. Sharp, minor.
          April 1815.   1813: Jan. 19th: Paid to W.P. Harrison;
May 19th Paid to: Jn. Andrews, W. Hulme, Geo. Hulmes; Feb. 24
paid to John Carson.   1814: March 12 paid to Geo. Hilme; Oct.
31 paid to Jas. Hicks; also for schooling & clothing.   Income:
1814: Aug. 10: 2 bonds on A. McPhail; 1 bond on Jno. P. Brodenax,
1 bond on Jas. G. Jones, bond on Jno. J. Henry; by John Swinney
for Rock; by hire of negro girl China for 1813 & 1814; by bond
on Geo. Hulme for hire of China & child due 25th.   Dec. 1815:
by bond on Geo. Hulme for hire of Cherry due 1st Jan. 1816; by
Zachariah Drake for wood.

          Henry Cook, guardian of Sumner M. Sharp, minor.
April session 1815.   1813 Expenses: Jan. 19 paid to W.P. Harrison; May 19 paid to Jno. Andrews, W. Hulme & Geo. Hulme; Dec.
24 paid to Jno. Carson.   1814: March 12 paid to Geo. Hulme; paid
for schooling & clothing; paid to John T. Henry.   Income: for
wood from B. Gholson; bonds on B. Gholson; for wood from T.
Saunders; bond on A. McPhail; balance received from John T.
Henry; hire of Rachel & child for 1813 & 1814; hire of Zacheal
& child due Jan. 1, 1815.

P. 141.   Henry Cook, guardian of Sala N. Sharp.   April session
          1815.   1813: Jan. 19th, W.P. Harrison; May 19th, John
Andrews, W. Hulme; June 11, James Depree, Geo. Hulme; Decr. 16
paid to James Hicks; Decr. 24 paid to John Carson.   1814: April
5, slate & pencil; Mar. 12 paid to Geo. Hulme; Aug. 25 paid to
Chas. McCollister; Oct. 31 paid to Jas. Hicks; Nov. 15 paid to
Benj. White; expenses also for schooling & clothing.   Income:
A. Johnson for use of land; A. Johnson by bonds; A. Lester by
bonds & for use of land; A. Johnson hire of Peter in 1813; A.
Sharp for a bond; John J. Henry balance in settlement; John
Swiney for a tree; John J. Henry for hire Peter due Jan. 1, 1815.

P. 142.   Henry Cook, guardian of Peggy N. Sharp, minor.   April
          1815.   1813: Jan. 19 paid to W.P. Harrison, W. Hulme,
John Berkley.   1814: Geo. Hulme; decr. paid to Chas. McAlister;
also expenses for clothing.   Income: 1814, bond on James G.
Jones for rent of land in 1813; for wood from T. Saunders; rent
1813 Ben White; hire of Jose in 1813; bond on Jno. P. Brodenax;
balance due from A. Sharp; received from Jno. J. Henry; by rent
of Ben White Jan. 1, 1815; by a bond on John J. Henry for hire
of Rose in 1814 & 1815; by a bond on Ben White for rent of land
in 1815; by James G. Jones for rent of land near town; by bond
on John P. Broadnax for rent of land Jan. 1st 1816.

P. 143.   Hendley Stone, guardian of Peter & Green Pryor, minors.
          April 1815.   Expenses: tax on land in Wilson Co.; paid
to Majr. Maury, Harpool, McAlister; for expenses to Virginia &
back; for half the expenses Green going with Agnes to a ball in
Franklin; cash to go to Brother Bartons; cash to Mrs. Ham for
Suckeys expenses; to Thos. Reynolds for gun for Green; to Mr.
Blackburn for tuition for Green's schooling; Peter Pryor to hire
of Sam (to D. Dunn); cash paid to Richard Orton; paid for Alsey's
hire (who dec'd. to Hobbs); to Cloes' expense & lost time at
Hobbs; to physick got for Sam to Dr. Reynolds; cash paid for
doctoring Joe; cash paid for doctoring Sam to Dr. Crockett; also
expenses for clothing, etc.   Income: By hire of Jude & 2 children
to Hendly Stone, Cloe to Joel Hobbs, Ailsey to Joel Hobbs,

Hanner & 3 children to Wm. Bond; Geo. to Wm. Guthrey; Suckey & 3 children to Green Pryor; John to John Porter; Frank & Sam to Peter Pryor; Joe to James Hughes; Jesse to Wm. Bond.

P. 145. LITTLETON BROWN, dec'd. Will. July session 1815.
Having enlisted into the service of the United States of America during the present war & not knowing if it may be my happy lot to survive------. Brother James Brown all my possessions either in land or what pay may be coming to me for my military services. Bro. James Brown, Exr. 7th June 1814. Wit: Wm. Bond Sr. & M.L. Bond. Probated July session 1815.

ABSOLEN TAYLOR, dec'd. Will. July session 1815. To Lewis Heath, 1 feather bed, furniture & horse; wife Lany Taylor the rest of my property. If Lewis Heath should die with out any heir, property to go to my sister Dorcas Arnold's two youngest sons, Jeremiah Arnold & Asa Arnold. Wife Lany Taylor & Meriman Landrum my exr. 3rd Nov. 1814. Test: Needham Bryan & G. West. Probated July session 1815.

P. 146. JAMES MOORE, JR., dec'd. Account of Sales. Sold on
27 April 1815. July session 1815. Those buying: Radford Butts, James Alexander, Samuel Akin, Alexander Moore, Richard Cragg, John Moore, Benj. Troter, Joseph McCollister. John Moore, Admr.

RICHARD CARTER, dec'd. Account of Sales. July session 1815. Sold on April 22, 1815. Those buying: Sally Carter, Admr. most of the items & hire of negro girl; Benjamin Roberts, John Johnson, William Wilson, Matthias Rozenbum, Alexander Johnson (hired old negro man), John W. Crunk (lease of land), Jacob Garrett, Joseph Fitts, John Brim. Sally Carter, Admr.

P. 147. ROBERTS MURRY, dec'd. Inventory. July session 1815.
Clothing & $5 note. Gen. L. Nolen, Admr.

SAMUEL MAIRS, dec'd. Inventory. July session 1815.
Court order dated April 1815. Inventory made: livestock, household furniture, shoemakers tools, rent of the crop now growing on 12 acres land. He is entitled to the pay as a private for 6 mos. tour of duty. Mary Mairs & Jas. McEwen, Admrs.

PETER POTTS, dec'd. Inventory. July session 1815.
July 8, 1815. 1 negro man, 1 negro woman, 3 children, livestock, farm tools, household items, & notes on Stephen Tomasan & Adam Meek. James McEwen, Admr.

P. 148. JOHN RADFORD, dec'd. Inventory. July session 1815.
Household items, furniture, livestock, note on Haroatio Pettice for 30 bbl. corn. Samuel Shelburn, Admr.

THOMAS MORTON, dec'd. Inventory. July session 1815.
Livestock, discharge for serving tour of 4 mo. & 7 days. July 3, 1815. Elizabeth Morton & Barnet, Admr.

P. 149. WILLIAM WITHERINTON, dec'd. Inventory. July session 1815. Livestock, household items. William Sparkman, Admr.

WILLIAM OWENS, dec'd. Inventory. July session 1815.
Mare, discharge for services on campaign for 5 mo. & 16 days; account on Wm. Goodrick, Elijah Owens; notes in Capt. Keneades

hands for the price of his clothes sold on campaign at his death. July 4, 1815. Mordica Skelley, Admr.

RICHARD CARTER, dec'd. Inventory. July session 1815. Livestock, household items, books. April 1. 1815. Sally Carter.

JAMES ROGERS, dec'd. Inventory. July session 1815. June 29, 1815, livestock, farm tools, household items, cotton, wheat & corn, flax, box of shoe tools. Robert Rogers, Admr.

P. 150. JOHN McSWINE, dec'd. Inventory. July session 1815. Furniture, household items, livestock. 3 pecks of blew grass seed, 400 lbs. tobaco, & $5 note on Alexander & Whitehead Lester. John & Samuel Andrews, Admrs.

JAMES E. EDMISTON, dec'd. Inventory. July session 1815. Clothing, note of $50, cash & morocco pocket book. D. Edmiston, Admr.

HANCH WALKER, dec'd. Inventory. July session 1815. Clothing, cash in hand $5.00 & marocco pocket book. John Walker, Admr.

PHILIP JACOB IRON, dec'd. Inventory. July session 1815. 10 negroes, furniture, few items. Thos. P. Iron, Admr.

SARAH IRON, dec'd. Inventory. July session 1815. 90 acres land, & household items. N.P. Hardeman, clerk.

P. 151. JOHN SHORES, dec'd. Inventory. July session 1815. Livestock, farm tools, breast pin, cert. of property lost in a battle at Orleans; note on: Wm. Floyd, Edw. Warren, Frederick Dill, John Gracy, Mason Richardson, Benijah Bateman, Simeon Motherhead, Thos. McCutchan, John Jones, James Vaughts, Newel Gracy, Isaac Jones. July 4, 1815. Samuel Mays, Admr.

ARMSTEAD BOYD, dec'd. Inventory. July session 1815. Tom age 40 yrs., Daniel 30 yrs., Charles 28 yrs., Barney 28 yrs., Dick 24 yrs., Seller 50 yrs., Suckey 30 yrs., Aggy 9 yrs., Winney 8 yrs., Daniel 7 yrs., Jefferson 1 yr. 6 mo.; several head of horses, livestock, furniture & household items. July 15, 1815. Wm. J. Boyd & Paul Dismuke, Admr.

P. 152. ISAAC CROW, dec'd. Account of hire of slaves. Decr. 12, 1814. July session 1815. Abram B. Morton hire of negro boy, Jas. (Herren)? hire of negro boy, John Herren, Abram B. Morton, Andrew Herren & Joanna Crow all hire of negro woman; Samuel Bird, Jeremiah Deen & Mary Green, corn. John Atkinson & Andrew Herren, Admr.

GEORGE REYNOLDS, dec'd. Inventory. July session 1815. July 4, 1815. Livestock; account on: Green Pryor, John Warren, Glen Owen, Thos. Reynolds, John Oliver, John McCarlin, Edw. Swanson, Micheal Hail, Zebulan Edmiston. Pryor Reynolds, Admr.

WILLIAM PARKS, dec'd. Inventory. July session 1815. 4 July 1815. Mare, livestock, furniture, & farm tools. Malinda Parks, Admrx. & J.B. Thompson, Admr.

P. 153. JAMES MCFADDEN, dec'd. Inventory. July session 1815. July 4, 1815. Mare & colt, notes on Willie McCall, Samuel N. Martin & Robert McCutchun. Robt. McFadden, Admr.

ROBT. NEELLY, dec'd. Inventory. July session 1815. Wages due him for about 1 month services. July 7, 1815. Wm. Neelly, Admr.

JOSEPH HALL, dec'd. Inventory. July session 1815. 8th April 1815. Livestock, furniture, household items, set shoemakers tools, one discharge for 3 months & 6 days services in General Caroll's Division of Tenn. Militia. $25 in cash. Robt. McLemore, Admr.

P. 154. STEPHEN ELAM, dec'd. Settlement. July session 1815. Wm. Logan, Thos. Wilson, & Wm. B. Nunn, Just. of the Peace. Heirs: Dianna Elam, Robt. Elam, Mathew Elam, Polly Elam, Nancy Elam, Elizabeth Elam, Joel Elam. Moses Ridley & Dianna Elam, Admrs.

LITTLEBERRY EPERSON, dec'd. Settlement. July session 1815. Divided into 8 shares viz: Nancy Eperson, James Joice, John Eperson, Levi Underwood, Creasy Armstron, Anderson Eperson, Littleberry Epperson & Nancy Eperson, guardian for Elizabeth Eperson. James Joice, Admr.

P. 155. JANE WHEATON, dec'd. Settlement. July session 1815. Thos. T. Maury Dr. in account with the estate; J. Bruff a note amount of Kemps note for rent of Lot #15; T.J. Reams note in Nashville, 1813; E. Marshall note collected from Naddox for rent N 175 in Nashville 1813; T. Saunders rent of Lots 22, 36, & 8 ft. front of no. 12 in Franklin 1813 & 1814; Clarissa Bethshears rent of above lot in 1815; T. Talbots note for hire of Harriett, Lucy & Ouid 1814; Garner for hire of Polly 1813; paid taxes in Davidson Co. 1810, 1811, 1812, 1813, 1814, 1815; paid T. Saunders for repairing building on Lot #11 in Franklin; paid taxes in Wmson. Co. 1814. Thos. T. Maury, Admr.

P. 156. RICHARD PUCKETT, dec'd. Settlement. July session 1815. 1813: paid to Jacob Coddington, N. Hardeman, William Faughn, James Short, Peter R. Booker, atty., Jarrot C. Puckett, Jason Hopkins, Ruffin Brown, Chiles McGabe, Jacob Halfire, Estate of Benj. Coddington; note on: Samuel Curry & Eli Stacey, John Norton living in Chocktaw Nation & John McNeal. Garner McConnico, Admr.

P. 158. FREDERICK BROWDER, dec'd. Will. Oct. session 1815. Four beloved children: Jane M. Combs, Wm. H. Browder, Nancy C. Browder, & Lucindey N. Browder. The houses on land I now live on & four slaves by the name of Henry, Silvey, Jack & Peggy; slaves Soloman & Joe be sold with certain livestock. To each of my daughters a black silk dress to be bought. Grand-dau. Ann P. Shelburn share equally with my children & the children of my dau. Patsy W. Gentry. Exr. to sell my land. Friends Samuel Perkins & Archer Jordan, Exrs. Aug. 14, 1815. Wit: Alexander Rolston & W. H. Downing. Probated Oct. 1815.

P. 159. EPHRAIM STANFIELD, dec'd. Will. Oct. session 1815. Wife, Heah Stanfield all my estate; son Durrett Stanfield, negro man Steph, with other property I have heretofore given him; son Shakespear Stanfield; son Geo. W. Stanfield; son Marmaduke Stanfield; son Goodloe Stanfield; 2 married dau. Elizabeth Butler & Philisha Stanfield; 2 daughters Polly Stanfield & Drucilla Stanfield; my negroe man Nelson has a wife belonging to Jas. Davis Esq. & Davis can purchase Nelson; if my son George should not return from the expedition, or tour of duty, he has now gone on, that his wife nor any of his children shall not be

entittled to any of my estate. Wife Leah Stanfield & sons Marmaduke & Goodloe, Exrs. March 30, 1815. Wit: Henry Talley,
Joseph Crockett, James Brooks, Jr. Probated Oct. session 1815.

P. 161. BENJAMIN HUMPHREYS, dec'd. Will. Oct. 1815. All my
family live on my land and keep all my livestock &
possession until 1822 & then divided between my heirs: Jincy
Orton, Daniel Jones Humphreys, Polly Humphreys, Willie Jones
Humphreys, Elijah Humphreys, Sally Humphreys, Anna Humphreys,
Hariet Humphreys, Hester Humphreys. My son Daniel Jones, Wily
Jones or Elijah to all have a part of my tract of land. Friend
Robt. Hudspeth & son Daniel Jones, Exrs. 10 Sept. 1809. Wit:
Henry Laurence & John P. Iron. Probated Oct. session 1815.

CHARLES JOHNSON, dec'd. Will. Oct. session 1815.
Loving wife, Patsey Johnson the tract of land I now live on.
Son, Andrew M. Johnson, the west end of my tract of land. Son,
Wm. Johnson east end of tract of land including the house I now
live in, reserving the house & etc. for my wife during her
lifetime. Children: Polly C. Williams, & Nancy Tuller. 21 April
1815. Wit: Wm. Anthony, Samuel Morton Jr. & Barth Stovall.
Prob. Oct. 1815.

P. 163. CHARLES JOHNSON. dec'd. Inventory. Oct. session
1815. Tract of land 162½ acres, claim against the
United States for service 3 mo. as private in a Vol. company of
mounted gun men 3 months & 13 days as Capt. Drafted Militia;
furniture, farm tools, livestock. surveying chain & 1 power of
atty. for a privates services 1 mo. & 22 days. Andrew M. Johnson, Exr.

P. 164. LOAMI STEPHENS, dec'd. Will. Oct. session 1815.
27th Sept. 1814. Children: Catharine, Feriby, Elizabeth, Loami, Hareitt, Polly, Rhody, Willie, Latty, Franny
Stephens all my estate. I being about to go into the Army & not
knowing whiter I shall ever return---Dau. Belinda & son Wm.
Stephens have had their share. Wife Polly Stephens, my land
during her lifetime. Exr. Joel Stephens, Geo. Kennard & wife
Polly Stephens. Wit: Charles Stephens & Richard Tanner. Probated Oct. session 1815.

THOS. COLE, dec'd. Will. Oct. session 1815. All
property be kept together until youngest child come of age.
Wife & children (no names given). Exr: Friends, Wm. Phillips
Sr. & Archer Jordan, Esqr. 9 May 1815. Wit: James Burns Sr.,
Wm. Phillips, Jr. & James Burnes, Jr. Prob. Oct. 1815.

P. 165. WM. SMITH, dec'd. Inventory. Oct. session 1815.
Sept. 28, 1815. Money, 3 months tour of duty under
Gen'l John Coffee, a certificate in amount of $12.00. James
Smith, Admr.

JAMES E. EDMISTON, dec'd. Supplentment Inventory.
Oct. session 1815. 1 discharge for 7 mo. tour as mounted gun
men & personal items. D. Edmiston.

JAMES RADFORD, dec'd. Supplement Inventory. Oct.
session 1815. Note on: Joseph Cole & S. Martin dated 27 Feb.
1815, James Shelburne & James P. Barret, David Lankaster &
James Patterson, Mesback Hail & S. Martin. Samuel Shelburn,
Admr.

P. 166. WM. WEATHERINTON, dec'd. Inventory. Oct. session

1815. Livestock, farm tools, furniture & etc., discharge for
4 mo. & 28 days. Wm. Sparkman, Admr.

CHRISTOPHER VANNATTA, dec'd. Inventory. Oct. session
1815. Livestock, furniture, farm tools, & etc; note on Baker,
Smith, N. Adams, John D. Hill & discharge for 3 mo. & 27 days.
Nancy Vanatta & Allen Bolston, Admr.

JOHN TARPLEY, dec'd. Inventory. Oct. session 1815.
Livestock, furniture, farm tools, note on Wm. Gilliam; Wm. Le-
gate Dr. by book account; discharge for 6 mo. in the Militia of
W. Tenn. Mary Tarpley.

P. 167.   CLEMENT SMITHSON, dec'd. Supplementary Inventory.
          Oct. session 1815. Received from the state of
Virginia money from his agent, Wm. Pettice. Nancy Smithson &
Horatio Pettice, Admr.

ROBERT MURRY, dec'd. Additional Inventory. Oct.
session 1815. Gun & silver watch. G.L. Nolen, Admr.

ANTHONY H. THOMAS, dec'd. Inventory. Oct. session
1815. 3 slaves, notes on Robert Sayers, Aran Askew & John H.
Crockett. Job H. Thomas, Admr.

PARKER BATEMAN, dec'd. Inventory. Oct. session 1815.
2 Oct. 1815. 2 horses, saddle & bridle, discharge of the United
States Mounted Rangers for term of 12 months. Enoch Bateman,
Admr.

P. 168.   JAMES ROGERS, dec'd. Supplementary Inventory. Oct.
          session 1815. Notes, money, gun, clothing & etc.;
service right for 2 mo. & 24 days. Robert Rogers, Admr.

ABSOLAM TAYLOR, dec'd. Inventory. Oct. session 1815.
Sept. 15, 1815. Livestock, furniture & etc. Laney Taylor,
Extrix.

JONATHAN MCPHERSON, dec'd. Inventory. Oct. session
1815. Was in the army under Gen'l Carroll at New Orleans; very
few possession. Hannah McPherson, Admrx.

P. 169.   JOHN RADFORD, dec'd. Account of Sales. Oct. session
          1815. Those buying: Sally Radford (most of the furni-
ture), Henry Walker, Richard Hay (shoemaker tools), John Roberts,
James Radford, James Shelburn, David Lankaster, John P. Shelburn.
Samuel Shelburn, Admr.

JAMES ROGERS, dec'd. Account of Sales. Oct. session
1815. Those buying: Benjamin Russell, John Tilman, John West,
Wm. Wilson, Martha Rogers, Richard Ogilvie, Philip Manier, Ro-
bert Biggers, John Boyd, Robert Cannon, Daniel Wall, Maths
Rosenbum, Wm. Edmiston, Jas. B. Parsley, Wm. King, Wm. Hill,
Jonathan Mobley, John Brim, Zachr. Smith, Archilus Hughes, A.
Arnold, Wm. Hooker, Robt. Rogers, Spencer Reynolds, Harder Til-
man, Isaac Ledbetter, John Dalton, Drury Floyd, Wm. Wall, Nath'l
Warmoth, Zadock Riggs, Thomas Mayfield, James Gambrill, Frances
Tilman, Jas. Marchant, Baly Pratt, Samuel N. Martin. Robert
Rogers, Admr.

P. 170.   THOS. SIMMONS, dec'd. Sale. Oct. 1815 session. 27
          April 1811. 6 negroes: Aaran, Phillis, Charles, Ruben,
Lee & Stephen Scott, 1 tin trumpet, Daniel Adams bought furniture

& Jonathan Soloman, 1 ax. Thomas Simmons, Admr.

P. 171.   PETER POTTS, dec'd. Account of Sales. Oct. session
          1815. Those buying: David McEwen, Price W. Brooks,
James McEwen, John Reese, Martin Stanley, Charles Hood, Thos.
Walker, John Mairs, Isham Cole, Abram Secrest, Edmond Sayers,
Stephen Thomason, Mary Potts (most of furniture), Christopher E.
McEwen, Terry Bradley, Wm. Evans, John Carothers, Thos. Haines,
Jas. B. Thompson, Arthur Fulgham, Benj. Williamson, James Hughes,
Benj. Evans. James McEwen, Admr.

P. 172.   GEO. REYNOLDS, JR., dec'd. Sales. Oct. session 1815.
          Aug. 5, 1815. Those buying: Pryor Reynolds, Thos.
Reynolds, Henry Cook, Samuel Cox, Joel Hobbs, James Tomblin,
Joseph Waddle, James Hughes, Peter Pryor, John Witherspoon.
Pryor Reynolds, Admr.

          SAMUEL CARSON, dec'd. Account of Sales. Oct. session
1815. Those buying: Terry Bradley, David Johnston, Joshua Butler, Sally Carson (most of furniture), Isham Cole. Terry Bradley, Admr.

P. 173.   SAMUEL MAIRS, dec'd. Account of Sales. Oct. session
          1815. Those buying: Mary Maires (most of furniture &
household goods), Martin Stanley, John Douglas, James Hughes,
Michael Long, John Haines, Aaron Houston, John Maires, John
Buchannon, Benj. Williamson, Isaac Maire, Amos Bullock, James B.
Thompson, Geo. Davidson, Christopher McEwen, Lucy Harris, Julis
Burton. James McEwen & Mary Mairs, Admr.

P. 174.   SARAH IRON, dec'd. Account of Sales. Oct. session
          1815. Those buying: Daniel Ireland, Henry Mullins,
Geo. A. Iron, Ann Chawning, Stephen Morton, Malichi Watts, John
McLain, Thos. White, Geo. Buchannon. John P. Iron, Admr.

          JAMES NORRIS, dec'd. Account of Sales. Oct. session
1815. Those buying: Elizabeth Norris (most of furniture & etc.),
John Peak, Ebenezar Perkins, Meady White, Stephen White, Geo.
Sulivan, Hugh Cooper, Henry Worldley, Samuel Baker, Jeremiah
Sulivan. Elizabeth Norris, Admrx.

P. 175.   SUSANNA BARNES, dec'd. Account of Sales. Sold 23rd
          Sept. 1815. Oct. session 1815. Those buying: Jacob
Adams, Wm. S. Webb, Watson Gentry, Joseph H. Scales (wearing
apparrel). Joseph H. Scales, Admr.

          JOHN SHORES, dec'd. Account of Sales. Oct. session
1815. Those buying: John Gracy, Charles Shores, Wm. Shores,
John H. Davis, Newel Gracy, Wm. Bond, Samuel Williams. Samuel
Mays, Admr.

P. 176.   WILLIS CARSON, dec'd. Account of Sales. Oct. session
          1815. Those buying: Peggy Carson, Jesse Bugg, Nicho-
las Lanier, James Burgess, Robt. Pateson, Wm. Wilson. James
Burgess & Peggy Carson, Admrs.

          THOMAS MORTON, dec'd. Account of Sales. Oct. session
1815. Elizabeth Morton & Barnet Donelson, Admrs.

          JAMES MCFADEN, dec'd. Account of Sales. Oct. session
1815. Those buying: Barnett McFaden, Wm. McFaden, Wm. Page.
Robt. McFaden, Admr.

WM. OWENS, dec'd. Account of Sales. Oct. session
1815. Those buying: Adam Cooper & Mordica Kelly. Mordica Kelly,
Admr.

P. 177.   HANCH WALKER, dec'd. Account of Sales. Oct. session
           1815. Sold Sept. 30, 1815. Wearing appearrel $5.00
and pocket book $1.00. John Walker, Admr.

WM. WITHERINTON. dec'd. Account of Sales. Oct.
session 1815. Wm. Sparkman, Admr.

WM. C. DEVORIX, dec'd. Account of Sales. Oct. session
1815. Wm. Wilson, Admr.

Peggy Carson, widdow of WILLIS CARSON, dec'd. Allotment for widow & orphans. Oct. 1815. Thos. Wilson, Jesse Bugg
& Ephraim M. Bugg, Commr.

P. 178.   Polly Potts, widdow of PETER POTTS, dec'd. Allotment
           for widow & orphans. Oct. 1815. Benj. Evans, Robert
Hodge & John Maires, Commr.

Mary Mairs, widdow of SAMUEL MAIRS, dec'd. Allotment
for widow & family. Oct. 1815. Years support from time of
death of SAMUEL MAIRS which was about the first of Feb. of this
year. David McEwen, Alston Edney & Martin Adams, commr.

PHILIP JACOB IRON, dec'd. Division of slaves. Oct.
session 1815. To: Fredrick Wilt Iron, Armstead, man; Geo.
Anderson Iron, Pettis, man; Ann P. Iron, Rose, woman; John P.
Iron, Ned, boy; Sarah C. Iron, Juba, boy; Frances A. White,
Lucy, girl; Robt. A. Iron, Alexander, boy.

P. 179.   GURDON SQUIER. dec'd. Settlement. Oct. session 1815.
           Paid to Amza Jones, Wm. Neelly, Joshua Farrington,
Thos. A. Martin, Young A. Gray, Daniel & Harden Perkins, James
Gordon, Daniel C. Snow, Wm. Banks, Thos. E. Sumner, Thos. G.
Bradford, Sappington & Brethitt, Sam'l. Winstead, Bradly &
Bookly, Judge Haywood, Turner Pinkston, John Mays, Benj. White,
Abram Maury, Wilkins Tanvehill, Wm. Smith. J. & L. Thompson,
Gideon Blackburn, Daniel McMahan, Dr. Nunan, James Gordon & Dr.
Sam'l. Crockett. David Squire, Admr.

P. 180.   SAMUEL CLARK. dec'd. Memorandam of negroes. Oct.
           session 1815. 1. Wall about 43 yrs.; 2. Frank about
16 yrs.; 3. Allen about 10 yrs.; 4. Jacob about 4 yrs.; 5. Jim
about 2 yrs.; 6. Jerry about 1 yr.; 7. Jude about 1 yr.; 8.
Oney about 27 yrs.; 9. Molley about 22 yrs.; 10. Marcy about 18
yrs.; 11. Caroline about 6 yrs.; 12. Ruth about 4 yrs.; 13.
Harriet about 3 yrs.; 14. Minerva about 6 mo.; 15. Lucindy 3
weeks. S. Green, Guardian.

SAMUEL CLARK, dec'd. Settlement. Oct. session 1815.
Paid expenses for Martin Clark, Samuel Clark, Salley Clark, &
Wm. Clark.

P. 181.   BENJ. BUGG, dec'd. Hire of slaves. July session
           1815. Hired by: John Carothers, Charles; David Pink-
ston, Peter; Terry Brandley, Starling; Nancy Bugg, Jacob, Allen,
Nelly, Dorcas & child; Wm. Young, Lucy & child, small girl for
his victuals & clothers; Ephraim Bugg, Rachel. Nancy Bugg &
David Pinkston, Admrs.

P. 182. FRANCIS NUNN, dec'd. Will. Jan. session 1816. Beloved wife, Marcy Nunn the land & plantation I live
on & all slaves; tract of land in Bedford Co. to my sons, Elijah
Nunn, Thos. Nunn & John Nunn; Zopheniah Nunn, all the land he
lives on in Maury Co.; Wm. R. Nunn may have the land he claims
in Maury Co.; dau. Sally Mayfield, have negro girl called Mourning; dau. Polly Nunn have negro & 1/3 of land I now live on;
son Joel. Marcy Nunn & Wm. R. Nunn, Exrs. 7 Oct. 1815. Wit:
Richard Ogilvie, Mark L. Jackson & Geo. Cohoon. Probated Jan.
session 1816.

P. 183. SAMUEL ROGERS, dec'd. Will. Jan. session 1816. Bro,
Robert Rogers; sister Martha Hughs. Robt. Hughs &
Archilus Hughs, Exrs. Wit: Watson Gentry & Jonathan Mobley.
July 13, 1815. Probated Jan. session 1816.

P. 184. WM. STEVENS, SENR., dec'd. Inventory. Jan. session
1816. Joel & Lewis Stevens, Admrs. The following
slaves: Lewis, Kaid, Rier, Peter, Cain, Ned, Taine, Sealy, Mary
Ann, Sal, Larymore, Berrell, Nelson, Caroline, Charity & Sarah.
Livestock, furniture & etc., & 1 silver watch; bonds on John
Lyon, Milton Gambill & Samuel Braden.

CHARLES JOHNSON, dec'd. Additional Inventory. Jan.
1816. Andrew M. Johnson, Admr.

P. 187. LOAMMI STEVENS, dec'd. Inventory. Jan. session 1816.
July 3, 1815. Livestock, furniture, farm tools, etc.
Mary Stevens, Admr.

BENJAMIN HUMPHREYS, dec'd. Inventory. Jan. session
1816. 5 negroes, livestock, furniture & etc.; receipt on Jo
Culberson, desperate; note on Sam'l Lawrence, desperate. Robt.
Hudspeth, Exr.

P. 188. ELISHA M. HASEL. dec'd. Inventory. Jan. session 1816.
Livestock & a few farm tools; 1 discharge for 4 mo.
& 10 days. Allen Hill, Admr.

FREDRICK W. IRON. dec'd. Inventory. Jan. session
1816. Interest in a negro fellow. Geo. A. Iron, Admr.

EPHRAIM STANFIELD, dec'd. Inventory. Jan. session
1816. Nov. 25, 1815. Livestock, furniture, farm tools & etc.;
note on James Davis. Marmaduke Stanfield & Gooler Stanfield,
Exr.

P. 189. RICHARDSON PERRY, dec'd. Inventory. Jan. session
1816. 1 discharge for 5 mo. & 3 days in the foot
service. Robt. Bates, Admr.

FREDRICK BROWDER, dec'd. Inventory & Sales. Jan.
session 1816. Those buying: Jacob Adams, Benjamin J. Bass,
Jesse Day, H. Bailey, John Dalton, Geo. Little, Nicholas Gentry,
Fredrick Browder (negro Saul), Wm. H. Downing, Jerman Winset,
John Bostic (negro boy Joe), Kinchun Pate, Edw. McNeal, Edw.
Elam, Sam'l. Hale, Geo. Taylor, Archer Jordan, James Gault, P.
Hailey, James Wilson, Wm. Edmiston, Thos. Joyce, Alex. Rolston,
Christopher Wood, Benj. Carr, John Morton, Dan'l. Potts, Hart-
well Hyde, Benj. Russell, John Johnson, John Pratt, Archilus
Winn, Elijha Downing, Sam'l. Perkins, James W. Parsons, Sam'l
D. Waddel, John Coffee, John P. Shelburn, Stephen Johnson, Ro.
F. Atkinson, Gilbert Hays, Dan'l Sumake, Elam Lewis, Geo. Gentry,

Zachs. Smith, Wm. R. Nunn, Wm. Patterson, John Tilman, Andrew
Fitzpatrick, Alex. Johnson, Wm. Johnson, D. Chadwell, Wm. Hayes,
E. Lewis, Thos. Smith, B. Yeargin, Franklin McCariam, Charles
Lock, Amos Winset, Wm. H. Browder, Wm. Webb, Wm. Ray, Wm. Jordan,
Moses Worly, David McKey; property disposed of by the will for
certain number of years & for the use of the youngest children;
negro man Hall, negro child Peggy, negro woman Silvy, negro boy
Jack; tract of land where the dec'd. lived; note due on Christo-
pher Wood, Johnson Jordan, Pugh Cannon & John Johnson. Sam'l
Perkins & Archer Jordan, Exrs.

P. 191.   EDWARD REED. dec'd. Inventory. Jan. session 1816.
          Bank notes; a discharge for services done at Orleans.
Josiah Reed, Admr.

          MARK THOMAS, dec'd. Inventory. Jan. session 1816.
Livestock, furniture & etc. Thos. Nolen, Admr.

P. 192.   WM. GOWEN, dec'd. Inventory. Jan. session 1816.
          Livestock, furniture, farm tools & etc. Jenning Gowen.

          Mary Boyd, widdow of ARMSTEAD BOYD, dec'd. Allotment.
Jan. session 1816. Dec. 1. 1815. Commrs. N. Perkins, C. White,
Wm. White, John Witherspoon & Robt. McLemore.

P. 193.   WM. STEVENS, dec'd. Widow allotment. Jan. session
          1816. Nov. 2, for widow & orphans. Shannon & Thos.
Wilson, Commr.

          DAVID CRAIG, JR., dec'd. Settlement. Jan. session
1816. One note on: Margaret Craig, John Crafton, James Craig,
John M. King, Mary Craig, Andrew Cole, Andrew Craig; Credit to:
Peter Pinkston for services as an officer, Gurdon Squires account,
James Craig account against D. Craig, Robert P. Currin account,
Robt. Edmiston account, Bradley & James. James Craig & Samuel
Buchannon, Admr.

P. 194.   JAMES KENNEY, dec'd. Account of Sales. Jan. session
          1816. Nov. 11, 1815. Those buying: Mary Kenney
bought everything. Jonathan Stepleton & Mary Kenney, Admr.

          GEO. REYNOLDS, dec'd. Division of land. Jan. session
1816. Tract of land belonging to Geo. Reynolds, Jr., dec'd.,
116½ acres; John Johnson drew lot #1; Pryor Reynolds drew lot
#2; Walter Bennett drew lot #3; Richard Reynolds drew lot #4;
James Hughes drew lot #5; Sally Reynolds drew lot #6; Samuel Cox
drew lot #7; Bethenia Reynolds drew lot #8; Thos. Reynolds drew
lot #9; Richard Hughes drew lot #10. By the following commrs:
Sam'l. Moore, Wm. Ashlin, Wm. Bond, Edw. Warren, Rich. Steele &
Joel Hobbs.

P. 197.   JAMES E. EDMISTON, dec'd. Account of Sales. Jan.
          session 1816. David Edmiston, Admr.

          PARKER BATEMAN, dec'd. Account of Sales. Jan. session
1816. Oct. 20, 1815. Those buying: Rosannah Stevens, Simeon
Bateman & Price W. Brooks. Enoch Bateman, Admr.

          WM. GOWEN, dec'd. Account of Sales. Jan. session
1816. Nov. 3, 1815. Those buying: Jamima Gowen, A. Johnston,
Caleb Mandley, Geo. Burnett, Daniel Deens, John Bridges, Wm. H.
Witts, Edw. Harris, Eph. Sampson, Bryant Gray, John Fuzzell,
Dampsey Deens, Geo. Glascock, John Wells, Elish Williams,

Jonathan Potts, Isaac Bizzell, Allse Capps, Michael Dooley, Glen Owen, Betsy Hood, John Wise, Sally Kerby, Benj. Sampson, Joseph Allen, Anderson Berryman, John Johnston, Littleton Johnston. Jemima Gowen, Admrx.

P. 199.   WM. PARKS, dec'd. Account of Sales. Jan. session
           1816. July 29, 1815. Those buying: Malinda Parks,
Cader Boleam, Arthur Stewart, Benjah Goodman, Cornelius Matthews,
Archabaid Goodman, Martin Standley, Samuel Braden. James B.
Thompson, Admr.

           ABRAHAM ANDERSON, dec'd. Account of Sales. Jan.
session 1816. Does not give the names of those buying. James
Marchant & Azariah Anderson, Admrs.

P. 200.   ROBERT MURRAY, dec'd. Account of Sales. Jan. session
           1816. G. L. Nolen sold on 28 Oct. 1815. Those buying: James
Turner, Marmaduke Stanfield, Anslum Nolen. Gen'l. L. Nolen,
Admr.

           WM. STONE, SENR., dec'd. Settlement. Jan. session
1816. Commissioners G. Hunt & G. Barnes. Wm. Stone & James
Stone, Admrs. Jane Stone has removed from this state; expenses
paid to Wm. Stone as Admr; expenses of going to S. Carolina.

P. 201.   ARMSTEAD BOYD, dec'd. Account of Sales. Jan. session
           1816. Dec. 1, 1815. Those buying: Mary Boyd (most
of the furniture), Wm. J. Boyd, Thos. Reynolds, James G. Jones,
John Witherspoon, Lazarus Dodson, Martin Standley, Hendley Stone,
Chas. McCabe, Joel Hobbs, H. Cook, John Atkinson, Jacob Critz,
John Gee, James Tune, Wiate Haley, John P. Gholston, Chas. A.
Dabney, A. Wood, Jas. Haley, Jas. Tune, Lewis Tune, Francis
Carter, John Cook, C. White, Wm. Shute.

P. 202.   Mary Kenney widow of JAMES KENNEY, dec'd. Widow
           allotment Nov. 4, 1815. Jan. session 1816. Commr.
Samuel Williams, John Edgar, Wm. McMillin.

           WILLIAM PATTERSON, dec'd. Will. Probated July ses-
sion 1816. Wife Margaret, all of my estate; children: James,
Carson, Thomas, Elizabeth & Mary; this tract of land to Thomas
& Carson; sons Wm., John & Robert have already received their
share. 6 Feb. 1812. Test: Wm. Patterson, Jr. & Elizabeth
Patterson.

P. 203.   Nancy Walton, widow of JOSAIH WALTON, dec'd. Widow
           allotment July session 1816. April 22nd, 1816. Sign-
ed: Thos. Berry, Wm. Bateman & Zacheus German.

           Ann B. Stringfellow, widow of WILLIAM STRINGFELLOW,
dec'd. Widow allotment. July session 1816. 26 April 1816.
Signed: D.D. Stone, N. Perkins, Sr., Edw. Warren & John Witherspoon.

P. 204.   BENJAMIN BUGG, dec'd. Settlement. July session 1816.
           Hire of slaves 1814 & 1815; note due from Jesse Bugg
to Jinkins Whiteside as atty; to Peter Pinkston as auctioner;
to Nancy Bugg for maintaining negro woman & 4 children. Admr.
James Allison & Thomas Wilson.

           MOSES MOORE, dec'd. Settlement. July session 1816.
Balance due Amos Moore & Ester Moore; to Joshua Cutchen, guardian.

P. 205.   THOMAS TAYLOR. dec'd. Account of Sales. Sold 7 May
          1816. Those buying: Martha Taylor, Benj. Kidd, M.
Taylor, Wm. Jemeson, Wm. Kidd (Bible), Sterling Brown, Jas. Kidd,
Silas Morton, Thos. Simmons, Wm. Anthony, Osburne Reeves. Sign-
ed Patcy K. Taylor & Wm. Kidd.

P. 206.   JOSIAH WALTON, dec'd. Account of Sales. July ses-
          sion 1816. 22 April 1816. (No names given of buyers)

          THOMAS BELOU, dec'd. Settlement. No names given of
heirs. Alexander Smith, Admr.

P. 207.   JAMES SKELLEY, dec'd. Inventory. July session 1816.
          Livestock, farm tools, gun, personal items. Stephen
Pigg, Admr.

          ALEXANDER REID, dec'd. Inventory. July session 1816.
7 negroes, livestock, furniture, silver watch, gun, tools, 46
bound books, other books & etc; note on: Peter Coffery due 1797,
on Joseph Shaw due 1809, on John Boyd due Jan. 1797, Jas. Kerr
due 1796, James Johnson, Gidem Johnson & Wm. McCastland due 1809,
Adam Hampton; notes on: D. Hays due 1789, James McAlister & John
McCasland due 1816, Thos. Watts due 1809, Isaac Mayfield due
1809, Joseph Erwin due 1816, Levina Erwin due 1813, _____? &
Cox, John Lenier & Absalum Hopper due 1817, Norfleet Perry &
Wm. Davis due 1817, Wm. Leafever & John McCasland due 1817,
Wm. Davis & John Beasley due 1817, John Beasley & Wm. Davis due
1817, Necpliel? Perry due 1817, Thos. Powell & Wm. Davis due
1817, James Frazier & Moses B. Frazier due 1816, James & Geo.
Reed due 1813; bank stock in Nashville Bank. Spencer Buford,
Admr.

P. 209.   JOHN WELLS, dec'd. Inventory. July session 1816.
          26 June 1816. 8 negroes, livestock, farm tools, furni-
ture, books, clothing & etc. Samuel Wells & James Carperten,
Admrs.

          JAOHN REID, dec'd. Will. Tract of land given me by
Major Abram Maury in this Co. on the dividing ridge between the
waters of Harpeth & Duck Rivers containing about 250 acres be
sold; any estate I am possessed of or entitled to by inheritance
from my father; wife Elizabeth; dau. Sophia; child of which my
wife is now pregnant with; my wish for my children to have a
good education. 30 Sept. 1813. Wit: Arch D. Potter & Arch d
Lytle. Probated April 1816.

P. 210.   JOHN JOHNSTON, dec'd. Will. To Henry Rutherford the
          negroes & property already received; heirs of James
Bryan, property already received by them; James Hibbitts property he has already received; Richard Orton, negroes & property
he has already received; son John Johnston, property he has
already received; son Robt. Johnston, property he has already
received & 1/3 of remaining balance of 5000 acres on the Miss.
surveyed by James M. Lewis; Benj. Jordan, property he has already
received; son Matthew Johnston, property he has already received
& tract of land I now live on & 2/3 of the 5000 acres tract on
the Miss. & negro boy Jacob; to Wm. Whiteall, the property he
has already received & balance of tract of land of 1500 acres on
Pine River which remains unsold supposed to contain about 690
acres; to James M. Lewis, 250 acres of land out of the 5000 acre
tract on the Miss.; sons Robt. & Matthew, negro boy Ben; negro
woman Charity given her freedom; I give her 1 cow and any other
property my exrs. may think proper; 5 grand dau. Elizabeth C.

Johnston, Betcy Johnston, dau. of Robt., Elizabeth dau. of Matthew Johnston, Elizabeth Lock Moody & Elizabeth the dau. of Benj. Jordan; grandsons: John Rutherford, Abner White, John Lock Johnston, the balance of a land warrant in the hands of Henry Rutherford about 1600 acres; sons John, Robt. & Matthew Johnston, Exrs. 18 Feb. 1816. Probated April 1816. Wit: Thos. McCrory, T. Hiter, Legate McCrory & Wm. McCrory.

P. 212.   JOHN JOHNSON, dec'd. Inventory. April session 1816.
          When he died possessed of on 4th March 1816, livestock, furniture, & etc. Robt. Johnston & Matthew Johnston, Exr.

          MOORE BRAGG. Will. Being very sick; dau. Sally, son-in-law James Tomblin. Feb. 29, 1816. Wit: John K. Campbell & John Bragg. Probated April session 1816.

P. 213.   SPENCER HILL. Will. Son Wm. Hill, 100 acres land in
          Bedford Co. on Weakleys Creek from a 400 acres tract of land I purchased from Jenkins Whiteside; son Joseph Hill, 100 acres land in Bedford Co. from the above tract; son Benjamin Hill 100 acres from the above tract of land in Bedford Co.; dau. Fanny Black, 100 acres from the above tract of land in Bedford Co. and at her decease goes to my grandson Thos. Hill Black; son Spencer, 68 acres land in Bedford Co. where he now lives; wife Penelope Hill, the plantation I now live on and at her death goes to 3 sons: Jonathan, Jeremiah & Hezekiah; negro woman Judah left to wife Penelope during her lifetime. Penelope Hill & Jonathan Hill, Exrs. 6 May 1813. Wit: Elisha Fly & Lawrence Fly & G. Hill. Probated April 1816.

P. 214.   DEZIAH SHINALLS. Will. Minnerva Porter, my sister
          Sarah's dau. all the negro property that is coming to me in N.C. at my mother's death; sister Sarah's son Wm. Porter; sister Sarah Porter, balance of my property except a frock parron & counterpane I leave to Margaret Berry to discharge so much of the trouble & expense they have been at in my sickness; sister Sarah Porter, Extrx. 18 Oct. 1815. Wit: W. Wilson & Bassil Berry. Probated April session 1816.

P. 215.   Widow Bland of ARTHUR BLAND, dec'd. Widow & orphans
          allotment April session 1816. Test: Enoch Ensley.
Commr. John Holt, Edwin Austin & John Frost.

          JOSIAH WATLON, dec'd. Inventory. 2nd April 1816.
5 negroes: Man Joe, woman Larah, girl Becky, girl Creasey, boy Aaron. Livestock, furniture, books, guns, farm tools, cash, account on James McGavock & 1 note on Thos. Berry & 1 note on Zacheus German.

          WILLIAM OWEN, dec'd. Account of Sales. Oct. session
1815. Returned by Mordicia Kelly, Admr. Those buying: Adam Cooper, 1 mare & pr. of shoes; Mordecia Kelly, 1 pr. of shoes.

P. 216.   WILLIAM MCEWEN, dec'd. Inventory. July session 1816.
          2 July 1816. Negro woman & two children, livestock, farm tools, gun, furniture, books, & etc. Sally McEwen & Jas. McEwen, Admrs.

          SPENCER HILL, dec'd. Inventory. 180 acres land, livestock, farm tools, carpenter tools, furniture, gun & etc. Jonathan Hill, Exr.

P. 217.   RICHARD L. LOCK, dec'd. Account of Sales. July

74

session 1816. 10 May 1816 by John Secrest. Those buying: John Thomas, Benagah Goodman, John Secrest, Isaac White, Geo. White, Wdw. Locke, Nath. Smithson, Ephraim M. Bugg, John Baker, Spencer Reynolds, James Brown, John Morton, Wm. Andrews, Allen Scruggs, Patrick Gibson, Obediah Driskill, Peter Pinkston, Joseph Spratt, Gideon Hulsley, Samuel Shelburn, Richard Hay, Chas. Pyron, John Tankersly, John Robeson, Joshua Stinson, Wm. Alexander, Murrel Bracey, Sam'l. Brooks, Joseph Hubbard, Tapley Andrews, Charles Peron, Pamphlet Shelburn, Wm. Williams, Maj. Ralston, Wm. Young, E. M. Bugg, Isach White, Hugh Pinkston, Joseph Hubbard.

P. 218.   WILLIAM R. BELL, dec'd. Will. July session 1816.
Wife, Martha all my possession & she school my children as she thinks proper; to my wife negro Wench named Candis. Hugh George & Robt. Bell. Exrs. 20 June 1809. Wit: Robert Bell & E. B. House (her mark). Probated July session 1816.

P. 219.   THOMAS COOR, dec'd. Inventory. 1 July 1816. July
session 1816. 7 negroes: Nat, Nan, Ned, Jerry, All, Nat. & Ale, furniture, & note on Micajah Cox in N.C. in Wayne Co. due 1817. Jonathan Coor, Admr.

EBENIZAR MCKINNEY, dec'd. Account of Sale. July
session 1816. July 1, 1816. Mare & colt, saddle, bridle, saddle bags, book & pocket book. (no names given). Moses Oldham, Admr.

WILLIAM SAMPLE, dec'd. Will. Apr. session 1816.
Wife, Peggy Sample, my watch, negro girl Maria & her child, Jolear (among other things); two children (not named); negro boy Burrel be sold by Hugh F. Bell, Exr; Father-in-law Hugh F. Bell & Bro-in-law John Sample, Exrs. Feb. 1, 1816. Wit: J. Gordan, R.P. Currin & James Sample. Probated April session 1816.

P. 220.   NATHANIEL BARNES. Will. April session 1816. Wife,
Elizabeth Barnes, the plantation and land I now live on & negro boy Jim; at her death land be divided between my 2 sons, Geo. & Samuel Barnes, daughters Anna Barnes & Polly Barnes (Polly the youngest dau.). Lamuel Barnes & G. Hunt, Exrs. 12 Feb. 1816. Wit: John Cochran, Thos. Gooch & Sterling Brown. Probated April session 1816.

JOHN CRAFTON, dec'd. Will. April session 1816. Wife
Elizabeth, the tract of land I now live on & negro men, Miles & Morton, negro woman Edy, girl Dill; son Robert Crafton, my still; grandsons, Geo. Crafton, Dennis Crafton, Richard Crafton, & Daniel Crafton, negro man Pleasant & boy Adam; dau. Jemima Craig, negro boy Willie; grand dau. Faney Wade Craig, negro girl Aney; dau. Sarah Bennet Shelburn; dau. Elizabeth Sampson; dau. Mary Singleton Cole, negro man Peter; Mary Singleton Cole, wife of Geo. Cole; grandson, Daniel Wilkes, a bond due me by Joseph Parsons. Exrs: wife Elizabeth Crafton, Andrew Craig & Daniel Wilkes. 23 Dec. 1815. Wit: James Harder & Samuel Cole. Probated April session 1816.

P. 221.   JARED MCCONNICO. Will. April session 1816. Nancy
B. Hudson $100; wife Ann McConico all my estate; my wife Ann may dispose of ½ of my property as she shall see fit, before her death; the other half of my estate at the death of my wife be left to the heirs of my dau. Nancy B. Hudson; my watch to my wife but if she should marry it goes to my nephew Jared McConnico, son of Garner & recommend that he not part

with it but leave it to one of the same name. Wife Ann McConnico & bro. Garner McConnico & friend Henry Brown, Exrs. 16 Dec.
1815. Wit: Robt. Shannon, Jas. Lauderdale, John Gerbison, John
Davy, Abel Garrett & Lazrus Inman. Probated April session 1816.

P. 222. JOHN CRAFTON, dec'd. Inventory. April session 1816.
        Those buying: James Harder, Elizabeth Crafton, John B.
Crafton, James Radford, Miles Priest, Jesse Jackson, Alexr.
Montgomery, Adam Coon, Andrew Thomas, John H. McLemore, Josiah
Wooldridge, John McClelen, James Boland, Owen Hughes, Benj.
Parks, Wm. Griffin, James Standley, Andrew Cole, John Cohea,
James Gee, James Carrel, Wm. Saunders, Mordeica Pillow, David
Craig, James Neelly, Sam'l. Shelburn, John Nichols, Henry Step-
hens, Robt. Crafton, Presley Harden, John Leygroon, Wm. Williams,
Robt. Sammons, Abel Corzine, Thos. Hilliday, Benj. Merrit,
Andrew Thomas, Sr., James Craig, William Dilliard, Horatio Pet-
tis, Tazwell Burge; 1 note on John Williams due, bad debt; 1 note
due on Robt. Sammons payable to Campbell & Baily due 1807; notes
on the following: John Pettus, bad debt; Geo. Lester, Pleasant
Crenshaw, bad debt; Thos. Crenshaw, bad debt; Robt. Shannon & M.
Pillow; Andrew Fitzpatrick & Robt. McKnight as guardian for Geo.;
Jas. Craig & Benj. Parks as guardian for Dennis Crafton; D.
Wilson as guardian for Geo. Crafton; Robt. Crafton & J.B. Crafton as guardian for Dennis Crafton; James Radford & John B.
Crafton as guardian for Geo. Crafton; Aron Askew & David Craig
as guardian for Geo. Crafton. Robert Sammons.

P. 225. JOHN CRAFTON, dec'd. Additional Inventory. April
        session 1816. Account on: John Sammon, Andrew Coles,
Thos. Pritchett, of Geo. & Dennis Crafton with John Crafton,
their guard., of Doct. Crockett for visit to Sam belonging to
Geo.

        JARRED MCCONNICO. dec'd. Account of Sales. July
session 1816, sold by Gared McConnico, Exr. Those buying:
Lundy Barnes, Jehu Davy, James Pritchett, Lazarus Inman, Wm.
McMillin, Robt. Kennady, John Inman, Jas. Burnham, Wm. Roach,
John Demoss, Chas. C. Burns, Thos. Thompson, Robt. Shannon, John
Jones, Jacob C. Harress, Samuel Smith, John Ketchorn, Jonathan
Stepleton, Frederick Holland, Thos. Loftin, Annian Williams,
David Montgomery, Daniel Gray, Huston Cooper, John Corthorn,
Nehemiah Smith, Demsey Sawyers, John Harveson, Jas. Kenny, Thos.
Findley.

P. 226. JOHN MCKINNEY, dec'd. Account of Sales. July session
        1816. No names given. Moses Oldham, Admr.

P. 227. HENRY CHILDRESS, dec'd. Additional Inventory. Aug.
        session 1816. His attendance at witness for Gov. of
Tenn. against Robt. Searcy; his attendance at witness & fees as
sheriff in the suit: Tabbs Eners vs. A. Whiteside in Wmson. Co.
circuit court; account from Doct. Wm. Dickson which he collected
from Dr. Guy.

        JOHN REID, dec'd. Inventory. July session 1816. 11
negroes: Fanny, Sidney, Nancy, Sally, Geo., Edw., Sam, Nelson,
Alfred, Minerva, & Rebecca; gold in possession of E.B. Reid;
debt E.B. Reid; 1 horse, A. Maury; 1 horse, T. Jenkins; 1 mare,
C. Staggs; 1 horse, J. Carothers; 1 horse, M. Horse; 1 horse;
above sold 7 May 1816; John H. Eaton rent due 1815; accounts due
on the following: Harrison Boyd, R. Corlett & Andw. Johnson.
Archd. Potter bought the books May 7, 1816.

76

P. 228.   WILLIAM LIVINGFELLOW, dec'd. Account of Sales. July
          session 1816. Those buying: Ann B. Stringfellow,
Caty Waddel, Ezekiel Blackshear, Benj. Gholston, Pryor Reynolds,
Richard Hughes, Henry Gray, Frederick Ivy, Wm. Smith, Catherine
Waddel, Wm. Bond, John Witherspoon, N.B. Stringfellow, Henry
Cook, Thos. Reynolds, Luke Blackshire. Ann B. Stringfellow,
Admrx.

P. 230.   WILLIAM SAMPLE, dec'd. Inventory. July session 1816.
          Furniture & etc.; 1 negro fellow sold to W.O. & W.P.
Perkins; note on Daniel Crenshaw; account against H.F. Bell and
1 against Wm. M. Bell; 1 negro woman & child left to widow & 2
children. Hugh F. Bell, Exr.

          CHARLES BROWN, dec'd. Inventory. Oct. session 1816.
Furniture, notes, livestock, gun, farm tools & crops. Micha
Brown & Jesse Cox, Admrs.

P. 231.   JOHN REDFORD. dec'd. Additional Inventory. July
          session 1816. Received of the district paymaster
$75.37; received of Robt. Sammons, $5.91 3/4. Sam'l. Shelburn,
Admr.

          SAMUEL GENTRY, dec'd. Account of Sales. July session
1816. April 27, 1816. Those buying: Famey Gentry (furniture and
hogs), Mincy Cannon, Mark L. Jackson, Geo. Little, Elias May-
field, Geo. Gentry, James Carton, Doctor Webb, James Boyd, Wm.
Young, John Tankersley, John Cloud, James Walker, Milton Gambrel,
Wm. Logan, James Carson, Senr., Wm. Carson, Mary Landrum, Rich.
Gentry, Archelous Huse, Wm. Akin, John Adams, Rich. C. Reynolds,
Kador Parker, Gedeon Riggs, James Carson, Nicholas Gentry. Minos
Cannon, Jas. Boyd & Famey Gentry, Admr.

P. 232.   FREDERICK W. IRION, dec'd. Additional Inventory. Oct.
          session 1816. Geo. A. Irion, Admr. Bond on John L.
Irion, good and John Moody, doubtful.

          JOHN SHORES, dec'd. Additional Inventory. Oct.
session 1816. Samuel Mays, Admr.

          BENJ. BUGG, dec'd. Account of hire of slaves. July
session 1816. N.T. Perkins hired Charles; David Pinkston hired
Jacob; Nancy Bugg hired Peter; David Pinkston hired Nelly &
child; Wm. Young hired Peter; Nicholas T. Perkins hired Starling;
Benj. T. Harrison hired Lucy & child; Nancy hired Rachel. Nancy
Bugg, Ephriam M. Bugg & David Pinkston, Admrs.

          ZADOCK RIGGS, dec'd. Inventory. July session 1816.
9 negroes, livestock, furniture & etc. Nancy Riggs and Richard
Ogilvie, Admr.

P. 233.   Margaret Sample, widow of JAS. SAMPLE, dec'd. Allot-
          ment. July session 1816.

          MOORE BRAGG. Account of Sales. July session 1816.
Those buying: James Tomlin, Wm. Ashley, Abraham Manuel, Geo.
Glascock, Reuben Littleton, Wm. Willet, Joel Hobbs, Luk Black-
share, David Tomlin, James Armstrong, Kemp Holland, John Bragg,
Fred Izrall, Wm. Bright, Sally Bragg. John Bragg, Adm.

          HIZEKIAH PURYEAR, dec'd. Inventory. July session
1816. Slaves: Joe, Will, Chelsey, Peter, Claibourn, Geo.,
Brister, Frank, Jim, Amus, Charles, Isaac, Joe, Billey, John

Granderson, Sam, Terry, Dick (an idiot), Elsey, Maria, Mary,
Nancy, Silva, Peggy, Dilsey, America, Palina, Moses, Davy, Selic,
Oliver, Asa, Beckey, Jinny, Letta, Jenny, Ursey, Diner, Lucy
Harrison, Nelly, Lucy & Easter; books, livestock, furniture,
silver watch, carpenter tools; bonds on the following: John
Waddle, Drury Tucker, Spencer Buford, John Hart, Wm. & Alexr.
Glass, R. Puryear, Jas. Pugh, Jas. Murfree, Daniel Carter, John
McMeens, Wm. Brue, Nich. Lavender, Wm. Hadley, Wm. Grimes, Dab-
ney Wade, Nath. Scott, Geo. Howser, Robt. Nichols, Mark Harder,
Col. Jas. T. Sanford, Wm. Kirk, Jas. Neely, Wm. Samson, Robt.
Campbell, Rich. Jones, Chas. Lavender, John Pope, Sr., Capt.
Hardeman; 1 discharge from Leonard Dunivant 1st Sgr. for 6 mos.
tour; 1 discharge from Alexr. Glass, atty. for Robt. Glass as
Sgt. from 28 Sept. 1814 till 28 April 1815; 1 discharge from
Alexr. Glass as Leutinant from 28 Sept. 1814 to 28 April 1815.
July 4, 1816. John Watson, Admr.

Catharine McCutchen, allotment. July session 1816.
30 April 1816 for Catherine & children. Commr. Sam'l. Edmiston.

NATHANIEL BARNES, dec'd. Inventory. April session
1816. 1 negro boy (willed away to 2 daus.); livestock. blacksmith tools. April 2, 1816. G. Hunt, Admr.

P. 236. ARMSTEAD BOYD. dec'd. Account of hire of negroes.
April session 1816. Jan. 1, 1816. James G. Jones
hired Daniel & Charles; Nicholas T. Perkins hired Tom; D.H.
Legu Davis & Co. hired Barney; Mary Boyd hired Dick.

COL. PETER PERKINS, dec'd. Settlement. April session
1816. Cash paid to: Wm. Murphrey, John Sample & Co., tax for
land in N.C., Petway & Maury, Henry Perkins, Doctor Sappington,
Thos. Hulme, John Newman, Stephen Smith, Jas. Gordon, Doctor
Champncy, Martin Tranthan, Doctor Crockett, Hendley Stone;
account for expenses traveling to N.C. Nicholas Perkins &
Nicholas Scales, Exr.

P. 237. Hendley Stone, guardian for Peter & Green Pryor, minors.
April session 1816. Tax paid for land in Virginia
1813; expenses paid for Doct. & coffin for Sam (slave); expenses
for clothing, schooling & etc.

P. 238. RICHARD S. LOCK, dec'd. Inventory. April session
1816. 3 slaves, livestock, 1 set wheel right tools.
blacksmith tools, farm tools, furniture, books, note & cash.

PETER POTTS, dec'd. Account of Sale. April session
1816. Those buying: Polly Potts (hired Jude & children). Atheldred Evans, Stephen Thomason, Henry Bradley, John Goff, Laurence
Murfree, Wm. Peebles (hired Peter), Arthur Fulghum, Jesse Beavers, Robert Smith, Benj. Evans, David McEwen, Charles Hood.
Jesse Veavers. James McEwen, Admr.

P. 239. JOHN MCKINNEY, dec'd. Inventory. April session 1816.
Farm tools, little furniture, 1 set of tools for
blowing rock, livestock. Moses Oldham, Admr.

EBENEZER MCKINNEY, dec'd. Inventory. April session
1816. Cash. bridle & saddle, rifle gun, saddle bags, pocket
book. coffee mill, 4 head cattle. Estate was admr. by John
McKinney who departed this life before he made an inventory.

MOORE BRAGG, dec'd. Inventory. April session 1816.

farm tools, crops, household utensils & etc. John Bragg, Admr.

P. 240.   WILLIAM STRINGFELLOW, dec'd. Inventory. April session 1816. The following negroes: Man Lic, boy Fountain, 14 yr.; boy Jack, 9 yr.; boy Harry, 9 yr.; woman Leah 38 yr.; woman Milly 20 yr.; woman Anaky 17 yr.; girl Aggy 3 yr.; furniture, rifle & shot bag, books, farm tools, livestock, set shoemakers tools, farm tools & crops. 2 April 1816. Ann B. Stringfellow, Admr.

P. 241.   JARED MCCONNICO, dec'd. Inventory. April session 1816. Negro man Sam 24 yrs.; negro girl Harriot 15 yr.; negro man Sampson 30 yrs.; negro woman Molly 60 yrs.; negro girl Rose 11 yrs.; furniture, guns, farm tools, livestock, deer skins, & family books; notes on Wm. B. Smith & R.P. Currin; Thos. Mothers Shed & John Harvertson; 336½ acre land on South Harpeth. Garner McConnico & Ann McConnico.

ISAAC CROW, dec'd. Settlement. April session 1816. John Atkinson & Andrew Herron, Admrs. No names of heirs given.

P. 242.   SAMUEL GENTRY, dec'd. Inventory. April session 1816. Livestock, furniture, part of a wagon in co. with Nicholas Gentry; 3 slaves: Peg, Charles & Nancy; 223 acre of land. Minos Cannon, Jas. Boyd & Fanny Gentry.

P. 243.   NATHANIEL BARNES, dec'd. Inventory. April session 1816. April 4, 1816. Household furniture & etc. G. Hunt.

SAMUEL MCCUTCHEN, dec'd. Inventory. April session 1816. Livestock, farm tools, books, clock, & etc. Catharine McCutchen & Robt. McCutchen.

GEO. L. WALTON, dec'd. Inventory. April session 1816. Jesse Walton, Admr. For services rendered as a ranger; note on John C. Williams and Ebenezer McKinney; order on Henry McPeak for substitute as ranger, Capt. Hammons Co.; note on William May; and rifle.

P. 244.   THOMAS TAYLOR, dec'd. Inventory. April session 1816. Livestock, rifle & shot pouch, furniture, books & etc. Patsey Taylor & W. Hill, Admr.

FREDERICK W. IRION, dec'd. Account of Sales. April session 1816. Those buying: John P. Irion. Geo. A. Irion, Admr.

ELISHA M. HASSELL, dec'd. Account of Sales. April session 1816. 15 Nov. 1815. Those buying: Nancy Hassell, Henson Estes, Margaret Hankins, Joshua Tarkenton, Wm. Hail, Geo. Glascock, Geo. Ganter, James Tailor, Amos Atkins, Allen Hill. Allen Hill, Admr.

P. 245.   ARTHUR BLAND, dec'd. Account of Sale. April session 1816, by Nomy Bland, Admrx. Those buying: Enoch Ensley, John Holt, John Edmondson, Jeremiah Gibson, Wm. Pumroy, G.A. Irion, Adam Carper, Roby Stone, Mordecia Kelly, Ambros Lacy, Thos. Warmouth, Samuel Thompson, Bennet Sulivan, Nelson Fields, Stephen Thomeson, Gersham Hunt, J.C. Hill, Edwin Austin, Hugh Lockhart, Rhoden Tucker, Nath'l. Hubbart, John C. Fielder, Wm. Stone, Nomy Bland, Green Hill.

P. 246.   ARTHUR BLAND, dec'd. Inventory. April session 1816.
           March 23, 1816. Furniture, livestock, gun & etc.;
notes on John McCain, Leven Dillen, Robt. Roger, Wm. McCandles,
James Turbeville, Edwin Austin & Wm. Lorrel. Nomy Bland, Admr.

           ANTHONY THOMAS, dec'd. Account of Sales. April
session 1816. Sold by Job H. Thomas, Admr. 1 negro man; 1
negro woman & 1 saddle.

P. 247.   WILLIAM STEVENS, dec'd. Additional Inventory. July
           session 1816.

           Fanny (Famey written in Pencil) Gentry, widow of
SAMUEL GENTRY, dec'd. Allotment. July session 1816. Commr.:
Moses Ridley, Wm. Logan & Richard Ogilvie.

           JAMES SHUMATE, dec'd. Settlement. April session 1816.
No names given. Joseph H. Bell, Admr.

           WILLIAM OWEN, dec'd. Settlement. April session
1816. Mordecia Kelly, Admr. Discharge for service as a soldier;
cash paid to Elizabeth Owen, wife of the dec'd.; cash from the
sale of his clothes.

P. 248.   SAMUEL MCCUTCHEN. dec'd. Account of Sales. July
           session 1816. Those buying: Catharine McCutchen,
Robert McCutchen, C. McCutchen, Mary McCutchen, James McCutchen,
Wm. McCutchen, Charles Walker, Hugh F. Bell, Wm. Neelly, Morris
Garrett, Benj. Rutherford, John Compton, James Sneed, Wm. Sneed,
Jesse Porter, Young E. Bone, Samuel Bell, Thos. Garrett, David
Pinkston, James Coner, Peter Conly, J.R. Ruble, Francis Slaugh-
ter, John Webb, Frederick Ivy, James Shaw, Dempsey Nash. James
Crowder, Alexr. Davis, Philip Mabry, Henry Barnes, Wilkin
Whitfield, Gabriel Smith, James Marlin, John Edmiston, Martin
Standley. Thos. McCutchen & Catherine McCutchen, Admrs.

P. 250.   SAMUEL MCCUTCHEN, dec'd. Additional Inventory. July
           session 1816. Notes not yet collected on the follow-
ing: Wm. Morrow, Joseph McBride, Elia F. Pope, Rich. Compton
& William Cowen.

           SAMUEL ROGERS, dec'd. Account of Sales. April ses-
sion 1816. Those buying: David Luty, Jesse Conally, John Hale,
Isaiah White, Franklin McCaren, Stephen Hargrove, John Oglesvey,
John Robertson, Wm. Bennett, Meshack Haile, John Brim, Azeriah
Anderson, Clement Wade, Stephen Nance, Cader Parker, John Cook,
Samuel Patton, Watson Gentry, Nathaniel Wamith, John Dillin,
Wm. Gentry, Mark L. Jackson, John Howard, Philip Beasley, Samuel
N. Martin, Woodson Hubbard, Robt. Rogers, Jonathan Mobley,
Nelson Chapman, Josep Morris, Thomas Thompson, Wm. Downing, Wm.
Wilson, Esqr., Rich. Ogilvie, Wm. L. Webb, Edw. Riggs, Henry
Bailey, Wm. Nolen, Moses Edmondson, Drury Wall, John Tilmon,
John Pastly, Joel Riggs, Benj. Russell, Francis Smith, John
Johnson, Minos Cannon, Archilus Hughes Sr., Archilus Hughes, Jr.,
Wm. Jordan, Watson Gentry; property that was divided: 131 acres
land; 2 negroes; furniture. Robt. Rogers & A. Hughes, Exrs.

           NATHANIEL BARNES, dec'd. Account of Sales. July
session 1816. Those buying: Elizabeth Barnes, Anna Barnes, Leeh
Barnes, G.A. Iron, Rodus Tucker, D. Chadwell, T.F. Cook, Luk(?)
Barnes, John W. Prim, Anna Leek, T. Gooch. N. Fields, Darcus
McClain, D.S. Humphreys, J. Holt, J. Primm. 26 April 1816.
W. Kidd & A. Barnes.

P. 252.   THOS. WILLIAMSON, dec'd.   Will.   July session 1816.
            Son, Wm. W., 100 acre land; son Benjamin, 78 acre land;
John, 75 acre bought of Wheaton; Anne; Susan; Elizabeth; Sarah
W.; Henry G., land I now live on & part of 50 acre tract; Patsey
G.; Minerva, part of land I now live on; Wife Martha, cleared
land on plantation I now live and improved land in a 50 acre
tract; part of 125 acre all cleared land belonging to 250 acre
tract; 3 lots in Franklin, #63, #64 & #72: dau. Polly Fulghum,
50 acre land part of 228 acre tract conveyed to me by Jas.
Robertson Jr. in Davidson Co.; daus. Nancy, Susan, Betsey, Sally,
& Patsey 50 acre land on Harpeth apart of 78 acre balance of my
228 acre tract I bought of A. Maury on Dry Fork of Spencers
Creek. Sion Hunt, Martha Williamson, Wm. W. Wmson, Benj. Wmson
& John Williamson, Exrs. Dec. 11, 1815. Wit: Andrew Ewing,
John Maires & James Brooks. Probated July session 1816.

P. 254.   THOMAS WILLIAMSON. dec'd.   Inventory.   Oct. session
            1816. Furniture, livestock, tools, & etc. Benj.
Wmson, Exr.

P. 255.   JOHN WHITE, dec'd.   Bill of Sales.   July session 1816.
            Nicholas P. Perkins sold to John White a bright mulatto
boy slave, about 6 yrs. old, called Anderson. 26 April 1816.
Test: David Squire.

            LAWRENCE NEWSOM, dec'd.   Inventory.   Oct. session
1816. Nov. 16, 1815. Livestock, furniture, 1 negro girl 9 yrs.
old; tools and notes.

P. 256.   LAWRENCE NEWSOM, dec'd.   Account of Sales.   Oct.
            session 1816, sold 16 Dec. 1815. Those buying: Nathan
Stancell, Rebecca Newsom, Wm. Lasley, Jas. D. Ross, Alexander
Morton, Jonathan Pratter, Jacob Coorfman, Francis Mays, Wm.
Morton, Edw. Hall, John H. Hall. Nathan Stancill, Admr.

            ZADOCK RIGGS, dec'd.   Account of Sales.   Oct. session
1816, sold 17 Aug. 1816. Those buying: Nancy Riggs, John M.
Reynolds, Daniel Riggs, Reuben Hamilton, Wm. Sheffield, Robt.
Bruice, James Joice, Edw. Riggs, Reuben Reynolds, Joseph Boyd,
David Orton, John Tucker, John Riggs. Rich. Ogilvie & Nancy
Riggs, Admrs.

P. 257.   JAMES SAMPLE, dec'd.   Account of Sales.   July session
            1816, sold 30 April 1816. No names given. 2 July
1816. Negroes sold as follows: Sarah & her 4 children, Maria,
Nancy, Bedford & Levian $1223.00; Martin, negro fellow $737.00.

P. 259.   JOSEPH HALL. dec'd.   Account of Sales.   Oct. session
            1816, sold Aug. 12, 1815 by Robt. McLemore & Sion
Hunt, Admr. Those buying: Sarah Hall, Young McLemore, Wm. W.
Woods, Abraham Mason, Isaac Mason, Robt. McLemore.

            Received of Wm. Nolen on the North Carolina bank, a
discharge for 3 mo. and 8 days.

            Allen Stephenson's emancipation state of Indiana, Co.
of Givson, I, Robt. M. Evans of the circuit court of Givson Co.
do hereby certify that the bearer here of Allen Stephenson, a
man of colour was brought into said Co. of Givson by John L.
Russwurm, under authority of a power of atty. from Thos. E.
Sumner of Wmson. Co. Tennessee for the purpose of emancipating
& discharging from a state of slavery the said Allen Stephenson
as well as other person of colour in the aforesaid power of atty.

named which power of atty. was duly proven by John Depriest &
Abraham Glenn subscribing wit. thereto before John J. Neelly
Esqr. a legal qualified Justice of the Peace for said Co. of
Givson & recorded in my office _____ 20 Nov. 1816.

P. 260.   State of Indiana, Givson Co. I, Wm. Prince, Judge of
           the first circuit in the state of Indiana and for the
Co. of Givson, do certify that Robt. M. Evans has signed the
foregoing certificate, _____ 16 April 1817.

           CHARLES BROWN. dec'd. Account of Sales. Jan. session
1817, sold 1 Nov. 1816 by Jesse Cox & Michael Brown, Admrs.
Those buying: Cash notes: Thos. Brown, John Stump & Cox, Casey
Williams, Ephraim Brown, Wm. Batey. Sold to: Michael Brown
(most of the furniture), Jesse Cox, Matthew Johnston, Gabriel
Smith, John Hill, James Co? (Cox), Joel Williams, John Cartwright,
Adam Bond, Henry Cox, James Dupree, Cornelius McCaslin, Hugh
Bell, John Whitby, Negro Jack, Sam'l. Edmiston, Ephraim Brown,
Levin Catoe, John Garet, Luther Brown, David Pinkston, John
Hogan, Samuel Betts, Jas. M. Sims, Jas. Stockett, Jas. Shaw,
Wm. Sneed, Henry Stewart, Thomas Cox.

           HEZEKIAH PURYEAR, dec'd. Account of Sales. Jan.
session 1817. 12 Dec. 1816. Matilda Puryear (most of the items),
Z. Drake, Henry Justice, Alexander Bennett, Geo. Glascock,
Francis Wilkerson, John Sweeney, John Pope, Patrick Reese, Wm. H.
Wells, Ksaac Dancy, W. Hays, John Watson, Henry Reams, Caleb
Mandley, Beverly Reese, Henry Cook, P.M. Puryear, Geo. Meband.

P. 262.   Micha Brown, widow of CHAS. BROWN, dec'd. Allotment.
           Jan. session 1817. 26 Oct. 1816 by Daniel Perkins &
Sam'l Edmiston.

           CORNELIUS CRENSHAW, dec'd. Inventory. Jan. session
1817. Livestock, furniture & tools. Sarah Crenshaw, Admrx.

P. 263.   Henry Cook, guardian for Sala N. Sharp, minor. Jan.
           session 1817. Paid: James Hicke, expenses; A. Goff,
expenses; W. Short; R.P. Currin; Gideon Blackburn; Currin &
Mason; Chas. McAlister. Credits: rent of lands, Geo. Hulme; rent
from Lesters; rent from Andrew Johnson.

           Henry Cook, guardian of Sumner M. Sharp. Jan. session
1817.

P. 264.   Henry Cook. guardian of Searcy D. Sharp. Jan. session
           1817.

P. 265.   Henry Cook, guardian for Peggy N. Sharp. Jan. session
           1817. (The last three are almost like Sala M. Sharps
report.)

           WM. HULME, dec'd. Inventory. Jan. session 1817. made
July 1816. Furniture & household items, 1 large Bible, books,
negro woman Celia @ 40 yrs.; girl Maria @ 8 yrs.; boy Ned @ 14
yrs.; & livestock. Bonds on the following: John Carothers, Wm.
McEwen, John J. Henry, Joseph Wright, Wm. Peebles, Geo. Hulme,
Henry Lester, Wm. Hulme, Thos. H. Perkins, John Dabney, Robt.
Todd, Wm. J. Yarborough, Wm. Miller, James G. Jones, Edw. Russell,
Wm. Clark, Francis Gunter, John Boyles, Charles Kavanaugh,
Philip Maury, Robt. Parrish, Geo. & Robt. Hulme, Deaderick &
Sumners, D. Campbell, P.R. Booker, Geo. Stremlar, Wm. Park,
Ephraim Brown, Wm. Willet, Thos. & E.A. Cox, John Warden,

Joel T. Rivers, Levi Oliver, John & Thos. Deaderich, John White,
Stephen Browder, Henry Childress, Wm. Hempheill, John Haray,
H. Clayton, Gideon Husley, Stephen Brooks, John Duffiel, Work
Smith, Thos. McPhail, Wm. McGaugh, Eli Garrett. Henry Cook &
John Witherspoon, Admrs.

P. 266.   WILLIAM MCEWEN. dec'd. Account of Sales. Those buy-
          ing: Sarah McEwen, James McEwen, Cyrus McEwen, Riley
Slocumb, Andrew Ewing, Allin Cotton, Wm. McKey, Michael Kinnard,
Henry Rutherford, Ephraim McEwen, Wm. Pinkston, E.E. McEwen,
John Douglas, Thos. Goff, Joel Stevens, John Buchanan, Richard
Orton, Ephraim Beasley, Stephen Barfield, Andrew Ewen, Thos. L.
West, James Brooks, Wm. Hope, Peter Pinkston, John Carothers,
Stephen Haynes, Simon Bateman, Adam Jackson, P.W. Brooks, Aaron
Houston, Michael Long, Enoch Bateman, Thos. Walker, Robt. Gray,
Thos. Stacy, Wm. Hope, Charles Stephens, Aaron Houston, Riley
Slocumb, Stephen Haynes, Abner Holt, Turner Pinkston.

P. 268.   An agreement between the several ---------- of JAMES
          SAMPLE, dec'd. 1816. JAMES SAMPLE of Wmson. Co.
Tennessee died 3rd of April 1816 intestate, owning the following
negro slaves: man Martin, woman Sarah & her 4 children: Maria,
Nancy, Redford & Levina. Left the following heirs: wife Margaret Sample; children: James Sample & Martha Sample; child, Ann
& the wife of Thos. Carrol. The 3 former entitled in their own
right, & said Thos. Carrol in right of his wife Ann. James
Sample was the Admr. of the estate of his dec'd. father & these
slaves must be sold to pay off the debts. Wit: Ephraim Anderson, Samuel Ragsdale, Benona Dicky & Geo. Dicky.

P. 269.   WILLIAM HULME. dec'd. Account of Sales. Jan. session
          1817, by H. Cook & John Witherspoon, Admrs. Those
buying: Henry Cook, John Witherspoon, John Nichol, Nicholas T.
Perkins, Zachariah Drake (negro woman Celia 35 yrs. old), James
Cox (negro girl Maria 9 yrs.), Henson Estes, Matthew Lee, Robt.
McLemore (Bible), John Wilkins, Charles Hood.

P. 271.   WILLIAM R. BELL, dec'd. Inventory. Oct. session 1816.
          Negro man Dick about 45 yrs.; negro woman Condis about
25 yrs.; negro woman Violet about 28 yrs.; negro girl Arabella
11 yrs.; negro girl Dinah 9 yrs.; negro girl Indiana 7 yrs.;
negro girl Jane 5 yrs.; negro boy Charley 7 yrs.; negro boy
Claracy 8 yrs.; negro girl susan 6 yrs.; negro boy Charles 2 yrs.;
livestock. furniture, farm tools, gun, note on Daniel Perkins.
8 Oct. 1816. Geo. Bell, Admr.

P. 270.   ALSTON EDNEY, dec'd. Inventory. Oct. session 1816.
          4 Oct. 1816. Furniture, books, compass, shoe tools,
farm tools, livestock, cash & notes, 2 negroes. Polly Edney,
Admrx.

P. 271.   JOHN WELLS, dec'd. Account of Sales. Oct. session
          1816. Those buying: Suan Wells, Samuel Well, Thos.
Wells, John McCollin, Isaac Owen, Jas. Miller, Cordy Nicholson,
Jas. McCaslin, Joseph Brook, Wm. Fleming, Wm. H. Winter, Wm.
Polk, Wm. Webb, Alexander Bennett, Lewis Turner, Allegary Mc-
Guire, Thos. Ragsdale, Geo. Hancock, Abram Hamon, Wm. Courtice,
Malachi Nicholson, Donalson Potter, Nicholas Lavender, John
McClellin, James Neelly, Wm. Sherod, Jas. Stevens, Thos. Rags-
dale, John Smith, Richard Cock. John Thompson, Richard Jones,
Jesse Walton, Pleasant Todd, Daniel Carter, Stephen A. Groom,
Wm. Timmons, Geo. W. Barker, Hutson Dawson, Felix Staggs, James
Hamer, James Slevins, Abigail Blake, Green Duke, Wm. Hill.

Garner Mays, David Bowers, Ezekiel McEley, Isaac Patton, James
Giddens. The following negro slaves: man named Wax to James
Caperton, boy Alexander & man Charles to Thos. Wells, girl
Franky to Richard Calaway, boy Benj. to Sasan Wells, birl lydia
to Jas. Caperton, girl Lynda to Richard Calaway, boy Arm to Wm.
Wells.

P. 273.   Nancy Riggs allotment. Oct. session 1817 for widow
            and orphans of ZADOCK RIGGS by James Wilson, Minos
Cannon & Thos. Wilson.

            NATHANIEL BARNES, dec'd. Oct. session 1816. List of
debts: Abner Morton, Geo. & Ephrain & Goodloe Standirld, G. Hunt,
Solomon Humphries, Geo. Golady, Jas. Taylor, John Edmonson,
Widow Iron, Wm. Fuller, John Iron, Thos. Gooch, John W. Primm,
Ansoleum Nolen, Thos. Lightfoot, Joseph Taylor, Joel Barnes,
Jeremiah Primm, Archibd. Carmichael, Elias Lamkins, Jas. Ray,
Wm. Councill, John McClein, Jas. Copeland, John Strong, Wm.
Gimmerson, Jas. Moore, Henry Bibb, John Frost, Daniel Ireland,
Lawrence Fly, John Primm, Sr., John Holt, Jas. Kincade, Jas.
Kimbro, Joshua Butler, Hugh McCride, Edwin Austin, John Vaught,
Wm. Anthony, James Sneed, Hugh Ray, Steph. Morton, Thos. P.
Kearsey, Rice Hughes, Nimrod Fielder, Lawrence Newsom, Wm. Duf-
fill, Bud Hamlet, J.C. Hill, John Martin, Jas. Bradley, Philip
Woolf, Wm. Burnes, Onn(?) Leak, Abraham McGee, Wm. Stone, Nath.
Chitwood, Alexr. McDonnald, Elisha Fly, Alexr. Smith, Wm. Key,
G.L. Nolen, Ambrose Owen.

P. 274.   LAURENCE MURPHREY, dec'd. Inventory. Oct. session
            1816. Those buying: Tully Williams, John White,
Joseph Alexander, Abraham Secrest, Thos. Malone, Dempsey Nash,
Ann Cator, Geo. Davis, Polly Gambling, Benj. White, Levin Cator,
Benj. White. Benj. White, Admr.

            GEORGE PARKER, dec'd. Inventory. Oct. session 1816.
Furniture, household items, a few tools, livestock & slaves.
Sp. Reynolds.

            Sally McEwen, allotment. Oct. session 1816. For wi-
dow and orphan of WILLIAM MCEWEN, dec'd. Commr.: Wm. Hope,
Benja. Evans & Robt. Hodge.

P. 275.   CLEMENT SMITHSON, dec'd. Settlement. Oct. session
            1816. Nancy Smithson & Haratio Pettus, Admrs.

            ALEXANDER MCCLARNA, dec'd. Will. Oct. session 1816.
Son Franklin McClaron, part of my land on which I now live;
sons Daniel Clevies & Alexander Parker, part of my land on
which I now live; son Garland Anderson, 50 acre land known by
the name of the Cedar tract; sons John Duke & Thomas, the
balance of tract of land I now live on; wife Jane; children:
Garland Anderson, Polly, Sally, Jincy, Daniel Clevis, Alexander
Parker, Milcah, Wm. & Felix; 8 sons, 1000 acre on the Mississippi
which I purchased of Robt. Martin of North Carolina it being
part of a 5000 acre tract granted by North Carolina to Alexr.
Martin; son John Duke McClaran, negro boy Ben; son Thos. McClaran, negro man Clement & blacksmith tools; sons John & Thos.,
3 negro girls: Milly, Nancy & Silvey; wife Jane, 2 negro women:
Phillis & Rose; sons John Duke McClaran & Thos. McClaran, Exrs.
15 Feb. 1816. Wit: Alex. Johnson & Wm. Johnson. Probated Oct.
session 1816.

P. 277.   WILLIAM PATTERSON, dec'd. Inventory. Oct. session

84

1816. Livestock, furniture, tools & etc. Margaret
Patterson, Admr.

HARDEN P. HOLT, dec'd. Account of Sales. Oct. session
1816. Those buying: Piety Parker, widow, David Harrys, Jas.
Allison, Esqr., Spencer Reynolds, Cadar Parker. Spencer Reynolds, Admr.

P. 278.   THOMAS L. ATKINS, dec'd. Inventory. Jan. session
1817. The following negroes: Men Bagwell & Watt;
boys Booker, James, John, Sam, Jack; women Darkies & Harriett;
girl Catharine; furniture, household utensils, set of books, a
list of bonds on John Webb, Jas. Orton, D.A. Durham, Chas.
Slater & Benj. Thompson. Catharine Atkins, Admrx.

P. 278.   THOMAS L. ATKINS, dec'd. Account of Sales. Jan.
session 1817. Those buying: Wilkins Whitfield, Martha
Lee, Frederick Ivy, Samuel Orton, Elizabeth Atkins, Daniel Gray,
David Pinkston, Jas. Rhodes, Isaac Greer, Thos. B. Temple, John
Jones, Henry Forehand, Jas. Gillum, Ab Rhodes, Jas. McGavock,
Dempsey Sawyers, Thos. E. Jones, Wm. Jones, Cousten Sawyers,
Matthew Lee, Wm. Roach, Burrl. Temple, Jas. Giddens, Charles
Jones, Wm. Perkins, Abram Smith, Jas. Conner, Samuel Bryant,
Thomas Walton, Samuel Orton. Elizabeth Atkins, Admrx.

P. 279.   NATHANIEL BARNES, dec'd. Inventory or Account of
monies due the estate. Jan. session 1817. John
Cochorn, Daniel Humphrey, Nathan Stancil, Wm. Hamer, David
Chadwell, Spencer Hill, David Nolen, Jas. Sneed, Green Seah,
Thos. Lastly, Moses Lindsey, Geo. Buchanon, John Waters, Luke
Pryor, Joshua Cannon, Joshua Barnes.

JOHN HOOD, dec'd. Account of Sales. Jan. session
1817. No names given.

P. 280.   ISAAC CROW, dec'd. Division of estate. Personal
devisees Joanna Crow (widow), Thos. Crow, Isaac Crow,
Bryant Crow, Polly Crow, & James Crow, heirs; Lot #1, Levin &
Davis drawn by Isaac Crow; lot #2, Flora & Little Geo. drawn by
Thos. Crow; lot #3, Geo. & Abba drawn by Polly Crow; lot #4,
Crecey & Leah drawn by Joanna Crow; lot #5, Hotta & Southerd
drawn by Bryant Crow; lot #6, Isaac drawn by James Crow. Commr.
Chapman White, Abram Maury, H. Cook & G. Hulme.

John Watson, guardian settlement Jan. session 1817.
The estate of JORDAN REESE. 1813: suit of mourning for Mrs.
Reese ($30.87½); expenses at Nashville. Paid to Jason Hopkins,
Mrs. Tarkington, Tyre Yancey, Jenkins Whiteside, Joseph Rhodes,
Fendal Crump, Elisha Madden, Young A. Gray, Henry Spain, John
Spain, Leonard Dunnavas, Robt. Reese, Robt. P. Currin & Jas.
Gideon; paid expenses to Virginia & back; bond (insolvent) on
Wm. C. Wells, Thos. Worsham, Jas. McKinny & John Tally; paid
Wm. Old & Wm. Robinson. Credits: bond on: Young A. Gray, Isham
R. Trotter, Herb. Reese & Stephen Spain, Wm. C. Wills. Robt.
Neelly & Leon Dunnavant, Robt. Reese. W. French & B. Duvoll,
Benj. Bovill & Wm. Wills, Gabril Baughan & C. Old, Will Goode &
Herb. Reese, Wm. Featherston & Dan'l. Beasley, Patrick Poytress
& Lem Woodard, John Allen & Laban Eppes, Leon Wooard & Pactrick
Poytress, Jas. Moore, Thos. Woodard, John Watson, John Tally
(insolvent), Nelson Jones, Wm. Wells, John Allen, Eliza Old,
Geo. Smith, accounts on Robt. Richie, Robt. Reese, Turner Saun-
ders, Geo. & Wm. Parham, James McKinny, Lew Jones & Wm. Wills,
Wm. French, A. North, Herbert Reese, Geo. R. Claibourn,

David Jones, John Wells, Thos. Worsham (insolvent).

P. 282.   Henry Cook, guardian, Jan. session 1817.   John T.
          Cook to Henry Cook, his guardian paid to for expenses
A. Boyd, Jas. Clark, Currin & Mason, Mary Boyd, G. Blackburn,
Jas. Hicks, Hicks Daniel;   Credit, hire of Bob, 1814, 1815 &
1816.   John T. Cook, orphan of EDMUND COOK, dec'd.

P. 283.   Henry Cook, guardian Jan. session 1817, Geo. E. Cook.
          orphan of EDMUND COOK, dec'd.   Paid to for expenses:
James Hicks, A. Boyd, Mary Boyd, Jo. Clark, Chas. McAlister,
Wm. Yeatman, H. Petway, G. Blackburn.   Credits: by hire of Sam
& Milly 1814, 1815, & 1816.

P. 284.   Henry Cook, guardian for Henry Cook, Jr. Jan. session
          1817, orphan of EDMUND COOK. Paid to for expenses
(same list as above).

P. 285.   DAVID LEWIS. Account of Sales. April session 1816.
          March 13, 1816. Wm. Hogans bought 13 acre of land.
Francis Jackson, Exr.

          James T. Sandford, guardian for the heirs of ISAAC
CROW. Expenses for Bryant Crow, Isaac Crow, Thomas Crow, Polly
Crow & James Crow; expenses in going to North Carolina in search
of Wm. McDaniel. Credit: settlement with Mrs. Joanna Crow for
rent of lands and for rent of negroes 1815; 1816, rent of land
& hire of negroes having never received the slaves from Atkinson
and Andrew Herron, Admrs. of ISAAC CROW, dec'd.

P. 286.   JAMES HARRELL, dec'd. Inventory. Jan. session 1817.
          Pension allowed by the United States for the support
of his family for 5 yrs. and is also entitled to a land warrant
from the United States or money in line. Jan. 7, 1817. O.
Williams, Admr.

P. 287.   ALEXANDER REED, dec'd. Account of Sales. Jan. session
          at his estate at Whites Creek & L. Harpeth. Those
buying: David Balentine, Wm. Johnston, Joseph Chumley, James
Marshall, Wm. Hudgens, Robt. Goodlet, John Porter, David Pink-
ston, Spencer Buford, Joseph Caldwell, Chapman White, Jas. H.
Cobbs, Langhorn Terage, Richard C. Philin, Isaac Walton, James
McGavock, John Cleaves, James Lester, James Pinkerton, Francis
Slaughter, John Hill, Jas. Giddens, Wm. Hutcheson, Henry Compton,
Henry Rutherford, Jas. Rice, Wm. Byers, John Marlin, David
Cartwright, Erastus Collins, Edw. Buford (silver watch), Jas.
McCutchen, Francis Campbell, Henry Barnes, Francis Hodge, Joseph
Pinkerton, Jr., Tully Williams, Henry Slater, Terry Bradley,
Thos. Shannon, Geo. Ralston, Geo. Hodge, Young E. Bane, Luther
Brown, Thos. Dillihunty, John Ralston, John White, Ephraim Brown,
John Thompson, Andrew Luins, Gabriel Buford, Samuel Marlin, Abel
Lucas, Leven Cator. Spencer Buford, Admr.

P. 289.   WILLIAM C. DEVEREIX, dec'd. Settlement. Jan. session
          1817. To Wm. Wilson, going to Huntsville & back; 6½
weeks attendance when sick at my house; waistcoat for him when
buried; pr. stockings for him when buried; 1 handkerchief for him
when buried; coffin. 31st Oct. 1816. Test: Eliazar Hardeman.
Credits: for Devereix services in the Creek war.

P. 290.   MOSES MONTGOMERY, dec'd. Inventory of Sale. Rifle,
          saddle, & trunk to Alexr. Montgomery. Alexr. Montgo-
mery, Admr.

WILLIAM BERRY, dec'd. Settlement. Oct. session 1815.
Vouchers on the following: Thos. Hope, Wm. Hulme, Geo. Oliver,
Jas. Patterson, Wm. Sumners, Wright Williams, Richard Orton,
Adam Miller, Wm. Beaty, Thos. C. Benton, James Elliott, R. Camp-
bell, Samuel Buchanan, David McCord, John Depriest, John Beaty,
Wm. Wilson, John Denny, John McCravy, Caleb Mandley, John Clark,
Wm. Hulme, N.T. Perkins; taxes for 1810, 1811, 1812, 1813, 1814.
Nicholas Scales & Wm. Wilson, Commr.

P. 291.   Polly Edney, widow of ALSON EDNEY, dec'd. Allotment.
           Jan. session 1816.

           PATRICK GIBSON, dec'd. Will. April session 1817.
Wife Mary, 1/3 of all property, negro woman Winny; son John
Gibson, $200 and his son Patrick $50; son John Gibson, $100;
son-in-law Levi Hughes, $450; son-in-law Mark Wilson $12 and his
daus. Maria & Polly $100 ea.; son-in-law James Barnet, $450;
daughters Sarah, Mary, Elizabeth & Catharine remainder of my
estate; dau. Sarah Gibson, horse; daus. Sarah Gibson and Mary
Gibson, Exrs. 8 Feb. 1816. Wit: Erastus Collins, Joseph Burke
& Jenny Burke.   Probated April session 1817.

P. 293.   HUGH HENDERSON, dec'd. Inventory. July session 1815.
           (His inventory sounds like he had a gen. merch. store).
Notes on the following: John P. Broadnax, John Edwards, Wm.
Faulkner, Gragg & McEwen, Jason Hopkins, Geo. Neelly, Joel T.
Rivers, Wilson & Vaughan, Geo. Hulme, Jas. Pugh, Oliver Crenshaw,
Joseph Crenshaw, Benj. Gholson, John Huston, John W. Luster,
John R. Ruble, Wm. Saunders, Thos. Wilson, David Dickinson,
Samuel Braden. John H. Eaton and Ann E. Henderson, Admr.

P. 301.   JOHN REID, dec'd. Division of land. Land on waters
           of L. Harpeth; lot #1, 84½ acres Wm. Reid; lot #2,
84½ acres John Reid; lot #3, 110½ acres Andrew Reid; lot #4,
32½ acres Levian Reid the widow; lot #5, 78 acres Shadrick
Robt. & Levina Reid, minor heirs.

P. 302.   Widow Locks Allotment July session 1816 for widow &
           orphans of RICHARD COOK, dec'd. Commr. Sam'l. Shel-
burn, Geo. Kinnard & John Robertson.

           JAMES BERRY, dec'd. Settlement. Jan. session 1817.
Cash received of the following: John McEwen, John Allen, Azariah
Anderson, J. Mobley, John Watt, Alexander Johnson, Job Loward,
Joseph Morris, David Berry, Sam'l. Campbell; for JAMES BERRY'S
Military services; expenses paid to the following: Azariah
Anderson, Doctor Crockett, Doctor Webb, P.R. Booker, B.M. Garner,
Jas. Campbell, P. Pinkston, tax for 1816, Wm. Wilson, Rebecca
Berry, Wm. Berry estate, Thos. Berry; cash paid the estate of
WILLIAM BERRY, dec'd.; cash paid Jas. Campbell, Thos. Berry by
D. Berry, D. Wall & wife, legatees. A. Johnson and Rebecca
Bery, Admr.

P. 304.   RICHARD S. LOCK, dec'd. Account of sales. Jan.
           session 1817. Sold 1 Jan. 1817. Those buying:
Elizabeth Lock (negroes: Stepney, Rose & Mingo), Thos. Wilson
(Jeffery), David Pinkston, Reuben Dodson, Levi Oliver (rent of
farm), Wm. Andrews. Henry Andrews & Elizabeth Lock, Admrs.

           ELISHA M. HASSELL, dec'd. Additional inventory. Oct
session 1816. The pay of a private from 20 Sept. 1814 to 31 Jan.
1815. Allen Hill, Admr.

87

JOHN ECHOLS, dec'd. Inventory. Livestock, $40 cash, wages subsistance & transportation allowed a 3rd Leiut. for 7 mo. service of the United States. Allen Hill, Admr.

JOEL PARRISH, dec'd. Division. Oct. session 1816. To the following legatees: Henchey Petway, 10 acres from tract adjoining Franklin; Matthew D.M. Parrish, 10 acre; Joel Parrish, 10 acre; Henchey Petway, negro man William & negro boy Phanteroy; Matthew F.M. Parrish, negro girl Maria & Dilsey; Joel Parrish, negro man Tom & negroe girl Mary; the old negro man aged about 60 was to remain with Susanna Parrish, the relict of said deceased. R.P. Currin, Henry Cook & B. Reese.

P. 305. MOSES MONTGOMERY, dec'd. Inventory. 1 partnership keel boat & rigging; 1 partnership note on Wm. Allman; saddle and gun. Alex. Montgomery, Admr.

P. 306. PARKER BATEMAN, dec'd. Inventory. Discharge of $284.12½. Enoch Bateman, Admr.

JAMES SKELLY, dec'd. Account of Sales. Those buying: Frank Secrest, John Wautlin, Stephen Pigg, Jesse White, John Pigg, Wm. Sparkman, Wm. Demoss, Wm. Hendley, Joseph Witherington, Henry Lester, Alexr. Thompson, Sarah Skelly, John McCaslin, Nicholas Branch, Hanner Hamilton, John Thomas, Wm. Blythe, Thorton Perry, Alexander Haverson, Chas. White, Abraham Wetherington, Geo. Wrenn.

P. 307. ISAAC CROW, dec'd. Additional Inventory. Jan. session 1817. Cash received from Barfield through Ariah Bass. John Atkinson & Andrew Herron, Admrs.

FREDERICK BROWDER, dec'd. Settlement. April session 1817. 27 Feb. 1817. Received of Samuel Perkins, John Bostick, Thos. Joice & John Morton. Credits: Paid Joel Childress for 2 silk dresses for Nancy C. & Lucinda N. Browder, Alexr. Rolston, Doct. W.S. Webb, Wm. H. Browder, Peter Pinkston, John Coffee, Jas. Allison, Thos. Parsons, Geo. Oliver, Haratio Burnes, N.T. Perkins, Wm. H. Browder; note on bond on Pugh Cannon that can't be collected.

JAMES JACKSON, dec'd. Inventory & account of Sales. April session 1817. April 5, 1816. No names given. Samuel Jackson, Admr.

P. 309. ELIJAH HUNTER, dec'd. Inventory. April session 1817. 2 negroes: Sarah & Bob; livestock, farm tools, furniture, books, household items & etc. Catherine Hunter & Elisha Hunter, Exrs.

Sally Chrisman, allotment. April session 1817. Widow of ARON CHRISMAN. Commrs. John Ogilvie, J. Hubbard & Sam'l. Brown.

P. 310. JOHN CRENSHAW, dec'd. Account of Sales. April 1817. Negro woman Philis. Oliver Crenshaw, Admr.

CAPT. WILLIAM JACKSON, dec'd. Inventory. July session 1817. Amount of discharge $29.50; note on Henry Russell (no good); little furniture. Wm. L. Webb, Admr.

SAMUEL SMITH, dec'd. Inventory. July session 1817. Received notes on: Bernard M. Patterson, Wm. Price, Riley D.

Murry, Samuel Cummins, Thos. Jenkins, John Matthews, David
Gooch.

P. 311.   JOHN A. LAGRON, dec'd.   Inventory & Account of Sale.
          July 1817. Those buying: Lemon Bateman, Jesse Jackson,
Andrew Cole, Josiah Wooldridge, David Huston, Michael Kinnard,
George Chadwell, Mary Lagron, Adam Coon, John McClellen, Dennis
Lark, Joseph Wallace, Solomon Whitmon, Eli Corzine, Allin Nich-
ols, John Tisdale, John McClellen, Elisha Walker, John R.
Bittick, Thos. Merritt, Wm. Lagron, Wm. Saunders, Chas. Pistole,
Frances Rice, Slolman Whitman, Ruffin Brown, John Stacy, Jacob
Halfacre, Michael Laton, John Record, Hugh Moore, Daniel Cren-
shaw, Turner Pinkston, Thos. Merritt, Amos Roundsavall, Benj.
Merritt; 1 note on Adam Lagroon and Adam Coon. Wm. Lagroon, Admr.

P. 312.   Malinda Parks, Allotment, widow of WILLIAM PARKS,
          dec'd. and orphan children. Commr. Wm. Gatlin, David
Byers and Cornelius Matthews.

          DOCT. SOLOMON HUMPHRIES, dec'd. Inventory. Horse
saddle, silver watch, medicine, 7 medical books, accounts on
books. Daniel J. Humphrey, Admr.

P. 313.   JOHN SAMPLE. Will. Bro. Thos. Sample; friend Archi-
          bald Potter; Peggy Sample, wife of Wm. Sample. In
addition to what I have already subscribed toward completing the
Presby. Church in Franklin, I leave to Elijah Hunter $100 toward
completing said church; sister Sally Sample, part of estate to
be paid out of Nashville Bank Stock; children of Wm. Sample;
bro.-in-law Wm. Brandon; bro-in-law Thos. Brandon; bro-in-law
John Buchanon; children of my bro. James Sample with exception
to Ann Carroll's part to my bro-in-law John Buchanon in trust
for her & to be during the life of her present husband. Exrs.
Robt. P. Currin and John White. 6 April 1816. Wit: Joel Stevens, Michael Long & Jas. Salisbury. Probated July session 1817.

          Codecil-Exrs. to pay to sis. Sally Sample & bro-in-law
John Buchanon $100 in addition to what I have already left them.
          Codecil-having made first will while in a very low
state of health and since making said will I had some hope of
recovering my health, I purchased a family of negroes of my
father-I now being very weak and low of body,-I give to my sis.
Sally a negro girl I purchased of my father named Sal, about 11
yrs. old; nephew John Sample Buchanon; friends, John White &
Robt. P. Currin sell remainder of slaves to some good master;
even if they sell for a less sum, so they will be kept together
as it was my object for buying them from my father. 22 July 1816.
Test: A. Potter and M.L. Bond.
          Codecil-to Margaret Sample widow of Wm. Sample, my
sister-in-law. 29 July 1816. Wit: W.L. Bond and Alex. White.

P. 315.   ALSON EDNEY. Sales of Estate. Nov. 1, 1816. Those
          buying: Polly Edney (most of furniture, dishes, books
and some livestock), Nancy Edney, John D. Edney, Alfred Edney,
Leven Edney, Abraham Truett, Jas. Hughes, Wm. F. Maury, Daniel
Perkins, Martin Stanley, Sion Hunt, Newton Edney, James Brown,
Stephen Childress, Wm. Harrison, Jas. Stanley, Francis Carter,
John Berry, Jacob Vanatta, Jas. Grimes, John Meak, John Dunham,
Harris Cobler. Polly Edney, Admr.

P. 316.   JAMES MCEWEN. Settlement. July session 1817.. The
          estate of Samuel Mairs, dec'd; note paid Martin Stan-
ley; to David Squier rect.; Coopers rect.; tax 1815 & 1816;

Sion Hunt account; John Douglas rect. Commr. Berry Nolen & Sion Hunt. Jas. McEwen has authority to collect the amount due Samuel Mairs for a tour of about 6 mo. duty in the late war. 11 July 1817.

James McEwen, Settlement, July session 1817, on Estate of PETER POTTS, dec'd. To: Wm. Evans rect, John Sample rect., Thos. Bradley rect., Sappington & Breathett, A. Gray, Polly Jones Potts rect., tax 1815 & 1816, Benj. White, Benj. Evans (crying sale), Caleb Manley, Thompsons rect., Wm. Peebles, Tally account, Geo. Hulme, David Johnson, 5 children and widow, makes 6 parts; by hire of: Peter to Woods, woman & children to Jas. Woods, girl to Crockett; Beavers note for corn; (no names of heirs given).

P. 317. JARED MCCONNICO, dec'd. Account of Sales. Those buying: Reuben Dodson, Jas. Stanley, Angus McPhail, Wm. Hill, Chiles McGee, Geo. Bennett, Stephen Barfield, Michael Kinnard, Lemuel B. McConnico, Christopher McConnico, John R. Bitticks, Lewis Stevens, Silas Stevens, John House, Hugh Pinkston, Harry Brown, Wm. Wakins, Elisha Walker, Horatio Pettus, Samuel Pratt, Charles Harrel, Reuben Dodson (1 negro woman & 1 negro man Samson), Jas. Williams (1 negro man Samuel), Chiles McGee (2 negro girls Harriet & Rose), Jacob Halfacre, Henry Brown, John Stacy, Ruffin Brown. Garner McConnico, Admr.

P. 318. Ezekiel Blackshare, guardian. July session 1817. 11 July 1817. Settlement with guardian of Luke, David, Elijah, Jacob & Jesse Blackshare, heirs of JESSE BLACKSHARE, dec'd. We the Commr. find by a settlement with Isaac Mairs, guardian with said heirs that he was indebted to the heirs. 25 Nov. 1816. Stephen Childress, Jas. B. Thompson, Marlin Stanley rect.; taxes for 1816-1817. Commrs. Sion Hunt & Joseph Braden.

P. 319. Sherwood Green. Settlement. April session 1817. To the heirs of SAMUEL CLARK; to the hire of negroes for 1816 and 1817; expenses for schooling, clothing, boarding & etc. for Sally, Martin, William and Samuel Clark.

P. 320. WILLIS CARSON, dec'd. Settlement. April session 1817. Commrs: Jas. Allison & Thos. Wilson. (No names given).

P. 321. HENRY WHITE. Settlement. April session. Commrs: Thos. Berry, Dan'l. Perkins & Sion Hunt; paid to widow Fanny White; receipt on Jas. Tilford; note on Jas. Bradley and John Higneth and David Reid; guardian has been appointed for widow and children (no names given); expenses paid to: Ephraim Brown, Elias F. Pope, Perkins Hardeman, F. Ivy. Credits received from: Robt. Searcy, F. Ivy, Wm. Edminston, Chambers note.

P. 322. HENRY WHITE, dec'd. Account of Sales. April 1817. Sold 12 May 1815. Those buying: Fanny White (Bible, bed & furniture, and a few items), John Motheral. Henry Hodge, Samuel Edmiston, John Stobuck.

ARMSTEAD BOYD, dec'd. Account of Sales. April 1817. Jan. 8, 1817. Negro man to Henry Cook, Dick about 23 yrs. old; $620.

LEWIS TOON, dec'd. Inventory. April session 1817. Jan. 6, 1817. 890 # tobacco, gun, few farm items & etc.

HENRY CHILDRESS, dec'd. Division. April session 1817. Eliza C. Childress, widow, negroes Milly & Charlotte; children of dec'd.: Eliza A. Childress, negro Jesse; Margaret L. Childress, negroes Easter and Allin; Thomas M. Childress, negroe Geo.; Sally C. Childress, negroes Perry and Harriet. Commrs.: John Watson, Wm. Banks and R.P. Currin.

P. 323.   Piety Parker, widow allotment. April 1817. Commrs.: Watson Gentry, James Ridley and Thomas Wilson. Feb. 10, 1817.

JOHN C. CRENSHAW, dec'd. Additional Inventory. April session 1817. Negro woman, Phillis. Oliver Crenshaw, Admr.

LEWIS TOON, dec'd. Account of Sales. April session 1817, sold 23 Jan. 1817. Those buying: Elias Dodson, Henry Cook, Henry Clark. Laneon Allin, John Witherspoon, Henry Short, Daniel Sinclair, Branch H. Anderson, Jas. Toon, Jonathan Clark, Fanny Toon. James Toon, Admr.

P. 324.   SAMUEL GENTRY, dec'd. Account of Sales. April session 1817, sold 16 Dec. 1816. Those buying: John Rushing, Milton Gambrel, Fanny Gentry (hire of negro girl), Geo. Little, John Merchant, Clement Cameron(?) (1 negro girl and 1 negro boy hired), Nicholas Gentry. Minos Cannon, James Boyd & Fanny Gentry, Admr.

AARON CRISMAN, dec'd. Inventory. April 1817. 1 set shoemakers tools; household items and furniture; livestock and farm tools.

ALEXANDER REID. dec'd. Supplement account of Sales. 7 April 1817. 20 shares bank stock to Joseph Philips, Esqr.; Spencer Buford, 6 months hire of 3 negroes, at public auction in town of Nashville. Spencer Buford, Admr.

NATHAN TRULL, dec'd. Account of Sales. April 1817, sold Jan. 15, 1817. Those buying: Mrs. Trull, Thos. Gillespie, Wm. Walker, Wm. Weatherby, Christopher Irvin, Ambrose Hill, Wm. Hooker (set of shoemakers tools), Wm. Tucker, John Dowdy. Penelope Trull, Admr.

P. 325.   Penelope Trull, Allotment. April session 1817 for Mrs. Trull and family. Commrs.: Thos. Gillepie and Moses Steele.

WILLIAM STEVENS, dec'd. Settlement. April session 1817. Note due: Samuel Wilson, Lovey Page, James Berry, Lovet Stevens, Gregory Wilson, John Stevens, Doct. Sappington & Breathet, Andrew Campbell, Beverly Ridley, Henry Jordan, Nicholas T. Perkins, Joseph Braden, Henry Tally, James Stewart, Wm. Ridley, O.T. Watkins (making coffin), Samuel Parker, Jason Wilson, Richard Tanner, Wm. Stevens, Benj. White, J.H. Eaton; Rec'd. from: Wm. Hulme, Peter Pinkston, Shelby Corzine, Joel Stevens. Proven account on Thos. T. Maury. Commrs.: Geo. Hulme, Berry Nolen and Owen T. Watkins.

P. 326.   JOHN HIGHTWOER, dec'd. Settlement. July session 1817. Credits: hire of negroes. Expenses: coming from Sumner Co. and back; boarding and clothing 2 children; taking deposition of Thos. Davidson and Smith Loftin in Logan Co., Ky. Notes on: John Dickinson, O.B. Hay, Geo. W. Campbell, John Carson; receipt from Wm. Smith; copies of records in

Rutherford Co.; Wm. Martin & James Tremblis, receipt. Commrs.: Joshua Farrington and Sion Hunt. Settle with Wm. Saunders in place of his wife Mary Saunders, Admrx. of John Hightwoer. Richard Hightower is indebted to estate.

P. 327.   PACTRICK GIBSON, dec'd.   Inventory.   July session 1817.
          9 negroes, furniture, livestock. household items, farm
tools, 1200# prime tobacco.   Exrx. Sarah Gibson & Mary Gibson.

P. 328.   Catherine Hunter.   Allotment.   July session 1817,
          widow of ELIJAH HUNTER, for families use 12 July 1817.
Wm. Bond Sr., Jas. Wilkins & Geo. Bennett.

          Susanna Wells.   Allotment.   July 1817. $100 account
of the estate of JOHN WELLS, dec'd.   Commrs.: Henry Yarbrough,
Wm. Bond & James Miller.

          JOHN HIGHTOWER, dec'd.   Division.   July 1817.   To:
Wm. Saunders, 2 negroes, Frank and Reuben; Alfred Hightower, 3
negroes, Jacob, Bick and Dilce; Delia Hightower, 2 negroes, Luke
and Jourdan.

P. 329.   WILLIAM PARKS, dec'd.   Supplemental Inventory.   July
          1817.   Cash drawn from the United States for his
service $28.04½; note on myself.

          JOHN MCKINNEY, dec'd.   Settlement with Admr.   July
session 1817.   Moses Oldham, Admr.   James Boyd and Alex Mebone,
J.P.

          THOMAS T. MAURY, dec'd.   Inventory.   Oct. session
1817.   List of open accounts due on the books belonging to the
firm of Maury & Reese, 1 Sept. 1817.   Elisha Dotson, Gardner
Mays, M.L. Bond, Wm. Carr, Wm. Banks, Martin True, Wm. Swanson,
Presley Dotson, Daniel McMahan, Jas. Priest, Saunders & Orgain,
Bernard Beasley, Currin & Mason, Andrew Campbell, Jas. S. Clemen,
Mary Ann Degraffenreid, Robt. Davis, Hudson Dawson, William
Eastin, Robt. C. Foster, Jr., Cordial Faircloth, John Gholson,
Lewis Garrett, James M. Gray, Nicholas P. Hardeman, John Allen,
Jeremiah Tranham, James Brooks, Doct. Edw. Breathett, Hugh F.
Bell, John Bell (atty.), James Brown, Jesse Benton, Archbd.
Lytle, Ephraim Brown, Jas. Swanson, Wm. White (atty.), Wm.
Croucher, Jas. Cavanaugh. John W. Crunk, David Dickerson, Leo-
nard Dunavant, Moses Davis, Benj. Evans, John Floyd, Benj.
Gholson, Doct. Young A. Gray, Nathan Garner, James Gordon, Wm.
Hemphill, Kemp Holland, John Inman & Jesse, James Jordan, Andrew
Johnston, Abraham Maury, Frederick Milchie, Angus McPhaie, Caleb
Mandley, John Murrell, Moses Moore, John Nichols, Wm. Nelson,
Jordan R. Old, John E. Old, Nicholas T. Perkins, Constantine
Perkins, Thomas H. Perkins Jr., Nicholas P. Perkins, John Ried's
Estate, Wm. Smith, Turner Saunders, Silas Stephens. Nathan Smith-
son, Johusa Thweatt, James B. Thompson, Lewis Turner, Thomas
Terry, John Wells, Estate Hezekiah Puryear, John Watson, John H.
Eaton, James Hicks, Wm. Saunders, Joshua Cameron, Wm. Graham,
Sion Hunt, Frederick Holland, Samuel Martin, Daniel Perkins,
John Roberts, David Bowers, Simon Balaman, Elisha North, Henry
Stevens, Job Mayberry, Wm. Bond, John Neelly Jr., Thomas H.
Perkins Sr., John Brown, Thomas Craig, John Cohan, Lawarus
Dotson, Fountain Parrish, Hardin Perkins, Mansfield House,
Zachariah Jackson, Joshua Jackson, Robt. McLemore, Philip Maury,
Richard Maury, John Mayse, Christopher McEwen, Abram North,
Malachi Nicholson, Thomas Old, Wm. E. Owen, H. Petway, Millieun
(?) Peebles, Nicholas Perkins, Sr., Jose Parrish, Sally Ruse,

92

Wm. Robertson, E. Sampson, John Swenny, Thomas Sappington,
Joham R. Trotter, Laurence & Joseph Thompson, Dixon Vaughan,
James Turner, John White, Estate of John Wheaton, Samuel Erscken,
James Gosey, Wiley Roy, John Thompson, Jacob Reader, Wm. Clark.
Thomas Hays, Taylor Jones, Samuel Cox, James G. Jones, Doct.
Samuel Crockett, Wm. O. Perkins, Toliver Burnett, Thomas Reynolds,
John Garey, James McEwen, Jeremiah Pope, Michael Saxton, John
Mallory, Nathan Garner Sr., James McGuire, Henry Pilly, Jeri-
miah Terry, Ezekiel Blackshare, Wm. Denson, Stephen Childress,
A.M. Degraffenreid, John Estes, Susan Reynolds, Armistead Atkin-
son, Susan Gray, Drury Palkum, Gaavis Thurman, Abram Wright,
Susan Wright, Susan Parrish, Allen Hill, Ishaim House, Thomas
Deaderick, James Andrews, Nathan Cheers, Alexander M. Gray,
Allen Bugg, Joseph Burke, Moses Parrish, Samuel Wood, Henry
Hunter, W.W. Cunningham, John Watson, Perry Cohea, M.I. House,
Thomas Fowler, John Floyd, John Little, Josiah Knight, Wm. Mil-
ler, Matthew Meggs, James Hughes, Wm. H. Wells, Billington Tay-
lor, Josh. Human, Wm. Banks, Elizabeth Mandly, Thomas H. & Dan
Perkins, C. White, Fielding Hulme, Wiley Johnson, Hugh F. Bell,
Wm. Ray, Walter Texmis, Wm. Campbell, Joshua Reams, Isaac Mason,
Jackey Jones, Frederick Browder Sr., Peter Beasley, Robt. Spriggs,
Sarah Malone, Joel Parrish & Co., Matthew Wiggs, Andrew Craig,
Bird Dotson, John Gee, Robt. White, Wm. Ashlin, Wm. Manning,
David H. True, John Atkinson Jr., Polly Estes, James Baugh,
David Gee, Wm. Hill, Henson Estes, James Hughes Sr., John Hamble-
ton, James Salisbury, Charles Perkins, Robt. Gordan, Bell Palle-
son, Frederick Broadnax, Wm. P. Hays, Joseph Wallace, Josiah
Doyal, Hudson Dawson, Benj. Gholson, E.W., James G. Jones, James
Pritchett, John Knight, Thomas Spence, Benj. Goodman, Edward
Hood, Joshua Farrington, John Grubbs, J.C. Williams, A. Maury,
Susan Parrish, Edward Rupil. Young A. Gray, Thomas Hamilton,
Henry Marlin, Wm. McCory, Samuel Martin, Wm. Beard, Thomas Her-
rin, Wm. McKey, Knight & Gray, John M. Walker, Terry Bradley,
Elisha Rhodes, Clary Bushawney, Turner Saunders, Richard Vaughan,
Samuel Tripp, Nicholas Scales, Wm. Stephens Jr., W. Stevens,
Samuel Hemphill, K.P. Bass & Co., Gholson & Reese, L. Dotson,
A.P. Hamilton, Reuben & Isham Jackson, Belhmy & Perkins, Nash-
ville Bank, John Sweeney, Stacy & Walker, P. Maury, F. Holland,
Currin & Petway, Wm. Hungorford, Sam'l. Atkinson, Chas. Kaven-
augh, Z. May, George T. Stark.

P. 332.   A list of accounts belonging to the late firm of Pet-
           way & Maury.   Jesse Benton, James L. Armstrong, Robt.
W. Carter, James M. Crackin, H.B. Pilway, Wm. Maddox, Wm. Step-
henson, Hugh R. Orr, Thompson Paxton, John Cook, Jesse M. Mahan,
Thomas Tarpley, John Burns, Richard Hungarford, Wm. Hess, Hugh
M. Black, Alexander Lester, John Miller, Humphrey Baker, Thomas
H. Perkins, Henry Atkinson, Jesse Hutchinson, Deaderick & Pett-
way, Wm. Bell, Estate of Joel Parrish, Joel T. Rivers, Lemuel
Childress. Abram Maury, Admr.

P. 333.   WILLIAM STRINGFELLOW, dec'd. Division. Oct. session
           1817. Met at home of Ann B. Stringfellow, widow;
divided negroes between widow and her daughter Caty Waddle;
widow, Harry, Leah & Aggy; Caty Waddle, Cye, Fountain, Jack,
Anaky & Esther. 2 Aug. 1817. Commrs.: Hendley Stone, Richard
Hues, Henry Cook, Wm. Orr & Wm. Bond, Sr.

P. 334.   JOHN GHOLSON, dec'd. Account of Sales. Oct. 1817.
           Furniture, household items, books, farm tools, live-
stock & etc.; note on Bank of Salam(?) State of Ohio; cash
received of: Mrs. John Gholson, John White, Robt. White. Benj.
Gholson, Admr.

P. 335.   EBENEZER MCKINNY, dec'd.   Settlement.   Oct. session
          1817.   (No names given).   Commrs.: Jas. Boyd & Alexr.
Mebane.   Moses Oldham, Admr.

          JOHN GHOLSON, dec'd.   Account of Sales.   Oct. session
1817.   Sold Aug. 21, 1817.   Those buying: Sally G. Gholson
(furniture, Bible & household items), Benj. Gholson, Isham
Thweat, Armstead Atkinson, A. Johnston, Sam'l. Word, Wm. Ashlin,
Richard Orton, John Stacy, A. Andrews, Wiley Johnson, John Tom-
lin, Fountain Parrish, Samuel F. Glass, Robt. Carter, Holland
Davis, Wm. Bright, Henry Cook, A. McPhail, Thos. Reynolds,
Wright Stanley, James G. Jones, Henry Stewart, John Cook, John
McDaniel, John Old, Wm. Hemphill, Samuel Cox, Samuel Atkinson,
Adam Jackson, John Graham, Thomas Old, C. Andrews, B. Andrews,
Leonard Dunavans, Dempsey Nash, John Knight, Lewis Garrett, H.
Petway (hire of Sawyer).

P. 336.   Henry Cook, guardian.   Settlement.   Oct. session 1817.
          Sala N. Sharp to H. Cook, guardian; expenses: Rent of
land to Geo. Hulme, 16 acres to A. Johnson, Lester(?), place
17 acres; hire of Peter; for wood, Wm. Eastin, Faircloth, T.
Hiter.

P. 337.   Henry Cook, guardian.   Settlement.   Oct. 1817.   Expen-
          ses paid to: David Hicks, W. Banks, Y.A. Gray, Doct.
Gray, Geo. Hulme, Jas. Hicks, McPhail.   Credits from: Angus
McPhail, James G. Jones, John P. Broadnax.

P. 338.   Henry Cook, guardian for Sumner M. Sharp.   Settlement.
          Oct. 1817.   Expenses, for tax; Paid to: Daniel Hicks,
Jordan & McPhail, Geo. Hulme, James Hicks, Wm. Banks.   Credits:
hire of Rachel and child, hire of Stephen, rent of land to
Roper and Hilliard; 3 tember trees from Benj. Gholson.

P. 339.   Henry Cook, guardian for Peggy N. Sharp.   Settlement.
          Oct. session 1817.   Expenses: tax, clothing for Rose,
paid to Geo. Hulme & Jas. Hicks; credits: hire of Rose & Esther;
rent of land: McCandles place, 14½ acres fork of road, 11 1/8
acres west of Nashville; cash received of R.P. Currin.

P. 340.   WILLIAM JACKSON, dec'd.   Account of Sales.   Oct.
          session 1817, sold 30 Aug. 1817.   Those buying: Mary
Landrum, Wm. Summers, Zachariah Smith, John Webb.

          JAMES SAMPLE, dec'd.   Inventory.   April session 1817.
6 negroes, livestock, furniture, household items, books, clothing and etc.; notes on the following: Robt. Sample, Thos. Taylor,
Wilie Barer, Joshua Taylor; accounts on: Daniel Crenshaw, John
Sample, Wm. Morris, Wm. Ashburn, Joel Stephens, Wm. Smith;
received from estate of Robt. Sample, Jr. and Willie Barrer.

P. 342.   THOMAS GOOCH, dec'd.   Will.   Oct. session 1817.
          Beloved wife, Elizabeth Gooch, negro man; Patrick,
negro woman Sarah, negro girl Chaney, livestock & etc.; children:
Matilda Gooch, Meriller Barnes & David Gooch; oldest dau. Matilda Gooch, negro girl Fann; second dau. Meriller Barnes, negro
girl Edy and all her husband Jeremiah Barnes, has in his possession; son David Gooch, negro boy Jacob; son-in-law Jeremiah
Barnes, rifle gun.   Exrs. friends: Sherwood Green and Wm. S.
Webb.   29 Sept. 1817.   Test: N. Gooch, W.S. Webb & Jeremiah
Barnes.   Probated Oct. session 1817.

P. 343.   JOHN C. CRENSHAW, dec'd.   Settlement.   Oct. session

1817. Oliver Crenshaw indebted to the estate of his dec'd. brother John C. Crenshaw. 30 Sept. 1817. Commrs: C. McDaniel and Joseph Crockett.

JOHN SAMPLE. dec'd. Inventory. Oct. session 1817. Receipt on the following: Joshua Farrington, Harison Boyd, Daniel Dean, Philip Maury, A.M. Degraffenreid, Chas. Cavender, Wyatt Cheatham's discharge $40.00 & $60.00, Silas Stephens account against quarter master $1.25, N.B. Rose order on quartermaster $36.62½. Robt. & Wm. Sample, John Buchannon, Wm. Logan, Wm. Smith, Thos. Hulme, Robt. B. Curry, Thomas Wilson, M.C. Bond, Peggy Sample, Gilbert Washington, Daniel Montgomery, John M. Clay, James Duncan, Armistead Boyd, Wm. Farrer, Charles Kavenaugh, Beverly Ridley, Robt. Smith, John Buchannon, Edw. Breather, John K. Campbell, Andrew Campbell, N.P. Hardeman, B. Gholson, Jas. Knight, John Mallory, James Meadow, Robt. McDaniel, M.B. Murfree, N. Perkins Sr., Joseph Stevens, N. Scales, Tho. Staggs, Turner Saunders, H.D. Thompson, John C. Wormby, Thos. Hiter, Peter Estes, C. Martin, M.O. Hiter, Wiley & Jas. Smith, Iaasa Hughes, Wm. Hulme, Wm. Montgomery, John Rice, Jesse Evans, Wm. Carr, Lavallin Phipps, James Sample Sr., Thos. Bradley, John Montgomery, Charles Burton, Andrew Campbell, J. & F. Woods, Stephen Cambel, Eli Harris, Alex McCowen, Robt. Sample Jr., Joel Stevens, Edw. Bevell, Hugh F. Bell, Robt. Davis, Wm. Eastin, D. Hammons, Kemp Holland, Thos. Jenkins, Robt. McLemore, Kineth Morrison, D. Mason, N.T. Perkins, James Sample, John Smith, Wm. Sample, G.W. Roper, Peter Randolph, Wm. Wilson, Jas. Hungarford, Hamilton & Clingan, F. Maury, C. Pyall, John Farren, Thos. Resse; cash received of Morris L. Bond; 75 shares Nashville Bank stock; Cash by Thompson, Crockett & Bell; the following negroes: negro man Squier about 35 yrs.; woman Polly 27 yrs.; girl Sally 12 yrs.; boy Dick 10 yrs.; girl Lucky 8 yrs.; boy Nead 7 yrs.; girl Caroline 5 yrs.; girl Abey 4 yrs.; boy Isaac 2½ yrs.; girl Fany 1 yr.

P. 345.   BURWELL THORNTON, dec'd. Settlement. Oct. session
          1817. Edw. Swanson, Admr. Expenses paid to: Doct.
Sappington, Benj. Carson. Commrs: Isham R. Trotter & Allen Hill.

THOMAS GOFF, dec'd. Inventory. Oct. session 1817.
9 Oct. 1817. Livestock, furniture, household items, & etc.
James McEwen, Jr., Admr.

SAMUEL SMITH, dec'd. Account of Sales. Oct. session
1817, sold 31 July 1817. Those buying: Berry Nolen, David D.
Page, Hugh Pinkston, John R. Bittick, John Holt, David Keigler,
Wm. Stevens, Th. McMullin, Owen T. Watkins, Peter Smith, Stephen
Nolen, Henry Cook, Arthur Pierce, Wm. Orr, John Woods, Leonard
Woods, John Beard(?), M. Stanfield, John Smith, Val. Shadwell,
Geo. Oldham, Peter Pinkston, John Stacy, John McDaniel, Ruffin
Brown, Lewis Stevens, Augustin Denton, Daniel Vaughn.

P. 347.   ELIJAH HUNTER, dec'd. Account of Sales. Oct. session
          1817. Those buying: Oran Moffitt, Catherine Hunter,
Hendley Stone, John D. Bennett, Samuel Benton, John Wilkins,
Garland Cosby, John Gardner, Wm. Philips, Wilkins Whitfield,
Frances Carter, John K. Campbell, Geo. Bennett, Henry Hunter,
James Brown, Andrew Hunter, Wm. Bright, Caleb Mandley, Meredith
Hulme, Wm. T. Northern, David Robertson, Wilkins Harper, Thomas
Ward.

P. 348.   SAMUEL MCCUTCHEN. dec'd. Division. Oct. session 1817.
          Division between the legatees after the dower of the
widow, it being 610 acres; lot #1 Robt. McCutche, lot #2 James

McCutchen, lot #3 Mary McCutchen, lot #4 John McCutchen, lot #5
Patrick McCutchen, lot #6 Wm. McCutchen, lot #7 Samuel B. Mc-
Cutchen, lot #8 Washington C. McCutchen, all receiving 76½ acres.
Commr.: Timothy Shaw, John Motheral, James Hardgrave and Samuel
Edmiston.

P. 350.   JOSEPH HALL, dec'd. Settlement. Oct. session 1817.
           Robt. McLemore and Sion Hunt, Admrs. Cash for a dis-
charge of 3 mo. 6 days of Hall's service; expenses: traveling
to head of Mill Creek and selling property; cash paid to Robt.
McLemore. Commrs.: Joshua Farrington, Joseph Motheral and
Timothy Shaw.

P. 351.   JAMES BERRY, dec'd. Division of Real Estate. July
           session 1817. Commrs: John Bostick, Nicholas Scales,
Joseph H. Scales, Edward McNail & Alexander Johnson. Division
of the land that James Berry lived on before his death; heirs:
widow Rebecca Berry, having had her dower previously laid off;
beginning for the resurvey of the whole residence of the tract
at a walnut, on which Richard Rudder, who purchased of Basil
Berry corners and running South with Rudders line ------ in the
West boundary of the original survey which was deeded by Thos.
Berry to his 3 sons Wm., James, Basil Berry ------ to a stake in
the Harpeth River ------ the Northwest corner of the widows
dower ----- containing 258½ acres; to be divided into five
parcels for the following legatees: Mary Wall, William Berry,
Robert Berry, James Berry and Thos. Berry; lot #1 Thomas Berry,
51 acres; lot #2 James Berry, 47 acres; lot #3 Robert Berry,
47 acres; lot #4 Wm. Berry, 60 acres; lot #5 Mary Wall 51 acres.

P. 352.   James McEwen, guardian, Oct. session 1817. James
           McEwen, Sr., guardian of the heirs of PETER POTTS,
dec'd. 61 1/3 acres land lying on the main road from Franklin
to Nashville, it being 2/3 of 92 acres of land that said Potts
owned; about 12 or 13 acres under cultivation; 1 negro woman
Jude (middle aged), 1 negro girl Dilsey about 9 or 10; 1 negro
girl Phillis about 7 yrs., 1 boy Isam about 4 yrs., 1 negro boy
Manson about 18 mo.; cash.

P. 353.   SAMUEL SMITH, dec'd. Inventory. July 1817. Received
           of Bernard M. Patterson; note on: Thos. Jinkins,
Wm. Price, John Matthews, Riley Murry, David Gooch; received of
Samuel Cummins; furniture, livestock, books, household items
and etc. Berry Nolen, Admr.

           GEORGE NEELLY, JR., dec'd. Settlement. Oct. session
1817. Credits: Received of Capt. Donelson, U.S. paymaster, T.
Turnage, Murry Alston & Wm. Gillespie (insolvent), John Hulme &
Ebenezer McKinnes (insolvent); expenses: Paid to: Hugh Henderson,
Eli McGan, R.P. Currin on Judgement of F.M. Dean, Loves paid S.
Cox, judgment of Geo. Neelly, Sr., Wm. McGileries. John H.
Eaton, Admr.

P. 354.   RICHARD CARTER, dec'd. Settlement. Oct. session 1817.
           Commrs: Eleazer Hardeman and Nicholas Scales. Credits:
James Carothers and Wm. L. Webb account; Nicholas Perkins for
direct tax; Sally Carter proven account. Sally Carter, Admrx.

           NATHANIEL TRULL, dec'd. Inventory. Oct. session 1817.
Few head livestock, household items and etc. Penelope Trull,
Admr.

           ALEXANDER REID, dec'd. Supplementary Inventory. April

1817. 1 loom. Spencer Buford, Admr.

P. 355. SOLOMON HUMPHRIES, dec'd. Account of Sales. (?)
         session 1817. Estate of Doctor Solomon Humphries.
Sold to the following: David Humphries, David Orton, John Hurley,
Thos. Gooch, D. Humphries, T.T. Young, J. Lauderdale, Samuel
Morton, Jr., Wm. Kidd, Ansalem Burnes. Daniel Humphries, Admr.

         FREDERICK BROWDER, dec'd. Additional inventory of
Sales. April 1816. Those buying: James Gault, John Johnson,
John Coffee, Nathaniel Lunn, Nathaniel Warren, Archer Jordan,
Samuel Perkins, Alexander Raulston, James Wilson, Richard
Ogilvie.

         ALEXANDER MCCLARAN, dec'd. Inventory. Jan. session
1817. 7 negroes, livestock, farm tools, household items, furniture, cash, bond for 100 acres land executed by Samuel Long to
David Orton and from Orton conveyed to James Walker and from
Walker assigned to said dec'd. Thos. McClaran, Exr.

P. 356. MATTHIAS MURFREE. Settlement. Jan. session 1817.
         Martha A.C. Murfree in account with Matthias B. Mur-
free, guardian. December: Paid to McPhail, R.P. Currin, Doct.
Wilson, Hilliards acct., Jas. Banks acct, James Terrell; expen-
ses of going to Stewart Co., taxes in Wmson. Co., Overton Co.,
Rutherford Co., Montgomery Co.; expenses for clothing and etc.
Credits: hire of negroes and some accounts paid.

P. 357. Thomas T. Maury, Admr. Supplement. Jan. session
         1817. In account with the heirs of JANE WHEATON.
J. Buffs note due 1809; E. Marshall & Wm. Lintz note; E. Talbot
note; G. Poysers note; J. Wards note; J. Metcalfs note; Wm. & J.
Knights note; Cook & Ewing note; T. Rushes note; Doct. F. Robert-
sons note; J. Perry's note; cash received of Wm. Pitman; hire of
Harriet for present year; Harris, Jackson, & Erwins note for
rent of lot #15 in Nashville; White & Williams note for rent of
#175 in Nashville, for hire of Hagar & children; Hobbs & Hart-
leys note for hire of Ovid; T. Talbots note for hire of Lucy;
O.B. Hays note; E. Marshall & Wm. Lintz note; J. Wards note;
J. Metcalfs note; Wm. Bell for hire of Polly & children. Expenses: to Doct. F. Robertson; tax in Franklin & Nashville; misc.
expenses.

P. 358. ZADOCK RIGGS, dec'd. Account of Sales. Jan. session
         1817. Nancy Riggs hired 2 negroes; Wm. Jackson hired
1 negro; James Wortham hired 1 negro; Gideon Riggs hired 1 negro.
Richard Ogilvie & Nancy Riggs, Admrs.

         BENJAMIN HUMPHREIS, dec'd. April 1816. 21 Feb. 1816.
Received of Joseph Culbertson for cotton, of Samuel Laurence for
1 mare. D. J. Humphries, Exr.

P. 359. Hendley Stone, Receipt. July session 1817. We, Peter
         Pryor and Green Pryor, have received all the negroes
belonging to us, and in the possession of Hendley Stone, agreeable to a division made 15th day Jan. 1799 between us and our
mother. And on 11 June 1817 we received our part of negroes in
full of our mother's share, being 1/3 part, that is 3 negroes,
Stepney, Nance & Jacob, the balance of our mother's part of
negroes: Pat, Jane, Henry, Fanney, Easter, Manuel, Simon & Sally
and their increase to be divided between our 2 sisters: Agnes P.
Jenkins and Mary W. Stone and our 2 brothers: Alfred Stone and
Nicholas P. Stone. Our sister Agnes P. Jenkins is to have

Easter & Simon for her part. 11 June 1817. Test: Wm. Orr and
Wyatt Haley.

JOHN DUNHAM, dec'd. Will. Jan. session 1818. Wife
Polly Dunham and son Wm. Dunham. Exrs. to sell my lands on West
Harpeth and use money to purchase another tract of land for the
benefit of all my children (to wit) William Dunham, Betsey Dunham, Susan Dunham, Jinny M. Dunham, Deborah Dunham, Polly Dunham,
Anna Dunham, John Dunham, Henry M. Dunham, Richard Leonard Dunham and Joseph Waller Dunham; to be divided when youngest child
comes of age; my negro man Beck to be sold; to my wife Polly
Dunham, the following negroes: Nance, Edmund, and Sarah during
her widowhood. 28 Sept. 1817. Test: Wm. Harrison, James Hughes,
Mary Edney and John Witherspoon. Probated Jan. session 1818.

P. 360.   THOMAS GOOCH, dec'd. Inventory. Jan. session 1818.
2 negro men Patrick & Jacob, 3 negro women Sarah,
Fanny, & Eadey, 1 negro girl Cherry; all divised or willed away;
livestock, furniture, household items, farm tools, parcel of
medicine, cotton in Giles County; note on Stump & Cox; note on
James Gooch (doubtful), note on Jeremiah Burnes, note on John
Jemmerson; money received of Nathaniel Gooch, Admr. of Thos.
Gooch, dec'd. of North Caroliner. S. Green, Exr.

P. 361.   THOMAS GOOCH, dec'd. Account of Sales. Jan. session
1818. Those buying: David Bell, Ansolum Barnes, John
Blackman, Thos. Bibb, Stephen Nolen, Geo. Kidd, Jeremiah Barnes,
G. Hunt, Daniel Humphries, E. Ouin, J. Hill, James Owen, John L.
Fielder, Rodon Tucker, Nathan Gooch, Elizabeth Gooch, David
Gooch, Matilda Gooch, James Jemmerson, E.B. Morton, T. Owens,
J. Roy, Wm. Fields. S. Green, Exr.

P. 362.   REBECCA PARHAM, dec'd. Will. Jan. session 1818.
Son Wm. Parham; son George Parham, negro man Toon;
grand-daughters Frances Hadley, saddle & trunk, Susan Hadley,
bed and furniture; four granddaughters: Mary Butts, Frances
Walker, Susan Jones, and Nancy Heath, money due by bond on Fendal
Crump. Exr. son William Parham. Wit: Thomas Parham, Sarah Parham & Geo. Parham. Probated Jan. session 1818.

WILLIS CARSON, dec'd. Inventory. Jan. session 1818.
Livestock, furniture and etc.; notes taken for his property
after his decease in New Orleans for services due him for serving a tour of duty in Gen'l. Coffee's brigade of mounted gunmen
from 28 Sept. until 23 Feb. 1815. June 30, 1815.

P. 365.   JAMES TOMLINSON, dec'd. Inventory. Jan. session
1818. Furniture and household items, notes and etc.

THOMAS GOFF, dec'd. Account of Sales. Jan. session
1818. Those buying: Peggy Goff, Holland White, Simeon Bateman,
John Douglas, James Brooks, Wm. Goff, Price W. Brooks, James
McEwen, Jr., Benjamin White, Wm. Bright, James McEwen, Sr.,
Ephraim McEwen, John R. Bittick, Michael Long, Dickson Vaughn,
John McDaniel, James Moore, Wm. Hope. James McEwen, Jr., Admr.

P. 364.   David D. Page, Receipt. Jan. session 1817. Received
Nov. 6, 1816 of Samuel Wilson account in full which
was coming from Wilson as guardian for me, David D. Page.
Wit: Elisha Davis and Jason Wilson.

JOHN EATON, dec'd. Division of land. Jan. session
1817. Commrs: David Shannon, Frederick Davis and Elisha Davis

have laid off 500 acres for Elizabeth Eaton. Lot #1 A. Henderson, 660 acres; lot #2 J.H. Eaton, 510 acres; lot #3 E. Breathitt, 640 acres.

P. 365.   CHARLES BROWN, dec'd.   Additional Sale.   Jan. session
           1818.   Property sold by Jesse Cox.   Nov. 1, 1817.   2
coves to the widow; Michael Brown, 1 negro man Jack; Thomas
Reynolds, 1 negro man Ned.   James G. Jones and Caleb Manley,
securities.   Jesse Cox and Michael Brown, Admr.

           ISAAC CROW, dec'd.   Settlement.   Jan. session 1818.
Taxes for Wmson. Co.; for copy of deed from Thos. Spratt to
Esaac Crow; H. Crabb for services in suit of said heirs against
J. Blythe; Spratt & Sam'l. Gordon; for court order to divide
estate; for Jas. Herron witness for heirs in suit; for N. Perkins fee in suit for services; for H. Crabb fee in suit for
services; tax in Rutherford Co.; credits for rent of town lots
in Wmson. Co.   James T. Sandford, guardian.

P. 366.   James T. Sandford, guardian.   Settlement.   Thomas Crow
           heir and minor of ISAAC CROW.   Jan. 1818.   To Joanna
Crow for boarding, clothing and schooling; credit for hire of
negro Flora.

           Bryant Crow heir and minor of ISAAC CROW, dec'd. in
account with James T. Sandford, his guardian; to Joanna Crow for
clothing, boarding, and expenses; hire of negro girl Hetty.

           Isaac Crow, heir and minor of ISAAC CROW, dec'd. paid
to Joanna Crow for expenses, boarding and clothing; by hire of
negro man Leven.

           WILLIAM HULME, dec'd.   Settlement.   Jan. session 1818.
John Witherspoon, Admr.   Expenses: paid to J. Witherspoon, Jam.
Trembler, J. Whiteside, A. Patterson, & Wm. Eastin.   Credits:
Received of H. Cook, Kemp Holland, for wolfs scalfs; James Hicks.

P. 367.   WILLIAM HULME, dec'd.   Settlement with Admr.   Jan.
           session 1818.   C. Manley, Lawyer Mack, John Witherspoon, tax in 1816, James G. Jones, W. Smith, Charles McAlister,
A. Gray, John B. Carter; Credits: received of: E. Brown, Hemp
Hill, W. McEwen's estate, Kemp Holland, John Carothers, W. Willet,
W. Smith for hire of Celia, cash for sales of Celia, Maria & Ned,
C. Kavenaugh, Robt. Hulme, John P. Broadnax, John J. Henry, Anne
Henderson, James G. Jones, Jas. Knight, B. Reese for rent of lots
in 1817 and 1818.   Henry Cook and John Witherspoon, Admrs.

P. 368.   JOHN RADFORD, dec'd.   Settlement.   Jan. session 1818.
           Commr: Wm. Wilson, Geo. Kinnard & Eleazar Hardeman.
Samuel Shelburn, Admr.   Credits: money received from paymaster
and Robt. Sammons; received from sales at Orleans.

           WILLIAM WERTHINGTON, dec'd.   Settlement.   Jan. 1818.
Wm. Sparkman, Admr.   Paid to: Noal Walker, Burkew & Bradley,
Doctor Geo. Bennett, Abraham Werthington, Andrew Roundtree, Wm.
Simpson, Alexander Thompson, Noah Walker.

P. 364.   SAMUEL HUSTON, dec'd.   Settlement.   Jan. session 1818.
           The heirs in account with H. Petway, their guardian
cash paid Lydia Huston her proportion of the estate; cash paid
to John Stubbs & his wife, Margaret's share of estate.   Credits:
by hire of Alyce to John McKenney.

ELISHA M. HASSELL. dec'd. Settlement. Jan. session
1818. Allen Hill, Admr. Paid to John Miller & Wm. W. ___?___ .
2 Jan. 1818. Commr: Isham R. Trotter & Tristram Patton.

Sally Crisman, widow allotment. Jan. session 1818.
Sally Crisman widow of ARON CRISMAN. Commr: John Ogilvie, J.
Hubbard and Samuel Brown.

P. 370. THOMAS COORE, dec'd. Account of Sale and hire of
negroes. Jan. session 1817. Those buying: Milly
Coor, negroes Nat & Nan; Isaac Bizzel, negroes Ab; Jones Glover,
negroes Ann & child; Thos. Rags negro Ally; Wm. Redford negro
Little Nat; Geo. Burnett negro Jerry, John Oliver, Benj. Blythe,
John Blythe, Elisha North, Wm. Brown, Joseph Blythe, Allin
Harrison, John Fuller, John Gibson, Patrick Gibson, Isaac Biz-
zell, Wm. Giles, Arch Goodman, Robt. Clark, Blythe Spratt.

THOMAS TAYLOR, dec'd. Settlement. Jan. session 1818.
3 Jan. 1818. Commr: George Barnes & G. Hunt, Esqrs. Wm. Kidd,
Admr.

JAMES MCKINNEY, dec'd. Settlement. Jan. session 1818.
Mary McKinney and Jonathan Stepleton, Admrs. Paid account:
Stephen Smith, Lewis Demoss, Thos. L. Robertson, Henry McWave,
Swanson Johnson. Commr: Hendley Stone, Wm. Bond, Sr., and John
Witherspoon.

P. 371. NATHAN TRULL, dec'd. Account of Sales. April ses-
sion 1817. Sold 15 Jan. 1817. Those buying: Mrs.
Trull, Thomas Gillespie, Ambrose Hill (shoemakers tools), Wm.
Weatherley, Christopher Irvin.

Peggy Goff, widow of THOMAS GOFF, dec'd. Allotment.
Jan. session 1818.

Henry Rutherford, Admr. & Guardian. Settlement.
Jan. session 1818. The estate of JOHN CRAWFORD, dec'd. Expen-
ses: Robt. Weakley & L. Crawford's note, David Jone, Currin &
Mason, Petway & Maury, Wm. Lytle by note, John S. Campbell,
Thomas G. Bradford, Peter Pinkston, Bradley & James, Richard
Orton, Wm. Edger, Jas. & Washington Jackson, Edw. Criddle, John
T. Pickering, Robert Johnston, Robert Carothers, Puleskie Com-
missioners, Thos. W. Stockett, Henry Bickerstaff, Robt. German,
Cornelius McPherson, John Swinny, Doctor John Newman, Jas.
Stewart by note, Thos. Reid, John K. Campbell. Samuel Wilson,
Campbell Martin, Terry Bradley, Mrs. Carothers, John Carothers,
Caleb Manley, Samuel Nesbit, James Latemore, James Gordon,
Joseph Thompson, John Sample, Alexander Campbell, Benjamin Pri-
get, Richard Law, John C. McLemore, Wm. G. Blunt fees for 21
grants; tax for 1812 & 1813; Survey fee to John Davis; expense
for land near Columbia; John C. McLemore for copy of 20 entries;
Jas. Rutherford for his services for attending to the factory.
Credits: judgment against Thos. Connelly; cash from paymaster
for said Crawfords services in the United States in 1812; cash
for certificate bought of John Campbell; cash from Zachus German for note; cash for his allowance as a witness in the suit
Sappington vs. White; cash from Robt. Weakley for partnership
in land near Columbia.

P. 373. Henry Rutherford, guardian. Jan. session 1818. To
the heirs of JOHN CRAWFORD, dec'd. Hire of negroes
for the years 1814, 1815 and 1816; rent of land for 1816.
Expenses: Tax for 1814, 1815, and 1816. Commrs: Robert Johnson

Alexander Smith.

SAMUEL ROGERS, dec'd. Division. Robert Rogers, 30 acres of land on Big Harpeth, a negro woman Scillar and girl Susan; Archeleus Hughes, Jr., balance of tract of land containing 107 acres. 1st Feb. 1816.

KINCHEN P. BASS, dec'd. Inventory. April session 1818. 4 Dec. 1817. Furniture, shot gun, silver watch, and etc. Accounts: Elisha Roades, Estate of Wm. Hulme, William Banks, Estate of John Dunham, Thos. Turnage, Taswell Burge, Nathaniel Osburn, James Hicks, James Short, Toberton Alexander, Wm. Holland, Archibald Potter, James Kelly(?) or Nelly(?), Philip Maury, Jeremiah Capps, Peter Estes, Isham House, V.B. Holmes, Charles Tomlin, Abram Washington, Abel Olive, Joshua Roberts, Sol. Watts & Col. Johnson, Spencer Paitman, John McAbe, Wm. Peebles, Allen Scruggs, Col. Thos. McCrory; Notes: Samuel Andrews, Isaac Oakes, Chas. Tomlin, Raisen L. Bishop, John Baker, James Crawford, Moses & Wm. Moore, Whitehead & Lester, Edw. E. Russell, John R. Tankersly, Ephraim Foster, David Orton; 1 receipt on James Coreathers for 2 executions on John Austin & Daniel Wilson, 2 discharges on Taylor & Prichett; 1 discharge D. Skeleton, dec'd.; 1 receipt on Wm. Bond; 1 note on Elisha Roades.

P. 375. JOHN GHOLSON, dec'd. Additional Inventory. April session 1818. Received money from Robt. White and others. Benj. Gholson, Admr.

JACOB ROLAND, dec'd. Settlement. April session 1818. Paid to: John Sample, Petway & Maury, Samuel Cox, Joel T. Rivers, Amos Bulock, Nicholas T. Perkins, Berryman Harper, James Terrill, Burwell McLemore, Doct. Samuel Crockett, Robt. Depart, Mary Roland. Received of: McKinney, Boyles & Porter, Elliott Hockman, John Sweeney, Geo. Galaspie, Woodson Hubbard, Elisha North. James C. O. Riley, Thomas Old, Bradley & Berkley, Peter Minten, Abraham Roland; taxes for 1813, 1814, 1815, 1816, and 1817; Wm. T. Roland, John Roland. Commrs: H. Petway, H. Cook and John Watson. Polly Roland, Admr.

P. 376. JOHN C. HULME. dec'd. Inventory. April session 1818. Clothing, accounts of school against: Wm. Moor, Joshua Doyl, Mrs. Walton, Josiah S. Walton, Henry Stuart, George Prewit, Hannah Tarkington, Thomas Cooper, Demsey Nash, Thomas Berry, Henry Gray, Polly Edney, Rebecca McLaughlin, Daniel German, James Cox, Wm. Betts, John Porter. S. Hunt, Admr.

CHARLES KAVANAUGH, dec'd. Inventory. April session 1818. Horse, saddle, furniture, household items & cash. A. Meband & Wm. Kavanaugh, Admrs.

P. 377. SAMUEL CLARK, dec'd. Division of Negroes. April session 1818. To Russworm in right of his wife, dau. of the said dec'd. Molly $600.00, Jerry $225.00, Wate $450.00, Harritt $250.00, Ben $175.00. Commrs: Nathan Stancile, S. Green, Wm. (Atkinson?).

REBECAH PARHAM, dec'd. Inventory. April session 1818. Widow of Thomas Parham, by Wm. Parham, Exr. to the last will of Rebecah at April term of court 1818; 1 negro man Tom; mare & saddle in state of Georgia; 1 note on Fendal Crump.

THOMAS WILSON, dec'd. Inventory. April session 1818. 8 negroes, livestock. Wm. Wilson, Admr.

JONATHAN BATEMAN, dec'd. Inventory. April session
1818. 13 April 1818. Livestock, furniture, farm tools & etc.
Polly Bateman, Admr.

KEZIAH MCCONNICO, dec'd. Inventory. April session
1818. Furniture & etc. by Garner McConnico. (botton of page
is so worn that it cannot be read).

P. 378. STEPHEN BARFIELD, dec'd. Will. April session 1818.
Son Lewis Barfield, $1 in addition to what I have
already given him; son John Barfield $1 in addition to what I
have already given him; son Blake Barfield $200 in addition to
what I have already given him; wife Nancy Barfield, tract of land
where I now live during her widowhood; son Willie Blount Barfield
where I now live consisting of 2 tracts of land of 125 acres
conveyed to me by John Blackman and the other tract of 6½ acres
conveyed to me by Wm. & Betsey Spencer to become his property
at the death of my wife and $200 to help with his education;
to my 4 daughters: Tabitha House Barfield, Penelope House Barfield, Harriot Barfield, & Polly (Sam?) Barfield, my 12 negroes
and balance of my estate. Exr: Majr. James McEwen and Lewis
Barfield. 3rd Nov. 1817. Wit: Ephraim McEwen, James McEwen &
S. Hunt. Probated April session 1818.

P. 378. HARRISON BOYD, dec'd. Will. April session 1818.
Wife Rhoda Boyd, the land where I now live; 1 negro
woman, Celia Hannah and her boys, Hampton & Dicey; wife Rhoda
Boyd, Exr. 24 Feb. 1818. Wit: H. Petway, Wm. Ewin, Page Bond,
H. Boyd. Probated April session 1818.

HENRY INGRAM, dec'd. Will. April session 1818.
Being sick and my affliction may prove mortal; brother Benjamin
Ingram, my tract of land in Brunswick, Virginia on Wagar Creek
containing 330 acres; he is also to collect my debts; at the
death of my wife, I give to my brother and his heirs the following negroes: John, Lillah, & Sinah; to my wife Susan, tract of
land where I now live containing 130 acres. 4 Aug. 1814. Wit:
Josiah Walton, Geo.(?) & Turner Saunders. Probated April session
1818.

P. 379. Patience Fields, widow of BENNETT FIELDS, dec'd.
April session 1818. For widow & children, 17 Jan.
1818. Commrs: Tristram Patton, Charles Madon & Isaac Farguson.

P. 380. Nancy Tolinson, widow of JAMES TOMLINSON. dec'd.
Allotment, April session 1818. Commr: R. Russell, Jas.
Thompson & Wm. White.

JOHN DUNHAM, dec'd. Inventory. April session 1818.
April 4, 1818. 4 negroes, livestock, furniture, farm tools and
etc. Wm. Dunham, Admr.

BENNETT FIELDS, dec'd. Inventory. April session 1818.
Furniture, farm tools, livestock and etc.

P. 381. WILLIAM PARKS, dec'd. Settlement. April session
1818. Money for his services in the army $28.06½;
Thompson note; money paid to Henry Cook; money paid on Watson's
voucher. James B. Thompson, Admr. Commr: Sion Hunt & P. Russell.

JAMES RODGERS, dec'd. Settlement. April session
1818. Bond, Archilus Hughes to Jas. Rodgers; money for his
services in the United States service for 1 mo. & 24 days; to

To cash received of John Dalton, amount of cash found in the possession of James Rodgers at his death; by amount paid Wm. Wilson; by amount paid A.M. Rodgers. 10 Jan. 1818. Robert Rodgers, Admr. Commrs: Nicholas Scales & Samuel Perkins.

P. 382. JARED MCCONNICO, dec'd. Settlement. April 1818.
         In account with: Garner McConnico-Robt. McMillen, Robert McLemore, Dr. John Sappington, schooling for Sally Carlisle, Daniel Craig, Peters Pinkston, Wm. Miller, for tax 1815, Jarred Carrel (building stable), R.P. Currin, Issac N. Henry, A. Campbell, Thomas L. Robinson, Wm. Henry, James Demoss, Lewis Demoss, Benj. White. Credits: land sold. Garner McConnico, Exr.

P. 384. JAMES SAMPLE, dec'd. Settlement. April session 1818.
         Paid: Wm. Donelson, Richard Smith, Archbald Potter, Gilbert Marshall, Gideon Blackburn, McGuire, Dr. Neaman, John White (Atty.), Burrus & Mathenys note (insolvent). Peter Pinkston, Michael Long, John Buchanan, James McCombs, Daniel Crenshaw (hauling corn), Gray & Dickinson, taxes for 1816, John Sample. James Sample, Admr. Commrs: H. Patway, Archibald Lytle, & G. McConnico.

P. 384. HEZEKIAH PURYEAR, dec'd. Settlement. April session
         1818. Paid to: Duncan Brown, Preacher, Thomas Baker, John Watson, Gideon Blackburn, Mordeca & John Tabb, Elijah Hambleton, Caleb Manley, Mrs. Coleman, James Davies, Doctor Gray, Lazarus Andrews, tax for Maury Co., Beverly Reese, Fendal Crump, John White, Sterling Davis, David Bowers, Joel Parrish. H. Puryear, Garner Gill, Bradford (printer), Mrs. Puryear (cash). Leonard Dunivant, Petway Hantsell, Wm. Fitzgerald, North & Watson (schooling), taxes for 1816, Frederick Mitchel (overseer 1817), Gray & Dickeson, Thomas Old, John Hambleton, Sanders & Organ, Currin & Mason, Turner Sanders, James Terrell, Hartwell Hobbs, Tristram Patton, Thomas Hardeman; Dabney Wade account insolvent; James Pugh account, no good; James T. Sanford account, he swore was unjust, James Logue. Credits: Cash of: John Hart, bond on Spencer Buford, Robt. Nichols, Wm. Alexr. Glass; bond on Geo. Howser; 1 discharge of Leonard Dunevant as first sargent for 6 mo.; bond on Robert Nichols; 1 discharge on Alexr. Glass atty. for Robt. Glass as Sargt.; also discharge from Alex Glass as Lieutenant; sold hogs to Ben Trotter; cash of Nicholas Perkins and Doctor Gray (butter & flour); account on Robt. Campbell; Sterling Davies (cotton); F. Mitchel (pork); Joel Parrish account. John Watson, Admr. Commrs: G. Hulme, H. Petway, Alexr. Clark and Edw. Swanson.

P. 387. NICHOLAS P. HARDEMAN, dec'd. Will. July 1818. To:
         Daniel Goodman & Joseph Royal a tract of land in Maury Co. on Globe Creek; Exr. to sell southwestern section of land in Maury Co. on Globe Creek; Thomas J. Hardeman to locate, for the use of my heirs, a warrent which I have for 274 acres & received ¼ part for his services; son William, money to complete his education; sons Thomas Hardeman & William Hardeman & son-in-law, Thomas H. Perkins, Exrs. 22 May 1818. Wit: John Hardeman, Chas. McAlister & D. Squier. Probated July session 1818.

P. 388. JANE GARDNER, dec'd. Will. July 1818. Brother
         William Gardner; niece Ann Berry, bed & furniture; niece Jane Berry, Sally Berry, nephews Robert Berry, William Berry, niece Ann Berry, lands on Arrington Creek belonging to me as an heir of my brother Ritchey Gardner, dec'd. Exr.: Robert McClellan & Robert Sharp. Probated July session 1818.

P. 389.   JOHN LITTLETON, dec'd. Will. July 1818. 5 May 1818.
          Being very sick & weak in body; wife Ellinor Littleton;
daughter Mary Littleton; rest of my children, 1 shilling (no
names). Test: James Armstrong & Geo. Glascock. Probated July
session 1818.

          RICHARD SAMPSON, dec'd. Will. July session 1818.
My family to live together & have the use of the dwelling house
and other houses, lot & orchard, & rent out rest of plantation.
My children (no names given) be bound to some proper persons to
teach them a useful trade; my exr. to sell my property & divide
it among my children when they are married or of age. Exr.
John Hail & Polly Sampson. 23 day May 1818. Test: Samuel
Willson, Wm. Alexander & Thos. L. White. Probated July session
1818.

P. 390.   JOHN DYER, dec'd. Inventory. July session 1818.
          Negroes: woman Sina about 40 yrs.; man Gilbert about
38 yrs.; woman Peggy about 34 yrs.; girl Milly about 14 yrs.;
boy Grey about 12 yrs.; boy Anthony about 10 yrs.; girl Phillis
about 8 yrs.; boy Ben about 8 yrs.; girl Betty about 4 or 5 yrs.;
boy Gabriel about 3 or 4 yrs.; boy Jim about 2 yrs.; livestock,
furnture, household items. Lavina Dyer, Admrx.

P. 391.   BENNETT FIELD, dec'd. Inventory. July session 1818.
          July 9, 1818. Receided of Wm. Fields as Admr. to
Bennett Fields, dec'd. by Patience Fields & Tristram Patton now
Admrs. Notes: Cloud McCollum, Stephen Sharrock, John Hood,
Elizabeth Cruse, Carey Pope, Donaldson Potter, Burwell Akin,
Green Duke, Fieldon Fields, Daniel Carter, Patience Fields, Wm.
Fields.

          HARRISON BOYD, dec'd. Inventory. July session 1818.
Names of persons paying: Wm. Eoff, Geo. Parker, Isaac Turman,
Elijah Lincoln, Phillip McMemor, Wm. G. Boid, Joel T. Rivers,
Robt. Clark, Absolam Holt, Mark Thomas, James Smith, Sam. Meri-
field, Wm. Hess, Frances Dean, Wm. Hungerford, Wigton King, D.
Caldwell, Robt. Sammons, Ja. Lewis, H.L. Hennel, L. Curry, Henry
Coleman, L. Marsh, John Crecy, S. Ingland, E. Ellam, Ballard
Caldwell, Sam Gardner, J. Neeley, John Dixon, H.G. Kearney,
John Hanks; notes in the hands of officers; officers names and
Drawers names: Joel T. Rivers, James Cox; Joel T. Rivers, Robt.
Todd & Jas. Reese; H. Pernal, Jas. Reese; D. Caldwell, John
McCullock; furniture & household items; negro women: Scily,
Hannah, Dycy & Hampton.

P. 392.   JANE GARRETT, dec'd. Inventory. July session 1818.
          9 July 1818. Negro woman Hannah, negro girl Ritter,
livestock, furniture, household items. Vinson Greer, Admr.

          AMOSA HAWKINS, dec'd. Inventory. July session 1818.
Livestock, furniture, household items; account on John Grayham;
note on Samuel B. Hammons; order on Wm. Grayham. Mary Hawkins,
Admrx.

P. 393.   TYRE WYMPEE, dec'd. Inventory. July session 1818.
          Very little inventory. Mary Wimper, Admrx.

          STEPHEN BARFIELD, dec'd. Inventory. July session
1818. 13 negroes: David, Peter, Daniel, Dennis, Curtis, Patrick,
Larkin, Pleasant, Clary, Mary, Lucy, Phillis & Mariah; livestock,
furniture, farm tools; execution on Henry Marlin (desperate);
notes on: John Godd, dec'd. (desperate); Wm. L. Corder,

(desperate); accounts in favor of firm of Barfield & Stramler desperate-over 3 years old: Frances Parker, Nat Goodrich, Wm. Stephens, John Ray, John Patterson, David Campbell, John Carden, Aron Willson, James Hill, Wm. Willet, John Fletcher, Nathan Garner, Thos. Sappington, John Carder, Hardeman Stone, Benj. Dean, Thos. Willice, Isaac Crow, Richard Davies, Sherrod Dean, Isaac Long, Frederick Simpson, James Little, James Leach, Sterlin Davis, Wm. Helm, Wm. Stevens Sr., John Cohoon, Ewill Ship, Wm. Fillerton, Phillip Maury, James Harrett, Geo. Davidson, Jesse Foster, Wm. P. Harrison, Thos. Thompson, John Pratt, Ezekiel Hughs, Wm. Roberts, Wm. Dickey, Chas. Huggins, Thos. Willea, Green Williamson, John Hill, Demo (y or s?) Nash, Wm. Grey, Hardy Bizzill, Benj. Almary, John Russell, Mary Brickle, Bryan Stone, John Whaley, Robt. Reed, Jeremiah Hay, Thos. Polite, Thos. Doyle, Wm. McGaugh, John J. Henry, James Hill, John B. Matthews, John Fletcher, Benj. Almary, Wm. Willson (schoolmaster), Chas. Stephens. James McEwen Sr. & Lewis Barfield, Exr.

P. 394.   HENRY INGRAM, dec'd. Inventory. July session 1818.
           July 18, 1818. Negroes: man John age 30 yrs.; woman Sina age 26 yrs.; woman Rachel age 24 yrs.; boy Charles age 8 yrs.; girl Edea age 6 yrs.; boy Jim age 6 yrs.; boy Dick age 3 yrs.; girl Sinth age 3 yrs.; girl Nancy age 16 mo.; girl Bets age 15 mo.; livestock, furniture, household items, & etc. Susannah Ingram, Exrx.

P. 395.   JOHN MONTGOMERY, dec'd. Sales. July session 1818, sold 23 April 1818. Those buying: Elizabeth Montgomery, Prudunce Montgomery, Patsy Montgomery, Francis Hoges, Aron Boyd, Reuben Reynolds, James Hughston, John Smith, Phillis Britton, Spence Reynolds, Zachariah Willson, I. Kennedy, Robt. Collett, Emay Field, Polly Montgomery, Cyrus Montgomery, S. Morton, John Allerson, Jas. McCraken, Wm. H. Vaden, Hudson Dawson, James Joyce, E. Cherry, John Hudson, Isaac Gillespie, Edw. Rigs, J. Cole.

P. 396.   CHARLES KAVENAUGH, dec'd. Account of Sales. July session 1818. (The names of buyers not given.) A. Mebane & Wm. Kavanaugh, Admrs.

P. 397.   JONATHAN BATEMAN, dec'd. Account of Sales. July session 1818. Those buying: Widow Bateman, Simeon Bateman, Geo H. Pruit, Beniah Bateman, Evan Bateman, Jesse Tarketon, Matthew Lee, Wm. Edmondson, Joel Rigeon, Joseph Angles, Bazzel Berry, John Gillespie, Thos. Garrett, Henry Slater, Roderick Temple, Geo. Brown, Harden Perkins, Jesse Spruit, Nosea Bateman, Wm. Shute, John Stephenson. Polly Bateman, Admrx.

P. 398.   BENNETT FIELDS, dec'd. Account of Sales. July session 1818, sold 24 Jany. 1818. Those buying: Henry Sorrow, Donelson Poetter, Fielden Fields, Patience Fields, Wm. Fields, John Hood, Solomon Patterson, Cloud McCollum, Stephen Sharrock, Burrell Akin, Daniel Carter, Carey Pope, Wm. McKee.

P. 399.   CHRISTOPHER VANATTA, dec'd. Sale of Property. 27 July 1815. Those buying: Nancy Vinetta (most of the furniture), Charles Lock, Andrew Hays, John L. Haines, Nathan Warren, Daniel Boatright, James Prisley, Alexr. McClarin, Baling Reams, Thos. Parsons, Elijah Downing, Wm. Downing, Zeecheus Smith, John Walker, John Dupriest, David E. Page, Archer Jordan.

           CALVIN WHEATON, dec'd. Account of Sales. July session 1818. Those buying: Wm. Wilkinson, David Chadwell, Matthew

Pinkston, Hugh Pinkston, John Holt, Beverly Ridley, Alexr. Wood, Goodler Stanfield, Edw. Robberson, Elisha Davis, Geo. Shannon, Hugh McBride, John Allen, Thos. Capeheart, James Gray, David Hughson, Wm. Hollen, Liles Stephens, Sterling Wheaton, David Cadwell, Gustavus Hollen, Geo. Barnes, James Arnot, Jonathan Hill, Henry Gray, John Howard, Calvin Wheaton, Thos. McMullin, John Bennett, David Chadwell, Elias Lampkins. 22 June 1818.

P. 401.   JOHN GHOLSON, dec'd. Settlement. July session 1818.
          Benj. Gholson, Admr. Expenses paid to: Thos. Ridley,
Thos. Old, John E. Old, J. Parrish, Maury Reese, John White,
Joel Parrish, John Tomlin, warrent against Ledbetter, Peter
Hardeman, Joshea Farrington, Andrew Johnston, John Gee, G.B.
Andrews, John Lemming, A. Campbell, S. Cox, Wm. Veal, P. Russell,
Wm. Shute, A. McPhail, H. Cook, James Wilkins, L. & J. Thompson,
Elisha North, Robt. Smith. Credits: Robert & John White, Geo.
Burnet, Wm. Shute, A. Campbell. Commrs: John Nichols, Archibald
Lytle & H. Cook.

P. 402.   ZADOCK RIGGS, dec'd. Settlement. July session 1818.
          30 May 1818. (No names given of heirs). Commrs:
Thos. Wilson, Wm. Logan & Wm. R. Nunn.

          JAMES SHELBURNE, dec'd. Settlement. July session
1818. Commrs: Wm. Wilson, Eleazar Hardeman, Samuel Shelburne,
& Sarah B. Shelburne, Admrs. (Names of heirs not given.)

          Polly Bateman, Allotment, July session 1818. Widow
of JONATHAN BATEMAN, dec'd. Commrs: J. Childress, Thos. Berry,
James Smith & Geo. H. Pruitt.

P. 403.   LAWRANCE MURPHEY, dec'd. Settlement. July session
          1818. Expenses paid to: B. White, Anna Caton, Geo.
Davis, John T. Wyne, James McEwen, James Carothers, Geo. Davies,
for tax, Benj. Rutherford, Patrick Corgon, Joshua Burnham,
Dempsy Jones, David Johnston, Gray & Dickison, Adam Barnes,
Peter Pinkston. Credit: rent of land & corn sold. Benj. White,
Admr. Commr: David Squier, Henry Cook & Geo. Hulme.

P. 403.   NATHANIEL BARNES, dec'd. Settlement. July session
          1818. Gersham Hunt, Exr. Credits by: John Edmondson,
Wm. Key, Dorcas McLane, James Sneed, Roden Tucker, David Adam,
Thos. Lightfoot, Luke Pryor, Nathan Stancil, Ansylam Barnes,
Alex Smith, Jas. Bradley, Thos. P. Hersey, John Winstead, Wm.
Nolin, John Primm, Jas. Taylor, John W. Primm, Geo. Barnes,
Sam'l. Morton Sr., Edwin Austin, Wm. Kidd, Wm. Roberts, Gersham
Hunt, David Chadwell, Step Morton, Wesley G. Nimmo, Abner Morton,
Joshua Butler (bad account), Thomas Gooch, Nimrod Fielder, Green
Scot, David Nolin, Jabez Owen, Isaac Lyttleton, John Waters,
Moses Lindsey, Solomon Humphreys, Alexander McDaniel, Elisha
Morton, John Frost, Elisha Fly, James Kincaide, Wm. Fielder,
Goodloe Stanfield, Joseph Taylor, Joshua C. Hill, Valentine
Chadwell, Thos. Gooch, Alexr. Buchanon, Nichs. T. Perkins, Wm.
Jameson, John P. Irion, Lawrence Fly, John Holt, Geo. Gollady
(bad account), Nathl. Chitwood (bad account), Rice Hughes (bad
account). 13 July 1818. Wm. Anthony & S. Green.

P. 405.   DAVID LEWIS, dec'd. Settlement. July session 1818.
          (No names given). Commrs: James O. Kellywood, W.
Nunn, & Moses Ridley. Frances Jackson, Exr.

          JOHN SHOARES, dec'd. Settlement. July session 1818.
Commrs: Wm. Byers, Timothy Shaw & Robt. Hulme. Samuel Mays,

Admr. Admr. has paid to 6 of the heirs that are of age (no
names given). June 20, 1818.

P. 406. JOHN WELLS, dec'd. Settlement. July session 1818.
          Commrs: Tristram Patton, J.P., James Miller, J.P.
James Caperton & Samuel Wells, Admrs.

          HENRY WHITE. dec'd. Settlement. July session 1818.
The heirs of HENRY WHITE. Sion Hunt, Guardian. Expenses: going
to Montgomery County to collect of Hignight & Reed; going to
Nashville to collect from Tilford; collection of Brady. Credits:
Rec'd. of Tilford, Jno. Hignight, Moulge; 1 note on James Brady.

P. 407. CHARLES MCCALISTER. dec'd. Will. Oct. session 1818.
          I, Charles McCalister of the town and state of Tenn.
To my dear wife, my property in the town of Franklin and at her
marriage or death to be divided between my children. Friend
John Nichol, merchant of Nashville, guardian of my children.
(No names given). Exr. John Nichols & wife Elizabeth. 7 Oct.
1818. Wit: Wm. McGee, S. Crockett & John White. Probated Oct.
session 1818.

P. 407. GEORGE MABANE. dec'd. Will. Oct. session 1818. 3
          April 1818. Brother Alexander Mebane; son George
Allen Mabane, negro boy Washington; to Louisa Mabane, dau. of
Alexander Mabane, negro girl Nancy; to James Mabane, Joseph
Mabane and Geo. Allen Mabane, sons of Alexander Mabane, 200 acres
of land in Wmson. Co. being the land that my father willed to
me, living in North Carolina; I give to Geo. Allen Mabane all
the money or property that will come to me from my deceased
father in North Carolina, after the decease of my mother; to
my brother Alexander Mabane, my silver watch. Exr. bro. Alexander Mabane. Wit: Anderson Berryman, Henry B. Jackson & John
Walton. Probated Oct. session 1818.

          AMOS ADKINS, dec'd. Will. Oct. session 1818. Being
very sick and weak; to Mary S. Ezell dau. of Balam Ezell, bed &
furniture; to Balam Ezell, 1 chest; to Frederick Ezell, my big
coat and 2 chairs; to Littlebury R. Ezell, my saddle and bridle;
the farm utensils & crops be sold. Exrs. Balam Ezell & Joshua
Tarkington. 11 June 1818. Wit: John Wirt & Taylor Jones.
Probated Oct. 1818.

P. 409. ROBERT SANDFORD, dec'd. Will. Oct. session 1818.
          Beloved wife Polly, all my property, 50 acres of land
during her widowhood; if my daughter Betsy should live to become
a woman, she is to have as much property out of my estate as will
make her equal with her sisters when they were married; at the
death of my wife or marriage, the land is to be divided between
my two sons, Wm. Heter Sandford & Willis Sandford. Exr. Richard
Polk & John Matthews. 1 Aug. 1818. Wit: Joseph Sumners &
Richard Polk. Probated Oct. session 1818.

P. 410. RICHARD SAMPSON, dec'd. Inventory. Oct. session 1818.
          Livestock, farm tools & little furniture. 23 July
1818, by John Hail & Polly Sampson.

          SALLY REDFORD, dec'd. Inventory. Oct. session 1818.
Little furniture & cow. Henry Walker.

          JOHN D. HILL, dec'd. Inventory. Oct. session 1818.
27 April & 9 May 1818. Farm tools, livestock, furniture & etc;
15 negroes hired out, plantation rented; note on: David Huddleston,

doubtful, John M. Clay, doubtful, Jacob (Wiseman?), desperate.
Nancy Hill, Admr.

P. 411.   JOHN NEELLY, SR., dec'd. Inventory. Oct. session
          1818. Livestock, farm tools, furniture, guns, silver
watch, books, etc.; slaves: Cruseley, Yorick. Hanalle, Milley,
Betsy, Anna, Nelly, Nancy, Patience,by James Neelly.

          GEORGE MABANE, dec'd. Inventory. Oct. session 1818.
200 acres land on W. Harpeth; 1 negro boy & 1 girl; furniture,
livestock, silver watch. 12 Oct. 1818. A. Mabane, Exr.

P. 412.   N. P. HARDEMAN, dec'd. Inventory. Oct. session 1818.
          Returned by Thos. H. Perkins & Thos. Hardeman Jr.
Negroes: girl Isabel about 18 yrs.; girl Silva about 13 yrs.;
boy Hannibal Farmer about 9 yrs.; girl Scerrina about 8 yrs.;
boy Cato about 7 yrs.; furniture, household items, livestock,
farm tools, many books, fanily Bible, 2 Testaments, book on
Methodist Episcopal Church & etc.; note on the following: Jas.
Kennedy & Jas. Dysart, Robt. Powers, John Nichols Jr., Black-
stone Hardeman & Robt. McNutt, Joel T. Rivers, John Dabney,
James C. Hill, Wm. Sparkman, Edw. Ragsdale, Jason Willson Sr.,
John Bell, Andrew Campbell, Moses Davis, Rhod Boyd, Wm. Woodfold,
Ephraim Brown, Nashville Steam Mill Co., Daniel Goodman & Joseph
Royal. Hardin P. Holt, John T. Bennett, Dempsey Nash, Thos. P.
Carney, Henry R.W. Hill, Wm. Wilson, Philip Maury, Jesse Benton,
John White, John Witherspoon, Chapman White, Nicholas P. Perkins,
Jason Thompson, Andrew Craig, Alexander Boyd (desperate).

P. 414.   ANDREW CAMPBELL, dec'd. Inventory. Oct. session 1818.
          Inventory of store & personal inventory. Oct. 16,
1818. Jane B. Campbell.

P. 431.   Ann Hardeman, widow of N.P. HARDEMAN, dec'd. Allotment.
          Oct. session 1818. For widow & minor children. Commrs:
S. Crockett, B. Reese, & Robt. Davis.

          Nancy Hill, widow of JOHN D. HILL, dec'd. Allotment.
Oct. session 1818. For widow & family. Commrs: Nathan Adams,
Joseph H. Scales & John R. Boyd.

          NICHOLAS P. HARDEMAN, dec'd. Account of Sales. Oct.
1818. Aug. 8, 1818. Those buying: Thomas Hardeman, David
Squire (family Bible). Wm. Moor, Enoch Bateman, Ann Hardeman,
Thos. J. Hardeman, Thomas H. Perkins, Peter Pinkston, Wm. McKey,
James Parks, Joel Waller. Some articles sold at the farm on
Mill Creek in Davidson Co.

P. 433.   STEPHEN BARFIELD, dec'd. Account of Sales. Oct.
          session 1818. 13 Aug. 1818. Those buying: Wm. H.
Hill, Wm. Hemphill, John Stephens, Nancy Barfield, Andrew Goff,
Stephen Sutton, Stephen Barfield, John Barfield, Richard Wm.
Hicks, James McEwen, John Stephens, Ephraim McEwen, Blake Bar-
field, Lewis Barfield, Penelope Barfield, Henry C. Carter, Hugh
Pinkston, Wm. Stephens, Enoch Bateman, Howel Peebles, John Stacy,
Mahlon Stacy, Benj. Williamson, David D. Page, Wm. Dickson,
Leonard Wood, James A. Brown, Matthew Pope, Joel Stephens, Larkin
Burch. Abraham Secrest, Simon Bateman, John Miller, Alexander
Wood, John Waggoner, Jas. A. Brown, Nicholas Tomlin, C.E. McEwen,
Michael Long. James McEwen & Lewis Barfield, Exr.

P. 435.   JOHN D. HILL, dec'd. Account of Sales. Oct. session
          1818. Sold on 27th April & 9th May 1818. Those

buying: Nancy Hill. Samuel Morton, Jacob Morton, Nicholas Scales·, Levi Measles, John Scales, G. Lewis, Jacob Adams, Jason C. Wilson, John Holmes, Wm. Edmondson, Robert Rogers, Thos. Boaz, John R. Boyd, Thos. Wood, Jacob Denton, Wm. Wall, John Williams, Charles Good, Silas Morton, James H. Ganbil. Jordan Black, John Rusworm, Wm. Depriest, Augustin Loftin, John West, John Bostick. Charles Depriest, Samuel Morton, Richard W. Hyde, Wm. King, John Vincent, Wm. Watson, Eli Corzine, James Maddix, Hartwell Hyde, Stringer Potts, Philip Haley, Jesse Warren, Bennett Hargrove, John Johnston, Abram Glenn, John Depriest, Wm. Saunders, James McKnight, Alexander Ralston; Lucy Hill hired all of the slaves; 1 note on David Huddleston (doubtful); account on Jacob Curfman (desperate), 1 note on John M. Clay. Nancy Hill, Admr.

P. 437.   ALSON EDNEY, dec'd. Additional account of sale. Oct. session 1818. Sold Oct. 10, 1818. Those buying: Polly Edney. Polly Edney, Admr.

P. 438.   THOMAS WILSON, dec'd. Account of Sales. Oct. session 1818. John Wilson only person buying. Wm. Wilson, Admr.

JANE GARRET, dec'd. Account of Sales. Oct. session 1818. Those buying: Wm. Edmondson, Timothy Shaw, Thos. Garrett, Geo. Davis, John C. Bradshaw, John Hardgrove, Allen Hill (Ritta slave). Vinson Greer, Joseph Ansley, Samuel Edmondson, Jas. H. Thompson, Armstead H. Brown, Demsey Nash (slave Hannah). Vinson Greer, Admr.

RICHARD SAMPSON, dec'd. Additional account of Sales. Oct. session 1818. Those buying: Wm. A. Price, Thos. Wilson, Edw. Ragsdale, Sire Wilson, John Smith, John L. Hadley, Chas. Legate, Cader Parker, Archd. Goodman, James M. Wilson, Richd. Ogilvie, Reynold McCay, Wm. Wilson, Henry Daughtry. John Hail & Polly Sampson, Admr.

JOHN DYER, dec'd. Account of Sales. Oct. session 1818. Sold Aug. 12, 1818. Those buying: Lavina Dyer (most of the items sold), John Waters, John Laster, Robt. Dyer, Thos. Dedman, Henry Bright, Charles Goode, Henry Walker, C.C. Depriest, John Depriest, Burrel Walker, Jacob Morton, Wm. Morton, John Fester, Nathan Goode. Lavina Dyer, Admr.

P. 439.   AMASA HAWKINS, dec'd. Account of Sales. Oct. session 1818. 8th Aug. 1818. Those buying: Mary Hawkins, Thos. Hanks, David P. Hamilton, Saml. Graham, John Porter, Thos. Hertly, Jonathan Horton, John Graham, Thos. Hillard, Thos. Graham, Wm. Graham, Joseph Davis. Mary Hawkins, Admrx.

P. 440.   HENRY INGRAM, dec'd. Account of Sail. Oct. session 1818. Those buying: Susan Ingram (almost everything sold). Wm. Smith. Susan Ingram, Admrx.

CHARLES BROWN, dec'd. Settlement. Oct. session 1818. Jusse Cox & Michael Brown, Admrs. Commrs: Timothy Shaw, M. Johnston & Joseph Motheral. (no names of heirs given).

P. 441.   JAMES SKELLY, dec'd. Settlement. Oct. session 1818. Expenses paid to: John Pegg, Thorton Perry, Jesse Oakly, Robt. Bates, Wm. Bond, Mary McCollum, Westley Witherspoon, Younger McCaslin, E. McLeon, Stephen Pegg, John Andrew & Sam'l. Andrews, Henry Rustin, Joseph McCollister, John Wauthing, Jane Adkins, Robt. Bates, Wm. Blythe, Nicholas Branch, Richard Orton.

Stephen Pegg, Admr.

WILLIAM MCEWEN, dec'd. Settlement. Oct. session 1818. Expenses paid to: Gray Dickeson, B. Evans, McCalister (account), R.C. Foster. Sarah McEwen & Jas. McEwen, Admrs. Commrs: H. Petway, W. Smith & David Mason.

P. 442. SAMUEL C. SMITH, dec'd. Settlement. Oct. session 1818. Expenses paid to: Wm. Austin, Berry Griggs, Thos. Reddish, Thos. Pool, John Christian, Joseph May, David J. Robertson, James Scott, Currin & Mason, Wm. Black, Catharine Smith, Jesse Bonner, Nathan G. Pinson, Wm. Maddox, Wm. Duffiel, James McCollum, Wright Wilfield, Adam Cabal, Jesse Bonner, Philemon McLemore, Nathan Gooch, Wm. Banks, Joshua Cutchen, Charles Tully, David Loovit, Moses Clark, Berry Nolin. Commrs: John Nichols & Henery Brown. Berry Nolin, Admr.

ARTHUR BLAND, dec'd. Settlement. Oct. session 1818. Nancy Bland, Admrx. Accounts not collected: John McCain, Wm. McCanless, cash paid to Edw. Singleton, Levi Dillon & Robt. Rogers, James Turberville. Expenses paid to: J. Minnan, Jason Thompson, John McCain, Francis Hamelton, Nathan Ewing, Wm. Brown, John Primm, Constantine Perkins, Henry Wisenor, the heirs of Henry Alexander, John H. Eaton, Wm. P. Seal, Peter Pinkston, Nichs. Perkins, Absolam Wilhite, Edw. Austin, Samuel Morton, Jerusha Alexander, Enoch Ensley. Thos. Hardeman, clerk.

P. 443. CHRISTOPHER VENATTA, dec'd. Settlement. Oct. session 1818. Commrs: Nicholas Scales, Wm. Wilson & Nathan Adams. Expenses paid to: Newton Cannon, note; Elizabeth Berry, note; Doctor Wm. S. Webb, account; Archibald Hayes, account; Thos. Washington, account; Taxes for 1816, 1817, 1818; David E. Page, account; Thos. E. Sumner, account; Wm. Span, account; Peter Venatta, account; Hartwell Hyde, account.

P. 444. JOHN CRAFTEN, dec'd. Settlement. Oct. session 1818. Commrs: Nicholas Scales, Eleazar Hardeman & Berry Nolen. Expenses paid to: Taxes 1815-1816, N. Perkins, James Parks, Alexander Bennett, Benj. Wilks (as guardian of Dennis & Geo.), Thos. J. Pritchett, John McClellan, Geo. Lester (bad debt), Joseph Parson (bad debt), John Williams (bad debt), Daniel Wilks (account), Adm. of James Shelburn, dec'd, Tax on property of Jas. Crafton, heirs, Nichs. Wilburn, James Harder, John Peters (bad debt), Pleasant Crenshaw (bad debt), Robert Sammons (bad debt), John Sammons (bad debt).

P. 445. Wilkins Harper, guardian. Settlement. Oct. session 1818. Guardian to Martin W. Richardson. Expenses paid to: Charles McAlister, Martin W. Richardson, John Sample, Wm. McGilvery, Stephen Smith, Wm. Parham, Moses Priest, Wm. Bond Sr., Saunders & Organ, T.L. Bass, Gray & Dickinson, Edw. Scruggs, T. Miller, Thos. Richardson, Joel Parrish, Meeks the Taylor, Thos. H. Word, Isaac Oaks, P. Hardeman, P. Petway, Y.A. Gray, Jacob Carl, Kemp Holland. Commrs: Hendley Stone, Wm. Bond, Sr. & Robt. Davis.

JAMES BUFORD, dec'd. Settlement. Oct. session 1818. Expense paid to: G. Blackburn for funeral sermon, James Gordon, Thos. G. Bradford, Cornelies Wilson (making shoes), Manley (auctioneer), John E. Beck atty., Hugh L. White, E. Cannon (Judgt. vs. Estate), Jenkins Whiteside, Whiteside for suit vs. Bradshaw, John Sample, James C.O' Riley, Alexr. Reed, Elisha Dotson, Moses Turner (b. smith), Samuel Dotson, James Hicks,

Wm. Bradshaw (land suit); Grundy for suit vs. Cameron; Blicks
deposition at Fayetville; Longs deposition at Shelbyville;
Bookers deposition at Maury Co.; Bookers deposition; expenses
to Ky. to settle with Roberts; Edw. Ragsdale as a witness;
Lazarus Dotson as a witness; Clark's deposition in Fayetville;
Jas. Herndon deposition; Expenses of going to Murfreesboro; Joel
Brown as a witness; Alexr. Mebane as a witness; John Haley as a
witness; railing in grave yard; Jas. Trimble in suit vs. Rags-
dale; Petway & Maury. Credits: Notes on: Nicholas Lavender, N.
Johnstons, Byrd Lavender, B. Goodman, John Hughs, Joel Ferguson,
N. Armstrong, James Henry, Geo. Glascock, Samuel Byrd, Wm. Allen,
R. Roads, Peter Edwards, Wm. Wells, Wm. Flippin, John Wills,
Eli Hope, John Scott; account on: John Dawson, Francis Giddens,
Mr. Graves, Samuel Harris. Job H. Thomas, Thomas Old; note on:
C. Boyles, Ezekiel McKailey, Caleb Manley, Cornelius Wilson,
Richard Barnes, Elisha Dotson, James Bradley, C. White for Peter
Edwards, Jas. Buford, Edw. Buford, Chas. Buford, Daniel Carter,
Chas. Hulcy, Samuel Braden, C. Lavender, E. Coleman, Malachi
Nicholson, Allin Hill. Edw. Ragsdale, Geo. Glascock, Alexr.
Mebane, Geo. Mebane, James Giddens, C. Hulsey, Archd. Beasley,
Wm. Gurley, Andrew Horron, (admr. of Crow). Spencer Buford.
Cmmors: H. Petway, Henry Cook & John Watson. Spencer Buford &
Edw. Bufords, Exrs.

P. 447.   THOMAS S. ADKINS, dec'd. Settlement. Oct. session
           1818. Eliza Adkins, admrx. Expenses paid to: James
Coonce, C. McAlister, Jas. McCombs, Wm. Cloid, John Jones, J.H.
Maury, Alson Lynton, Mary Evans, Samuel Horton, James Horton.
Credits: W. Whitfield, Matthew Lea, W. Jones, Constan Sawyers,
D. Gray, D. Pinkston, J. Rhoades, N. Perkins, A. Smith. L.
Jones, F. Ivey, D. Sawyer, Saml. Orton, E.E. Adkins, Wm. Roach,
T. Walton, James Gillu, H. Forehand, J. Cannon, hire of negroes
for 1816-1817. Commrs: John Watson, Henry Cook & R.P. Currin.

P. 448.   James McEwen, guardian. Settlement. Oct. session
           1818. The heirs of PETER POTTS, dec'd. Expenses paid
to: Adam Jackson for schooling; taxes for 1817; Willis Maclin
tuition; Mrs. Goff attending negro woman; books for Susan &
Maria; Charles. McAlister, account; Gray & Dickerson, medical
services; Samuel Crockett, medical services.

P. 451.   ISAAC CROW, dec'd. Division. Oct. session 1818.
           David Gillespie, surveyor. Commrs: Jas. Caperton,
Edward Buford, Thos. Herrin & Ephraim Andrews on West Harpeth.
Lot #1 Bryant Crow, 728 acres in Rutherford Co. on Hurricane
Creek, a West branch of Stones River, 2 town lots, 1 lot in
Columbia, Maury Co. #47, 1 lot in Franklin, Wmson. Co. #154;
Lot #2 James Crow, part of tract of land in Wmson. Co. on West
Harpeth on road from Franklin to Columbia 74 acres, ½ a lot #176
in Franklin; Lot #3 Polly Crow, balance of tract of land on West
Harpeth on road from Franklin to Columbia 124½ acres & ½ lot
#176 in Franklin; Lot #4 Thomas Crow, part of tract of land in
Wmson. Co. on the ridge between Duck & Harpeth Rivers, 265 acres;
Lot #5 Isaac Crow, balance of tract of land on ridge between
Duck & Harpeth Rivers, 275 acres. 16 Sept. 1818.

P. 455.   ALEXANDER REID, dec'd. Settlement. Oct. session 1818.
           Expenses paid to: Jesse Cox for making shoes, Jas.
Condon, James Lester, William Wilson, Thos. Wates, Thos. White
making shoes, Jesse Wharton agent for Theodorick B. Rice, Young
A. Gray for sandals for Sarah Reid, paid to Garner McConnico for
schooling Mary Reid, paid to J.B. Houston for coffin, Andrew
Campbell, expenses for books & clothing, John Ralston for survey-

ing 2 plantations, for Priscilla & Catherine expenses to Rich.
land, Pleasant Craddock for boarding 3 Miss Reads, Wm. Williams,
Edw. Tignor shoes, James Philips, Gideon Blackburn schooling,
Robt. Bratton repairs on L. Harpeth plantation. Credits: cash
at sales at Whites Creek. cash at sales at Little Harpeth. Wm.
Davis note, P. Hudges rent of plantation at Whites Creek 1816,
sale of 3 negroes-Daniel, Nancy & Manah, John Ralston, Thos.
Watts, Chumsley note, Scruggs note, Chapman White, John & Isaac
McCa(shius?), Stump & Cox note, Jas. Erwin note, Lanier &
Hoppers note, Isaac Mayfield, C. Collins note, James Marshall,
Jas. Gidden, Frazier note, Geo. Reed note, Norfleet Perry, La-
fever & McCaslin, Powel & Davis note, C. Buford note, Timothy
Demumbro, Robt. C. Phelin, David Balentine, Frances Slaughter,
Levin Cator, Abel Lewis, Samuel Mullin, Jas. Colb, Campbell &
Baker, Jesse Cox, Henry Slater, Tulley Williams, Jas. Pinkerton
Sr.; note on: Frances Hodge, Ephraim Brown, Young E. Barnes,
Henry Rutherford, Geo. Reids, Wm. St(?), Jesse Cox, Robt. Brat-
ton, Congers & Campbell, Johnson & McCaslin, John Thompson, John
Marlin's, James Reeds, Terry Bradley, Jas. Caldwell, John Porter,
Thos. Shannon; Wm. & Pharoah Hudgins rent of White Creek Planta-
tion 627 acres 1817; boarding Priscilla & Polly. Spencer Buford,
Admr.

P. 458.   Jan. Term 1814.   Petition for Partition.   David
          Dickinson & Fanny his wife & Matthias B. Murfree-
complainants vs. Wm. H. Murfree, Isaac Hilliard & Mary his wife,
James Manney & Sally his wife, Lavinia B. Murfree & Martha A.C.
Murfree. Hardy Murfree died seized of the following tracts of
land: 1 tract 5120 acres balance of a 5760 acre tract grant to
H. Murfree by North Carolina, 14 March 1786 patent #39, & 1 tract
of 640 acres adjoining the above tract granted by North Carolina
7 March 1786 patent #169. 1 other tract of 228 acres granted by
North Carolina to John White 7 March 1786 grant #665 & conveyed
to Murfree; 1 other tract of 1114 acres granted by North Carolina
to James Martin 14 March 1786 grant #261 & conveyed to Murfree.
In Rutherford Co. 1 tract of 389 acres granted to North Carolina
to Henry Winburn 7 March 1786 grant #194; 1 tract of 318 acres
granted by North Carolina to Wm. Ponder 7 March 1786 #203; 1
tract of 640 acres granted by North Carolina to John Wills 7
March 1786 #195; 1 tract of 274 acres granted by North Carolina
to Ezekiel White 7 March 1786 #200; 1 tract of 320 acres granted
by North Carolina to Thos. Powel 7 March 1786 #201; 1 tract of
228 acres granted by North Carolina to John Butler 7 March 1786
#162; 1 tract of 342 acres granted by North Carolina to Bryant
Smith 7 March 1786 #223; 1 tract of 342 acres granted by North
Carolina to Joseph Mitchell by North Carolina 7 March 1786 #197:
1 tract of 640 acres granted to Anthony Gaines by North Carolina
7 March 1786 #112; 1 tract of 768 acres part of a tract granted
by North Carolina to Clement Hall 14 March 1786 #47; 1 tract of
320 acres granted by North Carolina to Dempsey Jenkins 7 March
1786 #218. In Wilson Co. 1 tract of 321 acres granted by North
Carolina to Wm. Slade 18 May 1789 #1022; 1 tract of 640 acres
granted to David Bizzel by North Carolina on 14 March 1786 #146
& conveyed to Solomon Bizzell to H. Murfree; 1 tract of 94 acres
part of a tract granted to Robertson dying on Stones Creek; 1
tract of 200 acres granted to Masson Williams; 1 tract of 1508
acres granted by North Carolina to John Pointer 20 May 1793
#2178; 1 tract of 773 acres granted by North Carolina to Archi-
bald Henderson 14 March 1786 #95. In Robertson Co. 1 tract of
640 acres granted to Nancy Sheppard, 1 tract of 640 acres granted
to Nancy Sheppard. In Stewart Co. 1 tract of 400 acres part of
tract granted by North Carolina to John B. Hammond 18 May 1789
#974, 1 tract of 384 acres part of a tract granted by North

Carolina to Thos. Calinder 14 March 1786 #49; 1 tract of 640
acres granted by North Carolina to Nancy Shepherd 8 Dec. 1787
#668. In Dixon Co. 1 tract of 640 acres part of a tract granted
by North Carolina to Hardy Murfree 20 May 1793 #2380. In Montgomery Co. 1 tract of 640 acres granted by North Carolina to
Baker Archer 7 Mar. 1786 #111, 1 tract of 640 acres granted by
North Carolina to Letitia Archer 7 March 1786 #240, 1 tract of
228 acres granted by North Carolina to Isaac Butler 7 March
1786 #245, 1 tract of 274 acres granted by North Carolina to Jas.
Caleson 7 Mar 1768 #238, 1 tract of 274 acres part of tract
granted by North Carolina to Benj. Bailey 14 March 1786 #38, 1
tract of 67 acres part of a tract granted by North Carolina to
John Madeares 6 Dec. 1797 #3249, 1 tract of 640 acres granted by
North Carolina to --------- 6 Dec. 1797 #3248. In Davidson Co.
1 tract of 256 acres part of a tract granted by North Carolina
to John Pierce 7 March 1780 #188, 1 tract of 390 acres granted
by North Carolina to Benj. Johnson 20 May 1793 #2354, 1 town lot
in Nashville #16. Commrs: Turner Saunders, Abraham Maury Sr.,
David Dunn, Oliver Williams, Thos. Olds, Garner McConnico and
John Watson.

P. 461.   Lot #1, Wm. H. Murfree, 604 acres grant #39, 342 acres
           granted to Bryan Smith. 640 acres acres granted to
John Mederus, 384 acres part of Thos. Calinders tract, 786 acres
part of Clement Holes tract, total 2740 acres. Lot #2, Isaac
Hilliard & Mary his wife, 1430 acres part of Hardy Murfree
survey #169, 320 acres granted to Thos. Powell #201, 640 acres
granted to Jane Manley assignee of Allen Manley, 490 acres in
Dixon Co. #2380, 400 acres part of Abraham Burgess tract,
Stewart Co. #91, 640 acres granted to David Bizzell. Wilson Co.,
62½ acres purchased of Jacob Thomas, Wilson Co., 773 acres granted to Archibald Henderson #95, Smith Co., 287 acres granted to
Nancy Shephard, Sumner Co. #12294, 640 acres granted to Nancy
Shephard, Jackson Co. #23100, 321 acres part of Wm. Slacks
tract, Wilson Co. #22, total 6003½ acres. Lot #3, James Manney
& Sally H., his wife, 1588 acres part of large survey, 252 acres
granted to Ezekiel White, Rutherford Co. #200, 386 acres granted
to Dempsey Jenkins, Rutherford Co. #218. 1508 acres granted to
John Pointer, Smith Co. #2178, 228 acres granted to Isaac Butler,
Montgomery Co. #245, 274 acres granted to James Calfon, Montgomery Co. #238, 640 acres granted to Nancy Shephard, Stewart Co.
#668. Lot #4, Lavenia B. Murfree, 1242 acres part of large
survey, 400 acres granted to Henry Winton, Rutherford Co., 216
acres granted to John Butler, Rutherford Co. #162, 640 acres
granted to Baker Archer, Rutherford Co., 256 acres granted to
John Pearce, Davidson Co., 228 acres granted to Massen Williams,
Wilson Co., total 2982 acres. Lot #5, Martha Ann C. Murfree,
1452 acres part of large survey, 714 acres granted to John Wells,
Rutherford Co., 640 acres granted to Saticia Archer. Montgomery
Co., 274 acres granted to John Hargrove, Montgomery Co., 477
acres granted to Nancy Sheppard, Overton Co., 640 acres granted
to Nancy Sheppard, Stewart Co. #666, 640 acres granted to Nancy
Sheppard, Davidson Co. Lot #6, David Dickinson & Fanny N., his
wife, 1076 acres Wmson. Co. part of large survey, 708 acres
granted to Anthony Goins, Rutherford Co. #112. 94 acres granted
to Robertson, Wilson Co., 300 acres granted to Wm. Ponder,
Rutherford Co., 466 2/3 acres granted to Hardy Murfree, Bedford
Co., 200 acres granted to Hardy Murfree, Lincoln Co., total
2784 2/3 acres. Lot #7, Matthias B. Murfree, 1089 acres granted
to John Martin, Wmson. Co., 265 acres granted to Joseph Mitchell,
Rutherford Co., 203 acres granted to John White, Wmson Co. #165,
390 acres granted to Benj. Johnson, Davidson Co. #2354, 301 acres
granted to Nancy Sheppard, Sumner Co., 640 acres granted to Nancy

Sheppard, Sumner Co., 640 acres granted to Nancy Sheppard, Stewart Co., 640 acres granted to Nancy Sheppard, Robinson Co. #693, total 3528 acres.   31st Dec. 1813.

Names preceding page 1 are not indexed.
--: Thos., 045
--?: Agnes, 062
--?: Wm. W., 100
-ELAM: --?. 041
AAMS: L. B.. 045
ABET: David. 059
ACUFF: Isaac. 015
ADAM: David. 106
ADAMS: Benj., 051; Benjamin, 007;
  Charles. 021; Daniel, 025. 067;
  H., 056; Howell. 005. 057. 058;
  Jacob. 041. 046. 068. 070. 109;
  John, 077; Martin, 050, 069; N.,
  067; Nathan, 060. 108. 110;
  Thomas, 014; William. 014;
  Wm.. 045
_ADKERSON: Jordan. 056
ADKINS: Amos. 107; E. E.. 111;
  Eliza. 111; Jane. 109; John, 040;
  Molly. 040; Patsey. 040; Polly
  Johnston. 040; Thomas S.. 111
ADKINSON: John. 041
ADMONSTON: Moses. 046
AKIN: Burrell. 105; Burwell, 104;
  Samuel, 063; Wm. 077
AKINS: Moses. 018
ALCORN: John. 058
ALDRIDGE: Nathaniel. 026
ALEN: David. 019
ALEXANDER: David T., 015; E., 058;
  Ebenezer. 038; Eloc. 035; Henry,
  110; James. 029. 063; Jerusha.
  110; Joseph. 028. 084; Robert.
  029; Toberton. 101; William, 012,
  016. 021. 024. 041; Wm.. 075. 104
ALFRED: William. 039
ALLEN: ?. 024; Car.. 020; Carr.
  020; David. 037; Geo. H.. 041;
  Geo.. 046; George H.. 024;
  George S.. 018; George. 021;
  Henry. 045; John. 026. 032. 054,
  085. 087. 092. 106; Joseph. 072;
  Sally. 033; Valentine. 021;
  Wm. 111
ALLERSON: John. 105
ALLIN: Laneon. 091
ALLISON: Hugh. 022; James. 019.
  021. 024. 031. 040. 041. 048.
  072; Jas.. Esq.. 085; Jas.. 041.
  088. 090; Nancy. 031; Sally.
  031; Thomas. 024
ALLMAN: Wm.. 088
ALMARY: Benj.. 105
ALSAP: John. 009
ALSTON: Murry. 096
ALSUP: John. 010; Thomas. 011
ANDERSON: Abraham. 072; Azariah.
  054. 072. 087; Azeriah. 080;
  Branch H.. 091; David P.. 023.
  045; Ephraim. 083; John. 017.
  025; Thos.. 046; William P.. 026
ANDREW: Felston. 045; John. 109
ANDREWS: A.. 037. 094; Ann. 005;
  Athelston. 049; B.. 094; C..
  094; Capt.. 045; Ephraim. 005,

022. 024. 040. 041. 046. 111;
  Ephraim, Jr.. 041; G. B.. 106;
  George. 005. 040; Henry. 087;
  James. 021. 093; Jn.. 062; Jno..
  062; John. 004. 027. 046. 062.
  064; Knacy H.. 005; Knacy. 022.
  024. 040. 041; Lazarus. 103;
  Nancy. 005; Nias. 057; Old Lady.
  041; Sam'l. 042. 109; Samuel.
  012. 035. 046. 048. 054. 064.
  101; Stacy. 005; Tapley. 024.
  075; Wm.. 075. 087
ANGLES: Joseph. 105. 109
ANTHONY: Wm.. 066. 073. 084. 106
APPLEBY: Agnes. 004; David. 004;
  James. 004; John. 004; Samuel,
  004; William. 004
ARCHER: Baker. 113; Letitia. 113;
  Luticia. 047; Saticia. 113
ARMISTEAD: Wm. H.. 045
ARMSTRON: Creasy. 065
ARMSTRONG: James L.. 093; James,
  033. 049. 050. 077. 104; Jas..
  049; John. 012; Lancelot. 010;
  N.. 111; Nathaniel. 010
ARNOLD: A.. 067; Asa. 063;
  Dorcas. 063; Jeremiah. 063
ARNOT: James. 106
ARTHUR: Benjamin. 011; Henry. 031
ARTHURS: Benjamin. 013
ASCUE: Aaron. 043
ASHBURN: Wm.. 094
ASHLEY: Wm.. 077
ASHLIN: Wm.. 071. 093. 094
ASKEW: Aran. 067; Aron. 076
ATKINS: Amos. 079; Catharine. 085;
  Elizabeth. 085; John. 014. 038;
  Thomas L.. 085
ATKINSON: Armistead. 045. 093;
  Armstead. 094; Henry. 025. 093;
  John. 043. 045. 046. 051. 059.
  064. 072. 079. 088; John, Jr..
  093; Mary. 046; Molley. 051;
  Molly. 051; Patsey. 051; Polley
  J.. 051; Ro. F.. 070; Sam'l.
  093; Samuel. 094
ATKINSON?: Wm.. 101
AUSTIN: Edw.. 110; Edwin. 074.
  079. 080. 084. 106; John. 101;
  Wm.. 110
AVERELL: Aaron. 008
AYDELOTT: Thomas. 003
BAILEY: Benj.. 113; H.. 070; Henry.
  004. 021. 041. 080; William. 003
BAILY: --. 076
BAKER: --. 112; Humphrey. 012.
  093; John. 024. 075. 101; Samuel.
  068; Thomas. 103; William. 016
BALAMAN: Simon. 092
BALCHAS: A.. 054
BALCK: D.. 058
BALDRIDGE: Andrew. 023; John.
  004. 011; Robert. 023;
  William. 009
BALENTINE: David. 086. 112
BALEW: William H.. 039; Wm. H.. 039

BALLOW: Ann. 035. 041; Thomas.
  035. 039. 041; Thos.. 054
BANE: Young E.. 086
BANKS: --. 039. 054; Jas.. 097;
  W.. 094; William. 021. 037. 044.
  101; Wm.. 061. 069. 091-094. 110
BARER: Wilie. 094
BARESHEAR: David H.. 045
BARFIELD: --. 088. 105; Blake.
  102. 108; Harriot. 102; John.
  102. 108; Lewis. 102. 015. 108;
  Nancy. 102. 108; Penelope House.
  102; Penelope. 108; Polly(Sam?).
  102; Stephen. 045. 049. 061.
  083. 090. 102. 104. 108; Tabitha
  House. 102; Willie Blount. 102
BARKER: Geo. W.. 083
BARLONS: Samuel. 059
BARNES: A.. 080; Adam. 106; Anna.
  075. 080; Ansolum 098; Ansylam.
  106; Daus.. 078; Elizabeth. 075.
  080; G.. 072; Geo.. 075. 106;
  George. 100; Henry. 080. 086;
  Jeremiah. 094. 098; Joel. 084;
  Joshua. 029. 085; Lamuel. 075;
  Leah. 080; Luk(?). 080; Lundy.
  076; Meriller. 094; Nathaniel.
  075. 078-080. 084. 085. 106;
  Polly. 075; Richard. 029. 111;
  Samuel. 075; Seth. 009; Susanna.
  068; Young E.. 112
BARNET: --. 063; James. 087
BARNETT: John. 056; Martha. 027
BARNHART: John. 012
BARNS: John. 046
BARR: Hugh. 028. 053
BARREN: --. 005
BARRER: Willie. 094
BARRET: James P.. 066
BARTH: Sarah. 066
BARTON: Bro.. 062; Samuel. 006. 058
BASS: Ariah. 088p Benjamin J.. 070;
  K. P.. 093; Kinchen P.. 101;
  Lawrence. 018. 030; Nancy. 021.
  022; T. L.. 110
BATEMAN: Beniah. 105; Benijah.
  064; Enoch. 067. 071. 083. 088.
  108; Enock. 009; Evan. 105;
  Isaac. 006; Jonathan. 102. 105.
  106; Lemon. 089; Nosea. 105;
  Parker. 067. 071. 088; Polly.
  102. 105. 106; Simeon. 071. 098.
  105; Simon. 049. 083. 108;
  Widow. 105; Wm.. 072
BATES: Robt.. 070. 109
BATEY: Wm.. 082
BATTLE: Isaac. 027
BAUGH: James. 093
BAUGHAN: Gabril. 085
BAUGHN: Gabriel. 032
BEARD: William. 014; Wm.. 093
BEARD?: John. 095
BEASLEY: Ann. 050; Archd.. 111;
  Archibald. 029. 045; Archie.
  045; Bernard. 092; Charles.
  039; Dan'l. 085; Ephraim W..

050; Ephraim, 061, 083; John
W., 050; John, 073; P., 043,
049; Peter, 093; Phillp, 050,
080; Robert, 050; Robt. E., 049
BEASLY: Daniel, 032
BEATY: John, 087; William, 021;
Wm., 087
BEAVER: Elizabeth, 003
BEAVERS: --, 089; Jesse, 078;
William, 013
BECK: John E., 110
BEDICK: --, 046
BEEL: Barnabus, 009
BEESLEY: --, 021
BELHMY: --, 093
BELL: --, 095; David, 098;
Elizabeth, 001; Geo., 083;
H. F., 077; H., 026; Hugh F.,
061, 075, 077, 080, 092, 093,
095; Hugh T., 026; Hugh, 053,
082; James, 001; John, 001, 092,
108; Joseph H., 046, 080; Joseph,
041; Martha, 075; Robert, 075;
Robt., 075; Sally, 001; Samuel,
080; Stenson, 001; Sterling,
001; Thomas, 001, 017; William
R., 075, 083; William, Jr., 001;
William, Sr., 001; Wm. M., 077;
Wm., 093, 097
BELLER: Abraham, 019
BELLS: Isaac, 015
BELLUE: Thomas, 029
BELOU: Thomas, 073
BENNET: Geo., 045
BENNETT: Alexander, 024, 045, 082,
083, 110; Anna, 050; Camper,
039; Drury, 041; Elizabeth, 050;
Geo., 045, 050, 090, 092, 095;
Geo., Dr., 099; George, 025,
034; Jenny, 050; Jincey, 044;
John D., 095; John T., 044, 108;
John, 050, 106; Peter, 056;
Walter, 071; Walter, Sr., 050;
William, 015; Wm., 080
BENSON: John, 054, 060; Labon,
055; Martin, 061
BENTHALL: Matthew, 015
BENTLY: Richard, 014
BENTON: Elizabeth, 019; H., 054;
Jesse, 003, 049, 052, 092, 093,
108; Mary, 052; Nancy, 003;
Nat'l, 052; Nathaniel, 060;
Peggy, 003; Polly, 003; Samuel,
003, 052, 060, 095; Susannah,
003; T. H., 057; Thomas H., 003;
Thos. G., 087; Thos. H., 052, 057
BERKELEY: John, 059
BERKLEY: --, 101; John, 062
BERRY: Ann, 103; Basil, 023, 060,
096; Bassel, 054; Bassil, 074;
Bazel, 052; Bazil, 043; Bazzel,
105; D., 087; David, 054, 087;
Elizabeth, 110; James, 020, 021,
033, 043, 052, 054, 060, 087,
091, 096; Jane, 103; John, 089;
Margaret, 074; Martha, 021;

Rebecca, 054. 060, 087, 096;
Robert, 096, 103; Sally, 103;
Thomas, 021, 023, 028, 050, 060,
096, 101; Thos., 050, 072, 074,
087, 090, 096, 106; William,
004, 020, 021, 023, 087, 096,
103; Wm., 087, 096
BERRYMAN: Anderson, 045, 072, 107
BERY: Rebecca, 087
BETHELL: Carter, 012
BETHSHEARS: Clarissa, 065
BETTS: Jonathan, 011; Samuel,
082; Wm., 101
BEVELL: Benjamin, 032; Edw., 095
BEVILE: Robert, 021
BEZLE: Isaac, 045
BEZZELL: Hardy, 046
BIBB: Henry, 084; Thos., 098;
William, 039
BICKERSTAFF: Henry, 100
BIGGER: --, 005
BIGGERS: Robert, 067
BILLINSLY: James, 013
BINKLEYS: Adam, 001
BINNETT: Walter, 044
BIRD: Samuel, 045, 064
BISHOP: Raisen L., 101
BITTICK: John R., 089, 095, 098
BITTICKS: John R., 090;
Robert, 028
BIZLE: Hardy, 045
BIZZEL: David, 112; Isaac, 100
BIZZELL: David, 113; Isaac, 072,
100; Solomon, 112
BIZZILL: Hardy, 105
BIZZLE: David, 047
BLACK: David, 059; Fanny, 074;
Hugh M., 093; James, 018, 023,
053; John, 014; Jordan, 109;
Theo., 057; Thos. Hill, 074;
Thos., 056; William, 033;
Wm., 110
BLACKAMORE: John, 001
BLACKBURN: --, 030; G., 086, 110;
Gideon, 069, 082, 103, 112;
Mr., 062
BLACKE: Huch, 018
BLACKEMORE: Thomas, 037
BLACKMAN: Benjamin, 027; John,
009, 049, 098, 102; Mr., 039
BLACKSHAIRE: Ezekiel, 055
BLACKSHARE: David, 055, 090;
Elijah, 055, 090; Elisha, 055;
Ezekiel, 090, 093; Hannah, 008,
055; Jacob, 055, 090; James,
055; Jesse, 008, 055, 090; Luk,
077; Luke, 055, 090; Penny, 055;
Thomas, 008
BLACKSHEAR: Ezekiel, 077
BLACKSHIRE: Luke, 077
BLAIR: John, 010
BLAKE: Abigail, 083
BLAKELY: Sarah, 003; William,
014, 029
BLAND: Arthur, 074, 079, 080,
110; Nancy, 110; Nomy, 079,

080; Orphans, 074; Widow, 074
BLEUFORD: Gabriel, 045
BLICK: --, 111
BLOUNT: J. G., 057
BLUNT: Wm. G., 100
BLYE: Joseph, 046
BLYTHE: Benj., 100; J., 099;
John, 100; Joseph, 045, 100;
Wm., 088, 109
BOATRIGHT: Daniel, 105; Thos., 061
BOAZ: Thos., 109
BOID: Wm. G., 104
BOLAND: James, 076
BOLEAM: Cader, 072
BOLSTON: Allen, 067
BOND: Adam, 082; M.C., 095; M.L.,
063, 089, 092; Morris L., 095;
Samuel, 029; Thomas, 002; W.L.,
089; Wm., 052, 063, 068, 071,
077, 092, 101, 109; Wm., Sr.,
063, 092, 093, 100, 110
BONE: Young E., 080
BONNER: Jesse, 110; Polly, 032
BOOKER: P. R., 082, 087; Peter
B., 061; Peter R., 005, 011,
019, 041, 065; R. P., 061;
Suckey, 005
BOOKERS: --, 111; Peter R., 017
BOOKLY: --, 069
BORIN: William, 024
BORING: Jacob, 031; William, 005
BORLAND: James, 007
BOSTIC: John, 031, 045, 070
BOSTICK: John, 021, 088, 096, 109
BOTTS: Jonathan, 010
BOVILL: Benj., 085
BOWEN: John, 027
BOWERS: David, 084, 092, 103
BOYD: --, 051; A., 009, 051, 086;
Alexander, 108; Armistead, 095;
Armstead, 064, 071, 072, 078,
090; Aron, 105; Harison, 095;
Harrison, 003, 049, 076, 104;
James, 077, 091, 092; Jas., 077,
079, 094; John R., 108, 109;
John, 015, 018, 029, 041, 067;
Joseph, 041, 081; Mary, 009,
071, 072, 078, 086; Rhod, 108;
Rhoda, 003; William G., 004;
Wm. J., 051, 064, 072
BOYER: John, 010
BOYET: Catharine, 060
BOYLES: --, 101; C., 111; Charles,
003, 019, 026, 029, 051, 054;
G., 034; John, 082
BRACEY: Murrel, 075
BRACKIN: W., 027
BRADDENN: John, 045
BRADDON: Samuel, 029
BRADEN: Joseph, 006, 034, 090,
091; Samuel, 070, 072, 087, 111
BRADFORD: --, 103; B., 056; G.T.,
057; G., 057; S., 051; Samuel,
042; T. G., 056; Thomas G.,
100; Thos. G., 069, 110
BRADLEY: --, 071, 099-101; Henry,

078; James, 021-022, 027, 111;
Jas., 084, 090, 106; Robert,
060; Terry, 039, 049, 061, 068,
086, 093, 100, 112; Thomas,
024; Thos.. 060-062, 090, 095
BRADLY: --, 069
BRADSHAW: --. 110; John C.. 109;
Wm., 111
BRADY: James. 107; Jeremiah, 029;
John, 014; Tolliver, 022
BRAGG: John. 074, 077, 079; Moore.
074, 077, 078; Sally, 074, 077
BRANCH: John, 024; Nicholas,
088, 109
BRANDLEY: Terry, 069
BRANDON: Thos., 089; Wm., 089
BRATTON: Robt.. 112
BREATHER: Edw., 095
BREATHET: --, 091
BREATHETT: --, 089; Edw., Dr., 092
BREATHITT: E., 099
BRETHITT: --. 069
BRICKLE: Mary, 105
BRIDGES: John, 060, 071; Nancy,
012; Terry. 012; William, 012
BRIGHT: Henry, 109; Jenny, 003;
William, 008; Wm., 043, 044,
049, 077, 094, 095, 098
BRIM: John. 021. 033. 063, 067, 080
BRITTON: Phillis. 105
BROADENAX: John, 045
BROADNAX: Frederick, 093; John
P., 051, 062, 087, 094, 099
BRODENAX: Frederick, 062; Jno.
P., 062; John P.. 062
BROOK: Joseph. 083
BROOKS: Isaac, 014; James. 081.
083. 092. 098; James, Jr., 066;
P.W., 083; Price W., 068, 071,
098; Sam'l, 058. 075; Samuel.
005; Stephen. 014. 083;
William, 026
BROWDER: Frederick, 065, 088, 097;
Frederick, Sr., 093; Fredrick,
070; John, 008; Lucinda N., 088;
Lucindey N., 065; Nancy C., 065,
088; Stephen. 083; Wm. H.. 065,
071, 088; Wm., 061
BROWN: Ann. 052, 053. 054; Armstead
H.. 109; Benj.. 049; Benjamin,
022; Charles, 010, 028, 053,
077, 082, 099, 109; Chas.. 053,
082; Daniel. 033; Duncan, 103;
E.. 099; Ephraim. 007. 010. 012,
020. 028. 053. 082, 086, 090,
092, 108, 112; Geo.. 105; George.
053; Harry, 090; Henery, 110;
Henry. 076, 090; James A., 108;
James, 012, 048, 049, 063, 075,
089. 092. 095; Jas. A., 108;
Joel. 111; John, 023, 053, 092;
Joseph. 052. 054; Littleton.
063; Luther. 082. 086; Micha.
077. 082; Michael. 082, 099,
109; Nancy. 003; Nathaniel, 053;
Richard. 053; Ruffin. 045, 065,

089, 090. 095; Ruth. 053; Sam'l,
088; Samuel, 028, 100; Silvey,
033; Sister, 053; Sterling, 013,
073, 075; Thomas, 053; Thos.,
082; William, 021, 042; William,
Sr., 042; Wm., 050, 100, 110
BROWNLEE: John, 018
BRUE: Wm., 078
BRUFF: Eliza, 033; J.,033. 053, 065
BRUFF?: J., 021
BRUICE: Robt., 081
BRYAN: James, 073; Needham, 063
BRYANT: Samuel, 085
BUCHANAN: John, 026, 083, 103;
Margaret, 031; Samuel, 038, 087
BUCHANNON: Geo.. 068; John, 068,
095; Samuel, 071
BUCHANON: Alexr., 106; Geo.. 085;
John Sample, 089; John, 089
BUCKLEY: Jacob, 015
BUFFORD: Edw., 029
BUFFS: J. 097
BUFORD: C., 112; Catherine, 025;
Charles, 025, 029; Charlotte,
025; Chas., 111; Edw., 086, 111;
Edward, 025, 029, 111; Frankey,
025; Gabriel, 025, 086; Hennery,
025; James, 025, 029, 110; Jas.,
111; Katharine, 025; Priscilla,
025; Sicila, 025; Spencer, 025,
029, 073, 078, 086, 091, 097,
103, 111, 112
BUFORDS: Edw., 111
BUGG: Allen, 093; Benj., 069, 077;
Benjamin, 005, 022, 024, 032,
040, 041, 046, 055, 072; E. M.,
046, 075; Ephraim M., 041, 055,
069, 075, 077; Ephraim, 024,
069; Jesse, 032, 040, 041, 060.
068, 069; Nancy, 041, 046, 055,
069, 072, 077
BULKS: --, 058
BULLOCK: Amos, 007, 014, 017, 026,
040, 051, 068; Elizabeth, 026;
Frances, 004; Nathan, 026;
William, 004, 007, 026
BULLOCKS: Amos, 004; Elizabeth,
004; Frances, 004; Nathan, 004;
William, 004
BULOCK: Amos, 101
BURCH: Larkin, 108
BURGE: Taswell, 101; Tazwell, 076
BURGES: Absalom, 047
BURGESS: Abraham, 113; J., 056;
James, 041, 068; John, 058
BURHAM: Joshua, 028
BURKE: Jenny, 087; Joseph, 087, 093
BURKEW: --, 099
BURNES: Ansalem, 097; Charles,
039; Haratio, 088; James, Jr..
066; Jeremiah, 098; Wm., 084
BURNET: G., 038; Geo., 106;
George, 033, 038
BURNETT: Geo., 071, 100;
Tolliver, 093
BURNHAM: Jas., 076;

Joshua, 015, 106
BURNS: Chas. C., 076; James, Sr.,
066; Jeremiah, 005; John, 045, 093
BURNUM: Ivy, 015
BURRASS: Wm., 060
BURTON: Charles A., 020; Charles,
095; Francis N., 056; Julis,
068; Julues, 049; Levenia B.,
055; Samuel, 001; T. N., 059
BUSBY: James, 033
BUSHAWNEY: Clary, 093
BUSSEO: George, 013
BUSSO: George, 013
BUSSUY: George, 019
BUTLER: Elizabeth Stanfield, 065;
Henry, 026; Isaac, 047, 113;
John, 047, 112, 113; Joshua,
068, 084, 106; Thomas Ryan, 006
BUTTERS: T. R., 058, 059
BUTTS: Mary, 098; Radford, 063
BUZBY: James, 054
BYERS: David, 089; Wm., 086, 106
BYRD: Samuel, 111
CABAL: Adam, 110
CADWELL: David. 106
CAHOON: Geo., 048
CALAWAY: Richard, 084
CALDWELL: Andrew, 054; Ballard,
104; D., 023, 104; Jas., 112;
Joseph, 086; Mary, 021, 054;
Thomas G., 021; Thomas, 014,
054; William, 018, 025
CALESON: Jas., 113
CALFON: James, 113
CALHOON: Chas., 041; Wilson, 041
CALINDER: Thos., 113
CALINDERS: Thos., 113
CALLEN: Thos., 056
CALLISTER: Chas. M., 042
CALPIN: Wm. M., 041
CALVERT: John, 004;
Robert, 014, 046
CAMBEL: Stephen, 095
CAMBELL: James, 054
CAMDEN: Jack, 029
CAMERON: --, 111; Ewen, 054;
Joshua, 092
CAMERON?: Clement, 091
CAMPBELL: --, 027, 076, 112; A.,
103, 106; Alexander, 100; Andrew,
062, 091, 092, 095, 108, 111;
Charles, 012, 014-016, 024; D.,
082; David, 007, 105; Francis,
086; Geo. W., 091; James, 014,
035, 039; Jane B., 108; Jas.,
087; John K., 026, 059, 060,
074, 095, 100; John S., 028,
045, 053, 100; John, 008, 010,
012, 014, 023, 100; Patrick,
012, 014; R., 087; Robt., 078,
103; Sal., 054; Sam'l), 087;
Wm., 093
CANIDAY: Robert, 022
CANNADY: Francis, 046; Robert, 022
CANNON: --, 039, 054; E.. 110;
J., 111; Joshua, 085; Mincy,

077: Minos, 011-012, 077, 079,
080, 084, 091; Newton, 006,
007, 110; Pugh, 071, 088;
Robert, 067; Wm., 045
CAPEHART: Thos., 106
CAPERTON: James, 084, 107;
Jas., 111
CAPPS: Allse, 072; Jeremiah, 101
CARDER: John, 105
CARETHERS: Robert, 029
CARL: Jacob, 110
CARLILE: Robert, 017, 018, 029;
Sarah, 018
CARLISLE: Sally, 103
CARLTON: Thomas, 061
CARMICHAEL: Archibd., 084
CARMICHAELE: Alexander, 059
CARNEY: Thos. P., 108
CAROLL: Gen., 065
CAROTHERS: J., 076; James, 096,
106; John, 029, 041, 068, 069,
082, 083, 099, 100; Mrs., 100;
Robert, 054, 100
CARPENTER: John, 001; William, 028
CARPER: Adam, 079
CARPERTEN: James, 073
CARR: Benj., 070; Benjamin, 028;
Wm., 092, 095
CARREL: James, 076; Jarred, 103
CARROL: Thos., 083;
Thos., Mrs., 083
CARROLL: Ann, 089; Betsy, 043
CARROTHERS: Robert, 046
CARSON: Benj., 095; James, 072,
077; James, Sr., 077; Jno.,
062; John, 062, 091; Peggy,
068, 069; Sally, 068; Samuel,
068; Thomas, 027; William, 028;
Willice, 041; Willis, 068, 069,
090, 098; Wm., 077
CARTER: Daniel, 029, 037, 078,
083, 104, 105, 111; Frances,
045, 095; Francis, 072, 089;
Henry C., 108; John B., 099;
John, 005, 058; Lazarus, 056;
Moulton, 058; Richard, 063,
064; Robt. W., 093; Robt., 094;
Sally, 063, 064, 096
CARTERS: John, 059; Moulton:059
CARTESS: Dan'l, 058
CARTON: James, 077
CARTWRIGHT: David, 086; John, 082
CASH: Elisha, 006; Howard, 006;
Joseph, 006
CASTLEMAN: Silvanus, 008
CATOE: Levin, 082
CATON: Anna, 106
CATOR: Ann, 084; Leven, 086;
Levin, 084, 112
CAVANAUGH: Jas., 092
CAVENDER: Chas., 095; Jas., 045
CHADWELL: D., 071, 080; David,
085, 105, 106; George, 089;
Valentine, 106
CHAMBERS: --, 089; Moses, 006,
042, 043, 049

CHAMP: John, 010, 017, 022, 023;
Mary, 023; Thomas, 022, 023
CHAMPNCY: Dr., 078
CHAMPS: John, 020; Robert, 020;
Thomas, 020
CHAPMAN: --, 024; Nelson, 024,
025, 028, 080; R., 010;
Robert, 010
CHARES: Black, 044
CHAWNING: Ann, 068
CHEATHAM: J. B., 059; P., 058;
Wm., 046; Wyatt, 095
CHEATUM: --, 034
CHEERS: Nathan, 093
CHERRY: E., 105
CHILDRESS: --, 058; Eliza A., 091;
Eliza C., 091; Elizabeth, 048,
049; Henry, 001, 044, 048, 049,
076, 083, 091; J., 106; Joel,
056, 057, 088; John, 019, 044;
John, Jr., 018; Lemuel, 093;
Margaret L., 091; Mrs., 056;
S., 023; Sally C., 091; Stephen,
006, 017, 018, 028-030, 037,
056, 062, 089, 090, 093; Thomas
M., 091; Thomas, 019;
William, 029
CHIPLEY: Stephen, 017
CHISNHALL: Alexander, 009
CHITTY: Benj., 045
CHITWOOD: Edmond, 017; Edmund,
026; John, 026; Nath., 084;
Nathl., 106
CHRISMAN: Aaron, 091; Aron, 088;
Sally, 088
CHRISTIAN: John, 110
CHRISTMAS: Abegal, 026; Col.,
013, 026; William, 026, 027;
Wm., 021
CHUMLEY: Joseph, 086
CHUMSLEY: --, 112
CHUN: Little Berry, 045; Wm., 045
CHURCHWELL: William, 015
CLAIBORNE: George R., 032
CLAIBOURN: Geo., R., 085
CLANTON: Drury, 051
CLARK: --, 111; A., 061; Alexr.,
103, Alexander, 029; Children
(4), 019; Henry, 091; Jas., 086;
Jo., 086; John, 015, 021, 023,
087; Jonathan, 091; Joseph, 043;
Martin, 042, 055, 069, 090;
Moses, 110; Robt., 100, 104; S.,
042, 055; Salley, 042, 069;
Sally, 030, 055, 090; Samuel,
013, 019, 020, 030, 042, 055,
069, 090, 101; Thomas, 028;
Virginia, 013, 020; William,
090; Willie, 055; Wm., 042,
069, 082, 093
CLARKE: Guilliam, 010; Joseph, 045
CLAY: John M., 095, 108, 109
CLAYTON: H., 083; Lambert, 006;
Robert, 007, 022; Stephen, 015;
William, 015
CLEAVES: John, 086

CLEMEN: Jas. S., 092
CLINGAN: --, 095
CLOID: Wm., 111
CLONLAN: Thomas, 027
CLOUD: John, 077
CLOUTON: Drury, 046
CO?(COX): James, 082
COALE: Elizabeth, 020; Joseph,
020; Samuel, 020; Thomas, 020
COALES: John, 020; Joseph, 020
COBB: Ambrose, 022; Jas. H., 086
COBLER: Harris, 089
COCHORN: John, 085
COCHRAN: John, 075
COCK: Richard, 083
COCKE: William, 017
COCKEY: Mary, 019
COCKRILL: James, 050
CODDINGTON: Benj., 043, 060, 065;
Jacob, 043, 052, 065; John, 043
CODINGTON: Benjamin, 006;
Catherine, 006
COFFEE: Gen., 098; John, 056,
070, 088, 097; John, Gen., 066
COFFERY: Peter, 073
COFFEY: James, 004
COHAN: John, 092
COHARN: Aaron D., 045
COHEA: John, 076; Perry, 093
COHOON: Geo., 070; John, 105
COLB: Jas., 112
COLE: Abram, 024; Andrew, 038,
043, 071, 076, 089; Elenor, 050;
Elizabeth, 019; Geo., 075;
Isham, 068; Isham, Jr., 050;
J., 105; John, 019; Joseph, 019,
066; Mary Singleton, 075; Nancy,
019; Philip, 019; Samuel, 019,
075; Thomas, 019; Thos., 061,
066; William, 019
COLEMAN: E., 111; Henry, 104; J.,
059; John, 026; Joseph, 026;
Mrs., 103
COLES: Andrew, 076; Joseph, 019
COLLETT: Robt., 105
COLLIE: John, 014
COLLINGSWORTH: William, 021
COLLINS: --, 057; C., 112;
Erastus, 086, 087; Joseph, 027
COLSON: James, 047
COMBS: Jane M., 065
COMMISSIONERS: Puleskie, 100
COMPTON: Henry, 086; John, 010,
080; Rich., 080; Wm., 044
CONALLY: Jesse, 080
CONDON: Jas., 111
CONER: James, 080
CONGERS: --, 112
CONLY: Peter, 080
CONNALLY: Thomas, 007
CONNELL: Enoch P., 026
CONNELLY: Polley Graves, 026;
Thos., 100
CONNER: Jas., 085
CONNEY: James, 022; Wllllam, 022
CONWAY: Henry, 027, 056

COOCK: James, 027
COOK: --, 097; Edmund, 008, 009,
051, 086; Geo. E., 051, 086; H.,
009, 044, 058, 072, 083, 085,
094, 099, 101, 106; Henry, 006,
008, 009, 037, 049, 051, 052,
058, 062, 068, 077, 082, 083,
086, 088, 090, 091-095, 099,
102, 106, 111; Henry, Jr., 086;
John T., 086; John, 051, 072,
080, 093, 094; Mary, 009;
Richard, 087; T. F., 080;
Thomas H., 054
COOL: Wm., 056
COON: Adam, 076, 089
COONCE: James, 111
COOPER: --, 089; Adam, 069, 074;
Hugh, 068; Huston, 076;
Jonathan, 028, 039; Thomas,
101; Wm., 053
COOR: Jonathan, 075; Milly, 100;
Thomas, 075
COORE: Thomas, 100
COORFMAN: Jacob, 081
COPELAND: James, 014; Jas., 084
CORDER: --, 030
CORDER: Wm. L., 104
CORE(?): Samuel, 044
COREATHERS: James, 101
CORETHERS: John, 049
CORGON: Patrick, 106
CORHAM: Jas., 045
CORHAN: John, 044
CORLETT: R., 076
CORNWAY: Henry, 056
CORNWELL: Joseph C., 007, 008
CORTHORN: John, 076
CORZINE: Abel, 076; Eli, 089,
109; Shelby, 091
COSBY: Garland, 095
COTTINGIM: Betsey, 003
COTTON: Allin, 083; Thos., 058
COUCH: John, 048
COUNCILL: Wm., 084
COURTICE: Wm., 083
COUSART: John F., 014
COWAN: Daniel, 016
COWEN: Daniel, 010, 024; Jas.,
058; Joseph, 059; William,
010, 080
COWSART: Andrew, 039
COWSORT: Andrew, 033
COX: --, 082, 098, 112; --?, 073;
Daniel, 006, 007; E. A., 082;
Henry, 082; James, 083, 101,
104; Jesse, 077, 082, 099, 111,
112; John, 059; Jusse, 109;
Micajah, 075; S., 045, 096, 106;
Samuel, 014, 044, 049, 068, 071,
093, 094, 101; Thomas, 015, 082
CRABB: H., 099
CRACKIN: James M., 093
CRADDOCK: Pleasant, 112
CRAFT: Mason, 046
CRAFTEN: John, 110
CRAFTEN?: Dennis, 110; Geo., 110

CRAFTON: Daniel, 035, 075;
Dennis, 035, 075, 076; Elizabeth,
075, 076; Geo., 075, 076; George,
035; J. B., 076; James, 019,
020, 035; Jas., 110; John B.,
060, 076; John, 019, 020, 038,
043, 071, 075, 076; Richard,
035, 075; Robert, 042, 043,
075; Robt., 043, 049, 076;
Widow, 035
CRAGG: Richard, 063
CRAIG: Andrew, 016, 043, 071,
075, 093, 108; D., 071; Daniel,
103; David, 014, 029, 035, 076;
David, Jr., 033, 038, 071;
Fanny Wade, 075; James, 014,
038, 060, 071, 076; Jas., 076;
Jemima, 075; Margaret, 038, 071;
Mary, 071; Mary, Jr., 038;
Thomas, 092
CRAINSHAW: Oliver, 044
CRANSHAW: James, 035
CRATCHER: E., 058
CRAWFORD: --, 035, 100; Alexander,
035; Elizabeth, 035, 038, 054;
Henry R., 054; James J., 054;
James, 101; John, 016, 020,
026, 035, 054, 100; L., 100;
Lazarus, 016; Samuel, 035;
Washington P., 054
CRAWFORDS: John, 038
CRECY: John, 104
CRENSHAW: Cornelius, 045; Cornelius,
082; Daniel, 077, 089, 094, 103;
James, 060; John C., 091, 094,
095; John, 038, 088; Joseph, 038,
060, 087; Oliver, 087, 088, 091,
095; Pleasant, 076, 110; Sarah,
082; Thos., 076
CRIDDLE: Edw., 100
CRISMAN: Aron, 100; David, 028;
Sally, 100
CRITHERS: James, 059
CRITZ: Jacob, 072
CROCKETT: --, 021, 089, 095; Dr.,
030, 039, 057, 062, 076, 078,
087; James, 054; John H., 021,
053, 067; Joseph, 066, 095; S.,
107, 108; S., Dr., 053, 056;
Sam'l, Dr., 069; Samuel, 028,
035, 049, 053, 111; Samuel,
Dr., 035, 093, 101
CROUCH: John, 045, 052, 053;
Susanna, 048, 052, 053
CROUCHER:
CROW: --, 111; Bryant, 085, 086,
099, 111; Essac, 099; George,
029; Isaac, 009, 043, 046, 064,
079, 085, 086, 088, 105, 111;
Issac, 045, 099; J., 045; James,
045, 085, 086, 111; Joanah, 045;
Joanna, 064, 085, 086, 099;
Polly, 085, 086, 111; Thomas,
086, 099, 111; Thos., 085;
Widow, 046
CROWDER: James, 080; John, 010

CRUMP: Fendal, 085, 098, 101,
103; Fendall, 032; John, 018;
Joseph, 085
CRUNK: John W., 063, 092
CRUSE: Elizabeth, 104
CRUTCHER: Larkin, 061
CUFF: Andrew, 029
CULBERSON: Jo, 070
CULBERTSON: Joseph, 097
CULWELL: William, 034
CUMMINS: David, 009, 018, 030;
Samuel, 089, 096
CUNNINGHAM: John, 021, 022;
Matthew, 001; Polly, 021; W.
W., 058, 093
CURFMAN: Jacob, 109
CURRAY: Samuel, 049
CURREN: Merchant, 046; R. P., 034
CURREY: John, 027; Samuel, 006
CURRIN: --, 034, 082, 086, 092,
093, 100, 103, 110; R.P., 019,
056, 057, 075, 079, 082, 088,
091, 094, 096, 097, 103, 111;
Ro. P., 021; Robert P., 071;
Robt. P., 059, 061, 085, 089
CURRY: John, 025, 034; L., 104;
Robt. B., 095; Samuel, 006,
007, 042, 065
CUTCHEN: Joshua, 042, 072, 110
C_MMERON: Duncan, 025
DABNEY: Chas. A., 072;
John, 017, 082, 108
DALTON: John, 024, 041, 067,
070, 103
DANCY: Isaac, 082
DANIEL: Hicks, 086
DAUGHTRY: Henry, 109
DAVES: Robt., 052
DAVEY: Isiah, 022
DAVID: James, 010; Jonathan, 015
DAVIDSON: Alexander, 006; E. B.,
057; Ephraim B., 026; Geo., 042,
049, 068, 105; George, 006, 017,
026; John, 011; Thos., 091
DAVIES: Geo., 106; James, 103;
Richard, 105; Sterling, 103
DAVIS: --, 112; Alexr., 080;
Ammon, 003; Amos, 015, 020,
021, 030; Augustin, 027;
Benjamin, 006; D. H. Legu, 078;
Daniel, 015; David, 009, 019;
Elisha, 098, 106; Elizabeth,
015; Frederick, 035, 098; Geo.,
084, 106, 109; Henry, 014, 029;
Holland, 094; James, 003, 009,
022, 029, 033, 042, 070; Jas.,
Esq., 065; Jesse, 015; John H.,
068; John, 003, 015, 026, 047,
058, 100; Jonathan, 020, 030;
Joseph, 037, 109; Margaret, 019;
Moses, 092, 108; Nancy, 015;
Robert, 008, 020, 035; Robt.,
046, 060, 092, 095, 108, 110;
Sally, 003; Sarah, 009, 019;
Sterling, 103, 105; William,
006, 015; Willie G., 061; Willie

L., 027; Wilson, 011, 012;
Wm., 073, 112
DAVSIN: Ezekiel, 028
DAVY: Jehu, 076; John, 076
DAWSON: Hudson, 092, 093, 105;
Hutson, 083; John, 111;
Joseph, 010
DAY: Jesse, 070
DEADERICH: John, 083; Thos., 083
DEADERICK: --, 082, 093;
Thomas, 093
DEADRICK: --, 019
DEAN: Benj., 105; Daniel, 095;
F. M., 096; Frances, 104;
Greenberry, 024; Luke, 058;
Sherrod, 105
DEANS: Jeremiah, 046
DEBOW: Stephen, 049
DEDERICK: --, 008
DEDMAN: Thos., 109
DEEN: Greanberry, 028;
Jeremiah, 064
DEENS: Dampsey, 071; Daniel, 071
DEGRAFENREID: Abram M., 008;
Mary Ann, 008
DEGRAFFENREID: A. M., 093, 095;
A. Maury, 002; Mary Ann, 092;
Metcalf, 008
DEGRAFFINREID: A. Maury, 003
DEMOSS: James, 103; John, 076;
Lewis, 100, 103; Wm., 088
DEMUMBRO: Timothy, 112
DENNY: John, 087
DENSON: William, 035; Wm., 042,
043, 052, 093
DENTON: Augustin, 095; Hannah,
001; Jacob, 109
DEPART: Robt., 101
DEPREE: James, 062
DEPRIEST: C. C., 109; Charles,
109; John, 013, 015, 016, 029,
082, 087, 109; Wm., 109
DERRYBERRY: Daniel, 029
DEVARIX: Wm. C., 055
DEVEREIX: William C., 086
DEVERS: Amos, 039, 046
DEVILING: Patrick, 010
DEVILLING: Patrick, 012
DEVORIX: Wm. C., 055, 060, 069
DEWERY: Joseph, 022
DIAL: James, 016
DICKERSON: --, 111; David, 092;
Philopina, 052
DICKESON: Gray, 110
DICKEY: Benona, 003, 004; John,
003; Mary, 003; Wm, 105
DICKINSON: --, 103, 110; D., 030,
055, 057-059; David, 006, 042,
047, 048, 055, 059, 087, 112,
113; Fanny N., 048, 113; Fanny,
112; J., 056; Jno., 056; John,
006, 042, 057, 058, 091;
William, 033
DICKISON: --, 106
DICKSON: David, 059; James, 059;
John, 008; Polly M., 002;

William, 002, 005, 026, 027;
William, Dr., 027; Wm., 108;
Wm., Dr., 076
DICKY: Benona, 083; Geo., 083
DILL: Frederick, 064
DILLARD: N., 050
DILLEN: Leven, 080
DILLIARD: William, 076
DILLIHUNTY: John, 018; Thos., 086
DILLIN: John, 080
DILLING: John, 028
DILLON: Levi, 110
DISMUKE: Paul, 064
DIXON: John, 104; Josiah, 041;
Thomas, 009
DIZART: John, 046
DOBBINS: David, 009, 012; Samuel,
034; W., 057
DOBSON: Reuben, 045
DODSON: Elias, 091; Elisha, 025,
029; Lazarus, 072;
Reuben, 087, 090
DOIL: Joshua, 061; Kitchen, 061
DOLLERSON: Thos., 058
DOMOMBRO: Capt., 016
DONALSON: Francis, 017
DONELSON: Barnaba, 059; Barnet,
068; Capt., 096; Sam'l, 018;
Wm., 103
DONNALSON: Robert, 021
DOOLEY: Michael, 072
DOOLY: Jacob, 039
DORTON: Andrew, 038
DOTSON: Bird, 093; Elisha, 092,
110, 111; L., 093; Lawarus,
092; Lazarus, 007, 111; Presley,
092; Reuben, 007; Sam'l, 058;
Samuel, 029, 110
DOUGLAS: John, 068, 083, 090, 098
DOWD: Charles, 024, 028; Jean,
028; John, 028
DOWDY: John, 091
DOWER: Jeremiah, 049
DOWN: Jeremiah, 043
DOWNING: Elijah, 011, 070, 105;
James, 008, 013, 016, 026;
Polly, 004; W. H., 065; Wm. H.,
070; Wm., 080, 105
DOYAL: Josiah, 093
DOYL: Joshua, 101
DOYLE: Thos., 105
DRAKE: Z., 082; Zachariah, 017,
059, 061, 062, 083
DRISKELL: Obediah, 024, 075
DRUMMOND: William, 005
DRUMRIGHT: W., 040
DUE: Thomas O., 008; Thomas, 002
DUFFEY: Salley, 026
DUFFIEL: John, 083; Wm., 110
DUFFIELD: John, 020
DUFFILL: Wm., 084
DUFFY: John, 026
DUGAN: Thomas, 037
DUGLASS: John, 045
DUISEY: Charles, 029
DUKE: Green, 083, 104

DUN: Denney, 046
DUNAVANS: Leonard, 094
DUNAVANT: Leonard, 092
DUNCAN: Amos, 029; James, 095
DUNCAS: William, 029
DUNEVANT: Leonard, 103
DUNHAM: Anna, 098; Betsey, 098;
Daniel A., 010, 044; Daniel,
011; Deborah, 098; Henry M.,
098; Jinny M., 098; John, 049,
089, 098, 101, 102; Joseph
Waller, 098; Polly, 098; Richard
Leonard, 098; Susan, 098;
William, 098; Wm., 098, 102
DUNIVANT: Leonard, 078, 103
DUNN: Benjamin, 010; D., 030,
048, 052, 058, 059, 062; David,
030, 057, 059, 113; Leonard,
032; M. C., 058
DUNNAGAN: Ashby, 009
DUNNAVANT: Leon, 085
DUNNAVAS: Leonard, 085
DUNVANT: Brook, 032; Leonard,
032; Robert, 032
DUPREE: James, 082
DUPRIEST: John, 105
DURHAM: D. A., 085; Thos., 058
DUVOLL: B., 085
DYER: Joel, 026, 027, 058; John,
104, 109; Lavina, 104, 109;
Robert H., 027; Robt., 109;
Sally Jane, 026
DYSART: Jas., 108
EACHEN: P. M., 058
EACKEM(?): P. M., 026
EASTIN: William, 092;
Wm., 094, 095, 099
EATON: Elizabeth, 099; J. H.,
091, 099; John H., 076, 087,
092, 096, 110; John, 015,
021, 098
ECHOLS: --, 058; John, 088
EDGAR: John, 072
EDGER: Wm., 100
EDMISTON: D., 064, 066; David,
071; James E., 064, 066, 071;
John, 080; Lemuel, 010; Robt.,
071; Sam'l, 019, 078, 082;
Samuel, 001, 012, 053, 090,
096; Thomas, 017; Wm., 067, 070,
090; Zebulan, 064
EDMONDSON: John, 079, 084, 106;
Moses, 080; Samuel, 020, 109;
William, 015; Wm., 105, 109
EDMONSON: David, 060
EDMONSTON: David, 040; Robt.,
042; Samuel, 020
EDNEY: Alfred, 089; Alson, 087,
089, 109; Alston, 069, 083;
John D., 089; Leven, 089; Mary,
098; Nancy, 089; Newton, 089;
Polly, 083, 087, 089, 101, 109;
Seven, 010
EDWARDS: John, 087; Mark, 014;
Peter, 006, 029, 046, 111
EHITESIDE: A., 076

ELAM: Dianna, 041, 065; Edw., 070;
Edward, 001, 012; Elizabeth,
065; Joel, 065; Mathew, 065;
Matthew, 041; Nancy, 065;
Polly, 065; Robt., 065; Stephen,
038, 039, 041, 065; Widow, 039
ELEXANDER: Joseph, 028
ELLAM: E., 104
ELLIOT: James, 037; John P., 060
ELLIOTT: Barnet, 013; James,
015, 087; John, 014
ELLISON: J. T., 016, 024;
Joseph T., 024
ELLISTON: J. T., 017;
Joseph T., 016
ELLOT (ELLIOT?): Jonah, 013
ENERS: Tabbs, 076
ENSLEY: Enoch, 074, 079, 110
EOFF?: Wm., 104
EPERSON: Anderson, 065; Elizabeth,
065; John, 065; Littleberry,
065; Nancy, 065
EPPERSON: Ann, 033; Little Berry,
032; Littleberry, 029
EPPES: Laban, 085
EPPS: John, 045; Labone, 032
ERSCKEN: Samuel, 093
ERWIN: Jas., 112; John, 024;
Joseph, 073; Levina, 073
ERWINS: --, 097
ESTEP: Lydal B., 021
ESTES: Henson, 079, 083, 093;
John, 093; Ludwell, 016; Peter,
095, 101; Polly, 093
EVANS: Atheldred, 078; B., 110;
Benj., 068, 069, 078, 090, 092;
Benja., 084; Daniel, 002; Isham,
055; Jesse, 002, 095; John, 002,
028, 044-045; Lewis, 026;
Martha, 028; Mary, 002, 111;
Rachel, 002; Rebecca, 002;
Robert, 002; Robin, 002; Robt.
M., 081, 082; Wm., 068, 090
EVINS: David, 050; Jenny, 050;
Martha Galaspie, 050
EWEN: Andrew, 083
EWING: --, 097; Andrew, 035, 081,
083; Edley, 023, 039; Nathan,
110; William, 039
EWINGS: Amelia, 002; Elijah, 002;
Nancy, 002
EZELL: Balam, 107; Frederick,
107; Littleberry R., 107;
Mary S., 107
FAIRCLOTH: Cordial, 092
FAIRCLOTH?: --?, 094
FARGUSON: Isaac, 102
FARIS: James, 009
FARMER: Hannibal, 108; John,
002; Nathan, 002, 008
FARRAR: John, 012
FARREN: John, 095
FARRER: Wm., 095
FARRINGTON: Joshea, 106; Joshua,
069, 092, 093, 095, 096
FAUGHN: William, 065

FAULKNER: Wm., 087
FAUTS: Lewis, 054
FEATHERSTON: Wm., 085
FEATHERTON: William, 032
FERGERSON: A., 026
FERGUSON: James, 041;
Joel, 059, 111
FERREL: James, 059
FERRELL: Levy, 015
FESTER: John, 109
FIELD: Emay, 105
FIELDER: I. L., 017; John C.,
079; John L., 020, 022, 034,
035, 098; John S., 023, 029;
John, 060; Nimrod, 084, 106;
Old Mr., 012; William, 026;
Wm., 106
FIELDS: Bennett, 102, 104, 105;
Fielden, 105; Fieldon, 104; N.,
080; Nelson, 023, 039, 042,
044, 079; Patience, 102, 104,
105; Wm., 098, 104, 105
FIGUER: Mathew, 057
FIGUERS: Mathew, 057
FILLERTON: Wm, 105
FINDLEY: Thos., 076
FINNELL: Achilles, 033; James, 033
FINNEY: R., 057; Robt., 057-059
FISHBURN: Phillip, 018
FISHER: William, 029
FISHERS: Frederic, 001
FISK: Moses, 026, 027
FITCH: Peter, 009
FITZ: Joseph, 043
FITZGERALD: James, 014, 029;
Wm., 103
FITZPATRICK: Andrew, 018, 071,
076; Morgan, 015; Samuel, 015
FLEMIN: David, 041
FLEMING: Hannah, 015; John, 059;
Wm., 083
FLEMNIR: Samuel, 046
FLETCHER: John, 105
FLIPPIN: Wm., 111
FLOWERS: Henry, 033
FLOYD: David, 003; Drury, 067;
John, 035, 092, 093; Wm., 064
FLUALLEN: William, 006
FLY: Elisha, 074, 084, 106; Ire,
058; John, 058; Lawrence, 074,
084, 106
FOILDS: Nelson, 027
FOLKS: John, 012
FOREHAND: H., 111; Henry, 085
FOSTER: Ephraim, 101; Jesse, 012,
105; R. C., 110; Robt.
C., Jr., 092
FOWLER: Thomas, 093
FOWLKES: John, 015
FRANCIS: Moses, 045
FRANKLIN: --, 088; Robert, 018
FRAZIER: --, 112; James, 073;
Moses B., 073
FREEMAN: Arthur, 018; Polly, 018;
Saunders, 061
FRENCH: W., 085; William, 032;

Wm., 085
FRIERSON: David, 003, 004; Isaac
Edwin, 003; Moses G., 003, 004;
Samuel, 004
FROST: John, 074, 084, 106
FULGHAM: Arthur, 068
FULGHUM: Arthur, 016, 078;
Polly, 081
FULGUM: Arthur, 041
FULLER: Arthur, 013; John, 100;
Wm., 084
FULTON: James, 029, 034
FUTRELL: Sampson, 056
FUTWELL: Crenshaw, 060
FUZZELL: John, 071
GABLE: Ezell, 059
GABRIEL: Benjamin, 019
GAINES: Anthony, 112
GAINS: Anthony, 048
GALASPIE: Geo., 101
GALLENDERS: Thos., 047
GAMBILL: Milton, 060, 070
GAMBLE: Benjamin, 027; John, 010
GAMBLIN: Polley, 015
GAMBLING: John, 015; Polly, 084
GAMBREL: Benjamin, 013;
Milton, 077, 091
GAMBRICK: Smith, 046
GAMBRILL: James, 067
GANBIL: James H., 109
GANDERSON: John, 077-078
GANTER: Geo., 045, 079
GARDNER: Ann, 002; Hannah, 002,
004; Jane, 002, 004, 103; John,
002, 004, 095; Martha, 004;
Richey, 002, 004; Ritchey, 103;
Sam, 104; Thomas, 002;
William, 002, 004, 103
GARDNER?: Joseph Richey, 004
GARET: John, 082
GAREY: John, 093
GARNER: --, 058, 065; B. M., 087;
Britain, 009; John, 009, 010;
Nathan, 009, 092, 105;
Nathan, Sr., 093
GARRATT: Jacob, 010
GARRET: Jacob, 040; Jane, 109
GARRETT(GARROTT): Jacob, 010
GARRETT: Abel, 076; Eli, 083;
Jacob, 008, 010, 011, 028, 041,
043, 052, 061, 063; Jane, 104;
Jenney, 010; John D., 011, 020;
John, 010, 011; Lewis, 092,
094; Morris, 080; Thomas, 011;
Thos., 010, 080, 105, 109
GARROTT: Jacob, 008; John D.,
010; Thomas, 007, 010
GATLIN: Wm., 089
GATLING: John, 016
GAULT: James, 007, 010, 012, 017,
070, 097
GAY: James, 011
GAZETER: Morses, 034
GEARY: John, 014
GEE: --, 040; David, 093; James,
076; John, 054, 072, 093, 106

GENTRY: Famey, 077; Fanny(Famey),
080; Fanny, 079, 091; Geo., 070,
077; Nicholas, 070, 077, 079,
091; Patsy W., 065; Rich., 077;
Samuel, 046, 077, 079, 080, 091;
Watson, 060, 068, 070, 080, 091;
Wm., 080
GEORDAN: James, 054
GEORDON: James, 057
GEORGE: Hugh, 075; Reuben, 013
GERBISON: John, 076
GERMAN: Daniel, 101; Robt., 100;
Stephen, 008; William, 021;
Zacheus, 072, 074; Zachus, 100
GHOLDSON: Benj., 062
GHOLSON: --, 093; B., 062, 095;
Benj., 044, 087, 092-094, 101,
106; John, 044, 092-094, 101,
106; John, Mrs., 093;
Sally G., 094
GHOLSTON: Benj., 049, 077;
Benjamin, 037; John P., 072;
John, 037
GIBSON: Catharine, 087; Elizabeth,
087; James, 014; Jeremiah, 079;
John B., 014; John P., 014;
John, 087, 100; Maria, 087;
Mary, 087, 092; Pactrick, 092;
Patrick, 014, 024, 075, 087,
100; Polly, 087; Sarah, 087, 092
GIDDEN: Jas., 112
GIDDENS: Francis, 111; James,
029, 061, 084, 111;
Jas., 085, 086
GIDEON: Jas., 085
GILBERT: Benjamin, 059
GILES: --, 034; Wm., 100
GILL: Garner, 103
GILLEPIE: Thos., 091
GILLESPIE: Alexander, 014; David,
028, 111; Francis, 061; Isaac,
105; James, 033; John, 014,
018, 105; Thomas, 028, 100;
Thos., 091; Wm., 096
GILLIAM: Wm., 067
GILLU: James, 111
GILLUM: Jas., 085; Peter, 026
GIMMERSON: Wm., 084
GINLEY: William, 029
GIVENS: Ephraim, 013
GIVIN: Edward, 005; John, 026
GIVINS: --, 027; Edward, 027
GLASCOCK: Geo., 071, 077, 079,
082, 111; George, 012, 014, 029
GLASS: Alex., 103; Alexr., 078,
103; Robt., 078, 103; Samuel
F., 094; Wm. Alexr., 103;
Wm., 078
GLENN: Abraham, 082; Abram, 109;
Wm., 045
GLOVER: James, 007; Jones, 004,
007, 100; Jones, Sr., 007;
Joseph, 024, 056; Lancaster,
007, 024, 025, 034; William,
006, 007, 014
GODD: John, 104

GOFF: A., 082; Andrew, 108; John,
006, 007, 078; Mrs., 111; Peggy,
098, 100; Thomas, 095, 098, 100;
Thos., 083; Wm., 098
GOFF?: Wm., 104
GOINE: John, 011
GOING: J., 011
GOINS: Anthony, 113
GOLADY: Geo., 084
GOLLADY: Geo., 106
GOLSON: John, 045
GOOCH: David, 089, 094, 096, 098;
Elizabeth, 094, 098; James,
098; Matilda, 094, 098; N.,
094; Nathan, 098, 110; Nathaniel,
098; T., 080; Thomas, 094, 098,
106; Thos., 075, 084, 097,
098, 106
GOOD: Charles, 109;
William, 027, 032
GOODE: Charles, 109; Nathan, 109;
Will, 085
GOODLET: Robt., 086
GOODMAN: Arch., 100; Archabaid,
072; Archd., 109; B., 111;
Benagah, 075; Benagy, 029;
Benajiah, 045; Benj., 093;
Benjah, 072; Daniel, 103, 108
GOODRICH: Nat, 105
GOODRICK: Wm., 063
GOODRIDGE: Samuel E., 017
GOOLOES: Garrott, heirs, 027
GORDAN: J., 075; James, 069;
Robt., 093
GORDON: James, 069, 092, 100,
110; Jas., 078; John, 016, 024;
Sam'l, 099; Spratt, 099
GOSEY: James, 093
GOULY: John, 040
GOURLEY: William, 044
GOWEN: Jamima, 071, 072; Jenning,
071; Wm., 071
GOWER: Alexander, 001
GOWERS: Elisha, 001
GOYNE: John, 011
GRA??: Stephen, 004
GRACY: John, 064, 068;
Newel, 064, 068
GRAGG: --, 087
GRAHAM: John, 094, 109; Richard,
059; Saml., 109; Thos., 109;
Wm., 092, 109
GRAMNER: Murrey, 034
GRAVES: Hannah, 024; Mr., 111;
Thomas, 024
GRAY: --, 093, 103, 106, 110, 111;
A., 090, 099; Alexander M., 093;
Bryant, 071; D., 111; Daniel,
076, 085; Dr., 094, 103; Henry
K., 002, 005; Henry, 077, 101,
106; J., 002; James M. K., 002;
James M., 005, 041, 061, 092;
James McK., 002; James, 005,
106; James, wife & children,
002; John, 035; John, Sr., 050;
Joseph, 005; Lucy, 061; Robt.,

045, 083; Sally L. R., 034,
038, 041; Sally L., 002; Sally
S. R., 005; Sally, 061; Suckey,
005; Sukey McK., 002; Sukey,
002; Susan, 093; Susanna, 048;
William, 005; Y. A., 094, 110;
Young A., 002, 005, 032, 034,
035, 038, 041, 069, 085, 093,
111; Young A., Dr., 092
GRAYHAM: John, 104; Wm., 104
GREEN: John, 006; Joshua, 053;
L., 027; Mary, 004, 064;
Nathaniel, 003; Patsey, 026;
S., 019-021, 023, 069, 098,
101, 106; Sherwood, 026, 027,
030, 042, 055, 090, 094; Thomas,
004; William, 004, 027
GREENLEE: John, 006
GREER: Isaac, 085; Vincent, 028;
Vinson, 104, 109
GREGORY: Edward, 026
GREY: Wm, 105
GRIDER: William M., 026
GRIFFIN: John, 026; Wm., 076
GRIFFITH: John, 058
GRIGGS: Berry, 110; Thomas, 027
GRIMES: Jas., 089; John, 007;
Wm., 078
GRINDER: Robert, 017
GRINDERS: John, 017
GROOM: Stephen A., 083
GRUBBS: John, 093
GRUNDY: --, 111; Felix, 034
GULLEY: Jesse, 054
GUNNAWAY: Burwell, 059
GUNTER: Francis, 008, 082;
Sterling, 053
GURLEY: Jeremiah, 039; William,
014, 016, 029; Wm., 111
GURLY: Wm., 045
GUTHREY: Wm., 063
GUTHRIE: Robert, 008, 033
GUY: Dr., 076
GWINN: Edw., 059
GWINNS: Edw., 058
HADLEY: Frances, 098; John L.,
109; Susan, 098; Wm., 078
HAERDON: Elisha, 037
HAIL: John, 012, 041, 104, 107,
109; Marshall, 046; Mesback,
066; Michael, 064; Wm., 079
HAILE: Mashach, 049; Meshack, 080
HAILEY: P., 070
HAINES: John L., 105; John, 068;
Thos., 061, 068
HAIRSTON: Peter, 031
HALBERT: John, 019; William, 027
HALE: John, 080; Sam'l, 070
HALEY: James, 027; Jas., 072;
John, 111; Philip, 109;
Wiate, 072; Wyatt, 098
HALFACRE: Jacob, 035, 089, 090
HALFIRE: Jacob, 065
HALL: Clement, 047, 112; E. S.,
056; Edw., 081; John H., 081;
John, 013, 053; Joseph, 065,

081, 096; Josiah, 027; Lemuel
  B., 061; Martin, 005, 059;
  Sarah, 081; William, 010
HALY: John, 054
HAM: Mrs., 062
HAMBLETON: --, 030; Elijah, 103;
  John, 093, 103
HAMELTON: Francis, 110
HAMER: James, 083; Wm., 085
HAMILTON: --, 095; A. P., 093;
  David P., 109; Hanner, 088;
  Reuben, 060, 081; Thomas, 093;
  William, 030
HAMLET: Bud, 084
HAMMOND: John B., 112
HAMMONS: Capt., 079; D., 095;
  Samuel B., 104
HAMON: Abram, 083
HAMPTON: Adam, 073; Presley, 012
HANCOCK: Geo., 083
HANDLIN: Elizabeth, 052
HANES: Thos., 045
HANKINS: Margaret, 079
HANKS: --, 016; -?, 024; John,
  104; Thos., 109
HANSLEY: Gideon, 024
HANTSELL: Petway, 103
HARAY: John, 083
HARDEMAN: Ann, 108; Blackstone,
  108; Capt., 078; Children, 108;
  Eleazar, 106; Eleazer, 096, 099,
  110; Eliazar, 086; John, 034,
  040, 103; N.B., 005; N.P., 041,
  043, 049, 064, 095, 108; N.,
  065; Nicholas P., 039, 092, 103;
  Nicholas, 039; P., 110; Perkins,
  090; Peter, 106; T. J., 049;
  T. P., 043; Thomas J., 103;
  Thomas, 031, 103, 108; Thos.
  J., 108; Thos., 110; Thos.,
  Jr., 108; William, 103
HARDEN: James, 043;
  Presley, 061, 076
HARDER: Jacob, 037; James, 035,
  052, 05, 076, 110; Jas., 045;
  Mark, 078; Wm., 061
HARDEWAY: Dr., 032
HARDGRAVE: James, 096
HARDGROVE: John, 109
HARDIN: John, 006;
  Presley, 006, 007
HARDING: John, 010
HARDNER: Jacob, 016, 023
HARE?: Bryan, 059
HARES: Hamblen, 019
HARGROVE: Bennett, 109; John,
  048, 113; Stephen, 080
HARGROVES: Stephen, 045
HARKINGS: John, 026
HARNES: John, 042, 049
HARNESS: John, 006
HARNEY: Thomas, 026
HARPER: Berryman, 101;
  Wilkins, 095, 110
HARPETH: L., 112
HARPOOL?: --, 062

HARRASS: Samuel, 029
HARREL: Charles, 090
HARRELL: James, 086
HARRELSON: Ezekiel, 012;
  William, 012
HARRESS: Jacob C., 076
HARRETT: James, 105
HARRIS: --, 048, 097; Andrew, 033,
  038; Arthur, 026; Benton, 025;
  Beverly, 027; Caro, 033;
  Cassandra, 033; Ede, 033, 038;
  Edith, 034; Edw., 071; Edward,
  033, 034; Eli, 095; Joseph
  Simpson, 027; Joseph, 017, 038;
  Josephus, 033, 034; Lucy, 068;
  Margaret, 004; Meekezeno, 033;
  Nathaniel, 012; Patsy, 033;
  Samuel, 033, 048, 111; Sarah,
  004; Shadrock, 046; Sidney, 033;
  Wm., 046, 051; Zens, 034
HARRISON: Allin, 100; Benj. T.,
  077; Edmund, 037; Edward, 023;
  W. P., 062; William P., 034;
  Wm. P., 035, 050, 105;
  Wm., 049, 089, 098
HARRYS: David, 085
HART: John, 078, 103; Richard,
  022; Thos., Col., 052
HARTGRAVE: James, 010
HARTGRAVES: James, 011
HARTLEY: John, 010
HARTLEYS: --, 097
HARVERTSON: John, 079
HARVESON: John, 076
HARVEY: John, 023
HASEL: Elisha M., 070
HASSELL: Elisha M., 079, 087,
  100; Elisha, 029; Nancy, 079
HAVERSON: Alexander, 088
HAWKINS: Amasa, 109; Amosa, 104;
  Mary, 104, 109
HAY: Ann, 002; Balaam, 014, 038,
  040, 045, 051; Balasm, 046;
  Edith, 014; Jeremiah, 105; John,
  026; O.B., 091; R.,006; Richard,
  014, 043, 061, 067, 075
HAYES: Archibald, 110; Dr., 008;
  Robert, 018; Wm., 071
HAYNES: Simeon, 015; Stephen, 083
HAYS: Andrew, 105; D., 073;
  Gilbert, 070; O. B., 097;
  Robert, 017; Thomas, 093;
  W., 082; Wm. P., 093
HAYWOOD: John, 026, 027, 054;
  Judge, 069
HAYWOODS: John, 042
HEATH: Lewis, 063; Nancy, 098
HEBEL: Frederic, 001
HEFFLIN: James, 027
HEIUSTON: James, 019
HELBON: James, 056
HELM: Wm, 105
HELMS: Fielding, 059
HEMPHEILL: Wm., 083
HEMPHILL: Samuel, 093; William,
  023; Wm., 092, 094, 108

HENDERSON: A., 099; Ann E., 087;
  Anne, 099; Archibald, 047, 112,
  113; Hugh, 087, 096; John, 009;
  Richard, 019; Robert, 023;
  Robt., 041; William S., 019
HENDLEY: Wm., 088
HENDRIX: Thomas, 027
HENNEL: H. L., 104
HENRY: Isaac N., 103; Isaac, 037;
  James, 111; Jno. J., 062; John
  J., 037, 043, 044, 049, 051,
  054, 062, 082, 099, 105; John
  T., 062; John, 045; Wm., 103
HENSLEY: Gideon, 061
HERBERT: Nathaniel, 023, 041
HERNDON: Jas., 111
HERREN: Andrew, 064; John, 064
HERREN?: Jas., 064
HERRIN: Andrew, 045, 061; Thomas,
  093; Thos., 046, 111
HERRON: Andrew, 043, 046, 079,
  086, 088; Atkinson, 086;
  Jas., 099
HERSEY: Thos. P., 106
HERTLY: Thos., 109
HESLIN: Jonathan, 061
HESS: William, 018; Wm., 093, 104
HEW: Elizabeth, 044
HEWEY: James, 029
HEWS: James, 030, 040; Rich.,
  044; Richard, 044; Susannah, 044
HEWSTEN/HOUSTON?: Alse, 046;
  Margaret, 046; Rachell, 046;
  Roy, 046; Ruth, 046; Sam, 047
HEWSTEN: Lydia, 046
HEWSTIN: Lydia, 050; Samuel, 050
HEWSTON: Lidey, 019
HIBBITTS: James, 073
HICKMAN: Dr., 039;
  William, 021, 039
HICKS: Daniel, 094; David, 094;
  Harrison, 005; J., 061; James,
  014, 032, 056, 062, 082, 086,
  092, 094, 099, 101, 110; Jas.,
  062, 094; John, 005; Richard
  Wm., 108
HIGGIN: James, 027
HIGGINS: Albert, 005, 019;
  Halbert, 027; James, 019; John,
  005, 018, 019, 027; Martha,
  005, 019; Phoebe, 027;
  William, 019, 027
HIGHTOWER: Alfred, 092; Della,
  092; John, 001, 006, 092;
  Polly, 001, 006; Richard, 001,
  006, 023, 092
HIGHTWOER: John, 091, 092
HIGNETH: John, 090
HIGNIGHT: Jno., 107
HILL: Allen, 029, 032, 070, 079,
  087, 088, 093, 095, 100, 109;
  Allin, 111; Ambrose, 091, 100;
  Benjamin, 074; Dan, 045; Dann,
  006; Eli F., 034; Ely F., 038;
  G., 030, 074; Green, 003, 079;
  H. W., 019, 023; Hemp, 099;

Henry R. W., 108; Henry W., 023,
030, 039; Hezekiah, 074; J. C.,
023, 079, 084; J., 098; James
C., 019, 023, 039, 048, 108;
James, 023, 030, 105; Jeremiah,
074; John D., 067, 107, 108;
John, 010, 023, 029, 039, 041,
053, 061, 082, 086, 105;
Jonathan, 074 106; Joseph, 074;
Joshua C., 106; Lucy, 109;
Martha, 019, 023, 024, 030;
Nancy, 108, 109; Nathaniel, 004;
Penelope, 074; Spencer, 074,
085; W., 079; William C., 019,
023, 030; William, 003; Wm. C.,
048; Wm. H., 108; Wm., 045,
067, 074, 083, 090, 093
HILLIARD: --, 094; Isaac, 047,
055, 059, 112, 113; Mary, 047,
112, 113; Thos., 109
HILLIARDS: --, 097
HILLIDAY: Thos., 076
HILME: Geo., 062
HILTON: Jas., 058
HINDS: John, 010; Simon, 015, 020
HINES: David, 014
HITER: M. O., 095; T., 074, 094;
Thomas, 039; Thos., 043,
049, 095
HOBBS: --, 040, 097; Ann, 032;
Hartwell, 032, 103; James, 009;
Joel, 009, 014, 049-051, 056,
059, 062, 068, 071, 072, 077;
Nancy, 032; Sally, 032
HOBES: Wm., 046
HOBS: --, 030
HOBSON: Lawson, 013
HOCKMAN: Elliott, 101
HODGE: Edmond, 013; Frances, 112;
Francis, 008, 049, 060, 086;
Geo., 086; Hannah, 040; Henry,
090; John, 046, 049; Robert,
069; Robt., 054, 084; Welcom,
013; William, 041, 060; Wm. H.,
049; Wm., 046, 049
HODGES: Edmund, 013; Elizabeth,
003; James, 003; Josiah, 040;
Lydda, 003; Philip, 003;
Welcom, 003
HOGAN: John, 082
HOGANS: Wm., 061, 086
HOGES: Francis, 105
HOGH: Frank, 046
HOIUSTON: David, 019
HOLBERT: John, 005; William, 041;
Wm., 061
HOLEMANS: Thomas, 001
HOLES: Clement, 113
HOLIDAY: Henry, 045
HOLLAM: John, Jr., 005
HOLLAND: Augusty, 026; F., 093;
Frederick, 076, 092; Gustis,
006; Kemp, 077, 092, 095, 099,
110; Kempt, 060; Wm., 101
HOLLEN: Gustavus, 106; Wm., 106
HOLLIDAY: Henry, 008

HOLLYDAY: Peter, 045
HOLMES: Elm, 026; Hannah, 001;
John, 109; V. B., 101
HOLSTEAD: Elizabeth, 052
HOLT: Abner, 049, 053, 083;
Absolam, 104; Harden P., 085;
Hardin P., 108; J., 080; John,
021, 024, 074, 079, 084,
095, 106
HOLTON: Thomas, 009
HOLTS: W., 058
HONELL: William, 010
HONOLL(HUNNELL?): Peter, 022
HONOLL: Peter, 022
HOOD: Betsy, 072; Charles, 068,
078, 083; Edward, 093; John,
014, 085, 104, 105
HOOKER: Thomas, 013; William,
013; Wm., 041, 067, 091
HOOKS: Betty, 025;
Curtis, 024, 025
HOPE: E., 058; Ell, 059, 111;
Thomas, 023; Thos., 087; Widow,
023; William, 050; Wm., 083,
084, 098
HOPKINS: Bitha, 001; Elizabeth,
001; Hannah, 001; James, 001;
Jason, 001, 023, 039, 043, 045,
049, 054, 055, 062, 065, 085,
087; John, 001; Jonathan, 001,
007, 022; Joseph, 001; Keziah,
001; Lucy, 001; Neal, 023;
Richard, 030; Winfred, 039;
Winifred, 001, 023
HOPPER: Absalum, 073
HOPPERS: --, 112
HORRON: Andrew, 111
HORSE: M., 076
HORTON: James, 111; Jonathan,
109; Samuel, 111
HOURLEY: Wm., 046
HOUSE: E. B., 075; Green, 034,
038; Isham, 093; Isham, 101;
James, 026, 034; James, Jr.,
013, 033; James, Sr., 013;
John, 018, 029, 090; M.I., 093;
Mansfield, 092; William, 013;
Wm., 060
HOUSTON: Aaron, 068, 083; David,
017; J. B., 111; Lydia, 019;
Samuel, 017, 019; Sidney, 017;
W., 058; Wm. M., 059;
Wm., 057, 058
HOWARD: John, 080, 106;
Richard, 026
HOWDESHELL: Jacob, 040
HOWELL: Joseph, 013, 016; Wm., 056
HOWSER: Geo., 078 103
HUBBARD: Daniel, 033; J., 088,
100; John, 033; Joseph, 075;
Woodson, 080, 101
HUBBART: Nath'l, 079
HUDDLESTON: David, 109
HUDGENS: Wm., 086
HUDGES: P., 112
HUDGINS: Pharoah, 112; Wm., 112

HUDLOW: Barbara, 029; George, 028
HUDSON: Dawsey, 026; John, 005,
058, 105; Nancy B., 075
HUDSPETH: David, 006;
Robt., 066, 070
HUES: Richard, 093
HUEY: James, 012
HUGGINS: Chas., 105;
Reuben, 008, 035
HUGHAH: Henry, 018
HUGHES: A., 080; Archeleus, Jr.,
101; Archilus, 067, 102;
Archilus, Jr., 080; Archilus,
Sr., 080; Christian, 023;
Elizabeth, 044; Iaasa, 095;
James, 063, 068, 071, 093, 098;
James, Sr., 093; Jas., 089;
Levi, 087; Owen, 076; Rice, 084,
106; Rich., 059; Richard, 045,
049, 071, 077; Susanna, 044
HUGHS: Archilus, 070; Ezekiel,
105; John, 111; Martha, 070;
Robt., 070
HUGHSON: David, 106
HUGHSTON: James, 105
HULCY: Chas., 111
HULL: John, 028
HULM: G., 039, 051; Geo., 054;
George, 039; Margaret, 054
HULME: Fielding, 093; G., 007,
009, 011, 051, 055, 085, 103;
Geo., 043, 049, 062, 082, 087,
090, 091, 094, 106; George,
008, 010, 012; John C., 101;
John, 008, 010, 096; Meredith,
095; Peggy, 051; Robert, 007,
008, 010, 022, 023; Robt., 082,
099, 106; Susanna, 007, 008;
Thomas, 012, 021; Thos., 078,
095; W., 062; William, 008,
083, 099; Wm., 035, 082, 087,
091, 095, 101
HULMES: Geo., 062; W., 057
HULSEY: C., 111; Charles, 029
HULSLEY: Gideon, 075
HUMAN: Josh., 093
HUMPHREY: --, 056; Daniel J., 089;
Daniel, 085; Mrs., 056
HUMPHREYS: Anna, 066; Benjamin,
066, 070; D. S., 080; Daniel
Jones, 066; Elijah, 066; Hariet,
066; Hester, 066; Polly, 066;
Sally, 066; Solomon, 106;
Willie Jones, 066
HUMPHRIES: Benjamin, 097; D. J.,
097; D., 097; Daniel, 097, 098;
David, 097; Solomon, 084;
Solomon, Dr., 089, 097
HUNGARFORD: Jas., 095; Richard, 093
HUNGERFORD: James, 015, 045;
Wm., 104, 093
HUNNEL: William, 022
HUNNELL: William, 022
HUNT: G., 023, 072, 075, 078, 079,
084, 098, 100; Gasham, 039;
Gersham, 042, 044, 079, 106;

Gorsham, 015; Gurshum, 034;
Gurson, 029; S., 039, 050, 101,
102; Sion, 011, 024, 030, 037,
055, 081, 089, 090, 092, 096,
102, 107
HUNTER: Andrew, 060, 095;
Catherine, 088, 092, 095;
Elijah, 005, 012, 058, 088,
089, 092, 095; Elisha, 088;
Elisha, Sr., 012; Henry, 011.
093, 095; William, 031
HURD: Jesse, 026
HURLERY: John, 006
HURLEY: John, 097
HUSE: Archelous, 077; Richard, 017
HUSLEY: Gideon, 083
HUSTON: David, 006, 007, 089;
John, 007, 087; Lydia, 099;
Samuel, 099
HUTCHESON: William, 015; Wm., 086
HUTCHINSON: Jesse, 093
HYDE: Hartwell, 015, 070, 109,
110; Richard W., 015, 109
INGLAND: S., 104
INGRAM: Benjamin, 102; Frances,
011, 012; Henry, 015, 019, 045,
102, 105, 109; John, 011;
Samuel, 011, 012; Susan, 102
109; Susanna, 011, 012; Susanna,
Jr., 011, 012; Susanna, Sr.,
011; Susannah, 105;
Thomas, 011, 012
INMAN: Henry, 022; John, 076,
092; Lazarus, 076; Lazrus, 076
INMAN?: Jesse, 092
IRELAND: Daniel, 068, 084;
Hardy, 057
IRION: Frederick W., 077. 079; G.
A., 079; Geo. A., 077. 079;
John L., 077; John P., 079, 106
IRON: Ann P., 069; Fredrick W..
070; Fredrick Wilt, 069; G.A.,
080; Geo. A., 068. 070; Geo.
Anderson, 069; John P., 066,
068, 069; John, 084; Philip
Jacob, 064 069; Robt. A., 069;
Sarah C., 069; Sarah, 064, 068;
Thos. P., 064; Widow, 084
IRVIN: Christopher, 091, 100
IRVINE: William, 012
IRVINE?: Edmiston, 012
IVEY: F., 111; William, 010; F.,
090; Frederick, 077, 080, 085
IZRALL: Fred, 077
JACKSON: --, 051, 097; Adam, 083,
094, 111; Frances, 061, 106;
Francis, 053, 054, 086; Henry
B., 107; Henry H., 028; Isham,
093; James, 010, 088; Jas., 057
100; Jesse, 076, 089; Joseph,
015; Joshua, 092; Mark L., 043.
070, 077; Reuben, 093; Richard,
061; Samuel, 002, 088; Sarah,
002; Washington, 100; William,
041, 094; William, Capt., 088;
Wm., 097; Zachariah, 045, 049,

092; Zacheriah, 043
JAMES: --, 071, 100; Geo. H.,
061; George H., 059, 060
JAMESON: Wm., 106
JAMISON: John, 014
JEMESON: Wm., 073
JEMMERSON: Andrew, 028; James,
098; John, 098
JENKINS: Agnes P., 097; Dempsey,
047, 112, 113; T., 076; Thos.,
089, 095; Walter, 051
JENTRY: Samuel, 010
JERMAIN: Daniel, 050
JINKINS: Thos., 096
JINNINS: Edward, 027
JOB: John, 026
JOBE: James, 029
JOHNSON: --, 112; A., 062, 087,
094; Alex., 054, 060, 071, 084;
Alexander, 021, 063, 087, 096;
Andrew M., 066, 070; Andrew,
082; Andw., 076; Benj., 048,
113; Charles, 066, 070; Col.,
101; David, 049, 090; Gldem,
073; Grace, 017; Isaac, 059;
James, 017, 073; Jessee, 049;
John, 001, 028, 059, 061, 063,
070, 071, 074, 080, 097, 109;
Joseph, 033; Neil, 029; Patsey,
066; Robert, 100; Stephen, 061,
070; Swanson, 012, 100; Thomas
026; Wiley, 093, 094; Wm., 066,
071, 084
JOHNSTON: (Sawn?), 014; A., 071,
094; Alexander, 024, 041;
Andrew, 035, 045, 092, 106;
Betcy, 074; David, 049, 050,
068, 106; Elizabeth C., 073-074;
Elizabeth, 074; James, 059;
Jese, 042; Jesse, 045; John
Lock, 074; John, 009, 072-074;
Littleton, 072; M., 109; Matt,
014; Matthew, 035, 073, 074,
082; Peter, 041; Robert, 002,
010, 049, 100; Robt., 073,
074; Wm., 045, 086
JOHNSTONS: N., 111
JOHSTON: David, 049
JOICE: James, 065, 081; Thos., 088
JONE: David, 100
JONES: Amsey, 061; Amza, 069;
Andrew, 056; Benj., 045;
Charles, 085; David C., 032;
David, 086; Dempsey, 106;
Edward, 034; Elizabeth, 038;
Gray, 049; Isaac, 064; J. G.,
045; Jackey, 093; James G., 041,
043-045, 049, 051, 054, 062,
072, 078, 082, 093, 094, 099;
James Gray, 037; James, 020;
Jarvis, 027; Jas. G., 043, 049,
062; John, 010, 011, 022, 026,
064, 076, 085, 111; Julia, 052;
L., 111; Lew, 085; Lewicing,
032; Nelson, 032, 085; Polly,
090; Rich., 078; Richard, 083;

Susan, 098; Taylor, 093, 107;
Thomas, 026; Thos. E., 085; W.,
111; Wily, 066; Wm, 085
JONES?: E. W., 093
JORDAN: --, 094; Archer, 030,
065, 070, 071, 097, 105; Archer,
Esq., 066; Benj., 073, 074;
Burton, 003, 008; Elizabeth,
074; Henry, 016, 091; James,
005 044, 092; John, 008, 025,
034; Johnson, 071; Nancy, 034;
Sally, 008; Sarah, 009; Susanna
G., 034; William, 034;
Wiltshire, 015; Wm., 071, 080
JORDOM: Jas., 058
JOSLIN: Daniel, 018
JOYCE: James, 024, 033, 041,
105; Thos., 070
JULIN: Geo., 041
JUSTICE: Henry, 082
KANADAY: Jesse, 041
KAVANAUGH: --, 058; Charles, 046,
082, 101; Wm., 101, 105
KAVANNAS: Charles, 045
KAVENAUGH: C., 099; Charles,
095, 105; Chas., 093
KAVENDER: Capt., 055
KEARNEY: H. G., 104; Henry G.,
002, 043, 049; Lucy D., 061;
Lucy Davis, 061
KEARNY: Lucy, 005
KEARSEY: Thos. P., 084
KEE: Jenny, 028; Jinea, 028;
Nancy, 028
KEETH: John, 003
KEIGLER: Andrew, 015; David, 095
KELLY: Mordecia, 074, 079, 080;
Mordica, 069; Mordicia, 074;
Thomas, 029
KELLY?/NELLY?: James, 101
KELLYWOOD: James O., 106
KENARD: Michael, 025
KENEADES: Capt., 063
KENNADY: Robt., 076
KENNARD: Anthony, 025; Geo., 066;
George, 025, 041; John, 025;
Michael, 025; Nathaniel, 025;
W., 041; Walter, 026
KENNEDY: Dempsey, 014; I., 105;
Jas., 108; John, 014
KENNEY: James, 071, 072;
Mary, 071, 072
KENNY: Jas., 076
KERBY: Sally, 072
KERNEY: Henry, 006
KETCHORN: John, 076
KEY: Henry, 016, 024;
Wm., 084, 106
KIDD: Benj., 073; Geo., 098;
Jas., 073; W., 080; Wm., 073,
097, 100, 106
KIMBRO: Jas., 084; Nathaniel, 013
KINCADE: Jas., 084
KINCAIDE: James, 106
KINDRAKE: William, 002
KINDRICKS: Olsimus, 014

KING: J. J., 054; John M., 071;
    Neelson, 057; Nielson, 024;
    Wigton, 104; William, 033;
    Wm., 067, 109
KINNARD: Anthony D., 020; Geo.,
    060, 087, 099; George, 020,
    024, 034; John, 020, 025;
    Michael, 020, 024, 034, 042,
    045, 083, 089, 090; Michael,
    Jr., 006; Michale, 025;
    Nathaniel, 020
KIRK: Wm., 078
KNIGHT: --, 093; J. 097; Jas.,
    095, 099; John, 093, 094; Josiah,
    093; M., 056; Wm., 097
KRYSTER: John, 060
KYLE: Rebekah, 005
LACY: Ambros, 079
LAFEVER: --, 112
LAGRON: John A., 089; Mary, 089;
    Wm., 089
LAGROON: Adam, 089; Wm., 089
LAGROUND: Adam, 061
LAMASTER: James, 004
LAMB: Aquilla, 061; David, 061;
    David, Jr., 061; John, 027
LAMKINS: Elias, 084
LAMPKINS: Elias, 106; Ezekiel, 014
LANCASTER: David, 041, 043
LANDRUM: Mary, 061, 077, 094;
    Meriannam, 041; Meriman, 005,
    063; Moriman, 027
LANE: Turner, 027
LANIER: --, 040, 112; Nicholas, 068
LANKASTER: David, 066, 067
LANKSTON: Jacob, 045
LARK: Dennis, 089
LARKIN: Elizabeth, 031
LARKINS: Elizabeth, 031; John,
    031; Margaret, 031
LASLEY: Wm., 081
LASTER: John, 109
LASTLY: Thos., 085
LATEMORE: James, 100
LATON: Michael, 089
LATTA: Thomas, 012
LAUDERDALE: J., 097; Jas., 076
LAURANCE: Jacob, 057; Henry, 066;
    Samuel, 097
LAVENDER: Bluff, 029; Bud, 029;
    Byrd, 111; C., 111; Chas.,
    078; Nich., 078; Nicholas,
    029, 083, 111
LAW: Richard, 100
LAWRANCE: Jacob, 004
LAWRENCE: Abraham, 004; Elizabeth,
    004; Jacob, 056; John, 004;
    Polly, 004; Sam'l, 070;
    Samuel, 004
LAWRY: David, 041
LAY: Isaac, 006
LAYGROUND: John Adam, 045
LEA: Matthew, 111; William, 012
LEACH: James, 105
LEADBETTER: Joseph, 044
LEAFEVER: Wm., 073

LEAK: Onn?, 084
LEDBETTER: --, 106; Isaac, 067
LEE: Benjamin, 001; Braxton, 001;
    Jenny, 001; John, 001; Martha,
    085; Mary, 001; Matthew, 045,
    053, 083, 085, 105
LEEK: Anna, 080
LEEPER: Allen, 004
LEGATE: Chas., 109; Wm., Dr., 067
LEMASTER: David, 016
LEMMING: John, 106
LENIER: John, 073; Nicholas, 041
LESTER: --, 082, 101; A., 062;
    Alexander, 037, 064, 093;
    Alexander, Sr., 045; Frederick,
    037; Geo., 076, 110; Henry, 045,
    046, 082, 088; James, 086, 111;
    Whitehead, 064
LESTER?: --?, 094
LEWIS: Abel, 112; Benj., 053;
    David, 053, 054, 061, 086, 106;
    E., 071; Elam, 070; Elizabeth,
    053; G., 109; Hannah, 053; Ja.,
    104; James M., 073; Joel, 018;
    Nancy, 053; Sarah, 053;
    William T., 018; Wm., 053
LEYGROON: John, 076
LIGHTFOOT: Thomas, 019;
    Thos., 084, 106
LINCOLN: Elijah, 104
LINDSEY: John, 014;
    Moses, 085, 106
LINISY: Jesse, 021
LINTZ: --?, 016; Wm., 097
LITTLE: Abraham, 008; Benjamin,
    024; Geo., 070, 077, 091; Isaac,
    049; James, 105; Jean, 004;
    John, 093; William, 026
LITTLETON: Ellinor, 104; John,
    104; Mary, 104; Reuben, 077
LIVINGFELLOW: William, 077
LOCK: Charles, 071, 105;
    Elizabeth, 087; Orphs., 087;
    Richard L., 074; Richard S.,
    040, 078, 087; Thos. B., 060;
    Widow, 087; William, 015, 016
LOCKE: Richard S., 024, 041;
    Richard, 022; Wdw., 075
LOCKHART: Hugh, 079
LOFTIN: Augustin, 109; Smith,
    091; Thos., 076
LOGAN: Wm., 065, 077, 080,
    095, 106
LOGANS: William, 011
LOGATE: William, 024
LOGICK: Duncan, 034
LOGUE: James, 103
LONE: David, 029
LONG: Isaac, 105; Michael, 035,
    045, 068, 083, 089, 098, 103,
    108; Samuel, 097
LONGS: --, 111
LOOVIT: David, 110
LORD: John, 033
LORREL: Wm., 080
LOVE: David B., 018, 039; James,

    001, 029, 039; John G., 018,
    039; Joseph, 018, 039; Peggy,
    003; Samuel, 039; Susan, 003;
    William M., 039;
    William, 003, 018
LOVET: David, 029
LOWARD: Job, 087
LOWRANCE?LAWRENCE: John, 004
LOWRY: Alborn, 059
LUCAS: Abel, 086
LUINS: Andrew, 086
LUNN: David, 041; Nathaniel, 097
LUSTER: James, 025; John W., 087
LUTON: William, 026
LUTY: David, 080
LYAN: H., 049; Mrs., 061
LYNTON: Alson, 111
LYNTZ: William, 039
LYON: H., 049; Henry, 043, 049,
    058; John, 070
LYONS: Henry, 026;
    Patrick, 018, 026
LYTLE: --, 058; Arch'd, 073;
    Archbd., 092; Archibald, 052,
    103, 106; Casse, 006; Wm., 100
LYTTE: W., 058
LYTTLETON: Isaac, 106
MABANE: See (MEBANE): A., 108;
    Alexander, 107; Geo. Allen, 107;
    George Allen, 107; George, 107,
    108; James, 107; Joseph, 107;
    Louisa, 107
MABARY: Frederick, 012
MABRY: Philip, 080
MACK: Lawyer, 099
MACKEY: William, 012
MACFADIN: Curnelis, 028
MACLIN: John, 018; Willis, 111
MADDEN: Elisha, 085
MADDIX: James, 109
MADDOX: Wm., 093, 110
MADEARES: John, 113
MADON: Charles, 102
MAGISON: William G., 026
MAGNOSS: Robert, 009
MAHAN: Andrew, 022; Jesse M., 093
MAIRE: Isaac, 068
MAIRES: John, 068, 069, 081;
    Mary, 068
MAIRS: Hannah, 055; Isaac, 055,
    090; John, 068; Joseph, 008;
    Mary, 063, 068, 069; Samuel,
    063, 068, 069, 089, 090
MALANI: Wesley, 060
MALLORY: John, 093, 095; M., 058
MALLOY: Thomas, 091
MALONE: Miles, 005, 041; Sarah,
    093; Thomas, 028, 049;
    Thos., 084
MALORY: Daniel, 059
MANCE: Lewis, 024
MANCO: George, 024
MANCUE: Benjamin, 026
MANDLEY: Caleb, 001, 017, 057,
    058, 071, 082, 087, 092, 095
MANDLY: Elizabeth, 093

MANEY: James, 047; Jas., 055, 059; Sally H., 047
MANIER: John, 031; Philip, 067
MANIRE: Betty, 033; John, 033; Patty, 031
MANKER: George, Sr., 026
MANLEY: --, 110; Allen, 047, 113; C., 099; Caleb, 012, 017, 029, 037, 090, 099, 100, 103, 111; Jane, 047, 113
MANLY: Cabb, 045; Caleb, 054; G., 054
MANNEY: James, 112, 113; Sally H., 113; Sally, 112
MANNING: Wm., 052, 093
MANSKER: George, 016; L. W., 033; William, 016
MANUEL: Abraham, 077
MARCHANT: James, 072; Jas., 067
MARCUM: Abner, 041
MARINE: John, 013
MARKIM: Barnet, 028
MARLIN: George, 018; Henry, 093, 104; James, 037, 080; John, 086, 112; Samuel, 086
MARR: John, 018, 019; W. S., 016
MARRITT: Benjamin, 044
MARRS: Josiah, 026; William Christmas, 026
MARS: William, 039
MARSH: L., 104
MARSHALL: E., 053, 065, 097; Gilbert, 103; James, 031, 086, 112; William, 031; Wm., 045
MARTIN: Alex, 053; C., 095; Campbell, 100; George, 007, 008, 037; Henry, 007, 010; James, 048, 112; John, 084, 113; Jonathan, 015; Joseph A., 044; S., 066; Samuel N., 064, 067, 080; Samuel, 092, 093; Thos. A., 069; William, 013, 019, 020, 030; Wm., 092; Zachariah, 015
MASON: --, 034, 082, 086, 092, 100, 103, 110; Abraham, 013, 081; Chas., 058; D., 095; David, 110; Isaac, 013, 026, 027, 081, 093; Thomas, 007
MASSEY: Adkins, 059; John, 060
MASTERSON: Thomas, 002, 008, 021; Thos., 057
MATHENYS: --, 103
MATHIS: Cornelious, 029
MATTHEWS: C., 040; Cornelius, 024, 072, 089; Dalton, 040; John B., 105; John, 013, 089, 096, 107; William, 020, 025
MATTOCKS: William, 011
MAURY: --, 034, 039, 045, 054, 078, 092, 093, 100, 101, 111; A., 059, 076, 081, 093; Abraham, 092; Abraham, Jr., 002; Abraham, Sr., 113; Abram, 004, 020, 021, 048, 069, 085, 093; Abram, Maj., 073; Abram, Sr., 008,

027, 037; F., 095; J. H., 111; James, 055; Maj., 040, 062; P., 093; Philip, 008, 082, 092, 095, 101, 108; Phillip, 105; Richard, 092; Thomas T., 092, 097; Thos. T., 053, 065, 091; William, 012; Wm. F., 089
MAXFIELD(MAFIELD): Daniel, 046
MAXWELL: Daniel, 041; Thomas, 049
MAY: John, 018; Joseph, 110; William, 026, 079; Z., 093
MAYBERRY: Job, 092
MAYFIELD: Elias, 077; Elijah, 024; George, 010; Isaac, 073, 112; Izrael, 010; James, 017; John, 017, 020, 022, 023, 028, 029; Sally, 070; Thomas, 018, 067; Thos., 043
MAYS: Armistead, 029; Francis, 081; Gardner, 092; Garner, 084; James, 043, 049; John, 043, 049, 069; Samuel, 064, 068, 077, 106
MAYSE: John, 092
MCABE: John, 101
MCAFEE: John, 008; Miles, 008
MCAFFEE: John, 023
MCALISTER: --, 019, 023, 062; C. H., 042; C., 111; Charles, 042, 046, 099, 110, 111; Chas., 082, 086, 103; David, 045; James, 073
MCALROY: James, 004
MCBRIDE: Hugh, 015, 024, 106; James, 016; Joseph, 080
MCCA(SHIUS?): Isaac, 112; John, 112
MCCABE: Chas., 072
MCCAIN: John, 080, 110
MCCALISTER: --, 110; Charles, 107; Children, 107
MCCALL: Cathren, 018; Francis, 014, 018; Willie, 064
MCCALPAN: John, 009, 010, 023; John, Jr., 010; John, Sr., 010; William, 010
MCCANDLES: --, 094; Wm., 080
MCCANDLESS: John, 017
MCCANLESS: Wm., 110
MCCAREN: Franklin, 080
MCCARIAM: Franklin, 071
MCCARLIN: John, 064
MCCARREL: Israel, 013; Isreal, 060; Izrael, 027, 029
MCCARRELL: Israel, 026; Izrall, 013
MCCASLAND: John, 073
MCCASLIN: --, 112; Cornelius, 082; Jas., 083; John, 088; Younger, 109
MCCASTLAND: Wm., 073
MCCAY: Reynold, 109
MCCLAIN: Darcus, 080
MCCLANNAHAN: Sheff., 057
MCCLARAN: Alexander Parker, 084; Alexander, 097; Daniel Clevies, 084; Felix, 084; Garland Anderson, 084; Jane, 084; Jincy, 084; John Duke, 084; Milcah, 084; Polly, 084; Sally, 084;

Thomas, 084; Thos., 084, 097; Wm., 084
MCCLARIN: Alexr., 105
MCCLARON: Franklin, 084; John, 060
MCCLEAN: William M., 014
MCCLEIN: John, 084
MCCLELAND: Robert, 035
MCCLELEN: John, 076
MCCLELLAN: John, 015, 110; Robert, 103
MCCLELLEN: John, 089; Robert, 013
MCCLELLIN: John, 083
MCCLENEN: Robert, 033
MCCLURE: Henry, 027; William, 026
MCCOLLIN: John, 083
MCCOLLISTER: Chas., 062; Joseph, 063, 109; Wm., 046
MCCOLLUM: Cloud, 012, 104, 105; Jacob, 012; James, 110; John, 010, 012; Mary, 109; Thrasher, 012
MCCOLPAN: John, 017
MCCOMBS: James, 103; Jas., 111
MCCONICO: Garner, 042, 054; James, 045
MCCONNEL: Robert, 024
MCCONNICO: --, 059; Ann, 007, 075, 076, 076; Christopher, 090; G., 048, 052, 103; Gared, 076; Garner, 006, 043, 045, 046, 049, 052, 058-060, 065, 075, 076, 079, 090, 102, 103, 111, 113; Jared, 007, 075, 079, 090, 103; Jarred, 076; Keziah, 007, 102; Lemuel B., 090
MCCORD: David, 021, 029, 033, 043, 052, 087
MCCORKLE: Andrew, 028
MCCORMAC: James, 008, 010
MCCORY: Wm., 093
MCCOWEN: Alex, 095
MCCOY: Robert, 034
MCCRACKEN: John, 014, 057
MCCRACKIN: Robt., 061
MCCRAKEN: Jas., 105
MCCRARY: Armer, 026; Thomas, 018
MCCRAVEN: James, 029
MCCRAVY: John, 087
MCCRIDE: Hugh, 084
MCCRORY: Legate, 074; Thos., 074; Thos., Col., 101; Wm., 074
MCCUISTIAN: John, 011, 012
MCCUISTION: Benjamin, 025; Benjamin, Mrs., 025
MCCUISTON: John, 001
MCCULLOCK: James, 009; John, 104
MCCURDY: David, 004; Elizabeth, 004; Grissy, 004
MCCUTCHAN: Hannah, 023; James, 023; John, 023, 029, 039; Sam'l, 028; Thos., 064; William, 023
MCCUTCHEN: C., 080; Catharine, 078-080; Children, 078; Hannah, 022, 031, 039; James, 007, 008, 021, 022, 031, 039, 080, 095-096;

Jas., 039, 086; John, 007, 008,
020, 031, 039, 096; Mary, 080,
096; Patrick, 031, 032, 096;
Robert, 080; Robt., 079, 095;
Sam'l, 019, 028; Samuel B.,
096; Samuel, 001, 007, 008,
010, 031, 079, 080, 095; Thos.,
080; Washington C., 096;
William, 031; Wm., 080, 096
MCCUTCHUN: Robert, 064
MCDANIEL: Alexander, 034, 106;
C., 095; John, 014, 094, 095,
098; Robt., 095; Wm., 086
MCDDOWELS: William, 001
MCDONALD: Alex, 026
MCDONNALD: Alexr., 084
MCELEVEE: Thomas, 029
MCELEY: Ezekiel, 084
MCELMORE: Robt., 083
MCELWEN: Thomas, 028
MCENLERS: William, 029
MCEWEN: --, 087; C. E., 108;
Christopher E., 068; Christopher,
068, 092; Cyrus, 083; David, 042,
049, 054, 068, 069, 078; E. E.,
083; Ephraim, 083, 098, 102,
108; James, 049, 063, 068, 078,
083, 089, 090, 093, 096, 102,
106, 108, 111; James, Jr., 054,
095, 098; James, Maj., 102;
James, Sr., 096, 098, 105; Jas.,
063, 074, 090, 110; John, 087;
Sally, 074, 084; Sarah, 083,
110; W., 099; William, 074, 083,
084, 110; Wm., 049, 082
MCFADDEN: James, 064; Robt., 064
MCFADEN: Barnett, 068; James,
068; Robt., 068; Wm., 068
MCFAIL: Nancy, 037
MCFALE: Angus, 051
MCGABE: Chiles, 065
MCGAH: William, 006
MCGAN: Eli, 096
MCGAUGH: Matthew, 011, 015; Wm.,
083, 105
MCGAVOCK: David, 018, 030; James,
045, 049, 074, 086; Jas., 085
MCGEE: Abraham, 084; Chiles, 090;
Wm., 107
MCGILERIES: Wm., 096
MCGILVERY: Wm., 110
MCGIMSEY: William, 026
MCGUIRE: --, 103; James, 049, 093
MCHUGH: James M., 010; James,
012; Jane, 010; Moses, 010;
Nancy, 010; Polly, 010;
Sarah, 010
MCHUGHES: Moses, 010
MCKAILEY: Ezekiel, 111
MCKEARLEY: Ezekiel, 029
MCKEE: Wm, 105
MCKENNEY: John, 051
MCKENNY: John, 099
MCKEY: David, 071; John, 004;
William, 008, 012; Wm., 083,
093, 108

MCKINNES: Ebenezer, 096
MCKINNEY: --, 101; Ebenezer, 078,
079; Ebenizar, 075; Francis,
037; James, 032, 100; John, 007,
040,076, 078, 092; Mary, 100
MCKINNY: Ebenezer, 094; James,
085; Jas., 085
MCKINSEY: John, 038
MCKNIGHT: James, 015, 109; John,
006, 011, 015, 016; Robert,
Jr., 015; Robert, Sr., 015;
Robt., 076; Samuel B., 015;
Samuel, 011, 060;
William, 002, 011
MCKNOWEN: A., 054
MCLAIN: John, 068; Robert, 014
MCLAMORE: Burrell, 006
MCLANE: Dorcas, 106
MCLARAN: Frank, 060
MCLARNA: John, 084
MCLAUGHLIN: Rebecca, 101
MCLELLAND: John, 016
MCLEMORE: --, 027; Burrell, 007;
Burwell, 101; John C., 026,
100; John H., 076; Philemon,
110; Robert, 017, 030, 040, 051,
103; Robt., 050, 065, 071, 081,
092, 095, 096; Young, 002, 081
MCLENNON: Robert, 016
MCLEON: E., 109
MCLIN (&MCLAIN): William, 014
MCMAHAN: Daniel, 054, 069, 092
MCMAHON: Andrew, 022; Daniel,
017; John B., 014
MCMEENS: John, 078
MCMEMOR: Phillip, 104
MCMILLAN: Wm., 072
MCMILLEN: Robt., 103
MCMILLIN: Wm., 076; Andrew, 007;
James, 007; Mary, 007; Th.,
095; Thos., 106; William, 006;
Williamson, 006
MCMUTT: Sarah, 031
MCNAIL: Edward, 096
MCNEAL: Edw., 070; Edward, 021;
John, 049, 065
MCNEELLY: James, 008
MCNEILLY: James, 010
MCNIN: David, 007
MCNUTT: Robt., 108
MCPEAK: Henry, 079
MCPHAIE: Angus, 092
MCPHAIL: --, 094, 097; A., 062,
094, 106; Angus, 049, 090, 094;
Ann, 038; Jas. Hicks?, 094;
Thos., 083
MCPHERSON: Cornelius, 100; Hannah,
067; Jonathan, 067
MCQUIRE: Allegary, 083
MCREYNOLDS: Archibald, 018
MCSWINE: John, 064
MCWAVE: Henry, 100
MEADOW: James, 095
MEAK: John, 089
MEASELS: Levie, 041
MEASLES: Levi, 109

MEAZELES: Levi, 061
MEBAND: A., 101; Geo., 082
MEBANE: A., 105; Alexander, 025,
029, 107; Alexr., 094, 111;
Geo., 111; George, 029
MEBONE: Alex, 092
MEDALNE: Wm., 046
MEDDLETON: Samuel, 010
MEDERIN: G. W., 059
MEDERUS: John, 047, 048, 113
MEEK: Adam, 063
MEEKS?: Taylor(the), 110
MEGGS: Matthew, 093
MELBANE: George, 024
MENDENALL: Ruth, 052
MENEER: John, 041
MERCHANT: David, 041; John, 091
MERIFIELD: Sam., 104
MERRIT: Benj., 076; Samuel, 045;
Shemey, 061
MERRITT: Benj., 089; Samuel, 006;
Thos., 089
METCALFE: J. 097
MICHEL: Mark, 025
MILCHIE: Frederick, 092
MILES: Heatwell, 011; Thomas, 013
MILLER: Adam, 021, 087; Alex,
014; Alexander, 014, 029; Jack,
042; James, 012, 020, 021, 033,
092, 107; Jas., 083; John, 014,
046, 093, 100, 108; T., 110;
William, 010; Wm., 082, 093, 103
MILLS: James, 060; Patsy, 060;
Sharod, 060
MINNAN: J., 110
MINTEN: Peter, 101
MITCHEL: F., 103; Frederick, 103;
Robert, 034
MITCHELL: --, 024, 027, 057;
Charity, 019; Edward, 027; Evan,
019, 021; John, 014, 048;Joseph,
047, 048, 112, 113; Samuel, 018;
Sarah, 032; William, 027
MOBLEY: J., 087; Jonathan, 067,
070, 080
MOBLY: Jonathan, 054
MOFFITT: Oran, 095
MONTGOMERY: Alex, 014; Alex., 088;
Alexr., 076, 086; Cyrus, 105;
Daniel, 095; David, 003, 076;
Elizabeth, 105; Hannah, 002,
003; Jacob, 058; Jane, 003;
John, 095, 105; Mary, 003;
Moses, 086, 088; Patsy, 105;
Polly, 105; Prudence, 105;
Stephen, 027; William, 027;
Wm., 095
MOODY: Elizabeth Lock, 074;
John, 077; Moses, 001
MOOR: Hardin, 046; Wm., 101, 108
MOORE: Alexander, 012, 063; Amos,
042, 072; Betsy, 009, 012;
Catherine, 009, 012; D., 059;
Ester, 072; Esther, 042; Henry,
012, 058; Hugh, 089; James,
009, 023, 098; James, Jr., 061,

063; Jas., 084, 085; John, 009,
012, 027, 061, 063; Joseph,
032; Moses, 042, 072, 092, 101;
Sam'l, 071; Somerset, 029;
William. 027; Wm., 101
MORE: Robert, 025
MORGAIN: Mathew, 053
MORGAN: Cary, 025; Eli, 035; Geo.,
044; James, 057
MORRES: Henry, 006
MORRIS: Josep, 080; Joseph, 054,
087; Wm., 094
MORRISON: Kineth, 095
MORROW: Wm., 080
MORTON: A. B., 029; Abner, 084,
106; Abram B., 064; Alexander,
081; E. B., 098; Elisha, 106;
- Elizabeth, 063, 068; Jacob,
109; John, 070, 075, 088; S.,
105; Sam'l., Sr., 106; Samuel,
109, 110; Samuel, Jr., 066, 097;
Silas, 073, 109; Step, 106;
Steph., 084; Stephen, 068;
Thomas, 063, 068; Wm., 081, 109
MOSES: Christopher, 001
MOTHERAL: John, 090, 096;
Joseph, 109
MOTHERHEAD: Simeon, 064
MOTHERS SHED: Thos., 079
MOULGE: --, 107
MOULTON: Michael, 056
MULHERRIN: James, 057, 058;
Jas., 058
MULHERRINS: James, 005; Jas., 056
MULLIN: Jesse, 016, 024; Joshua,
016, 024; Josiah, 016; Mary,
016, 017; Samuel, 112; William
S., 016; William, 016, 024;
William, Jr., 016, 024
MULLINS: Henry, 068
MURFREE: --, 048, 112; H., 006,
047, 048, 056, 058, 112; Hardy,
005, 047, 055, 059, 112, 113;
Hary, 047; Jas., 078; Laurence,
078; Lavinia B., 112, 113;
Levenea B., 047; M.B., 056-059,
095; Martha A. C., 097, 112;
Martha Ann C., 047, 059, 113;
Martha, 055; Mat. B., 057; Matt
B., 059; Matthias B., 048, 056,
059, 112, 113; Mattias B., 097;
Mattias, 097; W.H., 058; William
H., 047; Wm. H., 047, 055, 059,
112, 113
MURPHEY: Butler, 024;
Lawrance, 106
MURPHREY: Hardy, 010; Laurence,
084; Wm., 078
MURRAY: Robert, 072
MURRELL: John, 092
MURREY: John, 026; William, 008
MURRUS: --, 103
MURRY: Riley D., 088-089; Riley,
013, 096; Robert, 067;
Roberts, 063
NADDOX: --, 065

NAIL: Julian, 041
NANCE: Stephen, 080
NASH: Demo(y or s?), 105; Dempsey,
010, 080, 084, 094, 108; Demsey,
101, 109; John, 001; Patsy, 002
NEAL: James, 011, 041; John M.,
043; John P., 001; Julian, 024;
Julis, 005; Nicholas, 024
NEALY: Thos., 046
NEAMAN: Dr., 103
NEELEY: J., 104; Geo., 087; Geo.,
Sr., 096; George, 007, 026;
George, Jr., 096; James M.,
010; James, 003, 006, 043, 076,
083, 108; James, Esq., 007;
John J., Esq., 082; John, 009,
012, 043, 058; John, Jr., 092;
John, Sr., 108; Robert, 053;
Robt., 064, 085; W., 058;
William, 002, 005, 012, 040;
Wm., 057, 061, 065, 069, 080
NEELY: Geo., 041; George, 037;
James, 006, 009, 049; Jas.,
078; John, 049
NEGRO: Aaran, 067; Aaron, 024,
025, 032, 074; Ab, 100; Abba,
008, 085; Abby, 056, 059; Abel,
026; Abey, 095; Abigail, 007;
Abraham, 012, 024; Abram, 002,
005, 026, 055; Aby, 007; Ace,
008; Acy, 040; Adam, 026, 037,
075; Aggy, 017, 050, 064, 079,
093; Agnes, 060; Allse, 022;
Allsey, 062; Aim, 005; Ale, 075;
Alexander, 069, 084; Alfred,
076; All, 075; Allen, 013, 020,
030, 032, 041, 044, 046, 069;
Allin, 091; Ally, 100; Alsey,
062; ALyce, 099; America, 055,
078; Amerky, 038; Amey, 055;
Amos, 027; Amus, 077; Amy, 024;
Anaky, 079, 093; Anderson, 005,
038, 054; Andrew, 012, 025;
Anerkey, 054; Aney, 075; Ann,
100; Anna, 055; Annas, 056;
Anne, 030; Annekey, 012; Anney,
044; Anny, 044; Anthony, 104;
Arabella, 083; Arm, 084;
Armstead, 069; Arthur, 007;
NEGRO: Asa, 078; Aylee, 050;
Bagwell, 085; Barney, 064, 078;
Beck, 002, 098; Beckey, 078;
Becky, 074; Bedford, 054, 081;
Ben, 008, 018, 029, 031, 032,
049, 050, 073, 084, 101, 104;
Benj., 056 084; Benjamin, 032,
055; Berrell, 070; Bets, 105;
Betsy?, 012; Betty, 032, 055,
104; Bick, 092; Bidd, 042;
Biddy, 032; Big Bob, 032; Big
Frank, 042; Bill, 005; Billey,
042, 077; Billy, 032, 050, 061;
Blacksmith Isaac, 042; Bob,
005, 024, 031, 044, 051, 055,
059; Bob, 086, 088; Bobb, 026,
027; Booker, 085; Brazior(Ned),

055; Brister, 032, 077; Bristo,
059; Bristow, 055, 059;
NEGRO: Bromfield, 030; Broomfield,
023, 030; Burrel, 075; Burrell,
007; Cabe, 055; Cain, 070;
Candis, 075; Caroline, 020, 030,
069, 070, 095; Catharine, 085;
Cato, 108; Ceasar, 032; Celia,
082, 083, 099; Chane, 038;
Chaney, 094; Charity, 008, 070,
073; Charles, 005, 019, 024,
025, 031, 032, 035, 041, 046,
055, 059, 064, 067, 069, 077-079,
083, 084, 105; Charley, 083;
Charlotte, 032, 055, 091;
Cheary, 014; Chelsey, 032, 077;
Cherry, 056, 059, 062, 098;
Chiana, 037; Children, 028,
030, 046, 051, 053, 058, 059,
062, 063, 069, 072, 081, 097,
100; China, 062; Chloe, 030,
052; Chysick, 055; Claibourn,
077; Claracy, 083; Clary, 027,
104; Clement, 084; Clementina,
038; Clementine, 041; Cloe,
019, 029, 030, 040, 051, 055,
062; Cloey, 059; Condis, 083;
Congo, 050; Conkard, 002; Contra
Loose, 046; Creasey, 074;
Crecey, 085; Crecy, 043, 045;
NEGRO: Curtis, 104; Cye, 093;
Daniel, 004, 032, 050, 056,
059, 064, 078, 104, 112; Darby,
025; Darcas, 005; Darcass, 046;
Darcus, 024; Darkies, 085;
David, 032, 053, 056, 059, 104;
Davie, 056; Davis, 085; Davy,
002, 078; Del, 015; Deliah, 005;
Delilah, 050; Dennis, 104;
Diana, 012; Dick, 005, 013, 020,
024, 025, 050, 055, 064, 078,
083, 090, 095, 105; Dilce, 092;
Dilcey, 024, 032; Dilcoy, 024;
Dilcy, 027, 075; Dill, 005; Dilse,
005; Dilsey, 078, 088, 096;
Dinah, 026, 056, 083; Diner,
078; Doctor Scott, 055; Doll,
005, 009, 039; Dolly, 002, 024;
Dorcas, 032, 052, 069; Dover,
008; Dred, 055, 059; Dudley,
002, 038, 041; Dycy, 104; Eadey,
098; Easter, 023, 044, 078, 091,
097, 098; Eddy, 055, 056; Edea,
105; Edmund, 032, 098; Edw.,
076; Edy, 075, 094; Effey, 002;
NEGRO: Elenor, 032; Elick, 035;
Elisa, 031; Eliza, 056; Elley,
044; Ellick, 019; Elly, 044;
Elsey, 078; Enee, 035; Eny, 019;
Ephraim, 005; Essin, 002; Ester,
030, 044; Esther, 030, 031, 037,
038, 044, 093, 094; Fann, 094;
Fanney, 024, 032, 097; Fanny,
017, 025, 044, 076, 098; Fany,
095; Fill, 045, 050; Fillis,
059; Flora, 043, 045, 085, 099;

Fortune, 055, 59; Fountain, 079,
093; Frances, 055; Frank Will,
032; Frank, 013, 020, 027, 030,
032, 040, 050, 051, 056, 057,
059, 063, 069, 077, 092; Franky,
005, 084; Furry, 002; Gabriel,
104; Gardiner, 032; Gardner,
042; Geo Carr, 055; Geo. Porter,
056; Geo., 043-045, 049, 051,
059, 063, 076, 077, 085, 091;
NEGRO: George, 022, 030, 032, 038,
040, 054, 059; Gilbert, 104;
Gillum, 032; Gloster, 025; Grey,
104; Godfrey, 008; Guameny, 045;
Hagar, 053, 097; Hall, 071;
Hampton, 104; Hana, 059; Hanibal,
032; Hannah, 007, 030-032, 038,
040, 055, 059, 104; Hannen, 051;
Hanner, 063; Hannibal Farmer,
108; Hardy, 002, 005, 055, 056;
Harper, 002, 038, 041; Harriet,
053, 069, 090, 091, 097;
Harriett, 031; 065, 085;
Harriot, 079; Harriotte, 055;
Harrison, 078; Harritt, 101;
Harry, 004, 006, 025, 029, 055,
056, 059, 079, 093; Hartwell,
038; Harwell, 037; Henry, 055,
056, 065, 097; Hester, 002; Het,
045; Hetta, 043; Hetty, 055,
099; Hillard, 033; Hilliard,
038; Hirum, 060; Hotta, 085;
NEGRO: Indiana, 083; Isaac, 032,
043-045, 050, 077, 085, 095;
Isabel, 108; Isam, 039, 056,
059, 096; Isbell, 024; Isham,
023, 030, 048, 051; Israel, 027;
Ivice, 060; Jack, 002, 005, 008,
019, 020, 031-033, 038, 039,
045, 050, 055, 056, 059, 065,
071, 079, 082, 085, 093, 099;
Jacob, 005, 024, 030, 032, 041,
046, 056, 069, 073, 077, 092,
094, 097, 098; James, 002, 005,
008, 033, 085; Jane, 004, 008,
026, 038, 083, 097; Janey, 059;
Jared, 049; Jean, 054;
Jefferson, 064; Jeffery, 005,
024, 087; Jemima, 007; Jenney,
024, 032; Jenny, 005, 008, 019,
021, 044, 078; Jerry, 008,
022-024, 030, 032, 039, 048,
069, 075, 100, 101; Jesse, 030,
040, 051, 056, 059, 063, 091;
NEGRO: Jessee, 049; Jessie, 044;
Jim, 007, 018, 032, 038, 042,
050, 060, 069, 075, 077, 104,
105; Jimmy, 055; Jinney, 002,
042; Jinny, 032, 055, 061, 078;
Joan, 005; Joe, 005, 030, 040,
051, 061-063, 065, 070, 074,
077; John Ganderson, 077-078;
John, 024, 032, 042, 055, 063,
085, 102, 105; Jolear, 075;
Jose, 062; Joseph, 055; Jourdan,
092; Joyce, 002; Juba, 069;

Jubels, 026; Juda, 042; Judah,
013, 074; Jude, 020, 025, 030,
040, 050, 062, 069, 078, 096;
Judea, 032, 054; Judith, 005,
052, 055; Judy, 002, 032, 038,
055; Julia, 027; Juniper, 031;
Kaid, 070; Kissy, 005; Kitty,
055; Larah, 074; Larkin, 104;
NEGRO: Larymore, 070; Lawson, 017;
Leah, 043, 045, 079, 085, 093;
Lee, 024, 025, 067; Letta, 078;
Levan, 043, 045; Leven, 099;
Levena, 056; Levian, 081; Levin,
085; Levina, 083; Lew, 032;
Lewis, 013, 020, 023, 029, 030,
032, 035, 038, 044, 055, 056,
070; Lic, 079; Lige, 049;
Lillah, 102; Lina, 037; Linda,
040; Lindey, 019; Little Aaron,
032; Little Bob, 032; Little
Daniel, 032; Little Dilcey, 032;
Little Frank, 042; Little Geo.,
085; Little Nat, 100; London,
022; Lotte, 044; Louisa, 040;
Lovy, 051; Lucindy, 069; Lucky,
056, 095; Lucy, 002, 005, 024,
032, 041, 044, 053, 055, 065,
069, 077, 078, 097, 104; Luke,
006, 092; Lycy, 038; Lydia, 002,
037, 038, 084; Lynda, 084;
NEGRO: Magga, 005; Maho, 008;
Manah, 112; Manson, 096; Manuel,
029, 097; Marcy, 069; Maria,
031, 075, 078, 081-083, 088,
099; Mariah, 008, 027, 035, 104;
Martin, 081, 083; Mary Ann, 070;
Mary, 013, 019, 020, 026, 030,
035, 040, 053, 078, 088, 104;
Matilda, 052; Matt, 008; Melley,
051; Mercka, 032; Michael, 027;
Miles, 032, 042, 044, 075;
Milkey, 012; Milley, 007, 020,
022, 024, 029, 044; Milly, 002,
027, 035, 079, 084, 086, 091,
104; Minerva, 069, 076; Mingo,
007, 087; Minncy, 008; Minney,
007; Minty, 005; Mitchell, 052;
Moll, 041; Molley, 007, 013,
027, 030, 069; Molly, 056, 059,
079, 101; Moriah, 019; Morton,
075; Moses, 019, 032, 035, 037,
050, 056, 059, 078; Mouring,
030; Mourning, 070; Nan, 002,
075, 100; Nance, 022, 097, 098;
NEGRO: Nancy, 008, 027, 033, 038,
050, 051, 054-056, 076, 078,
079, 081, 083, 084, 105, 107,
112; Napper, 017; Nat, 075, 100;
Nat., 055, 075; Nathan, 038,
054; Nead, 095; Ned, 008, 026,
050, 055, 059, 069, 070, 075,
082, 099; Nelly, 005, 046, 069,
077, 078; Nelson, 005, 044, 050,
065, 070, 076; Nuney, 051; Old
Dilcy Maria, 032; Old Jack, 059;
Old Lucy, 024; Old Peter, 059;

Oliver, 032, 042, 078; Oney,
069; Orid, 053; Orra, 020;
Orrey, 013; Ouid, 065; Ovid,
097; Palina, 078; Pammey, 012;
Pat, 005, 097; Pate, 025;
Patrick, 094, 098, 104; Patsy,
005; Peg, 079; Peggy, 052, 055,
065, 071, 078, 104; Perkins,
055; Perry, 044, 091; Peter,
013, 025, 028, 032, 037, 038,
041, 046, 049, 050, 054, 056,
059, 062, 069, 070, 075, 077,
078, 090, 094, 104; Pettis, 069;
NEGRO: Phanteroy, 088; Phil, 023,
030; Philes, 059; Philip, 002;
Philis, 024, 088; Phill, 030;
Phillis, 024, 025, 055, 067,
084, 091, 096, 104; Pleasant,
055, 075, 104; Poll, 050; Polly,
053, 065, 095, 097; Pompey, 031;
Rachel, 005, 024, 032, 033, 037,
038, 046, 062, 069, 077, 094,
105; Rebecca, 055, 076; Redford,
083; Reuben, 006, 024, 092;
Rheuben, 032; Rhody, 045; Rier,
070; Ritta, 040; Ritter, 104;
Rose, 031, 037, 038, 050, 062,
069, 079, 084, 087, 090, 094;
Ross, 008; Ruben, 067; Rulien,
025; Rusey, 032; Ruth, 030, 069;
NEGRO: Sal, 070, 089; Sally, 050,
055, 058-060, 076, 095, 097;
Sam, 017, 019, 024, 025, 030,
032, 035, 040, 050-052, 056,
057, 062, 063, 076, 078, 079,
085, 086; Sampson, 055, 079;
Samson, 090; Samuel, 090; Sandy,
037, 038; Sarah, 005, 028, 056,
070, 081, 083, 088, 094, 098;
Saul, 070; Sawyer, 008, 094;
Scerrina, 108; Scillar, 101;
Scily, 104; Scinda, 035;
Scintha, 031; Seal, 050; Sealy,
050, 070; Season, 029; Selic,
078; Selina, 032; Seller, 064;
Selvy, 055; Sidney, 076; Silon,
008; Silva, 050, 078, 108;
Silvey, 044, 055, 065, 084;
Silvy, 071; Simon, 002, 004,
097, 098; Sina, 037, 104, 105;
NEGRO: Sinah, 102; Sinth, 105;
Size, 024; Sizo, 005; Solomon,
008, 065; Sook, 032; Southerd,
085; Squier, 095; Starling,
005, 024, 055, 069, 077; Steph,
065; Stephen Scott, 067;
Stephen, 002, 024, 025, 032,
037, 038, 042, 094; Stepney,
087, 097; Sterling, 041, 046;
Suck, 005, 050; Suckey, 025,
030, 062-064; Suk, 051; Suke,
038; Sukey, 040, 051, 054;
Susan, 024, 083, 101; Sutha,
043; Taine, 070; Tempathy, 007;
Tempy, 007; Terey, 092; Terry,
032, 078; Thomas, 007, 008, 031;

Tibe, 012; Tiller, 008; Tillman,
007; Tim, 055, 059; Timothy,
059; Tinney, 055; Tobey, 048;
NEGRO: Toby, 023, 030; Tom, 005,
007, 024, 027, 032, 040, 050,
052, 056, 064, 078, 088, 101;
Tona, 056; Toney, 055; Tony,
055; Toon, 098; Trace, 055;
Truce, 059; Un.N., 054, 063,
074, 080, 088, 091; Ursey, 032,
078; Ursula, 042; Venture, 032;
Venus, 055, 056; Vine, 005;
Viney, 032; Violet, 037, 083;
Virgil, 050; Wall, 069; Warrick,
005, 032, 056; Washington, 107;
Wat, 030; Wate, 101; Watt, 013,
020, 085; Wax, 084; Will, 005,
024, 042, 055, 059, 077;
William, 013, 027, 088; Willie,
057, 075; Willis, 044, 055, 056;
Winney, 032, 045, 055, 064;
Winny, 087; Worick, 024; Young
Doll, 005; Young Lucy, 024;
Zacheal, 062; Zilf, 050
NELSON: --, 017; William, 027;
Wm., 092
NESBIT: Samuel, 100
NEUSOM: Wm., 057
NEWGENT: John, 057
NEWMAN: Dr., 039; John, 078;
Thomas, 017
NEWSOM: Lawrence, 081, 084;
Rebecca, 081
NEWSOME: Eldridge, 057
NEWSON: Baalam, 007
NEWTON: John, Dr., 100
NICHOL: --, 023; John, 083, 107
NICHOLOS: John, 030
NICHOLS: --, 019; Allin, 089;
Elizabeth, 107; Geo., 058; John
H., 045; John, 015, 076, 092,
106, 107, 110; John, Jr., 108;
Robert, 103; Robt., 078, 103
NICHOLSON: Cordy, 083; Isaac,
027; Malachi, 029, 058, 083,
092, 111; Orsbourne, 058
NICKERSON: James, 056
NIMMO: Wesley G., 106
NOLAND: John, 013
NOLEN: Allen, 027; Anney, 026;
Anslum, 072; Ansoleum, 084;
Ansolum, 027; Berry, 045, 090,
091, 095, 096, 110; David, 085;
Davis, 026; Easter, 013; Ester,
013; Esther, 013; G. L., 067,
072, 084; G.S., 029; Golsby,
026; Isaac, 010; John, 013, 026;
L., Gen., 040, 063, 072;
Littleberry, 026; Stephen, 095,
098; Thos., 071; William, 013,
019, 027, 029; William, Sr.,
026; Wm., 044, 080, 081
NOLES: Berry, 045
NOLIN: Berry, 051, 110; David,
106; G. S., 027; John, 026;
L., Gen., 026; Lee, Gen., 026;

William, 026, 034; Wm., 106
NORRIS: Elizabeth, 061, 068;
James, 061, 068
NORTH: --, 103; A., 085; Abraham,
032; Abram, 092; Elisha, 045,
092, 100, 101, 106
NORTHERN: Wm. T., 095
NORTON: Eliza, 042, 046, 048, 054;
John, 043, 049, 065; William,
048; Wm., 042, 046, 054
NOWLIN: John, 026
NUGENT: --, 058
NUNAN: Dr., 069; J., Dr., 056
NUNN: Elijah, 070; Francis, 041,
070; Joel, 070; John, 070; Marcy,
070; Polly, 070; Thos., 070;
W., 106; Wm.B., 065; Wm.R., 041,
070, 071, 106; Zopheniah, 070
O'RILEY: James C., 110
OAKES: Charles, 044; Isaac, 101
OAKLY: Jesse, 109
OAKS: Isaac, 110
OGILSVIE: John, 046; Kimber, 046;
Richard, 046
OGILVIC: William, 019
OGILVIE: Harris, 031; John, 024,
031, 039, 041, 048, 088, 100;
K., 040; Kembro, 048; Kimbro,
005, 024, 040, 041, 049;
Kimbrough, 021, 031; Rich., 041,
080, 081; Richard, 021, 024,
031, 041, 042, 067, 070, 077,
080, 097; Richd., 109; Smith,
031; William, 031; Wm., 041
OGLESVEY: John, 080
OLD: C., 085; Eliza, 085;
Elizabeth, 032; John E., 092,
106; John, 094; Jordan R., 092;
T., 059; Thomas, 029, 032, 037,
042, 092, 094, 101, 103, 111;
Thos., 048, 058, 106; Wm., 085
OLDHAM: Geo., 095; Moses, 075,
076, 078, 092, 094
OLDS: Clement, 032; Elijah, 032;
Thos., 113
OLIVE: Abel, 101; Robert, 020
OLIVER: Geo., 087, 088; George,
041; John, 064, 100;
Levi, 083, 087
ORE: Robert, 012
ORGAIN: --, 092
ORGAN: --, 103, 110
ORLON: Richard, 037
ORR: Hugh R., 093; Robert, 013;
Wm., 093, 095, 098
ORTON: David, 014, 081, 097, 101;
Jas., 085; Jincy, 066; Richard,
006, 007, 009, 013, 042-044,
048, 049, 054, 062, 073, 083,
087, 094, 100, 109; Saml., 111;
Samuel, 085; William, 001, 010
OSBURN: Nathaniel, 101
OSLIN: John, 024
OSTEEN: Jesse, 026; William, 026
OUIN: E., 098
OUTLAW: W., 056; William, 027

OVERHALL: Robt., 059
OVERTON: John, 027
OWEN: Ambrose, 029, 039, 084;
Elizabeth, 080; Everit, 039;
Frederick, 023, 039; Frederick,
Sr., 023; Glen, 033, 064, 072;
Isaac, 083; Jabez, 029, 106;
James, 010, 029, 039, 098;
Walter B., 049; Walter, 039;
Watson, 046; William, 074, 080;
Wm. E., 092
OWENS: Elijah, 063; T., 098;
William, 063; Wm., 069
PAGE: David D., 095, 098, 108;
David E., 105, 110; David, 035;
David, Sr., 016; Harvey, 035;
Jacob, 035; John, 015, 019,
023, 035; Lovey, 015, 091;
Patsy, 035; R., 058; Robert,
012; Stokley, 035; Wm., 068
PAISLEY: Robert, 012
PAITMAN: Spencer, 101
PALKUM: Drury, 093
PALLESON: Bell, 093
PARHAM: Geo., 085; George, 098;
Rebecah, 101; Rebecca, 098;
Sarah, 098; Thomas, 098, 101;
William, 019, 030, 039, 048,
098; William, Dr., 023;
Wm., 042, 085, 101, 110
PARK: Joseph, 056; Wm., 082
PARKER: Cadar, 085; Cader, 080,
109; Frances, 105; George, 039,
084; Kador, 077; Parker, 104;
Piety, 085, 091; Samuel, 091
PARKERS: William, 018
PARKS: Benj., 076; James, 108,
110; John, 006; Malinda, 064,
072, 089; Moses, 014; Samuel,
061; William, 064, 089, 092,
102; Wm., 045, 072
PARMELY: Ephraim, 001; Giles,
001; Samuel, 001
PARRISH: Fountain, 092, 094; J.,
106; Joe, 027; Joel, 027, 088,
093, 103, 106, 110; John, 093;
Jose, 092; Matthew D. M., 088;
Matthew F. M., 088; Moses, 093;
Robt., 082; Susan, 093; Susanna,
088; Susannah, 027
PARSLEY: Jas. B., 067
PARSON: Joseph, 110
PARSONS: James W., 070; Joseph,
075; Thomas, 015; Thos., 088, 105
PASTLY: John, 080
PATE: Elizabeth, 025; Hardy, 025,
034; Kenchen, 041; Kinchun, 070;
Nancy, 025, 034; Persons, 034;
Polly, 024, 025; Porson G., 025
PATESON: Robt., 068
PATTERSON: A., 099; Anne, 004;
Bernard M., 088, 096; Charles,
016; Elizabeth, 072; Gilbert,
012; H., 004; Jacob, 012; James,
004, 012, 039, 066; Jas., 087;
John, 016, 027, 072, 105; Luke,

012; Margaret, 072, 085; Mary,
072; Robert, 072; Solomon, 105;
Thomas, 072; William, 072, 084;
Wm., 071, 072; Wm., Jr., 072
PATTON: Betsy, 021, 022; Charles,
016; Drucilla, 021; George,
018, 022; Hannah, 021, 022;
Isaac, 056, 057, 084; J., 030;
James, 011, 021, 022; John, 009,
018, 021, 022; Margaret, 011;
Nancy, 021; Robert, 011; Sally,
021, 022; Samuel, 080; Thomas,
021, 022; Tristram, 056, 100,
102-104, 107; William, 021,
022; Wm., 045, 056
PATWAY: H., 103
PAXTON: Thompson, 093
PAYTON: Joseph, 001
PEAK: John, 068
PEARCE: Arthur, 003, 019;
John, 047, 113
PECK: Jediah, 012; Josiah, 009
PEEBLES: Howel, 108; Millleun?,
092; Wm., 078, 082, 090, 101
PEGG: John, 109; Stephen, 109, 110
PERKINS: --, 093; Charles, 093;
Col., 030, 040, 051; Constantine,
092, 110; Dan', 057; Dan'l, 090;
Dan, 093; Daniel, 001, 013, 019,
023, 030, 040, 051, 069, 082,
083, 089, 092; Ebenezer, 068;
Harden, 031, 069, 105; Hardin,
018, 092; Henry, 051, 078; John
P., 012; Leah, 012; N.T., 077,
087, 088, 095; N., 030, 040,
052, 054, 071, 099, 110, 111;
N., Sr., 023, 051, 072, 095;
Nicholas P., 081, 092, 108;
Nicholas T., 017, 077, 078,
083, 091, 092, 101; Nicholas,
031, 035, 037, 044, 049, 053,
059, 078, 096, 103; Nicholas,
Sr., 092; Nicholas, 044; Nichs.
T., 106; Nichs., 110; Peter,
012, 017, 031, 044; Peter, Col.,
023, 031, 053, 078; Sam'l, 070,
071; Samuel, 065, 088, 097,
103; Thomas H., 017, 018, 093,
103, 108; Thomas H., Jr., 092;
Thomas H., Sr., 092; Thomas,
017; Thos. H., 044, 051, 082,
108; W.O., 077; W.P., 077; Wm.
O., 044, 093; Wm., 085
PERNAL: H., 104
PERON: Charles, 075
PERRY: Darling, 008; J. 097;
Necpllel?, 073; Norfleet, 073,
112; Richardson, 070; Thorton,
088, 109; William, 023
PERRYMAN: John, 011, 015
PETERS: John, 110
PETTICE: Haroatio, 063; Horatio,
061, 067; Wm., 067
PETTIENCE: Horatio, 043
PETTIS: Horatio, 076
PETTUS: Haratio, 084; Horatio,

054, 090; John, 076
PETTWAY: --, 093; Hinchey, 042
PETTY: Henry, 007
PETWAY: --, 034, 039, 045, 046,
054, 078, 093; --, 100, 101,
111; Caroline Parrish, 027; H.,
042, 054, 086, 092, 094, 101,
103, 110, 111; Henchey, 088;
Hinchey, 027, 030, 042, 044,
046, 050; P., 110
PEWITT: Geo. H., 053
PEYTON: George Y., 008
PHELIN: Robt. C., 112
PHILIN: Richard C., 086
PHILIPS: --, 027; Bennett, 026;
James, 112; Joseph, 091;
Wm., 061, 095
PHILLIPS: John C., 018; Jonathan,
012, 013; Rachel, 041; William,
041; Wm.,Jr., 066; Wm., Sr., 066
PHIPPS: Lavalllin, 095
PICKERIN: John, 001
PICKERING: James, 001;
John T., 100
PICKINS: Andrew, 016
PIERCE: Arthur, 009, 095;
John, 113
PIGG: John, 005, 027, 088;
Stephen, 073, 088
PILLOW: Abner, 027, 057, 058;
Gideon, 026; John, 015, 024,
038; M., 076; Mordecal, 060;
Mordelca, 076; Mordica, 033, 043
PILLY: Henry, 093
PILWAY: H. B., 093
PINKERTON: David, 023, 045;
James, 086; Jas., Sr., 112;
Joseph, 053; Joseph, Jr., 086
PINKLEY: Frederick, 009
PINKSTON: --, 010; D., 111;
David, 024, 041, 046, 069,
077, 080, 082, 085-087; Hugh,
024, 049, 075, 090, 095, 106,
108; Matthew, 105-106; P., 035,
087; Peter, 003, 015, 016, 024,
034, 041, 043, 045, 049, 053,
061, 071, 072, 075, 083, 088,
091, 095, 100, 106, 108, 110;
Peters, 103; Turner, 016, 049,
069, 083, 089; Wm., 083
PINSON: Nathan G., 110
PISTOLE: Chas., 089
PITMAN: Wm., 097
PITTS: Joseph, 063
POETTER: Donelson, 105
POINTED: John, 047
POINTER: John, 112, 113
POLITE: Thos., 105
POLK: Charles, 021; Richard, 107;
William, 019; Wm., 083
POLKE: Thos., 046
POLLARD: Joseph, 059
PONDER: Wm., 048, 112, 113
POOL: Thos., 110; Wiltshire
G., 011
POPE: Carey, 104, 105; Elia P.,

080; Elias F., 090; Jeremiah,
093; John, 003, 082; John, Sr.,
078; Matthew, 108
PORTER: --, 101; Dudley, 029,
033, 043, 052; George, 059;
Jesse, 080; John, 007, 008,
010, 018, 023, 028, 033, 059,
063, 086, 101, 109, 112;
Minnerva, 074; Rus, 002; Sara,
033; Sarah, 029, 033, 043, 052,
060, 074; Thos., 056; Wm., 074
POTTER: A., 089; Ann, 052; Arch.
D., 073; Archd., 076; Archibald,
061, 089, 101, 103; Donaldson,
104; Donalson, 083; Isaac, 053
POTTRESS: Patrick, 032
POTTS: --, 023, 089; Agnes, 049;
Dan'l, 070; John, 039; Jonathan,
072; Joseph, 028, 049, 053;
Mary, 068; Oswald, 061; Peter,
063, 068, 069, 078, 090, 096,
111; Polly, 069, 078;
Stringer, 109
POTTS?: Maria, 111; Susan, 111
POUGE: Thos., 046
POWEL: --, 112; Polly, 028;
Thos., 112
POWELL: Anderson, 028; Thomas,
047; Thos., 073, 113;
William, 027
POWERS: Robt., 108
POYSERS: G., 097
POYTRESS: Pactrick, 085;
Patrick, 032, 085
POYZER: George, 056
PRATT: Baly, 067; John, 070,
105; Samuel, 090
PRATTER: Jonathan, 081
PREACHER: --, 103
PREWETT: John, 012, 023;
Robert, 012
PREWIT: George, 101
PRICE: James, 041, 046; Thomas,
007; William A., 024; William,
025; Wm. A., 109; Wm., 088, 096
PRICKETT: James, 022
PRIEST: Abram, 020; David, 020;
Elizabeth, 020; Fanney, 020;
James, 020; Jas., 092; Jenney,
020; John T., 019; John, 020,
021; Mary, 019-021; Miles, 076;
Moses, 020, 110; Rodney Love,
020; Thomas, 020
PRIGET: Benjamin, 100
PRIM: John W., 080
PRIMM: J., 080; Jeremiah, 084;
John W., 084, 106; John, 027,
106, 110; John, Sr., 084
PRINCE: Frances, 056; Robert,
027; Robt., 056
PRISLEY: James, 105
PRITCHETT: --, 101; James, 076,
093; Thos. J., 110; Thos., 076
PRUET: John, 010; Robert, 012;
Thomas, 012
PRUETT: Elisha, 027; John, 014

PRUIT: Geo. H., 105
PRUITT: Geo. H., 106
PRYOR: Green, 023, 030, 040, 050;
 062-064, 078, 097; John, 023,
 030, 040, 050; Luke, 085, 106;
 Peter, 023, 030, 040, 050, 062,
 063, 068, 078, 097
PUCKETT: David, 059; Elizabeth,
 045; Harvey, 042, 049; Henry,
 045; Jared, 042, 043, 049;
 Jarrot C., 065; Jered, 022; R.,
 008; Richard, 006, 007, 035,
 039, 042, 043, 045, 046, 049,
 052, 060, 065; Robt. C., 045;
 Sally G., 045
PUGH: James, 035, 058, 059, 103;
 Jas., 058, 078, 087; John, 057
PUGHE: Henry, 027
PUGHES: James, 056
PULLAM: Drury, 045
PUMROY: Wm., 079
PURKINS: Donnald, 028
PURYEAR: H., 103; Hezekiah, 077,
 082, 092, 103; Matilda, 082;
 Mrs., 103; P.M., 082; R., 078
PYALL: C., 095
PYRON: Chas., 075
RADFORD: James, 066, 067, 076;
 John, 043, 063, 067, 099; Sally,
 067; William, 043; Wm., 043
RAGGER: Jacob, 013
RAGS: Thos., 100
RAGSDALE: --, 111; Edw., 045,
 048, 054, 062, 108, 109, 111;
 Edward, 029, 046; Peter, 029;
 Samuel, 083; Thos., 045, 083
RALSTON: Alexander, 109; Geo.,
 086; James, 027; John, 086,
 111, 112; Maj., 075
RAMSEY: Wm., 051
RANDOLPH: B., 043, 052;
 Peter, 095
RANGER: C., 057
RANKIN: John, 006
RANOLDS: Richard, 024
RAULSTON: Alexander, 011, 097
RAY: Alexander, 013; Hugh, 084;
 James, 027; Jas., 084; John,
 009, 014, 034, 105; William,
 027; Wm., 071, 093
READ: Miss(3), 112; Thos. J., 053
READER: Jacob, 093
REAMS: Baling, 105; Henry, 045,
 082; Joshua, 045, 093;
 T. J., 065
REARDON: Thomas, 014
REAVES: Peter, 023
RECORD: John, 003, 004, 034, 089;
 Sion, 012, 023, 057, 058
RECORDS: Sion, 005
REDDING: Maxamillion, 039
REDDISH: Thos., 110
REDFORD: John, 077; Sally, 107;
 Wm., 100
REED: --, 023, 107; Alexander,
 086; Alexr., 110; Ana, 049;

Edward, 071; Geo., 073, 112;
 James, 073; John, 049, 050;
 Josiah, 071; Robt., 105
REEDS: James, 112
REESE: --, 092, 093; B., 088,
 099, 108; Beverly, 029, 032,
 042, 045, 082, 103; Herb, 085;
 Herbert, 032, 085; I., 030;
 Jas., 104; John, 068; Jordan,
 032, 042, 061, 085; Jordon, 031;
 Matilda, 032, 042; Maury, 106;
 Mrs., 085; Patrick, 032, 042,
 061, 082; Robt., 085; Sally,
 031, 032; Thos., 095
REEVES: Nathan, 028; Osburne,
 073; Peter, 039; Sarah, 039
REID: Alexander, 073, 091, 096,
 111; Andrew, 087; Catherine,
 112; David, 090; E. B., 076;
 Elizabeth, 073; James, 039;
 Jaohn, 073; John, 076, 087;
 Levian, 087; Levina, 087; Mary,
 111; Polly, 112; Priscilla,
 112; Sarah, 111; Shadrick
 Robt., 087; Sophia, 073; Thos.,
 100; unborn child, 073;
 Wm., 087
REIDS: Geo., 112
RELEIUGH: Thomas, 034
RENNELS: Spencer, 041
RENSHAW: Elijah, 016
REY (KEY?): James, 061
REYNOLDS: Beathany, 044; Bethenia,
 071; Dr., 062; Elisha, 023;
 Geo., 044, 045, 071; Geo., Jr.,
 068, 071; George, 043, 064;
 John M., 081; Nancy, 044;
 Polly, 044; Pryor, 044, 048,
 053, 064, 068, 071, 077; Reuben,
 041, 081, 105; Rich. C., 077;
 Richard, 040, 044, 046, 071;
 Sally, 071; Sarah, 044; Sp.,
 084; Spence, 105; Spencer, 060,
 067, 075, 085; Susan, 093;
 Susanna, 044; Susannah, 044;
 Thomas, 044, 093, 099; Thos.,
 062, 064, 068, 071, 072, 077, 094
RHOADES: J., 111
RHODES: Ab, 085; Elisha, 093;
 Isaac, 058; Jas., 085; Wm., 085
RICE: Frances, 089; Jas., 086;
 John, 095; Theodorick B., 111
RICHARDSON: Elijah, 011; Martin
 W., 110; Mason, 064; Thos., 110
RICHEY: Joseph, 004
RICHIE: Robt., 085
RIDLEY: Beverly, 016, 091, 095,
 106; James, 033, 040, 091;
 Moses, 041, 065, 080, 106;
 Thomas, 041; Thos., 043, 052,
 106; Wm., 091
RIED: John, 092
RIEVES: Joel T., 043; Peter, 029;
 Robert C., 039; Robert, 039;
 Thomas, 022
RIGEON: Joel, 105

RIGGS: Daniel, 081; David, 034;
 E., 029; Edw., 080, 081;
 Gedeon, 077; Gideon, 097;
 James, 009; Joel, 023, 080;
 John, 081; Nancy, 077, 081,
 084, 097; Wright, 034; Zadock,
 067, 077, 081, 084, 097, 106
RIGS: David, 046; Edw., 105
RILEY: James C. O., 101
RITCHER: Robert, 032
RIVERS: Edmund, 015; Joel T.,
 045, 049, 083, 087, 093, 101,
 104, 108; Mary, 020
ROACH: Spear, 018; Wm., 076,
 085, 111
ROAD: Robert, 006
ROADES: Elisha, 101
ROADS: R., 111
ROANE: James, 059
ROBBINS: William, 015
ROBENSON: John, 024
ROBERSON: Edw., 106
ROBERTS: --, 111; B., 057;
 Benjamin, 063; John, 061, 067,
 092; Joseph, 021, 042; Joshua,
 101; Wm., 105, 106
ROBERTSON: --, 048, 112; David
 J., 110; David, 095; Duncan,
 035; F., Dr., 097; Gen'l, 002;
 Jackson, 058; James, 005; James,
 Gen., 018; Jas., Jr., 081; John,
 041, 049, 080, 087; Michael,
 012; Mrs., 018, 024; Sarah,
 016; Thomas S., 023; Thos. L.,
 054, 100; William, 012; Wm., 093
ROBESON: John, 075
ROBINS: Wm., 053
ROBINSON: --, 040; Charles, 012;
 David, 009, 012, 017; James,
 017; John, 012, 041, 060;
 Michael, 017; Thomas L., 103;
 Wm., 085
RODES: Richard, 025
RODGERS: A. M., 103; Abraham,
 009; James, 102, 103; Jas.,
 102; John, 006; Robert, 103
ROGER: Robt., 080
ROGERS: Greenberry, 014; Isaac,
 013; James, 064, 067; Martha,
 067; Robert, 024, 041, 064,
 067, 070, 101, 109; Robt., 067
 080, 110; Samuel, 070, 080,
 101; Sophia, 014; Thomas, 014
ROLAND: Abraham, 101; Jacob, 101;
 John, 101; Mary, 101; Polly,
 101; Wm. T., 101
ROLLAND: Jacob, 039;
 Polly, Mrs., 039
ROLSTON: Alex., 070; Alexander,
 013, 065; Alexr., 088;
 Joseph, 006
ROODS: Richard, 029
ROPER: --, 094; G. W., 095
ROSE: N. B., 095
ROSENBUM: Mathlas, 015; Maths,
 067; Matthias, 060

ROSEWELL?: --, 003
ROSS: Daniel, 005, 058; Jas. D.,
081; William B., 026
ROULSTON: Alexander, 012
ROUNDSVALL: Amos, 089
ROUNDTREE: Andrew, 099
ROUNSAVALL: Amos, 015
ROWLAND: Jacob, 026
ROY: J., 098; James, 041; Wiley,
093; Willie, 041
ROYAL: Joseph, 103, 108
ROZENBUM: Matthias, 063
RUBLE: J. R., 080
RUBLE: John R., 087
RUDDER: Richard, 096
RUPIL: Edward, 093
RUSE: Sally, 092
RUSHES: J. 097
RUSHING: John, 091
RUSSEL: Benjamin, 046; Edward,
035; P., 054; Wm., 060
RUSSELL: Benj., 041, 070, 080;
Benjamin, 060, 067; Edw. E.,
101; Edw., 059, 082; Henry,
088; John, 105; P., 102, 106;
R., 102
RUSSWORM: --, 101
RUSSWURM: John L., 081
RUSTIN: Henry, 109
RUSWORM: John, 109
RUTHERFORD: --, 035; Benj., 053,
080, 106; G. C., 035; Henry,
010, 035, 038, 041, 073, 074,
083, 086, 100, 112; James, 035;
Jas., 100; John, 074
RUTLEDGE: Alex. 012; Alexander,
012; Elijah, 012; Margaret,
012; William, 012, 026;
Wm., 061
S.(?): Lewis, 030
SALISBURY: James, 093; Jas., 089
SALLEN: William, 029
SALTER: Michael, 018
SAMMON: John, 076
SAMMONS: John, 110; Nancy, 034;
Robert, 076, 110; Robt., 076,
077, 099, 104; Sally, 043
SAMOLE: --, 046
SAMPLE: Ann, 083; J., 056; James,
075, 081, 083, 089, 094, 095,
103; James, Sr., 095; John, 021,
057, 058, 075, 078, 089, 090,
094, 095, 100, 101, 103, 110;
John, Col., 034; Margaret, 077,
083, 089; Martha, 083; Peggy,
075, 089, 095; Robt., 094, 095;
Robt., Jr., 094, 095; Sally,
089; Thos., 089; William, 075,
077; Wm., 061, 089, 095
SAMPSON: Benj., 072; E., 038,
093; Elizabeth, 075; Eph., 071;
Ephraim, 033; Polly, 104, 107,
109; Richard, 104, 107, 109
SAMSON: Wm., 078
SAND: Ray, 003
SANDERS: --, 103; Julius, 011;

Polly, 006; Turner, 032, 058,
103; William, 001, 006
SANDFORD: James T., 086, 099
SANFORD: Betsy, 107; James T.,
103; Jas. T., Col., 078; Polly,
107; Robert, 107; Willis, 107;
Wm. Heter, 107
SAPPINGTON: --, 069, 089, 100;
Dr., 011, 091, 095; John, 016,
019, 027, 034; John, Dr., 103;
Roger B., 006, 049; Thomas,
020, 093; Thos., 061, 105
SAPPINTON: Dr., 078
SARGENT: William, 023
SAUNDERS: --, 092, 110; Geo.?,
102; Mary, 092; S., 052; T.,
030, 048, 062, 065; Turner,
056, 057, 059, 085, 092, 093,
095, 102, 113; Wm., 044, 076,
087, 089, 092, 109
SAWYER: D., 111; John, 048;
Sampson, 019, 020; Virginia
Clark, 020
SAWYERS: Constan, 111; Cousten,
085; Dempsey, 085; Demsey, 076;
I., 030; Sampson, 019, 020,
026, 042, 055
SAXTON: Michael, 093
SAYERS: Edmond, 068; Robert, 067
SCALES: Anne P., 031; Henry, 021;
John, 109; Joseph H., 068, 096,
108; N., 095; Nich., 052;
Nicholas, 002, 011, 023, 030,
031, 034, 053, 060, 078, 087,
093, 096, 103, 109, 110;
Thomas H. P., 031
SCOT: Green, 106
SCOTT: James, 027, 110; John,
111; Nath., 078; Stephen, 067
SCRUGGS: --, 112; Allen, 075,
101; Edw., 110; Edward, 024;
Finch, 043, 050; Nathan, 016
SEA: Jane, 003; John, 003
SEAH: Green, 085
SEAL: Wm. P., 110
SEALES: Nicholas, 004
SEARCY: B., 026; R., 059; Robert,
027; Robt., 076, 090; Rouben, 027
SEATON: George, 025
SEAY: Eli A., 027; Elizabeth W.,
027; Jenny, 027; John, 027,
033; Martha A., 027; Polley
Any, 027
SECREST: Abraham, 084, 108; Abram,
068; Frank, 088; John, 075
SELLERS: Isaac, 014; Robert, 014
SERCY: Robt., 056
SETTLE: John, 008
SHACKLEFORD: John, 018
SHADWELL: Val., 095
SHANNON: D., 019; David, 011, 015,
016, 019, 044, 060, 098; David,
Sr., 016; Geo., 106; George,
003; James, 015, 033; Polly,
015; R. W., 033; Robert, 022;
Robt., 076; Thomas, 015;

Thos., 086, 112
SHARP: A., 062; Anthony, 037, 051,
054; Grove, 019, 046; Jane, 037;
Margaret, 054; Mrs., 037, 054;
Nancy, 037; Peggy N., 038, 051,
062, 082, 094; Peggy, 037, 051;
Robert, 103; Sala M., 082; Sala
N., 062, 082, 094; Sally N.,
038; Sally, 037; Searcy D., 038,
051-052, 062, 082; Sola N., 051;
Sumner M., 038, 051, 062, 082,
094; Thomas, 016
SHARROCK: Stephen, 104, 105
SHAW: Alexander, 059; Ben, 016;
James, 080; Jas., 082; Joseph,
073; N., 058; Stephen, 032;
Timothy, 096, 106, 109
SHEFFIELD: Wm., 081
SHELBOURN: James, 043, 061; John
P., 061; S., 043; Sam'l, 042;
Samuel, 043; Sarah B., 043
SHELBOURNE: John P., 043
SHELBURN: Ann P., 065; James, 048,
052, 067, 110; John P., 038,
060, 067, 070; Pamphlet, 075;
S., 052; Sam'l, 076, 077, 087;
Samuel, 039, 048, 044, 063, 066,
067, 075, 099; Sarah B., 048,
052; Sarah Bennet, 075
SHELBURNE: James, 040, 043, 066,
106; Samuel, 040, 042, 106;
Sarah B., 040, 043, 106
SHELTON: John, 053
SHEPARD: Jane, 031; John, 031
SHEPHARD: Nancy, 113
SHEPPARD: John, 033; Nancy,
047, 048, 112-114
SHEPPERD: Nancy, 113
SHEROD: Wm., 083
SHIELDS: Samuel, 003
SHINALLS: Deziah, 074
SHINAULT: Kizza, 043, 052
SHINOL: Kizey, 029
SHIP: Ewill, 105
SHOARES: John, 106
SHORES: Charles, 068; D., 026;
John, 064, 068, 077; Michael,
068; R., 026
SHORT: Henry, 091; James, 045,
065, 101; W., 082
SHUMAKE: Wm., 041
SHUMATE: Aney, 046; James, 041,
043, 046, 080; John, 015;
Thomas, 049; Thos., 046;
Widow, 046
SHUTE: Thomas, 026; Wm., 049,
053, 054, 072, 105, 106
SIMMONS: Alexander, 024, 025;
Keziah, 024; Martha, 024;
Priscilla, 024; Sarah, 024;
Thomas, 024, 025, 029, 068;
Thos., 024, 067, 073
SIMPKINS: William M., 049
SIMPSON: Alex, 026; Frederick,
105; W., 058; William, 012;
Wm., 099

SIMS: Gray, 012; James, 058, 059;
  Jas. M., 082; Jas., 057, 058
SINCLAIR: Daniel, 091
SINGLETON: Edw., 110
SKELETON: D., 101
SKELLEY: Mordice, 064
SKELLY: James, 073, 088, 109;
  Sarah, 088
SKIDMORE: Henry, 001
SLACKS: Wm., 113
SLADE: William, 047; Wm., 112
SLATER: Chas., 085;
  Henry, 086, 105, 112
SLAUGHTER: Frances, 112;
  Francis, 080, 086
SLAVE: Abley, 005; Anderson, 081;
  Anna, 108; Anthony, 001; Ben,
  001, 005; Betsy, 108; Bett,
  005; Bob, 005, 009; Brister,
  005; Charles, 009; Charlotte,
  005; Cloey, 006; Cruseley, 108;
  Dacey, 005; Daniel, 005; Dred,
  005; Edy, 005; Fortune, 005;
  Frances, 006; Frank, 005;
  Friday, 003; George, 005;
  Hanalle, 108; Hannah, 109;
SLAVE: Hanner, 006; Hardy, 005;
  Harriot, 005; Harvy, 005; Henry,
  001; Hetty, 005; Jacob, 005;
  James, 001; Jancy, 005; Joham,
  009; Juner, 009; Kitty, 005;
  Labina, 003; Levina, 009; Lucy,
  001; Maggy, 005; Milley, 009,
  108; Moses, 005; Nancy, 005,
  009, 108; Nanny, 003; Ned, 003,
  005; Nelly, 108; Old Lona, 003;
  Patience, 108; Peter, 005;
  Phillis, 006; Ritta, 109; Sally,
  005; Sam, 009; Selvy, 005; Tom
  Frank, 005; Tom, 001, 005; UnN.
  108; Will, 005; Yorick, 108
SLEEKER: George, 026
SLEVINS: James, 083
SLOCOLMB: Ryley, 035
SLOCUMB: Joseph, 009;
  Riley, 009, 083
SMILEY: Hugh, 029
SMITH: --, 046, 047, 058; A.,
  111; Abram, 085; Alex, 035,
  106; Alexander, 001, 041, 049,
  054, 073, 101; Alexr., 041,
  084; Baker, 067; Bennett, 034;
  Bryan, 113; Bryant, 047, 112;
  Catharine, 110; Charles, 017;
  David, 015; Edwin, 049;
  Elizabeth Burk, 060; Francis,
  033, 080; Gabriel, 080, 082;
  Geo., 085; George, 032; James,
  066, 104, 106; Jas., 095; John
  Crenshaw, 060; John, 021, 083,
  095, 105, 109; Luke, 005;
  Martin, 049; Molinde, 005;
  Nehemiah, 076; Peter, 095;
  Rich.. 041; Richard, 046, 049,
  103; Robert, 028, 078; Robt.,
  095, 106; Samuel C., 110;

  Samuel, 076, 088, 095, 096;
  Senneah, 005; Slone, 005;
  Stephen, 037, 046, 054, 078,
  100, 110; Thomas, 060; Thos.
  Wm., 061; Thos., 058, 059, 071;
  W., 052, 058, 099, 110; Wiley,
  095; William, 005, 006; Willie,
  039; Wm. B., 079; Wm., 044,
  049, 066, 069, 077, 091, 092,
  094, 095, 109; Work, 024, 083;
  Zachariah, 094; Zachr., 067;
  Zachs., 071; Zeecheus, 105
SMITHSON: Clement, 054, 060, 061,
  067, 084; Drucills, 061; Nancy,
  054, 060, 061, 067, 084; Nath.,
  075; Nathan, 092; Susanna, 061
SMOADE: Lewis, 045
SNEED: --?, 016; James, 080, 084,
  106; Jas., 051, 085; William,
  020, 028; Wm., 028, 049, 080, 082
SNEEDE: William, 020
SNELL: William, 015
SNOW: Daniel C., 069
SOCRESS: Abraham, 035
SOLOMAN: Jonathan, 068
SOLOMON: Jordan, 008, 025;
  Jordon, 026
SOMMERVILLE: --, 019
SON_LEG: Sheff., 057
SORROW: Henry, 105
SOUTHERLAND: Samuel, 009
SPAIN: David, 021; Henry, 085;
  John, 085; Stephen, 085
SPAN: Wm., 110
SPANN: Moses T., 061
SPARKMAN: Jesse, 012; W., 058;
  William, 012, 063; Wm., 067,
  069, 088, 099, 108
SPEAKS: Thomas, 007, 010
SPENCE: Thomas, 093
SPENCER: Betsey, 102; John, 006,
  007; Wm., 102
SPRATT: Blythe, 100; Joseph, 075;
  Thos., 099
SPRIGGS: Robt., 093
SPRINKLES: Moses, 012
SPRUIT: Jesse, 105
SPURLIN: Ell, 018
SQUIER: D., 049, 103; David, 043,
  044, 089, 106; Gurdon, 043,
  044, 069; Mary, 044
SQUIRE: David, 014, 017, 035,
  049, 051, 057, 061, 069, 081,
  108; Gurden, 049
SQUIRES: Gurdon, 071
ST(?): Wm., 112
STACY: --, 093; Eli, 006, 007,
  042, 049, 065; John, 037, 045,
  089, 090, 094, 095, 108; Mahlon,
  108; Thos., 083
STAGG: Felix, 045
STAGGS: C., 076; Felix, 083;
  Thos., 095
STAGS(?): Thomas, 029
STAINBACK: Drucilla, 021, 022
STALLINGS: Thos., 057

STANCELL: Nathan, 081
STANCIL: Nathan, 085, 106
STANCILE: Nathan, 101
STANCILL: Nathan, 081
STANDIRLD: Ephraim, 084; Geo.,
  084; Goodloe, 084
STANDLEY: James, 076;
  Martin, 045 072, 080
STANFIELD: Drucilla, 065; Durrett,
  065; Ephraim, 041, 065, 070;
  Geo. W., 065; George, 065;
  Goodler, 106; Goodloe, 065, 066,
  016; Gooler, 070; Heah, 065;
  Leah, 066; M., 095; Marmaduke,
  065, 066, 070, 072; Phillsha,
  065; Polly, 065; Shakespear, 065
STANLEY: J., 054; James, 037;
  Jas., 089, 090; Marlin, 090;
  Martin, 008, 016, 043, 049,
  068, 089; Wright, 094
STANLY: Martin, 054
STAPLES: Samuel, 042
STARK: George T., 093
STATON: George, 020
STEAVENS: Loamine, 024
STEEL: Robt., 045
STEELE: Moses, 091; Rich., 071
STEPHENS: Belinda, 066;
  Catharine, 066; Charles, 005,
  035, 066, 083; Chas., 105;
  Elizabeth, 066; Feriby, 066;
  Franny, 066; Hareitt, 066; Henry,
  035, 043, 045, 076; James, 054;
  Joel, 014, 043, 066, 094, 108;
  John, 038, 108; Latty, 066;
  Lewis, 034, 042, 045; Liles, 106;
  Loaml, 066; Loamy, 045; Polly,
  066; Rhody, 066; Silas, 092,
  095; William, 035; Willie, 066;
  Wm., 066, 105, 108; Wm.,Jr., 093
STEPHENSON: Allen, 081; John,
  105; Wm., 093
STEPLETON: Edward, 009; Jonathan,
  071, 076, 100
STEVENS: Charles, 015, 024; Edward,
  016; Henry, 015, 092; Jas., 083;
  Joel, 014, 016, 024, 070, 083,
  089, 091, 095; John, 025, 091;
  Joseph, 095; Lewis, 016, 020,
  025, 070, 090, 095; Loamie, 025;
  Loamml, 070; Lovet, 091; Mary,
  070; Rosannah, 071; Silas, 090;
  W., 056, 093; Will, 024; William,
  024, 080, 091; William, Jr.,
  015, 016; William, Sr., 016;
  Wm., 071, 091, 095; Wm., Jr.,
  060; Wm., Sr., 060, 070, 105
STEWARD: Ann, 028; George, 010;
  John, 001; Thomas, 001, 019
STEWART: Ann, 028; Arthur, 072;
  B. G., 026; Henry, 082, 094;
  James, 091; Jas., 100; Margaret,
  028; Sarah, 028; Thomas, 001;
  Thos., 059
STINSON: Joshua, 075
STOBUCK: John, 090

STOCKETT: Jas., 082; Joseph, 020; Noble, 007; Robert, 034; T. W., 020; Thos. W., 100; William, 007

STONE: Agnes, 029, 031; Alfred, 097; Betsey Perkins, 031; Bryan, 105; D. D., 072; Edward, 029; Elizabeth, 023; H.D.L.G., 044; Hardeman, 105; Hendley, 023, 030, 031, 040, 044, 050, 051, 062, 072, 078, 093, 095, 097, 100, 110; Hendly, 062; Hondley, 017; James, 072; Jane, 029, 034, 072; Mary W., 097; Mr., 044; Nicholas P., 097; Polly, 031; Roby, 079; Rowley, 029; Ruth, 031; William, 029, 034; William, Sr., 029; Wm., 072, 079, 084; Wm., Sr., 072; Wm.?, 023

STOVALL: Aggy, 026; Bartholomew, 010, 013, 026

STRAMLAR: George, 010, 017, 025

STRAMLER: --, 105

STRAMLOR: George, 007

STREMLAR: Geo., 082

STRICKLAND: Thomas, 009; Zilpha, 009

STRINGFELLOW: Ann B., 072, 077, 079, 093; N. B., 077; William, 072, 079, 093

STRONG: John, 084

STRUMLAR: George, 017

STUART: Henry, 028, 101; Thomas, 002, 028; Thos., 056

STUBBLEFIELD: A., 026

STUBBS: John, 099; Margaret, 099

STUMP: --, 098m 112; John, 082

STURDUVANT: Sylvanus, 026

SULIVAN: Bennet, 079; Geo., 068; Jeremiah, 068

SULLARD: James, 033; Samuel, 033

SUMAKE: Dan'l, 070

SUMMERS: Abram, 021; Adam, 021

SUMNER: Thos. E., 069, 081, 110

SUMNERS: --, 082; John, 004; Joseph, 002, 004, 107; Martha, 004; Molly, 004; Nancy, 004; Rebecca, 004; Wm., 087, 094

SUTHERLAND: Thomas, 012

SUTTON: Stephen, 108

SWANSON: Ed, 016; Edw., 042, 061, 064, 095, 103; Edward, 016, 034; James, 014; Jas., 092; Wm., 092

SWEENEY: John, 082, 093, 101

SWENNY: John, 093

SWINEY: John, 062

SWINNEY: John, 062, 100

TABB: John, 103; Mordeca, 103

TAILOR: James, 079

TAIT: William, 034

TALBOT: --, 058; E., 097; John T., 051; Matthew, 031; T., 065, 097; Thos., 056

TALBOTT: --, 023; Clayton, 016

TALLEY: Henry, 049, 066

TALLOTS: Thomas, 018

TALLY: --, 089; Henry, 053, 091;

John, 032, 085

TANKERSLEY: J. R., 040; John R., 024, 041; John, 077; Richd, 041

TANKERSLY: John R., 101; John, 075

TANNER: Richard, 066, 091

TANVEHILL: Wilkins, 069

TAPLEY: John, 017

TARKENTON: Joshua, 079

TARKETON: Jesse, 105

TARKINGTON: Hannah, 101; Jesse, 011; Joshua, 107; Mrs., 085

TARPLEY: John, 067; Mary, 067; Thomas, 093

TATE: David, 015

TATUM: --, 008; H., 056; Howell, 058

TAYLOR: --, 101; Absolam, 067; Absolen, 063; Billington, 005, 093; Billinton, 058; Charles, 024, 025, 028; Francis, 027; Geo., 070; Greenham (Grunham?), 003; James, 027; Jas., 084, 106; John, 026; Joseph, 084, 106; Joshua, 094; Laney, 067; Lany, 063; M., 073; Martha, 073; Mary Ann, 023; Meeks, 110; Patcy K., 073; Patsey, 079; Perry, 054; Thomas, 012, 073, 079, 100; Thos., 094; William, 027

TEAT: Joseph, 029

TEMPLE: Burrl., 085; Burwell, 002; Roderick, 105; Thos. B., 085

TERAGE: Langhorn, 086

TERBAVILLE: James, 046, 051; Jas., 051

TERBIVILL: James, 038

TERREL: Wm., 059

TERRELL: James, 097, 103

TERRILL: James, 101

TERRY: David, 061; Jeremiah, 093; Thomas, 059, 092; Thos., 061

TERRYL: James, 026

TEXMIS: Walter, 093

THAIGLER: David, 033

THOMAS: Andrew, 076; Andrew, Sr., 076; Anthony H., 067; Anthony, 080; David D., 014; Jacob, 047, 113; Jesse, 050; Jesse, Jr., 041; Jesse, Sr., 041; Job H., 080, 111; John, 075, 088; Mark, 071, 104; Nancy, 004; Phenis, 061

THOMASON: Stephen, 044, 045, 068, 078; William, 007

THOMESON: Stephen, 079

THOMPSON: --, 089, 095, 102; Ab, 056; Alexander, 099; Alexr., 088; Benj., 085; H. D., 095; Hall, 058; J. B., 031, 064; J., 069, 106; James B., 007, 068, 072, 092, 102; James, 020, 025, 034; Jas. B., 068, 090; Jas. H., 109; Jas., 102; Jason, 019, 108, 110; John, 056, 083, 086, 093, 112; Joseph, 093, 100; L., 069, 106; Laurence, 093; Samuel, 079; Thomas, 080; Thos., 076,

105; W., 057; Washington, 005, 058

THORNTON: Burwell, 016, 095; Yancy, 057

THURMAN: Gaavis, 093; James, 059

THWEAT: Isham, 094

THWEATT: Joshua, 092

TIGNOR: Edw., 059, 112; Isaac, 057, 059; Issac, 058

TILFORD: --, 107; Jas., 090; John M., 059

TILLMAN: Geo., 048; Jacob, 045, 050

TILMAN: Frances, 067; Geo., 048; Harder, 067; John, 067, 071

TILMON: John, 080

TIMMONS: Wm., 083

TISDALE: John, 089

TLEPPON(?): William, 029

TODD: Pleasant, 083; Robt., 082, 104

TOLBERT: Jno T., 051; John T., 051

TOLINSON: Nancy, 102

TOLLEY: William, 015

TOMASAN: Stephen, 063

TOMBLIN: James, 068, 074

TOMLIN: Charles, 101; Chas., 101; David, 077; James, 077; John, 094, 106; Nicholas, 108

TOMLINSON: James, 043, 098, 102; Jas., 049; Nancy, 102

TOON: Fanny, 091; J., 058; James, 091; Jas., 091; Lewis, 090, 091

TOONE: James, 049

TOWLER: William, 013

TOYL: Jas., 046

TRAINUM: Jeremiah, 045

TRANHAM: Jeremiah, 092

TRANTHAN: Martin, 078

TREMBLER: Jam., 099

TREMBLIS: James, 092

TRENTHAM: Martin, 045

TRIEL: Moses, 013

TRIMBLE: Jas., 111

TRIPP: Samuel, 093

TROTER: Benj., 063

TROTT: Henry, 059

TROTTER: --, 058; Ben, 103; Isham R., 032, 085, 095, 100; Joham R., 093

TRUE: David H., 093; Martin, 092

TRUETT: Abraham, 089

TRULL: Mrs., 091, 100; Nathan, 091, 100; Nathaniel, 096; Penelope, 091, 096

TRUNKHOUSER: C., 012

TUBERVILLE: J., 051

TUCKER: Drury, 078; John, 081; Rhoden, 079; Roden, 106; Rodon, 098; Rodus, 080; William, Sr., 024; Wm., 041, 091

TULLER: Nancy, 066

TULLY: Charles, 110

TUNE: James, 072; Jas., 072; Lewis, 072

TURBERVILLE: James, 110

TURBEVILLE: James, 080

TURMAN: Isaac, 104

TURNAGE: T.. 096; Thos., 101; Wm., 051
TURNER: James, 072, 093; Lewis, 083, 092; Moses, 110
TURNEY: Jas.. 058
TWINNER: James, 058
TYGARD: James, 027
UNDERWOOD: Levi, 065
UPSHAW: Charity, 011
VADEN: Wm. H. . 105
VANATTA: Christopher, 105; Jacob, 089; Nancy, 067
VANNATTA: Christopher, 067
VAUGHAN: Dixon, 093; Richard, 093
VAUGHN: --, 087; Abner, 015; Daniel, 095; Dickson, 098; Joel, 015, 016; Richard, 045
VAUGHT: John, 084
VAUGHTS: James, 064
VAULX: James, 026
VEAL: Wm., 106
VEAVERS: Jesse, 078
VENABLE: Richard, 015; Samuel, 015; William, 026; William, Old, 026
VENATTA: Christopher, 110; Peter. 110
VERILL: William, 027
VINCENT: John. 109
VINETTA: Nancy. 105
WADDEL: Catherine, 077; Caty, 077; James, 059; Sam'l D.. 070
WADDLE: Caty, 093; John, 078; Joseph, 068
WADE: Clement, 080; Dabney, 078, 103; Jeremiah, 015; John, 059' Obediah, 061
WADEY: Wm., 059
WADKINS: B., 016
WADSWORTH: Jason, 013; Obediance, 013
WAGGONER: Jacob, 013; John, 108
WAIT: Wm., 058
WAITE: W., 056; Wm., 056
WAKEFIELD: William, 026
WAKINS: Wm., 090
WALDRISS: James, 009
WALF(WARF?): Phillip, 008
WALK: Anthony. 041
WALKER: --, 093; Abraham, 009; Abram, 013, 058, 059; Burrel, 109; Charles, 080; Elisha. 089, 090; Frances, 098; Freeman, 035, 043, 045, 052; Gabriel, 041; Hanch, 064, 069; Henry, 002. 006, 008, 043, 049, 061, 067, 107, 109; James, 017, 018, 023, 035, 077, 097; John M., 093; John, 039, 064, 069, 105; Noah, 099; Noal, 099; Thomas, 007; Thos.. 045. 058. 068, 083; Wm.. 045, 061. 091
WALL: --, 058; Clem. 028, 045; D., 087; Daniel, 067; Drury, 080; Mary, 096; Mrs., 087; Wm., 060, 067, 109

WALLACE: Joseph, 089, 093
WALLER: Joel, 108; Samuel, 059
WALLIS: Matthew, 046; Thomas, 046; Thos., 045; William, 010
WALLS: Clement, 024; William, 021, 033
WALS: Drury, 046
WALTHALL: Thos. B., 060
WALTON: Geo. L., 079; Isaac, 086; Jesse, 079, 083; John, 107; Josiah S., 101; Josiah, 072, 073, 102; Mrs., 101; Nancy, 072; T., 111; Thomas, 085
WAMITH:: Nathaniel, 080
WARD: Thomas, 095
WARDEN: John, 082
WARDS: J. 097
WARMOTH: Nath'l, 067
WARMOUTH: Thos., 079
WARREN: Edw., 044, 064, 071, 072; Edward, 017, 023, 030, 040, 051, 052; Jesse, 109; John, 023, 064; Michael, 014, 029; Nathan, 105; Nathaniel, 097; Robt., 049
WASHINGTON: Abram, 101; G.G., 057; Gilbert, 095; Thos., 110
WATERS: John, 034, 085, 106, 109
WATES: Thos., 111
WATHER(?): John, 033
WATKINS: --, 027; B., 016; Noel, 001, 045; Nowel, 045; O.T., 091; Owen T., 035, 091, 095; Pleasant, 045
WATLON: Josiah, 074
WATSON: --, 102, 103; Jane, 032; John, 016, 032, 039, 042, 048, 078, 082, 085, 091-093, 101, 103, 111, 113; William L., 027; Wm., 109
WATT: John, 054, 087
WATTS: John, 024; Malichi, 068; Sol., 101; Thos., 073, 112
WAUTHING: John, 109
WAUTLIN: John, 088
WEAKLEY: John, 001; Robert, 027; Robt., 100; Samuel, 026, 058; Thomas, 001
WEATHERBY: Wm., 091
WEATHERINTON: Wm., 066
WEATHERLEY: Wm., 100
WEATHERS: Jesse, 007
WEATHERSPOON: Col., 059; Wesley, 059
WEBB: Dr., 077, 087; John, 027, 061, 080, 085, 094; W. S., 094; W. S., Dr., 088; Wm. L., 080, 088, 096; Wm. W. S., 061, 068, 094; Wm. S., Dr., 110; Wm., 041, 071, 083
WEBSTER: William, 033
WEIGHTMAN: Matthew, 045
WELCH: Jonathan, 061; W., 059
WELL: Samuel, 083
WELLS: John, 047, 071, 073, 083, 086, 092, 107, 113; Samuel, 073, 107; Sasan, 084; Suan, 083;

Susanna, 092; Thos., 083, 084; William, 029; Wm. C., 085; Wm. H., 082, 093; Wm., 084, 085, 111
WERTHINGTON: Abraham, 099; William, 099
WEST: Asa, 061; G., 063; Isaac, 061; Johathan, 061; John, 016, 035, 043, 049, 061, 067, 109; Micajah, 008; Thomas, 009, 049; Thos. J., 043; Thos. L., 083; Thos. S., 049; Thos., 045
WETHERINGTON: Abraham, 088
WEVSTER: William, 039
WHALEY: John, 046, 105
WHARTON: Jesse, 006, 011, 111
WHEALY: John, 029
WHEATON: Calvin, 026, 105, 106; Coleman, 016; Jane, 033, 053, 065, 097; John Lord, 033; John, 093; Sterling, 033, 106; Sterling, Dr., 033
WHITBY: John, 082
WHITE: --, 097, 100; Abner, 074; Alex., 089; Alexander, 045; B., 106; Ben, 062; Benj., 062, 069, 084, 090, 091, 103, 106; Benjamin, 010, 037, 098; C., 008, 050, 071, 072, 093, 111; Chapman, 001, 006, 008, 027, 048, 085; 086, 108, 112; Chas., 088; Daniel, 061; Elizabeth, 052; Ezekiel, 047, 112, 113; Fanny, 090; Frances A., 069; Geo., 075; George, 014; Henry, 061, 090, 107; Holland, 052, 098; Hugh L., 110; Isaac, 075; Isach, 075; Isaiah, 028, 080; Isiah, 024; WHITE: James, 004, 015; Jesse, 009, 012, 088; John, 008, 010, 015, 031, 035, 048, 054, 056, 061-062, 081, 083, 084, 086, 089, 093, 103, 106-108, 112, 113; John, Dr., 023; Lemuel, 010; Meady, 068; Robert, 106; Robt., 093, 101; Samuel, 010, 015; Stephen, 068; Thos. L., 104; Thos.. 068, 111; William, 008; Wm., 071, 092, 102
WHITEALL: Wm., 073
WHITEHEAD: --, 101; Jacob, 018
WHITESIDE: Adam, 008; J., 099; Jenkins, 057, 074, 085, 110; Jinkin, 058; Jinking, 072
WHITESIDES: Abraham, 009, 019
WHITFIELD: W., 111; Wilkin, 080; Wilkins, 085, 095
WHITLOCK: Dicey, 043
WHITMAN: Slolman, 089
WHITMON: Solomon, 089
WHOOTON: James, 035
WIGGS: Matthew, 093
WILBOURN: Nicholas, 035
WILBURN: James, 012; Nichs., 110
WILFIELD: Wright, 110
WILHITE: Absolam, 110
WILKERSON: Francis, 082

WILKES: Daniel, 019, 020, 043, 075
WILKEY: James, 045; John, 038
WILKINS: James, 002, 028, 034,
  106; Jas., 092; John, 002, 023,
  083, 095; Rebecca, 002; Robert,
  002, 012; Unborn child, 002;
  William, 002, 034
WILKINSON: Wm., 105
WILKOCKSON: William, 026
WILKS: Benj., 110; Daniel, 110
WILLEA: Thos., 105
WILLET: W., 099; Wm., 077, 082, 105
WILLETT: Charlotte, 035, 050; R.
  M., 050; Richard, 034,038, 050;
  William, 035
WILLEY: John, 058
WILLIAM: John, 006
WILLIAMS: --, 097; Annian, 076;
  Casey, 082; Claiborn, 046;
  Elijah, 002, 006; Elish, 071;
  Elisha, 022; Isaac, 011; J. C.,
  093; James, 006, 041, 060, 061;
  Jas., 090; Joel, 082; John C.,
  079; John, 007, 076, 109, 110;
  Massen, 113; Masson, 112; Nimrod,
  023; O., 019, 035, 048, 049, 052,
  086; Oliver, 015, 019, 024, 034,
  043, 045; 046, 052, 057, 058,
  113; Polly C., 066; Richard, 007;
  Robert, 010; Samuel, 019, 022,
  054, 060, 068, 072; Tulley, 112;
  Tully, 084, 086; W., 005, 041;
  William, 006, 014, 060; Wm., 008,
  034, 061, 075, 076, 112;
  Wright, 015, 087
WILLIAMSON: Anne, 081; Benj., 068,
  108; Benjamin, 081; Betsey, 081;
  Elizabeth, 081; Green, 005, 058,
  105; Henry G., 081; John, 004,
  007, 026, 030, 032, 081; Martha,
  081; Mary, 003; Minerva, 081;
  Nancy, 081; Patsey G., 081;
  Patsey, 081; Richard, 007;
  Salley, 081; Sarah W., 081;
  Susan, 081; Thomas, 030, 081;
  Thos., 081; Wm. W., 081
WILLICE: Thos., 105
WILLIS: Augusta, 002; Caleb, 027,
  029; Cubb, 034; Daniel, 026
WILLS: John, 111, 112; William C.,
  032; William, 032; Wm. C., 085;
  Wm., 085
WILLSON: Aron, 105; Jason, Sr.,
  108; Samuel, 104; Wm, 105;
  Zachariah, 105
WILSON: --, 058, 087; Aron, 031;
  Betsy, 031; Capt., 059;
  Cornelius, 029, 110, 111; D.,
  076; Daniel, 043, 101; Dr., 097;
  Edward, 026; Geo., 076; Gregory,
  017, 091; James M., 109; James,
  008, 018, 021, 030, 040, 070,
  084, 097; James, Jr., 040; Jason
  C., 109; Jason, 091, 098; John,
  109; Joseph, 040; Josiah, 024,
  031, 040; Margaret, 031; Mark,

087; Martha, 031, 039; Moses,
  031; Polley, 031; Respah(??),
  031; Robert, 030, 041; Sally,
  031; Samuel, 009, 022, 031, 039,
  040, 057, 091, 098, 100; Shannon,
  071; Sire, 109; Thomas, 009, 024,
  033, 040, 041, 072, 091, 095,
  101, 109; Thos., 048, 065, 069,
  071, 084, 087, 090, 106, 109;
  Vilate, 040; W., 043, 052, 074;
  William, 015, 021, 029, 041, 055,
  060, 063, 111; Wm., 048, 054,
  060, 067-069, 086, 087, 095, 099,
  101, 103, 106, 108-110; Wm.,
  Esq., 080; Zacheus, 031, 039
WIMPER: Mary, 104
WINBORN: Henry, 048
WINBORNE: Henry, 047
WINBURN: Henry, 112
WINDERS: John, 041
WINDROW: Elizabeth, 003; Henry,
  003, 028; John, 003, 027, 028,
  033; Millinder, 003; Richard,
  003; Sally, 003
WINN: Archilus, 070
WINSET: Amos, 033, 071; Jerman,
  070; Jesse, 033; John, 033;
  Milley, 033; Silas, 033; Silvo,
  033; William, 033
WINSETT: Amos, 038; Ann, 033;
  Jason, 033; Mille, 038; Robert,
  012, 033, 038; William, 038
WINSTEAD: John, 106; Sam'l, 069;
  Samuel, 044
WINTER: Wm. H., 083
WINTON: Henry, 113
WIRT: John, 107
WISE: John, 072
WISEMAN?: Jacob, 108
WISENOR: Henry, 110
WITHERINGTON: Joseph, 088
WITHERINTON: William, 063; Wm., 069
WITHERS: Edmond, 007, 061
WITHERSPOON: D., 040; David, 022,
  030; J., 099; John, 009, 017,
  030, 034, 044, 051, 053; 068,
  071, 072, 077, 083, 091; 098-100,
  108; Sam'l, 042; Samuel, 049;
  Wesley, 051; Westley, 109
WITHROW: William, 041
WITTET: William, 014
WITTS: Wm. H., 071
WMSON: --, 099; Wm. W., 081
WOMBUELL: Reading, 010
WOOARD: Leon, 085
WOOD: A., 072; Alexander, 108;
  Alexr., 106; Christopher, 070;
  071; Johnson, 012; Jonathan,
  045; Leonard, 108; Richard, 016;
  Samuel, 093; Stephen, 034;
  Thompson, 012; Thos., 109
WOODARD: Lem, 085; Linn, 032; Sim,
  032; Thomas, 032; Thos., 085
WOODFOLD: Wm., 108
WOODFORD: W., 056
WOODFORK: W., 057; Wm., 057

WOODS: --, 089; F., 095; J., 095;
  Jas., 090; John, 095; Leonard,
  095; Wm. W., 081
WOOLDREDGE: Jasiah, 042
WOOLDRIDGE: Josiah, 045, 076, 089
WOOLF: Philip, 084
WOOLFORK: Joseph, 027
WOOLRIDGE: Josiah, 015, 019
WOOTEN: Moses, 061
WOOTON: John, 017
WORD: Sam'l, 094; Thos. H., 110
WORLDLEY: Henry, 068
WORLEY: Joseph, 053; Moses, 060
WORLY: Moses, 071; Polly, 052
WORMBELLS(WOMBWELL?): Reading, 010
WORMBY: John C., 095
WORSHAM: Robert, 032; Thomas, 032;
  Thos., 085, 086
WORTHAM: James, 097
WOULDRIDGE: Josiah, 049
WREN: David, 010
WRENN: Geo., 088
WRIGHT: Abram, 093; Elizabeth,
  057; Isaac, 010, 011; John, 006;
  Joseph, 059, 082; Mr., 034;
  Susan, 093
WRITE: Merchant, 046
WYCH: Nathaniel, 004, 014
WYCHE: N., 030; Nathaniel, 026, 042
WYMPEE: Tyre, 104
WYNE: John T., 106
YANCEY: Tyre, 085
YARBOROUGH: Wm. J., 082
YARBROUGH: Henry, 092; Wm., 045
YEARGIN: B., 071
YEATMAN: Wm., 086
YOCUM: Jesse, 054
YOUN(?): Howard, 040
YOUNG: Elizabeth, 005; Howard,
  005, 041; John, 056; Larence,
  028; T. T., 097; William, 010,
  012, 016, 024, 041; Wm., 046,
  069, 075, 077